the martyrology of the sacred order of friars preachers

the <u>martyrology</u>
of
the sacred order
of
friars preachers

Translated by Rev. W. R. Bonniwell, O. P.

Published with the Approbation of
Most Rev. T. S. McDermott, O. P.
Vicar General of the Order of Preachers

THE NEWMAN PRESS · WESTMINSTER, MARYLAND
1955

18664

Nihil obstat: Francis N. Wendell, O.P.
Ferdinand N. Georges, O.P.
Censores Librorum

Imprimatur: Most Rev. T. S. McDermott, O.P.
Vicar General of the Order of Preachers

November 12, 1954

TO OUR BELOVED FATHERS, BROTHERS, AND SISTERS

OF THE ORDER OF FRIARS PREACHERS,

WE

FATHER TERENCE STEPHEN MCDERMOTT

MASTER OF SACRED THEOLOGY

AND THE HUMBLE VICAR GENERAL AND SERVANT

OF THE ENTIRE ORDER OF FRIARS PREACHERS

GREETINGS AND BLESSINGS:

With the rapid growth of the liturgical movement especially in the last quarter of a century, there has been an increasing volume of requests from Dominican Sisters and Lay Tertiaries for an English translation of both our Breviary and Martyrology. It is with pleasure, therefore, that I am able to announce the fulfillment of these desires. The Breviary, translated by Father Aquinas Byrnes, O.P., is now in the process of publication at Rome, while the translation of the Dominican Martyrology has just been completed.

The Martyrology is one of the six official books of the Church's liturgy, and its use in the choral recitation of the Divine Office is obligatory. Because of the salutary effects derived from the reading of this sacred volume, various Pontiffs have urged its use by those who recite the Office privately. Indeed, not a few pious laymen are wont to read daily this great book of the saints, and in many convents it is the custom to read in the refectory at the beginning of the evening meal the Martyrology for the following day.

This is indeed a praiseworthy practice and one that might well be introduced in all our houses. For, day after day, the sacred volume sets before us men, women, and children, from every walk of life, who chose God in

v

preference to anything the world could offer. Daily there is held up before our eyes the shining examples of heroic Christians who sacrificed all and endured all—even the most prolonged and agonizing tortures—rather than offend God. It is impossible to listen to this stirring narrative of the saints without being deeply moved by it.

We therefore recommend the following careful translation of the Dominican Martyrology to all our convents as well as to our devout Lay Tertiaries, in the confident belief that by its daily reading we will give glory to God and His saints, participate more fully in the liturgical spirit of the Church, and be spurred to a closer imitation of those heroes and heroines of God whose eternal happiness we hope one day to share.

Given at Rome, in our Venerable Monastery of Santa Sabina, on the Feast of All Saints of our Order, November 12, 1954.

FATHER TERENCE S. McDERMOTT, O. P.
Vicar General of the Order of Preachers

introduction

The origins of the Martyrology go back to the earliest period of the Church. During the persecutions that were waged century after century against the Christians, the local authorities of various churches compiled lists of the faithful who died for Christ. Gradually local lists were enriched with the names of illustrious martyrs from other churches, until finally the local lists gave way to general martyrologies which embraced the universal Church.

The most famous of the general martyrologies was the one compiled about the year 475 and which was erroneously attributed to St. Jerome. In the Middle Ages, varying versions of the so-called Hieronyman Martyrology were in circulation, the most popular being the one edited by the monk Usuard (d. c. 875). It was his version the Dominican Order adopted in the thirteenth century and which several centuries later became the official version of the Church.

The Roman Martyrology has undergone a number of revisions and corrections from Gregory XIII to Benedict XV. The Dominican Order has profited by these scholarly labors and incorporated the results in its own Martyrology. However, the Order has not issued a new Martyrology since 1925, and since then many additions and changes have been officially authorized. All these changes and additions have been incorporated in their proper places in this translation, so that we have the anomaly of a translation being up to date, while the official version is not.

The ancient compilers of the Martyrology presupposed in the reader a considerable knowledge of the lives of the saints. Without such a knowledge, many of the allusions are lost. To have explained all such references would have required too many footnotes; but in a number of instances an explanatory word or phrase (always in parentheses) has been inserted in the text or placed in a footnote. Everything in parentheses, and all footnotes, have been added by the translator; they are not in the original text.

The Latin edition has one hundred and eighty-five folio pages devoted to a *Tractatus de Pronuntiatione Lunae,* to the Office of *Pretiosa,* and to a complete index of all the saints. It has been regarded as unnecessary to add all this extra material. The modern *Ordo* renders the *Tractatus* superfluous, while the entire Office of *Pretiosa* is given in the Breviary. Instead of a huge index of some four thousand five hundred names, there is given an index of all the feasts and the saints special to the Dominican Order. In assigning ranks to the various feasts, I have followed the latest edition of our breviary—that of 1952.

W. R. B.

vii

the RUBRICS of the martyrology

The martyrology is read every day of the year and always a day in advance of the actual date of the lesson; thus, on December 31 is read the lesson for January 1; on January 1, the lesson for January 2, etc. When he finishes reading a lesson, the reader always adds:

"And elsewhere, many other holy martyrs, confessors and holy virgins." And the choir responds: "Thanks be to God."

Since the dates of movable feasts change from year to year, they could not be inserted in the text of the martyrology. The list of such feasts is herewith given so that the reader, immediately after announcing the date of the lesson, may insert the proper movable feast at the very beginning of the lesson for the day. A movable feast is always announced on the day before the date given below.

The Movable Feasts

1. SUNDAY BETWEEN THE CIRCUMCISION AND THE EPIPHANY:
   The Feast of the Holy Name of Jesus. *A totum duplex feast of the first class.*

2. SUNDAY WITHIN THE OCTAVE OF THE EPIPHANY:
   Feast of the Holy Family of Jesus, Mary and Joseph—a Family that offers Christian homes the most holy examples, and from it may be invoked opportune help. *A totum duplex feast.*

3. SEPTUAGESIMA SUNDAY:
   Septuagesima Sunday—the Sunday on which is discontinued the Canticle of the Lord—the Alleluia.

4. THURSDAY AFTER SEXAGESIMA SUNDAY:
   Transferal of the body of St. Catherine of Siena, virgin, of the Order of Preachers. *A totum duplex feast.*

5. WEDNESDAY AFTER QUINQUAGESIMA SUNDAY:
   Ash Wednesday and the beginning of the fast of the holy season of Lent.

6. FRIDAY AFTER PASSION SUNDAY:
   Feast of the Compassion of the most Blessed Virgin Mary. *A totum duplex feast.*

7. PALM SUNDAY.
   Palm Sunday, when our Lord Jesus Christ, in accordance with the prophecy of Zacharias, entered Jerusalem, seated on the colt of an ass, and the people met Him, with branches of palm-trees.

8. THURSDAY OF HOLY WEEK:
   The Lord's Supper, when Christ Jesus, on the day before He was crucified for our salvation, gave to His disciples the mysteries of His Body and Blood to be celebrated.

9. FOR THE HOLY DAY OF EASTER, BEFORE THE DAY OF THE MONTH IS ANNOUNCED:
   "On this day, which the Lord has made, the solemnity of solemnities and our Pasch—the Resurrection of our Saviour Jesus Christ according to the flesh. *A totum duplex feast of the first class with a most solemn octave.*" The date is now announced and then the lesson of the Martyrology for Easter is read.

10. THE THIRD WEDNESDAY AFTER EASTER:
    The Solemnity of St. Joseph, confessor, spouse of the Blessed Virgin Mary. The Sovereign Pontiff, Pius IX, acceding to the wishes and prayers of the entire Catholic world, declared him to be the patron of the universal Church. *A totum duplex feast of the first class with a solemn octave.*

11. THE ASCENSION:
    On Mount Olivet, the Ascension of our Lord Jesus Christ. *A totum duplex feast of the first class with a most solemn octave.*

12. PENTECOST:
    The day of Pentecost, on which the Holy Ghost came upon the disciples at Jerusalem in tongues of fire. *A totum duplex feast of the first class with a most solemn octave.*

13. SUNDAY AFTER PENTECOST:
    Feast of the Most Holy and Undivided Trinity. *A totum duplex feast of the first class with a solemn octave.*

14. THURSDAY AFTER TRINITY SUNDAY:
    Feast of the Most Holy Body of Christ, instituted by Urban IV. *A totum duplex feast of the first class with a most solemn octave.*

15. FRIDAY AFTER OCTAVE OF CORPUS CHRISTI:
    Feast of the Most Sacred Heart of Jesus. *A totum duplex feast of the first class with a most solemn octave.*

16. FIRST SUNDAY OF OCTOBER:

The Commemoration of Our Lady of Victory, which Pope Pius V instituted to be made annually, on account of the famous victory gained on this very day by the Christians in a naval battle against the Turks, by the assistance of the same Mother of God. However, Gregory XIII decreed that for the same victory there should be celebrated on the first Sunday of this month the annual solemnity of the Rosary of the Most Blessed Virgin. *A totum duplex feast of the first class with a solemn octave.*

17. LAST SUNDAY OF OCTOBER:

Feast of our Lord Jesus Christ, the King. *A totum duplex feast of the first class.*

the anniversaries of the order

Throughout the martyrology all anniversaries are indicated by a cross. When the anniversary is that of the death of a master general, the reader should prefix the words: "The death of the venerable brother . . ."

JANUARY
   8. Joseph Maria Larroca of Spain, 74th master general of the Order.
 18. Barnabas of Vercelli, 15th master general of the Order.

FEBRUARY
   4. Anniversary of our Fathers and Mothers; likewise, Vincent Ajello of Lucania, in the Kingdom of Naples, 72nd master general of the Order.
   9. Andrew Frühwirth of Austria, 75th master general of the Order. He was also a cardinal of the Holy Roman Church.
 19. Munio of Spain, 7th master general of the Order.
 21. Augustine Pipia, 61st master general of the Order. He was also a cardinal of the Holy Roman Church.
 23. John of Moulins, 20th master general of the Order. He was also a cardinal of the Holy Roman Church.
 26. Antoninus Cloche of France, 60th master general of the Order.

MARCH
   1. Peter of Palma, 18th master general of the Order.
   3. Stephen Usodimare, 46th master general of the Order.
   9. Francis Ferdinand Jabalot of Parma, 68th master general of the Order.
 16. Leonard Dati of Florence, 25th master general of the Order.

APRIL
   8. Garin of Gy in Gaul, 19th master general of the Order.
 12. Aylmer of Piacenza, 12th master general of the Order.
 21. Garcia of Loaysa, of Spain, 39th master general of the Order. He was also a cardinal of the Holy Roman Church.

MAY
   2. Louis Theissling of Alkmaar, 77th master general of the Order.
   6. John Baptist de Marinis of Rome, 57th master general of the Order.
 16. Peter Rochin, 27th master general of the Order.
 25. Nicholas Ridolfi of Florence, 55th master general of the Order.

JUNE

7. Simon of Langres, 21st master general of the Order.
11. Antoninus Bremond of Marseilles, 63rd master general of the Order.
13. John Thomas de Rocaberti of Spain, 58th master general of the Order.
16. Sixtus Fabri of Lucca, 50th master general of the Order.
20. Elias Raymond of Toulouse, 22nd master general of the Order; and Balthazar de Quiñones, 65th master general of the Order.
25. Leonard de Mansuetis of Perugia, 31st master general of the Order.

JULY

6. John du Feynier, 42nd master general of the Order.
9. Thomas Hyacinth Cipolletti of Ascoli, 70th master general of the Order.
12. Anniversary of all who are buried in our cemeteries.
14. Humbert of Romans, 5th master general of the Order.
20. Francis Romeo, 45th master general of the Order.
27. Gerard de Daumar, 17th master general of the Order. He was also a cardinal of the Holy Roman Church.
29. Barnabas Sassone of Naples, 34th master general of the Order.

AUGUST

1. Joachim Torriani of Venice, 35th master general of the Order.
3. Hippolytus Maria Beccaria of Monreale, 51st master general of the Order.
4. Bartholomew Comazio of Bologna, 33rd master general of the Order.
7. Thomas (Paccoroni) of Fermo, 24th master general of the Order.
8. Hugh de Vaucemain of Gaul, 16th master general of the Order.
9. Hervé de Nédellec of Brittainy, 14th master general of the Order; and John Clérée of Gaul, 37th master general of the Order.
12. Bonaventure Garcia de Paredes of Spain, 78th master general of the Order.
27. Vincent Bandelli of Lombardy, 36th master general of the Order.
28. Albert de Chiavari of Genoa, 10th master general of the Order.
29. Angelus Dominic Ancarani, of Faenza, 71st master general of the Order.
30. Augustine Galamini, 53rd master general of the Order. He was also a cardinal of the Holy Roman Church.

SEPTEMBER

1. Berengarius of Landorra, 13th master general of the Order.

4. Martin Stanislaus Gillet of France, 79th master general of the Order.

5. Anniversary of the *familiares* and benefactors of our Order.

9. Thomas de Vio Cajetan, 38th master general of the Order. He was also a cardinal of the Holy Roman Church.

12. Jerome Xavierre of Saragossa, 52nd master general of the Order. He was also a cardinal of the Holy Roman Church.

15. Salvo Casseta of Sicily, 32nd master general of the Order.

17. Bernard of Jusix, 11th master general of the Order; and Paul Constable of Ferrara, 49th master general of the Order.

21. Martial Auribelli of Avignon, 29th master general of the Order.

22. Thomas Ripoll of Tarragona, 62nd master general of the Order.

24. Francis Silvestri of Ferrara, 40th master general of the Order; and Seraphin Secci of Pavia, 54th master general of the Order.

27. Maurice Benedict Olivieri of Salluzo, 69th master general of the Order.

OCTOBER

9. Paul Butigella, 41st master general of the Order.

15. Bartholomew Texier, 26th master general of the Order.

28. Vincent Guistiniani of Chios, 47th master general of the Order. He was also a cardinal of the Holy Roman Church.

NOVEMBER

4. John the Teuton, 4th master general of the Order.

7. Anthony de Monroy of Mexico, 59th master general of the Order.

10. Anniversary of all the Brothers and Sisters of our Order.

16. Albert de las Casas of Spain, 44th master general of the Order.

18. Guido Flamochetti, 28th master general of the Order.

21. Stephen of Besançon, 8th master general of the Order; and Seraphin Cavalli of Brescia, 48th master general of the Order.

DECEMBER

1. Thomas Turco of Cremona, 56th master general of the Order.

3. Joachim Briz of Spain, 67th master general of the Order.

11. Alexander Vincent Jandel of Nancy in France, 73rd master general of the Order.

15. Conrad d'Asti, 30th master general of the Order.

16. John Thomas de Boxadors, 64th master general of the Order. He was also a cardinal of the Holy Roman Church.

17. Hyacinth Maria Cormier of Orleans, 76th master general of the Order.

20. Augustine Recuperati, 43rd master general of the Order.

23. Pius Joseph Gaddi, 66th master general of the Order.

the martyrology of the sacred order of friars preachers

JANUARY

The First Day of January

The Circumcision of Our Lord Jesus Christ, and the Octave of His Nativity. *A totum duplex feast of the second class.*

At Rome, the suffering of St. Martina, virgin and martyr. At the time of the Emperor Alexander, she was subjected to various kinds of torture and finally obtained the crown of martyrdom by the sword. Her feast is observed on January 30.

At Caesarea in Cappadocia, the death of St. Basil the Great, bishop, confessor, and Doctor of the Church. He lived at the time of the Emperor Valens, and was remarkable for his learning and wisdom. Adorned with every virtue, he was wonderfully distinguished by the unconquerable firmness with which he defended the Church against the Arians and Macedonians. His feast is fittingly celebrated on June 14, the day on which he was consecrated bishop.

At Monte Senario, in Etruria (Italy), St. Bonfilius, confessor, one of the seven founders of the Order of the Servants of the Blessed Virgin Mary. Since he had so faithfully served her, he was quickly called by her to heaven. His feast, with that of his companions, is observed on February 12.

At Rome, St. Almachius, martyr. At the command of Alipius, prefect of the city, he was slain by gladiators because he cried out: "Today is the Octave Day of the Lord; stop your idolatrous superstitions and your polluted sacrifices."

Also at Rome, on the Appian Way, the crowning of thirty holy soldiers, martyrs, under the Emperor Diocletian.

At Spoleto, St. Concordius, priest and martyr, in the time of the Emperor Antoninus. He was first beaten with clubs, and then stretched on the rack. Afterward, he was starved in prison, where he was consoled by the visit of an angel. At length his life was ended by the sword.

On the same day, St. Magnus, martyr.

1

In Africa, Blessed Fulgentius, Bishop of the church of Ruspe. During the Vandal persecution, he was greatly harassed by the Arians because of his Catholic faith and excellent teaching. He was exiled to Sardinia, but finally was allowed to return to his own church, where he died a holy death, renowned for his life and preaching.

At Chieti in Abruzzi (Italy), the birthday of St. Justin, bishop of that city, renowned for the holiness of his life and for his miracles.

In the country of Lyons, in the monastery of Mount Jura,[1] St. Eugendus, abbot, whose life was resplendent with miracles and virtues.

At Souvigny in Gaul, St. Odilo, Abbot of Cluny. He was the first to prescribe that the Commemoration of All the Faithful Departed should be kept in his monasteries on the first day after the Feast of All Saints. This custom the Universal Church afterward approved and adopted.

At Alexandria, the death of St. Euphrosyna, virgin, who was renowned in her monastery for the virtue of abstinence and for her miracles.

*And elsewhere many other holy martyrs, confessors, and holy virgins.
R. Thanks be to God.

The Second Day of January

The Octave of St. Stephen, the Protomartyr. *A memory.*

In the town of Socino, in the Diocese of Cremona (Italy), Blessed Stephana Quinzani, virgin, of the Order of Preachers, who on January 2 went to her heavenly Spouse. *A semi-duplex feast.*

At Rome, the commemoration of many holy martyrs. They refused to obey the edict of Diocletian by which they were commanded to surrender their sacred books. They chose rather to give their bodies to the executioners than holy things to dogs.

At Antioch, the suffering of Blessed Isidore, bishop.

At Tomis in Pontus, the three holy brothers, Argeus, Narcissus and the youth Marcellinus. The young man was drafted as a recruit at the time of the Emperor Licinius. When he refused to perform military service,[2] he was flogged almost to death, and kept for a long time in prison. At

---

[1] This was the abbey of Condate on Mount-Jou (Mount Jura). When St. Eugendus died, is was called after him, by his French name, St. Oyend. Then, many centuries later, it was re-named St. Claude.

* With this formula and its response the reading of the Martyrology is always concluded.

[2] Certain passages in the works of several early Christian writers gave some converts the impression that military service and the teachings of Christ were incompatible. The error was not widespread.

last he was thrown into the sea, and so completed his martyrdom. His brothers were slain by the sword.

At Milan, St. Martinian, bishop.

At Nitria in Egypt, blessed Isidore, bishop and confessor.

On the same day, St. Siridion, bishop.

In the Thebaid, St. Macarius of Alexandria, priest and abbot.

The Third Day of January

The Octave of St. John, Apostle and Evangelist. *A memory.*

At Jablona in Bohemia, Blessed Zedislava Berkiana, a noble matron. After receiving the habit of the Order of our holy Father Dominic from Blessed Ceslaus, she became celebrated during her life for her spirit of meditation, her penance and works of charity, and after her death, by her reputation for miracles. *A semi-duplex feast.*

At Rome, on the Appian Way, the birthday of St. Antherus, pope and martyr, who suffered under Julius Maximin, and was buried in the cemetery of Callistus.

At Vienne in Gaul, St. Florentius, bishop, who was sent into exile in the time of the Emperor Gallienus, and there completed his martyrdom.

In the city of Aulona in Palestine, the suffering of St. Peter (Balsam), who was put to death by crucifixion.

On the Hellespont, the holy martyrs Cyrinus, Primus, and Theogenes.

At Caesarea in Cappadocia, the centurion St. Gordius, martyr. On his feast day, St. Basil the Great delivered in his praise a famous sermon, which is still extant.

In Cilicia, the holy martyrs Zosimus and Athanasius the notary.

Also SS. Theopemptus and Theonas, who underwent a sublime martyrdom in the persecution of Diocletian.

At Padua, St. Daniel, martyr.

At Paris, St. Genevieve, virgin. She was consecrated to Christ by Blessed Germanus, Bishop of Auxerre, and was renowned for remarkable virtues and miracles.

The Fourth Day of January

The Octave of the Holy Innocents, martyrs. *A feast of three lessons.*

In Crete, the birthday of St. Titus, who was ordained Bishop of the Cretans by St. Paul the Apostle. After having faithfully fulfilled the office of preaching, he obtained a blessed death. He was buried in the church to which the holy Apostle had appointed him a worthy minister. His feast day is kept on February 6.

At Rome, the holy martyrs Priscus, priest, Priscillian, cleric, and Benedicta, a woman in religion, who, in the time of the wicked Julian, fulfilled their martyrdom by the sword.

Also at Rome, Blessed Dafrosa, the wife of the martyr St. Flavian, and mother of SS. Bibiana and Demetria, virgins and martyrs. After the execution of her husband, she was first sent into exile, and afterward beheaded in the reign of the same Emperor (Julian).

At Bologna, SS. Hermes, Aggaeus, and Caius, martyrs, who suffered under the Emperor Maximian.

At Adrumetum in Africa, the commemoration of St. Mavilus, martyr. In the persecution of the Emperor Severus, he was flung to the wild beasts by the cruel governor Scapula, and received the crown of martyrdom.

Also in Africa, the most illustrious martyrs Aquilinus, Geminus, Eugene, Marcian, Quinctius, Theodotus, and Trypho.

At Langres in Gaul, the Bishop St. Gregory, who was famous for miracles.

At Rheims in Gaul, St. Rigobert, bishop and confessor.

The Fifth Day of January

The Vigil of the Lord's Epiphany.

At Rome, St. Telesphorus, pope and martyr. In the reign of Antoninus Pius, he attained an illustrious martyrdom, after having endured much suffering in confessing Christ.

In England, the king St. Edward, confessor, famed for his chastity and the grace of miracles. His feast, by decree of Pope Innocent XI, is celebrated on October 13, on which day his holy body was transferred (to a shrine in the choir of Westminster Abbey).

In Egypt, the commemoration of many holy martyrs, who were slain in the Thebaid by various kinds of torments during the persecution of Diocletian.

At Antioch, the monk St. Simeon, who for many years persevered living on top of a column, whence he received the name Stylites. He was greatly renowned both for his life and conversation.

At Rome, St. Emiliana, virgin, aunt of Pope St. Gregory. On this day she went to her Lord at the call of her sister Tharsilla, who had gone to God before her.

At Alexandria, St. Syncletica, whose deeds St. Athanasius admirably commended in his writings.

In Egypt, St. Apollinaris, virgin.

The Sixth Day of January

The Epiphany of the Lord. *A totum duplex feast of the first class.*

At Florence, the birthday of St. Andrew Corsini, a Florentine Carmelite, Bishop of Fiesole, and confessor. Renowned for miracles, he was inscribed in the number of the saints by Urban VIII. His feast is observed on February 4.

At Barcelona in Spain, the birthday of St. Raymund of Peñafort, of the Order of Preachers, confessor. He is famous for his learning and sanctity. His feast day, however, is celebrated on January 23.

In Africa, the commemoration of many holy martyrs who, in the persecution of Severus, were bound to stakes and burned alive.

In the neighborhood of Rheims, the suffering of St. Macra, virgin. In the persecution of Diocletian, she was cast into a fire at the command of the governor Rictiovarus, but remained unhurt. Afterward she was mutilated and cast into a foul prison; then she was rolled upon jagged sherds and burning coals and, while praying, went to her Lord.

At Rennes in Gaul, St. Melanius, bishop and confessor. He manifested innumerable virtues and, always intent on Heaven, passed gloriously from the world.

At Gerras in Egypt, St. Nilammon, recluse, who gave up his spirit to God in prayer, while being urged against his will to accept a bishopric.

The Seventh Day of January

The Return of the Child Jesus from Egypt.

At Nicomedia, the birthday of Blessed Lucian, priest and martyr, of the Church of Antioch. He won unusually great renown for his doctrine and eloquence, and he suffered for confessing Christ in the persecution of Maximian Galerius. He was buried at Helenopolis in Bithynia. St. John Chrysostom highly praised him.

At Antioch, St. Clerus, deacon, who for his glorious confession of faith was tortured seven times. He was incarcerated for a long time and at last was beheaded, thus fulfilling his martyrdom.

In the city of Heracles, the holy martyrs Felix and Januarius.

On the same day, the martyr St. Julian.

In Denmark, St. Canute, king and martyr.

At Pavia (in Italy), St. Crispin, bishop and confessor.

In Dacia, St. Nicetas, bishop, who by preaching the Gospel made civilized and humane some nations that before were savage and barbarous.

In Egypt, Blessed Theodore, monk, who grew in holiness in the time of Constantine the Great. St. Athanasius mentions him in his life of St. Anthony.

The Eighth Day of January

At Venice, the death of Blessed Laurence Giustiniani, confessor, first Patriarch of that city. The Sovereign Pontiff, Alexander VIII, seeing him abundantly filled with learning and the heavenly graces of divine wisdom, inscribed him among the number of the saints. But his feast is kept on September 5, when he ascended the episcopal throne.

At Beauvais in Gaul, the holy martyrs Lucian, priest, Maximian, and Julian. The two latter were slain by the sword of the persecutors. Blessed Lucian, who came into Gaul with St. Dionysius, was severely tortured. As he did not fear to continue confessing the name of Christ in a loud voice, he also underwent the fate of the other two.

In Libya, the holy martyrs Theophilus, deacon, and Helladius. They were first mangled and pierced with sharp sherds; then they were cast into the fire, where they gave up their souls to God.

At Autun, St. Eugenian, martyr.

At Hierapolis in Asia, St. Apollinaris, bishop, who was eminent for holiness and learning, under Marcus Antoninus Verus.

At Naples in Campania, the birthday of the Bishop St. Severinus, brother of the blessed martyr Victorinus. After he performed many virtuous deeds, he entered into rest rich in sanctity.

At Metz in Gaul, St. Patiens, bishop.

At Pavia (in Italy), St. Maximus, bishop and confessor.

At Ratisbon in Bavaria, St. Erhard, bishop.

In Bavaria, St. Severinus, abbot, who preached the Gospel in that country, and is called the Apostle of the Bavarians. His body was miraculously brought to Lucullano, near Naples, and was afterward taken from there to the monastery of St. Severino. ✠

The Ninth Day of January

At Antioch, under Diocletian and Maximian, the birthday of St. Julian, martyr, and of the virgin Basilissa, his spouse. She remained a virgin during marriage, and (although persecuted for the faith) ended her days in peace. A number of priests and ministers of the Church, who had sought refuge with Julian owing to the barbarity of the persecution, were (notwithstanding) burned to death, and Julian himself, at the command of the governor Marcian, was tortured in many ways and then beheaded. With him there were martyred many others: a priest named Anthony, one Anastasius, who had been raised from the dead by Julian and converted to Christianity, Celsus, a boy, and his mother, Marcionilla, seven brothers, and many other Christians.

At Smyrna, the holy martyrs Vitalis, Revocatus, and Fortunatus.

In Africa, the holy martyrs Epictetus, Jucundus, Secundus, Vitalis, Felix, and seven others.

In Eastern Morocco, St. Marciana, virgin, who was thrown to the beasts, and so completed her martyrdom.

At Sebaste in Armenia, the Bishop St. Peter, the son of SS. Basil and Emmelia. He was also the brother of SS. Basil the Great, Gregory of Nyssa, bishops, and of the virgin Macrina.

At Ancona, St. Marcellinus, bishop, who, as St. Gregory mentions, delivered that city from fire by a miracle.

The Tenth Day of January

In the Thebaid, the birthday of the first hermit, St. Paul, confessor. He remained alone in the desert from the sixteenth to the one hundred and thirteenth year of his age. St. Anthony beheld his soul borne up to heaven by angels amid the choirs of Apostles and Prophets. His feast is celebrated on January 15.

In Cyprus, Blessed Nicanor, deacon, one of the first seven deacons (of the Church of Jerusalem).[3] Through the grace of faith and his admirable virtue, he received a most glorious crown.

At Rome, Pope St. Agatho, who was remarkable for his holiness and learning. He died a peaceful death.

At Bourges in Aquitaine, St. William, archbishop and confessor. He was renowned for miracles and virtues. Pope Honorius III inscribed him in the roll of the saints.

At Milan, St. John the Good, bishop and confessor.

At Constantinople, St. Marcian, priest.

In the monastery of Cuxa in Gaul, the birthday of St. Peter Urseolo, confessor. He was once Doge of Venice, and then monk of the Order of St. Benedict. He was noted for holiness and virtue.

At Arezzo in Tuscany, Blessed Gregory X of Piacenza. He was called from the archdeaconry of Liege to be Pope. He convoked the second Council of Lyons, received the Greeks to the unity of the faith, healed the strifes of Christians, and began the recovery of the Holy Land. He deserved well of the Universal Church which he governed in a most holy manner.

[3] See Acts, 6:5.

The Eleventh Day of January

At Rome, St. Hyginus, pope and martyr, who gloriously fulfilled his martyrdom in the persecution of Antoninus.

Also at Rome, the birthday of St. Melchiades, pope and martyr. He suffered much in the persecution of Maximian and, when peace returned to the Church, died peacefully in the Lord. His feast day is kept on December 10.

At Fermo in Piceno, St. Alexander, bishop and martyr.

At Amiens in Gaul, St. Salvius, bishop and martyr.

In Africa, Blessed Salvius, martyr, on whose birthday St. Augustine delivered a panegyric to the people of Carthage.

At Alexandria, the holy martyrs Peter, Severus, and Leucius.

At Brindisi, St. Leucius, bishop and confessor.

In Judea, St. Theodosius the Coenobiarch,[4] who was born in the village of Magarissus in Cappadocia. He suffered much for the Catholic faith, and at last rested in peace in the monastery he had erected on a lonely hill in the Diocese of Jerusalem.

In the Thebaid, St. Palaemon, abbot, who was the instructor of St. Pachomius.

At Suppentonia, near Mount Soracte, the monk St. Anastasius, and his companions. They were called (to heaven) in a miraculous way and so went happily to the Lord.

At Pavia, St. Honorata, virgin.

The Twelfth Day of January

At Rome, St. Tatiana, martyr, in the reign of the Emperor Alexander. She was mangled with hooks and iron combs, exposed to wild beasts, and cast into a fire, but was not harmed. At length, put to the sword, she passed into heaven.

At Constantinople, SS. Tigrius, priest, and Eutropius, lector. In the time of the Emperor Arcadius, they were falsely accused of the fire which destroyed the cathedral church and the Senate-hall. It was alleged that they had caused the fire to avenge the exile of St. John Chrysostom. They were martyred under Optatus, prefect of the city, a man attached to the worship of the false gods and a hater of the Christian religion.

In Achaia, St. Satyrus, martyr. As he passed before a certain idol, he breathed upon it and made the sign of the cross. Instantly the idol fell to the ground; for this reason he was beheaded.

---

[4] Sallust, bishop of Jerusalem, appointed Theodosius head of all the coenobites in Palestine; hence his title Coenobiarch.

On the same day, St. Arcadius, martyr, a man noted for his noble birth and for his miracles.

In Africa, the holy martyrs Zoticus, Rogatus, Modestus, Castulus, and forty soldiers, gloriously crowned.

At Tivoli, St. Zoticus, martyr.

At Ephesus, the suffering of forty-two holy monks. In the reign of Constantine Copronymus, they were most savagely tortured for their veneration of holy images, and so fulfilled their martyrdom.

At Ravenna, St. John, bishop and confessor.

At Verona, St. Probus, bishop.

In England, St. Benedict, abbot and confessor.

The Thirteenth Day of January

The Octave of the Lord's Epiphany. *A most solemn octave.*

At Poitiers in Gaul, the birthday of St. Hilary, bishop and confessor. On behalf of the Catholic faith which he defended valiantly, he was sent into exile in Phrygia for four years. Among his other miracles, he raised a man from the dead. Pope Pius IX declared him a Doctor of the Church. His feast is celebrated on January 14.

At Rheims in Gaul, St. Remigius, bishop and confessor. He converted the Franks to Christ, baptized their king, Clovis, and instructed him in the mysteries of the faith. After many years as bishop, during which he became famous for his holiness and the greatness of his miracles, he departed from this life. His feast is observed on October 1, when his holy body was transferred (to the abbey church at Rheims).

At Rome, on the Via Lavicana, the crowning of forty holy soldiers, which they merited to receive for their confession of the true faith under Gallienus the Emperor.

At Cordoba in Spain, the holy martyrs Gumesind, priest, and Servideus, monk.

In Sardinia, St. Potitus, martyr, who suffered much under the Emperor Antoninus and the governor Gelasius, and at last obtained martyrdom by the sword.

At Belgrade in Serbia, the holy martyrs Hermylus and Stratonicus. In the reign of the Emperor Licinius, they were drowned in the Danube, after enduring cruel tortures.

At Caesarea in Cappadocia, St. Leontius, bishop, who strove mightily against the heathens at the time of Licinius, and against the Arians at the time of Constantine.

At Treves, St. Agritius, bishop.

In the monastery of Verzy in Gaul, St. Viventius, confessor.

At Amasea in Pontus, St. Glaphyra, virgin.

At Milan, in the monastery of St. Martha, Blessed Veronica of Binasco, virgin, of the Order of St. Augustine.

The Fourteenth Day of January

St. Hilary, Bishop of Poitiers, confessor and Doctor of the Church, who on the previous day departed to heaven. *A duplex feast.*

At Nola in Campania (Italy), St. Felix, priest. Bishop St. Paulinus tells us that every time Felix was tortured and taken back to his prison, he was chained and laid upon sharp sherds; but every night he was unchained and led forth by an angel. After the persecution ceased, he converted many to the faith of Christ by the example of his life and his doctrine. Renowned for his miracles, he died a peaceful death. *A memory.*

In Judea, St. Malachy the Prophet.

On Mount Sinai, thirty-eight holy monks, slain by the Saracens for the Christian faith.

In Egypt, in the district of Rhaitis, forty-three monks, who were slain by the Blemmians [5] for the Christian religion.

At Milan, St. Datius, bishop and confessor, whom Pope St. Gregory mentions.

In Africa, St. Euphrasius, bishop.

At Neocaesarea in Pontus, St. Marcina. She was a disciple of St. Gregory the Wonderworker, and grandmother of St. Basil, whom she educated in the faith.

The Fifteenth Day of January

In the city of Fogan, in the Chinese Empire, the suffering of Blessed Francis de Capillas, a missionary priest of the Order of Preachers. He was the first among all the apostolic heralds in the Chinese Empire to seal the Faith of Christ with his blood. *A duplex feast.*

St. Paul the first hermit, confessor, who on January 10 was called to the company of the blessed. *A memory.*

In Anjou (Gaul), Blessed Maurus, abbot, who was a disciple of St. Benedict from boyhood. He made such progress in the monastic life under St. Benedict, that among other things he did in obedience to him was to walk upon the water; an extraordinary thing scarcely witnessed since the time of St. Peter. He was then sent by his teacher into Gaul, and

---

[5] An ancient savage tribe of Ethiopia.

built there a famous monastery, of which he was the superior for forty years. He died peacefully, renowned for his glorious miracles. *A memory*.

In Judea, SS. Habacuc and Michaeas, Prophets, whose bodies were discovered by divine revelation at the time of the Emperor Theodosius, the Elder.

At Cagliari in Sardinia, St. Ephysius, martyr. In Diocletian's persecution, under Flavian the judge, he endured by divine grace various tortures; at last, being beheaded, he passed triumphantly to Heaven.

At Anagni, St. Secundina, virgin and martyr, who suffered under the Emperor Decius.

At Nola in Campania, St. Maximus, bishop.

In Auvergne in Gaul, St. Bonitus, bishop and confessor.

In Egypt, the Abbot St. Macarius. He was a disciple of Blessed Antony, and was most renowned for his life and miracles.

At Alexandria, Blessed Isidore, famous for holiness of life, for his faith, and for his miracles.

At Constantinople, St. John Calybites.[6] He dwelt for some time, unrecognized by his parents, in a corner next to his father's house, and then in a (nearby) hut. At his death he was recognized by his parents, and became renowned for his miracles. His body was later removed to Rome and buried in the church erected in his honor on the island in the Tiber.

The Sixteenth Day of January

At Amarante in Portugal, Blessed Gonsalvo, confessor of the Order of Preachers. He was filled with the spirit of his holy Father Dominic, and confirmed his preaching of the Gospel both by the example of his life and by the number of his miracles. *A semi-duplex feast*.

At Rome, on the Via Salaria, the birthday of St. Marcellus I, pope and martyr. By orders of the tyrant Maxentius, St. Marcellus was beaten with clubs because he confessed the Catholic faith. Then he was sent under a public guard to take care of cattle. Clad only in a piece of sackcloth, he perished while toiling in this occupation. *A memory*.

At Morocco in Africa, the suffering of the five protomartyrs of the Order of Friars Minor: Berard, Peter, and Otho, priests, and Accursius and Adjutus, lay-brothers. For preaching the Catholic faith and because of their detestation of the Mohammedan Law, they were subjected to various tortures and mockeries by the Saracen caliph, and then beheaded.

---

[6] The Greek word *kalube* means a hut. Because the saint lived for so long in a hut, he became known as the "hut-dweller."

At Rhinocolura in Egypt, St. Melas, bishop. After he had suffered exile and other bitter trials under Valens for the Catholic faith, he had a peaceful death.

At Arles in Gaul, St. Honoratus, bishop and confessor, whose life was illustrious for doctrine and miracles.

At Oderzo near Venice, St. Titian, bishop and confessor.

At Fondi in Latium (Italy), St. Honoratus, abbot, whom Pope St. Gregory mentions.

At the village of Mézerolles on the river Authie in Gaul, St. Fursey, confessor; his body was later transferred to the monastery of Peronne.

At Rome, St. Priscilla, who dedicated herself and her goods to the service of the martyrs.

The Seventeenth Day of January

In the Thebaid, St. Anthony, abbot. He was the spiritual father of many monks, and was most renowned for his life and his miracles. St. Athanasius set forth his deeds in a famous book. His holy body was found by divine revelation at the time of the Emperor Justinian. It was brought to Alexandria and buried in the church of St. John the Baptist. *A duplex feast.*

At Langres in Gaul, three holy brothers, who were triplets, Speusippus, Eleusippus, and Meleusippus. Together with their grandmother Leonilla, they were crowned with martydrom in the time of the Emperor Marcus Aurelius.

At Bourges in Aquitaine, the death of the Bishop St. Sulpicius, called the Pious, whose life and precious death were approved by glorious miracles.

At Rome, in the monastery of St. Andrew, the holy monks Anthony, Merulus, and John; all are mentioned by Pope St. Gregory.

In the territory of Edessa in Mesopotamia, the hermit St. Julian, surnamed Sabas. In the reign of the Emperor Valens, when the Catholic faith at Antioch had almost died, he restored it by his miracles.

At Rome, the finding of the bodies of the holy martyrs Diodorus, priest, Marian, deacon, and their companions, who suffered martyrdom on December 1 during the pontificate of Pope St. Stephen.

The Eighteenth Day of January

The Chair of St. Peter the Apostle wherein he first exercised authority at Rome. *A totum duplex feast.*

In the same city, the suffering of St. Prisca, virgin and martyr, who, at the time of the Emperor Claudius, endured many tortures and received the crown of martyrdom. *A memory.*

At Buda in Hungary, the birthday of St. Margaret, virgin, who was the daughter of King Bela IV. As a nun of the Order of St. Dominic she became distinguished by the virtue of chastity, by the severity of her penance, and by her charity toward her neighbor. The Sovereign Pontiff, Pius XII, inscribed her on the roll of holy virgins; her feast is celebrated on January 19.

In Pontus, the birthday of the holy martyrs, Moseus and Ammonius, who were soldiers. They were first condemned to the mines, and later were burned alive.

In the same place, St. Athenogenes, (called) the Old Theologian. When he was about to complete his martyrdom by fire, he sang a hymn of joy, which he left in writing to his disciples.

At Tours in Gaul, St. Volusian, bishop, who was captured by the Goths, and gave up his spirit to God in exile.

In the monastery of Lure in Burgundy, St. Deicola, abbot, who was Irish by birth and a disciple of blessed Columbanus.

At Tours in Gaul, St. Leobard, recluse, who was famed for his wondrous abstinence and humility.

At Como (in Italy), St. Liberata, virgin. ✠

The Nineteenth Day of January

St. Margaret, virgin (of the Order of Preachers), who on January 18 went to her heavenly Spouse. *A totum duplex feast of the second class.*

At Rome, on the Via Cornelia, the holy martyrs Marius, Martha his wife, and their sons Audifax and Abachum. They were Persians of noble birth, who came to Rome on a pilgrimage in the time of the Emperor Claudius. After they had endured scourging, the rack, fire, iron hooks, and the cutting off of their hands, Martha was drowned at (a place called) Ninfa; the others were beheaded, and their bodies cremated.

Also St. Canute, king and martyr.

At Smyrna, the birthday of St. Germanicus, martyr. At the time of Marcus Antoninus and Lucius Aurelius, St. Germanicus cast aside by the mighty grace of God all bodily fears, although he was yet in the flower of his youth. Having been condemned to death by the judge, he deliberately provoked the wild beast let loose on him. Ground by the teeth of the beast, he merited to be united with the true Bread, the Lord Jesus Christ, by dying for His sake.

In Africa, the holy martyrs Paul, Gerontius, Januarius, Saturninus, Successus, Julius, Catus, Pia, and Germana.

At Spoleto, the suffering of St. Pontian, martyr, in the time of the Emperor Antoninus. For his confession of Christ, Fabian the judge ordered him to be beaten severely with rods, and to walk barefoot on live coals. Then he was tortured on the rack and hung from iron hooks; after this, he was cast into prison, where he merited to be consoled by the visit of an angel. Afterward, he was exposed to the lions, had molten lead poured over him, and was at last put to the sword.

At Lodi in Lombardy, St. Bassian, bishop and confessor, who, together with St. Ambrose, fought strenuously against the heretics.

At Worcester in England, St. Wulstan, bishop and confessor. He was outstanding for his merits and his miracles, and was numbered among the saints by Innocent III.

The Twentieth Day of January

At Rome, the birthday of Pope St. Fabian, who suffered martyrdom in the time of Decius, and was buried in the cemetery of Callistus.

Also at Rome near the Catacombs, St. Sebastian, martyr. He was in command of the first cohort under the Emperor Diocletian. On being accused of being a Christian, he was ordered to be tied in an open field and shot with arrows by the soldiers. Finally, he was beaten with clubs until he died. *A duplex feast.*

At Nicaea in Bithynia, St. Neophitus, martyr. When fifteen years old, he was scourged, cast into a furnace, and (then) thrown to the beasts; but he remained unhurt. As he continued to profess unswervingly the faith of Christ, he was finally slain with the sword.

At Cesena, St. Maurus, bishop, famed for virtues and miracles.

In Palestine, St. Euthymius, abbot. He flourished in the Church in the time of the Emperor Marcian, full of zeal for Catholic teaching and endowed with the power of miracles.

The Twenty-first Day of January

At Rome, the suffering of St. Agnes, virgin. At the time of Symphronius, the prefect of the city, she was cast into the flames; at her prayer they were extinguished, and she was slain with the sword. St. Jerome thus speaks of her: "The life of St. Agnes is praised in the writing and the tongues of all peoples, especially in the churches, because she rose superior both to her (youthful) age and to the tyrant, and consecrated by her martyrdom her claim to chastity." *A duplex feast.*

At Athens, the birthday of St. Publius, bishop. After St. Dionysius the Areopagite, he admirably ruled the church of Athens. Great in virtue and resplendent for doctrine, he was gloriously crowned by martyrdom for Christ.

At Tarragona in Spain, the holy martyrs Fructuosus, bishop, Augurius and Eulogius, deacons. In the time of Gallienus, they were first thrown into prison, and then cast into the flames. When their bonds were burnt through, they stretched out their hands in prayer in the form of a cross, and so fulfilled their martyrdom. St. Augustine delivered a panegyric to the people on this their birthday.

In the monastery of Einsiedeln in Switzerland, St. Meinrad, priest and monk. In that same place, where later the monastery arose, he lived as a recluse and was slain by robbers. The body of this blessed man, which was formerly buried in the monastery of Reichenau, in Germany, was brought back to the monastery of Einsiedeln.

At Troyes in Gaul, St. Patroclus, martyr, who merited the crown of martyrdom under the Emperor Aurelian.

At Pavia, St. Epiphanius, bishop and confessor.

The Twenty-second Day of January

At Valencia in Spain, in the province of Tarragona, St. Vincent, deacon and martyr. Under the wicked governor Dacian, he suffered prison, starvation, the rack, the disjointing of his limbs, red-hot metal plates, the blazing gridiron, and other kinds of torture. For the reward of his martyrdom, he went to heaven. Prudentius set forth in noble verse the glorious triumph of his suffering, and St. Augustine and Pope St. Leo commend him with the highest praise. *A totum duplex feast.*

At Barsaloe in Assyria, St. Anastasius, a Persian monk. After many tortures of imprisonment, floggings, and chains, which he had suffered at Caesarea in Palestine, he was delivered up to more torments under Chosroës, King of the Persians. He was at last beheaded, after sending before him to martyrdom seventy companions, who were drowned in a river. His head, together with his venerated image, was brought to (the monastery at) Aquae Salviae near Rome.[7] The Acts of the second Council of Nicaea testify that at the sight of his relics demons fled and diseases were cured.

At Embrun in Gaul, the holy martyrs Vincent, Orontius, and Victor, who were crowned with martyrdom in the persecution of Diocletian.

[7] Aquae Salviae is now known as Tre Fontane; the monastery is that of SS. Vincent and Anastasius.

At Novara (in Italy), St. Gaudentius, bishop and confessor.

At Sora (in Italy), St. Dominic, abbot, renowned for miracles.

The Twenty-third Day of January

At Barcelona in Spain, St. Raymond of Peñafort, confessor and third master-general of the Order of Preachers. He was celebrated for his doctrine, holiness, and the glory of his miracles. He founded the Order of Our Lady of Mercy, and it was at his advice that James, King of Aragon, instituted in his domains the sacred Office of the Inquisition. When about to return to Barcelona from the island of Majorca, he crossed the sea miraculously carried by his cloak spread on the water, and entered his monastery although the gates remained closed. He is said to have raised forty persons from the dead. He was almost one hundred years old when, on the feast of the Epiphany, he went to heavenly glory. From his sepulchre there comes, as an unceasing miracle, a fine dust which is never exhausted and by means of which various ailments are cured. He was canonized by Clement VIII. *A totum duplex feast of the second class.*

At Rome, St. Emerentiana, virgin and martyr. While she was yet a catechumen, she was stoned to death by the pagans while she was praying at the tomb of her foster-sister, St. Agnes. *A memory.*

At Philippi in Macedonia, St. Parmenas, who was one of the first seven deacons (of the Church of Jerusalem).[8] Surrendering himself to the grace of God, he perfectly fulfilled the office of preaching entrusted to him by his brethren, and under Trajan he obtained the glory of martyrdom.

At Ancyra in Galatia, St. Clement, bishop, who was tortured a number of times, and at the last completed his martyrdom under Diocletian.

In the same place and on the same day, St. Agathangelus, who suffered under the governor Lucius.

At Caesarea in Morocco, the holy martyrs Severian and Aquila, his wife, who were burned alive.

At Antinoe, a city of Egypt, St. Asclas, martyr. After many torments, he was thrown into a river, and thus rendered up his precious soul to God.

At Alexandria, St. John the Almsgiver, bishop of that city, most celebrated for his mercy toward the poor.

At Toledo in Spain, St. Ildefonsus, bishop. Because of the singular purity of his life and of the defence he made against heretics who denied the virginity of the Mother of God, he was by that same Blessed Mother

[8] See Acts, 6:5.

clothed with a pure white garment, and at last, famed for his holiness, was called to heaven.

In the province of Valeria (Italy), Blessed Martyrius, monk, whom Pope St. Gregory mentions.

The Twenty-fourth Day of January

At Forli, in Emilia (Italy), Blessed Marcolino, confessor of the Order of Preachers. *A semi-duplex feast.*

At Ephesus, St. Timothy, the disciple of St. Paul the Apostle, by whom he was ordained Bishop of Ephesus. After he had undergone many labors for Christ, he rebuked some pagans who were sacrificing to Diana. He was stoned by them, and shortly after he died in the Lord. *A memory.*

At Antioch, St. Babilas, bishop. In the persecution of Decius, after he had often glorified God by his sufferings and torments, he reached the end of his admirable life while bound in chains. He commanded that his body should be buried with the chains. It is said that there suffered with him also three youths, Urban, Prilidian, and Epolonius, whom he had instructed in the faith of Christ.

At Foligno in Umbria, St. Felician. He was ordained bishop of that city by Pope Victor I. After a life of many labors, he was crowned in his extreme old age with martyrdom, in the time of Decius.

At Neocaesarea in Mauretania, the holy martyrs Mardonius, Musonius, Eugene, and Metellus; all were delivered to the flames, and their relics were scattered in a river.

Also the holy martyrs Thyrsus and Projectus.

At Cingoli in Piceno, St. Exuperantius, confessor. He was bishop of that city, and was renowned for his miracles.

At Bologna, St. Zamas, first bishop of that city. He was consecrated by St. Dionysius, the Roman Pontiff, and he spread to a remarkable degree the Christian faith in that place.

Also Blessed Suranus, abbot, who flourished in holiness at the time of the Lombards.

The Twenty-fifth Day of January

The Conversion of St. Paul the Apostle, which took place in the second year from the Ascension of the Lord. *A totum duplex feast.*

At Damascus, the birthday of St. Ananias, a disciple of the Lord, who baptized the Apostle Paul. He preached the Gospel in Damascus, Eleutheropolis and elsewhere until, under the judge Licinius, he was scourged with thongs and mangled. At last, he was stoned to death and thus obtained martyrdom.

In Auvergne in Gaul, St. Praejectus, bishop, and St. Amarinus, abbot of Doroang; both suffered death at the command of the authorities of that city.

At Antioch, the holy martyrs Juventinus and Maximus who, under Julian the Apostate, were crowned with martyrdom. On (the anniversary of) their birthday, St. John Chrysostom delivered a panegyric to the people.

Also the holy martyrs Donatus, Sabinus, and Agape.

At Tomis in Scythia, St. Bretannio, bishop. In the reign of the Arian Emperor Valens, whom he fearlessly opposed, he flourished in the Church in wondrous sanctity and zealous devotion to the Catholic faith.

At Marchiennes in Gaul, St. Poppo, priest and abbot, famed for his miracles.

The Twenty-sixth Day of January

At Morbegno in Rhaetia (Italy), Blessed Andrew of Peschiera, a celebrated Friar Preacher. He left many great monuments in the Valtelline Valley of his holiness, doctrine, and remarkable charity. He was renowned for his miracles. *A semi-duplex feast.*

St. Polycarp, Bishop of Smyrna and martyr, who won the crown of martyrdom on February 23. *A memory.*

At Hippo in Africa, Bishop St. Theogenes and thirty-six others. In the persecution of Valerian, they despised the life of this world, and obtained the crown of eternal life.

At Bethlehem of Judea, the death of St. Paula, widow. Though she came of a noble senatorial family, in company with her daughter Eustochium, a virgin of Christ, she renounced the world, distributed her goods to the poor, and went to Bethlehem. There, enriched with many virtues and crowned with a prolonged martyrdom, she departed to the heavenly kingdom. Her life, which was remarkable for its many virtues, was written by St. Jerome.

The Twenty-seventh Day of January

St. John Chrysostom, Bishop of Constantinople, confessor, Doctor of the Church, and the heavenly patron of preachers. He died in the Lord on September 14. His holy body was transferred to Constantinople on this day, at the time of Theodosius the Younger; afterward, it was taken to

Rome, where it is buried in the Basilica of the Prince of the Apostles. *A duplex feast.*

At Brescia, the virgin St. Angela Merici, a Franciscan tertiary. She founded the Order of Nuns of St. Ursula, whose chief work is to direct young girls in the ways of the Lord. Pope Pius IX decreed that her feast should be observed on May 31.

At Le Mans in Gaul, the death of St. Julian, the first bishop of that city. He was sent there by St. Peter to preach the Gospel. *A memory.*

At Sora (in Italy), St. Julian, martyr. He was arrested in the persecution of Antoninus under the governor Flavian. While he was being tortured, a pagan temple fell to the ground. He received the crown of martyrdom by being beheaded.

In Africa, St. Avitus, martyr.

In the same place, the holy martyrs, Datius, Reatrus, and their companions, who suffered in the Vandal persecution.

Likewise, SS. Dativus, Julian, Vincent, and twenty-seven other martyrs.

At Rome, Pope St. Vitalianus.

In the monastery of Bobbio in Gaul, St. Maurus, abbot.

The Twenty-eighth Day of January

St. Peter Nolasco, confessor, who was founder of the Order of Our Lady of Mercy for the Redemption of Captives. He died in the Lord on December 25. *A duplex feast.*

At Rome, for the second time,[9] St. Agnes, virgin and martyr. *A memory.*

At Alexandria, the birthday of St. Cyril, bishop of that city, confessor and Doctor of the Church. He was a most renowned defender of the Catholic faith. He died in peace, illustrious for his teaching and holiness. His festival is, however, kept on February 9.

At Rome, St. Flavian, martyr, who suffered under Diocletian.

At Alexandria, the suffering of many holy martyrs. While they were in church at Mass on this day, they were put to death in various ways by the faction of the Arian leader Syrianus.

At Apollonia, the holy martyrs Leucius, Thyrsus, and Callinicus. In the reign of the Emperor Decius, they were subjected to various kinds of torture and all completed their martyrdom. Leucius and Callinicus were beheaded; but Thyrsus, summoned by a voice from Heaven, gave up his spirit.

[9] The phrase "for a second time" may mean either the octave day of her death, or a second feast in her honor, i.e., her birth into this world. The latter meaning is the more probable.

In the Thebaid, the holy martyrs Leonidas and his companions, who obtained the palm of martyrdom in the reign of Diocletian.

At Saragosa in Spain, St. Valerius, bishop.

At Cuenca in Spain, the birthday of St. Julian, bishop. He distributed to the poor the goods of the Church, and supported himself by the work of his hands after the example of the Apostles. He died in peace, renowned for miracles.

In the monastery of Reomay in Gaul, the burial of the priest, St. John, a man devoted to God.

In Palestine, St. James, a hermit. After having committed a grave sin, he lived for a long time in a sepulchre for penance. Famed for miracles, he went to the Lord.

The Twenty-ninth Day of January

St. Francis of Sales, Bishop of Geneva, confessor, and Doctor of the Church. He is the special patron of all Catholic writers, who explain, promote, or defend Christian Doctrine by publishing journals or other writings in the vernacular. He departed to heaven on December 28, but his feast is observed on this day, the date of the transferal of his body (to Savoy). *A duplex feast.*

At Treves, the death of blessed Valerius, bishop, a disciple of St. Peter the Apostle.

At Rome, on the Via Nomentana, the holy martyrs Papias and Maurus, soldiers, in the time of the Emperor Diocletian. At their first confession of Christ, Laodicius, the prefect of the city, ordered their mouths to be pounded with stones. After this, they were cast into prison and beaten with clubs; then they were flogged with lead-tipped scourges until they died.

At Perugia, St. Constantine, bishop and martyr. Together with his companions, he received the crown of martyrdom for his defence of the faith under the Emperor Marcus Aurelius.

At Milan, St. Aquilinus, priest, whose throat was pierced with a sword by the Arians, thus receiving the crown of martyrdom.

At Edessa in Syria, the holy martyrs Sarbellius and his sister Barbea, who were baptized by Bishop Blessed Barsimaeus. They were crowned with martyrdom under Lysias the governor in the persecution of Trajan.

Near Troyes (in Gaul), St. Sabinian, martyr, who was beheaded for the faith of Christ at the command of Aurelian the Emperor.

At Bourges in Aquitaine, St. Sulpicius Severus, bishop, remarkable for his learning and virtues.

The Thirtieth Day of January

At Pisa, in Etruria, Blessed Maria Mancini (widow, who joined the Order of Preachers). From childhood, she was devoted to works of piety. Later, when married, she showed the utmost commiseration toward the sick, and finally she entered the religious life where she pursued the path to perfection. *A semi-duplex feast.*

St. Martina, virgin and martyr, whose birthday is commemorated on January 1. *A memory.*

At Edessa in Syria, St. Barsimaeus, bishop. After converting many Gentiles to the faith and sending them to their crowns before him, in the reign of Trajan he followed them with the palm of martyrdom.

At Antioch, the suffering of Blessed Hippolytus, priest. For a while he was deceived by the schism of Novatus, but enlightened by grace he returned to the unity of the faith, and in behalf of it completed an illustrious martyrdom. Asked by his people which Church was the true one, he anathematized the doctrine of Novatus, declaring that he would keep the same faith as the See of Peter held. So saying, he presented his throat to the executioner.

In Africa, the suffering of the holy martyrs Felician, Philappian, and one hundred and twenty-four others.

Also Blessed Alexander, who was arrested in the persecution of Decius. He gave up his spirit amid the tortures of the executioners, glorious for his venerable age and his repeated confession (of faith).

At Edessa in Syria, St. Barses, bishop, famous for the power of healing. The Arian Emperor Valens exiled him because of his Catholic faith. His place of exile having been changed three times, each time for a distant region, Barses died of exhaustion.

At Jerusalem, the birthday of St. Mathias, bishop, of whom are told deeds wondrous and full of faith. In the reign of Hadrian, he suffered much for Christ, but at length died in peace.

At Pavia, St. Armentarius, bishop and confessor.

In Maubeuge, in a monastery of Hainault (Belgium), St. Aldegund, virgin, in the time of King Dagobert.

At Viterbo, the virgin St. Hyacintha Mariscotti, nun of the Third Order of St. Francis. She was noted for (her virtues of) penance and charity. Pope Pius VII numbered her among the saints.

At Milan, St. Savina, a most religious woman, who died in the Lord while praying at the tombs of the martyrs SS. Nabor and Felix.

Near Paris, St. Bathildis, queen, famed for the glory of her miracles and her sanctity.

The Thirty-first Day of January

At Turin, the birthday of St. John Bosco, confessor, the founder of the Salesian Congregation and of the Institute of the Daughters of Mary Help of Christians. He was outstanding in his zeal for souls and in propagating the faith. Pius XI inscribed him among the saints in 1934. *A duplex feast.*

At Rome, on the Via Portuensis, the holy martyrs Cyrus and John, who after many torments were beheaded for Christ.

At Alexandria, St. Metranus, martyr, under the Emperor Decius. When he refused the command of the pagans to utter impious words, they beat his entire body with clubs, and bored through his face and eyes with sharp stakes. Then driving him out of the city with fresh tortures, they stoned him to death.

In the same city, the holy martyrs Saturninus, Thyrsus, and Victor.

Also at Alexandria, the holy martyrs Tharsicius, Zoticus, Cyriacus, and their companions.

At Cyzicus in the Hellespont, St. Triphenes, martyr. She endured various torments and was at last killed by a bull, thus meriting the palm of martyrdom.

At Modena, St. Geminianus, bishop, famous for the glory of miracles.

In the province of Milan, St. Julius, priest and confessor, in the time of the Emperor Theodosius.

At Rome, St. Marcella, widow, whose excellent praises Jerome has written.

Also at Rome, blessed Louisa Albertoni, a Roman widow, of the Third Order of St. Francis, renowned for virtues.

On the same day, the transferal of (the body of) St. Mark the Evangelist. His holy body was brought from Alexandria, which was then occupied by the barbarians, to Venice, and was there honorably buried in the great church dedicated to his name.

fEBRUaRy

The First Day of February

St. Ignatius, Bishop of Antioch and martyr, who gloriously suffered martyrdom on December 20. *A duplex feast.*

At Smyrna, St. Pionius, priest and martyr, who wrote books defending the Christian faith. After enduring a foul prison, where by his exhortations he strengthened many of the brethren to suffer martyrdom, he was subjected to many tortures. Pierced with nails and placed upon a flaming pyre, he obtained for the sake of Christ a glorious end. With him there were martyred fifteen others.

At Ravenna, St. Severus, bishop who, on account of his excellent merit, indicated by a dove, was chosen (bishop).

At the city of Trou in Gaul, St. Paul, bishop, whose life was renowned for his virtues, and whose precious death was approved by miracles.

At Kildare in Ireland, St. Bridget, virgin. In proof of her virginity she touched the wood of an altar, and forthwith it became green.

At Castel-Fiorentino in Tuscany, blessed Veridiana, virgin and recluse, of the Order of Vallombrosa.

The Second Day of February

The Purification of the Blessed Virgin Mary, which is called by the Greeks the Hypapante of the Lord. *A totum duplex feast of the second class.*

At Caesarea in Palestine, St. Cornelius, the centurion whom St. Peter the Apostle baptized and raised to episcopal honor in that city.

At Rome, on the Via Salaria, the suffering of St. Apronianus, a notary. While he was still a heathen, he was leading St. Sisinius from prison to bring him before Laodicius the prefect, when he heard a voice from heaven: "Come, ye blessed of my Father, inherit the kingdom prepared for you from the foundation of the world." He believed and was baptized, and afterward was condemned to death for confessing the Lord.

Also at Rome, the holy martyrs Fortunatus, Felician, Firmus, and Candidus.

At Orleans in Gaul, St. Flosculus, bishop.

At Canterbury in England, the birthday of St. Laurence, bishop who, after St. Augustine, governed that Church and converted the king himself to the faith.

At Prato in Tuscany, St. Catherine de'Ricci, virgin of Florence, of the Order of Preachers. She was noted for her store of heavenly gifts. The Sovereign Pontiff, Pope Benedict XIV, inscribed her name on the roll of holy virgins. Her feast is celebrated February 13.

The Third Day of February

At Sebaste in Armenia, the suffering of St. Blaise, bishop and martyr. He performed numerous miracles. Under the governor Agricolaus, he was scourged for a long time; then, suspended from a rack, his flesh torn with iron combs, after which he was thrown into a prison totally devoid of light. Although he was cast into a lake, he emerged from it unhurt. Finally, at the command of the same judge, he was beheaded with two boys. However, before his death, seven women who had collected the drops of blood that flowed during his tortures, were arrested and for their Christian faith were slain by the sword after cruel tortures. *A feast of three lessons.*

In Africa, St. Celerinus, deacon, who was kept in a prison for nineteen days, and was a glorious confessor of Christ despite stocks, chains, and other afflictions. While he conquered his adversary by unconquerable firmness in his own trial, he showed others the way to be victorious.

In the same place, three holy martyrs, relatives of the same deacon St. Celerinus; namely, his two uncles Laurence and Ignatius, and his aunt Celerina. All three were crowned with martyrdom ahead of him. A letter of St. Cyprian is extant, setting forth the glorious praises of them all.

Likewise in Africa, the holy martyrs Felix, Symphronius, Hippolytus, and their companions.

In the town of Gap in Gaul, SS. Tigides and Remedius, bishops.

At Lyons in Gaul, SS. Lupicinus and Felix, likewise bishops.

At Bremen, St. Anschar, Bishop of Hamburg, then (Archbishop) of (both) Hamburg and Bremen. He converted the Swedes and Danes to the faith of Christ, and was appointed Apostolic Legate of all the North by Pope Gregory IV.

The Fourth Day of February

St. Andrew Corsini, confessor, of the Carmelite Order, and Bishop of Fiesole, of whom mention is made on January 6. *A duplex feast.*

At Rome, St. Eutychius, martyr, who completed an illustrious martyrdom and was buried in the cemetery of Callistus. Pope St. Damasus adorned his sepulchre with verses.

At Thmuis in Egypt, the suffering of blessed Philaeas, bishop of that city, and Philoromus, tribune of the soldiers. In the persecution of Diocletian, they could not be persuaded by their friends and kinsfolk to save themselves, but both offered up their lives and merited the rewards of victory from the Lord. With them, an innumerable multitude of the faithful from the same city who followed the example of their pastor and were crowned with martydrom.

At Fossombrone (in Italy), the holy martyrs Aquilinus, Geminus, Gelasius, Magnus, and Donatus.

At Troyes in Gaul, St. Aventinus, priest and confessor.

At Pelusium in Egypt, St. Isidore, priest and monk. He was noted for learning and doctrine.

At Sempringham in England, St. Gilbert, priest and confessor, who was the founder of a religious Order at Sempringham.

In the city of Amatrice in the Diocese of Rieti, the death of St. Joseph of Leonissa, a Capuchin priest. For his preaching of the faith, he was cruelly treated by the Mohammedans. Famous for his apostolic labors and for his miracles, he was canonized by the Sovereign Pontiff, Pope Benedict XIV.

At Bremen, the commemoration of St. Rembert. He was a disciple of St. Anschar and, after the death of his master, was elected on this day Bishop of Hamburg and Bremen in his stead. ✠ *An Anniversary.*

The Fifth Day of February

At Catania in Sicily, the birthday of St. Agatha, virgin and martyr. At the time of the Emperor Decius, under the judge Quinctian, she endured buffets, imprisonment, the rack, the disjointing of her limbs, mutilation, and torture by being rolled upon sherds and live coals. At last she died in prison while praying to God. *A duplex feast.*

At Nagasaki in Japan, the suffering of twenty-six martyrs. Three priests, one cleric, and two lay-brothers, were members of the Order of Friars Minor. One cleric belonged to the Society of Jesus. The seventeen others were tertiaries of the Third Order of St. Francis. All of them were crucified for the Catholic faith. They were pierced by spears, and died praising God and preaching the Catholic faith. They were canonized by the Sovereign Pontiff, Pope Pius IX.

In Pontus, the commemoration of many holy martyrs. In the persecution of Maximian, some were covered with molten lead while others were tortured by having sharp splinters thrust under their nails; they suffered many horrible tortures which were inflicted on them again and again. By their remarkable suffering, they merited palms and crowns from the Lord.

At Alexandria, St. Isidore, soldier and martyr. In the persecution of Decius, this soldier, because of his faith in Christ, was beheaded by order of Numerian, general of the army.

At Vienne, Blessed Avitus, bishop and confessor. By his faith, labors, and wonderful teaching, Gaul was preserved from the infection of the Arian heresy.

At Sabion in the Tyrol, St. Ingenuinus, bishop, whose life was renowned for his miracles. His sacred body was afterwards transferred to Brixen, and is there honorably preserved.

At Brixen, St. Albuinus, bishop, who transferred the episcopal see from Sabion to that city, and there, famous because of his miracles, died in the Lord.

The Sixth Day of February

St. Titus, Bishop of Crete and confessor, whose birthday occurs on January 4.

At Caesarea in Cappadocia, St. Dorothy, virgin and martyr. Under Sapricius, the governor of that province, she was first tortured by being stretched upon a rack, then she was whipped for a long time with palm-stems; at last she was punished by capital sentence. Because of her confession of faith, one Theophilus, a student, was converted to the faith of Christ; soon he too was cruelly tortured upon the rack, and at last put to the sword.

At Emesa in Phoenicia, St. Silvanus, bishop. After he had ruled that Church for forty years, he was cast to the beasts in the reign of the Emperor Maximian, together with two others. They were torn to pieces, limb from limb, and so received the palm of martyrdom.

On the same day the holy martyrs Saturninus, Theophilus, and Revocata.

In Auvergne in Gaul, St. Antholian, martyr.

At Arras in Gaul, St. Vedast, bishop of that city. His life and death were glorified by many miracles. *A memory.*

At Elnon in Gaul, St. Amand, Bishop of Maestricht. During his life and after death, he was renowned for his miracles; the town, in which he built the monastery and died, was later named after him. *A memory.*

At Bologna, St. Guarinus, Cardinal Bishop of Palestrina, remarkable for holiness of life.

The Seventh Day of February

St. Romuald, abbot, father of the Camaldolese monks. His birthday is commemorated on June 19, but his festival is observed on this day when his body was removed (to the town of Fabriano). *A duplex feast.*

At Augusta, now called London, in England, the birthday of Blessed Augulus, bishop. He fulfilled the course of his life by martyrdom, and merited to obtain everlasting rewards.

In Phrygia, St. Adaucus, martyr. He came of a noble Italian family, and was honored by the emperors with dignities of almost every rank. At length, while performing the office of quaestor, he was found worthy of a martyr's crown for his defence of the faith.

In the same place, many holy martyrs, citizens of one city, whose leader was this same Adaucus. Since they were all Christians and remained constant in the confession of the faith, they were burned alive by the Emperor Galerius Maximian.

At Heraclea in Pontus, St. Theodore, an army general. After he had undergone many torments in the reign of Licinius, he was beheaded, and entered Heaven as a victor.

In Egypt, St. Moses, a venerable bishop. At first he led a solitary life in the desert; then at the request of Mauvia, Sultana of the Saracens, he was made a bishop and converted that ferocious people in great part to the faith. Glorious for his merits, he died in peace.

At Lucca in Tuscany, the death of St. Richard, King of England. He was the father of St. Willebald, Bishop of Eichstadt, and of St. Walburga, virgin.

At Bologna, St. Juliana, widow.

The Eighth Day of February

St. John of Matha, priest and confessor, founder of the Order of the Most Holy Trinity for the redemption of captives. On December 17 he died in the Lord. *A duplex feast.*

At Somascha in the district of Bergamo, St. Jerome Emiliani, confessor, who was the founder of the Congregation of Somascha. He was celebrated both during life and after death for his many miracles, and was inscribed in the calendar of the Saints by the Sovereign Pontiff, Pope Clement XIII. However, his feast day is observed on July 20.

At Rome, the holy martyrs Paul, Lucius, and Cyriacus.

In Lesser Armenia, the birthday of the holy martyrs Dionysius, Emilian, and Sebastian.

At Constantinople, the birthday of the holy martyrs, monks of the monastery of Dirn. They were savagely slaughtered for their defence of the Catholic faith while carrying letters of Pope St. Felix against Acacius.

In Persia, commemoration of the holy martyrs who were slain, because of their Christian faith, by various kinds of torment under Cabades, King of the Persians.

At Alexandria, the suffering of St. Cointha, martyr, in the reign of the Emperor Decius. The pagans seized her and led her to their idols to compel her to worship, but she refused with horror. Then they fastened her ankles with chains and dragged her thus bound through the city streets until, by that inhuman torture, they had torn her body to pieces.

At Pavia, St. Juventius, bishop, who labored zealously for the Gospel.

At Milan, the death of St. Honoratus, bishop and confessor.

At Verdun in Gaul, St. Paul, bishop, noted for the power of working miracles.

At Muret in the district of Limoges, the birthday of St. Stephen, abbot, founder of the Order of Grandmont. He was renowned for his virtues and miracles.

In the monastery of Vallombrosa, Blessed Peter, Cardinal Bishop of Albano. He was a member of the Congregation of Vallombrosa (of the Order of St. Benedict), and was surnamed Igneus, because he passed through fire unharmed.

The Ninth Day of February

St. Cyril, bishop, confessor, and Doctor of the Church, of whom mention is made on January 28. *A duplex feast.*

At Alexandria, the birthday of St. Apollonia, virgin and martyr. During the reign of Decius, the executioners first knocked out her teeth, then they built and kindled a pyre, and threatened to burn her alive unless she would utter impious words with them. But she, deliberating with herself for a short space, suddenly tore herself from their wicked hands, and of her own accord leaped into the fire they had prepared, being kindled within by the greater fire of the Holy Spirit. As a result, the very authors of this cruelty were themselves terrified, since a woman was found more ready to meet death than were her persecutors to inflict it.[1]

At Rome, the suffering of the holy martyrs Alexander and thirty-eight others crowned (with him).

In the village of Lamelum in Africa, the holy martyrs Primus and Donatus, deacons. They were slain by the Donatists while they guarded the altar in a church.

At Soli in Cyprus, the holy martyrs Ammonius and Alexander.

At Antioch, St. Nicephorus, martyr, who was beheaded, thus receiving the crown of martyrdom under the Emperor Valerian.

In the monastery of Fontanelle, in Gaul, St. Ansbert, Bishop of Rouen.

At Canossa in Apulia, St. Sabinus, bishop and confessor. As Pope St. Gregory narrates, Sabinus was gifted with the spirit of prophecy and the power of miracles. Although he was blind, he instantly knew by divine enlightenment that a drink offered him by a bribed servant was poisoned. Declaring that God would punish the man who had corrupted his servant, he made the sign of the cross and confidently drank the poison from which he received no harm. ✠

The Tenth Day of February

At Monte Cassino, St. Scholastica, virgin, the sister of St. Benedict the abbot. He beheld her soul in the form of a dove leaving her body and entering heaven. *A duplex feast.*

At Rome, the holy martyrs Zoticus, Irenaeus, Hyacinth, and Amantius.

In the same place, on the Via Lavicana, ten holy martyrs (all of them) soldiers.

Likewise at Rome, on the Appian Way, St. Soteris, virgin and martyr. As St. Ambrose relates, she was of noble birth, and for the sake of Christ she held in little esteem the consulships and prefectures of her kinsfolk. Being ordered to sacrifice, she refused, and was severely struck with blows for a long time. When she had endured other kinds of torture, she was put to the sword, and so passed joyfully to her Bridegroom.

In Campania, St. Silvanus, bishop and confessor.

At Malavalle, near Siena, St. William, hermit.

In the territory of Rheims, St. Austreberta, virgin, famed for miracles.

---

[1] Self-destruction is not permissible unless God unmistakably demands it. St. Apollonia (and certain other martyrs) evidently acted under divine inspiration. See St. Thomas, *Summa Theol.,* IIa-IIae, Q. 64, art. 5, ad 4.

The Eleventh Day of February

At Lourdes, in France, the Apparition of the Blessed and Immaculate Virgin Mary. *A totum duplex feast.*

At Adrianople in Thrace, the holy martyrs Bishop Lucius and companions. In the reign of Constantius, the Bishop steadfastly suffered many things at the hands of the Arians and finished his martyrdom in chains. His companions, who were the more noble of the citizens, refused to receive the Arians who had already been condemned by the Council of Sardice; for this reason, they were sentenced to death by (the Arian) Count Philagrius.

In Africa, the birthday of the holy martyrs the priest Saturninus, Dativus, Felix, Ampelius, and their companions. In the persecution of Diocletian, when they had assembled according to their custom to celebrate the Lord's Supper, they were seized by the soldiers, and suffered death under the Proconsul Anolinus.

In Numidia, the commemoration of many holy martyrs, who were arrested in the same persecution. As they refused to give up the Holy Scriptures in accordance with the Emperor's edict, they were tortured by most severe punishments and finally put to death.

At Rome, Pope St. Gregory II, who boldly withstood the impiety of Leo the Isaurian, and who sent St. Boniface to preach the Gospel in Germany.

Likewise, Pope St. Paschal I, who removed the bodies of many holy martyrs from their tombs and buried them with honor in various churches of the city.

At Ravenna, St. Calocerus, bishop and confessor.

At Milan, St. Lazarus, bishop.

At Capua, St. Castrensis, bishop.

In the town of Landon in Gaul, St. Severinus, abbot of the monastery of St. Maurice d'Agaune. By his prayers, the Christian king Clovis was freed from a long-standing sickness.

In Egypt, St. Jonas, monk, renowned for his virtues.

At Vienne in France, the transferal of the body of St. Desiderius, bishop and martyr, from the neighborhood of Lyons where he had died on May 23.

The Twelfth Day of February

The seven holy founders of the Order of the Servants of the Blessed Virgin Mary, confessors, whose deaths are noted on their respective days. As in life one single spirit of true brotherhood drew them together, so after death an undivided veneration of the people followed them. The Sovereign Pontiff, Leo XIII inscribed them together in the roll of the saints. *A duplex feast.*

In Africa, St. Damian, soldier and martyr.

At Carthage, the holy martyrs Modestus and Julian.

At Alexandria, the holy children Modestus and Ammonius, both martyrs.

At Barcelona in Spain, St. Eulalia, virgin. In the time of the emperor Diocletian, she suffered the rack, iron hooks, and the flames. At last, she was crucified and so received the glorious crown of martyrdom.

At Constantinople, St. Meletius, Bishop of Antioch. He repeatedly suffered exile for the Catholic faith, and at last at Constantinople went to the Lord. SS. John Chrysostom and Gregory of Nyssa celebrated his virtues with highest praise.

Also at Constantinople, St. Anthony, bishop, in the time of the Emperor Leo VI.

At Verona, St. Gaudentius, bishop and confessor.

The Thirteenth Day of February

At Prato in Etruria, St. Catherine de'Ricci, of Florence, virgin, of the Order of Preachers. She was remarkable for the abundance of her divine gifts, and was canonized by the Sovereign Pontiff, Benedict XIV. She died rich in virtues and merit on February 2, but her feast is celebrated today. *A totum duplex feast of the second class.*

At Antioch, the birthday of St. Agabus, Prophet, whom Saint Luke mentions in the Acts of the Apostles.[2]

At Todi in Umbria, St. Benignus, priest and martyr. At the time of the Emperors Diocletian and Maximian, he refused to cease spreading the Christian faith by word and example. He was therefore arrested by the pagans, suffered various tortures, and finally enriched his priestly office with the honor of martyrdom.

At Melitina in Armenia, St. Polyeuctus, martyr, who suffered much in the persecution of Decius, and obtained a martyr's crown.

At Lyons in Gaul, St. Julian, martyr.

At Ravenna, SS. Fusca, virgin, and Maura, her nurse. In the time of the Emperor Decius, they suffered greatly under the governor Quinctian, and at last gained martyrdom, being pierced with the sword.

At Lyons in Gaul, St. Stephen, bishop and confessor.

At Rieti, the abbot St. Stephen, a man of marvellous patience. At his

[2] Acts, 11:28, 21:10.

death, as Pope St. Gregory relates, the holy angels who were present were seen by the by-standers.

The Fourteenth Day of February

At Perugia, Blessed Nicholas Palea of Giovinazzo, confessor, of our Order, and founder of the monasteries at Perugia and Trani. He was received into the Order by our holy Father Dominic, who selected him to be his companion in preaching the Word of God. He shone to a wonderful degree by the exercise of every virtue. *A semi-duplex feast.*

At Rome, on the Via Flaminia, the birthday of St. Valentine, priest and martyr. After many wondrous works of healing and teaching, he was beaten with clubs and beheaded in the reign of Claudius Caesar. *A memory.*

Also at Rome, the death of St. Cyril, bishop and confessor. Together with his brother Methodius, also a bishop, whose birthday falls on April 6, Cyril brought many people and the rulers of Moravia to the faith of Christ. Their feast is observed on July 7.

Also at Rome, the holy martyrs Vitalis, Felicula, and Zeno.

At Teramo, St. Valentine, bishop and martyr. After prolonged scourging, he was handed over to a guard; since he could not be made to yield, he was brought out of his prison in the dead of night, and beheaded at the command of Placidus, prefect of the city.

At Alexandria, the holy martyrs Cyrion, priest, Bassian, reader, Agatho, exorcist, and Moses. All were burned to death and thus passed to heaven.

At Teramo, SS. Proculus, Ephebus, and Apollonius, martyrs. They were keeping watch over the body of St. Valentine when, by the command of Leontius, the consular officer, they were seized and put to the sword.

At Alexandria, the holy martyrs Bassus, Anthony, and Protolicus, who were drowned in the sea.

Also at Alexandria, SS. Dionysius and Ammonius, who were beheaded.

At Naples in Campania, St. Nostrianus, bishop, who became famous for his defence of the Catholic faith against heretical attacks.

At Ravenna, St. Eleuchadius, bishop and confessor.

In Bithynia, St. Auxentius, abbot.

At Sorrento, St. Antoninus, abbot. When the monastery of Monte Cassino was laid waste by the Lombards, he departed to a solitary place near Sorrento, and there, renowned for miracles, died in the Lord. His body is glorified daily by many wonders, especially in the freeing of those possessed by demons.

The Fifteenth Day of February

The feast of Blessed Jordan (of Saxony). On account of the probity of his life and teaching, he was considered by our holy Father Dominic as being worthy to govern the Order. Placed in authority, his zeal for the salvation of souls greatly augmented the Order in a short time. Having been shipwrecked and drowned, he entered heaven as a victor rich in merit. *A duplex feast.*

At Brescia, the birthday of the holy brothers Faustinus and Jovita, martyrs. At the time of the Emperor Hadrian, they underwent many glorious trials for the faith of Christ and received the victorious crown of martyrdom.

At Rome, St. Craton, martyr. He was baptized by the Bishop St. Valentine, together with his wife and his whole household, and not long after was martyred with them.

At Teramo, the birthday of the holy martyrs Saturninus, Castulus, Magnus, and Lucius.

In the same place, St. Agape, virgin and martyr.

At Vaison in Gaul, St. Quinidius, bishop, whose death, as frequent miracles testify, was precious in the sight of the Lord.

At Capua, St. Decorosus, bishop and confessor.

In the province of Valeria, St. Severus, priest, of whom St. Gregory writes that by the shedding of his tears he recalled a dead man to life.

At Antioch, St. Joseph, deacon.

In Auvergne in Gaul, St. Georgia, virgin.

The Sixteenth Day of February

At Catania, in Sicily, Blessed Bernard, confessor, of the Order of Preachers. He was born of the patrician family of Scammacca. God made him wonderful by the contemplation of divine things, and by the glory of his virtue. *A semi-duplex feast.*

At Rome, blessed Onesimus, regarding whom St. Paul wrote to Philemon.[3] The apostle ordained him Bishop of Ephesus to succeed St. Timothy, and entrusted him with the office of preaching. Onesimus, however, was taken in chains to Rome where he was stoned to death for the Christian faith. He was first buried there but later his body was transferred to Ephesus where he had been ordained bishop.

In Egypt, St. Julian, martyr, with five thousand others.

At Caesarea in Palestine, the holy Egyptian martyrs Elias, Jeremias,

---

[3] Philemon, 5:10.

Isaias, Samuel and Daniel. They voluntarily ministered to the Christians condemned to the mines in Cilicia. On their return, they were arrested and most cruelly tortured by the governor Firmilian, in the reign of the Emperor Galerius Maximian. At length they were put to the sword. And after these, St. Porphyrius, servant of the martyr Pamphilus, and St. Seleucus the Cappadocian, triumphed in repeated trials. Being once more tortured, they obtained the crown of martyrdom, the one by fire, and the other by the sword.

At Nicomedia, St. Juliana, virgin and martyr. At the time of the Emperor Maximian, she was first grievously scourged by her father Africanus. Then she was tortured in various ways by the prefect Evilasius, whom she refused to marry. Next, she was cast into prison, where, in the presence of others, she fought with the devil. Finally, overcoming flames of fire and a boiling cauldron, she completed her martyrdom by being beheaded. Her body was later on transferred to Cumae in Campania.

At Brescia, St. Faustinus, bishop and confessor.

The Seventeenth Day of February

At Paris, Blessed Reginald, confessor. He was dean of the Church of St. Aignan in Orleans. While at Rome, he received from the hands of our holy Father Dominic, the Dominican habit which the glorious Virgin Mary had shown him a short time before when he was dangerously ill. *A semi-duplex feast.*

At Florence, the birthday of St. Alexius Falconieri, confessor, one of the seven founders of the Order of Servants of the Blessed Virgin Mary. In the 110th year of his life, he died in blessedness, comforted by the presence of Christ Jesus and of the angels. His feast, with that of his companions, is kept on February 12.

At Rome, the suffering of St. Faustinus, whom forty-four others followed to the crown.

In Persia, the birthday of Blessed Polychronius, Bishop of Babylon. In the persecution of Decius, his face was beaten with rocks. He died with hands extended and his eyes raised to heaven.

At Concordia near Venice, the holy martyrs Donatus, Secundian, and Romulus, with eighty-six others, sharers in the same crown (of victory).

At Caesarea in Palestine, St. Theodulus, an old man, who was of the household of Firmilian the governor. Roused by the example of the martyrs, he confessed firmly Christ, was nailed to a cross, and by his noble triumph merited the martyr's palm (of glory).

Likewise St. Julian the Cappadocian. He was denounced as a Christian because he had kissed the remains of the martyrs. Being taken before the governor, he was ordered to be burned to death over a slow fire.

In the district of Terouanne in Gaul, St. Silvinus, Bishop of Toulouse.

In the monastery of Cluainedhech in Ireland, St. Fintan, priest and abbot.

The Eighteenth Day of February

At Jerusalem, the birthday of St. Simeon, bishop and martyr. He is said to have been the son of Cleophas, and a kinsman of the Saviour according to the flesh. He was ordained Bishop of Jerusalem to succeed James, the cousin of our Lord. In the persecution of Trajan, he was subjected to many tortures, and gained martyrdom. All who were present, and even the judge himself, marvelled that a man one hundred and twenty years old should bear the torment of the cross so bravely and with such firmness.

At Ostia, the holy martyrs Maximus and Claudius, brothers, and Praepedigna, the wife of Claudius, with their two sons Alexander and Cutias. Though they were of most noble birth, they were arrested and exiled at Diocletian's command. Afterward they offered themselves to God as a sweet sacrifice of martyrdom, being burned to death. Their relics were cast into the river, but were found by the Christians and buried near the same city.

In Africa, the holy martyrs Lucius, Silvanus, Rutulus, Classicus, Secundinus, Fructulus, and Maximus.

At Constantinople, St. Flavian, bishop. He fought for the Catholic faith at Ephesus, and was attacked with kicks and blows by the faction of the impious Dioscorus. He was driven into exile where after three days he died.

At Toledo in Spain, St. Helladius, bishop and confessor; St. Ildefonsus, Bishop of Toledo, greatly praised him.

The Nineteenth Day of February

At Cordoba in Spain, Blessed Alvarus, confessor, of the Order of Preachers, and founder of the monastery of Scala Caeli (near Cordoba). *A semi-duplex feast.*

At Rome, the birthday of St. Gabinus, priest and martyr, and brother of Pope St. Caius. Kept chained in prison for a long time, by his precious death he gained the joys of heaven.

In Africa, the holy martyrs Publius, Julian, Marcellus, and others.

In Palestine, the commemoration of the holy monks and other martyrs, who were killed with the utmost cruelty for the faith of Christ by the Saracens under their general Almondhar.

At Naples in Campania, St. Quodvultdeus, Bishop of Carthage. Together with his clergy, he was placed in leaky boats without oars or sails by the Arian King Genseric; but contrary to expectations, he reached Naples, and died there in exile as a confessor.

At Jerusalem, St. Zambdas, bishop.

At Soli in Cyprus, St. Auxibius, bishop.

At Benevento (Italy), St. Barbatus, bishop, who was famed for holiness, and who converted the Lombards and their leader to Christ.

At Milan, St. Mansuetus, bishop and confessor. ✠

The Twentieth Day of February

At Tyre, in Phoenicia, the commemoration of many blessed martyrs whose number is known only to God. In the reign of the Emperor Diocletian, they were slaughtered by Veturius, a military officer. They were killed in turn by numerous varieties of torture. Their bodies were torn by scourges, and then they were thrown to different kinds of wild beasts. When by the power of God the beasts did not harm them, they gained their martyrdom by a barbarous use of fire and sword. The Bishops Tyrannio, Silvanus, Peleus, and Nilus, and the priest Zenobius, encouraged the glorious multitude to victory, and they too by a happy test obtained the palm of martyrdom, together with them.

At Constantinople, St. Eleutherius, bishop and martyr.

In Persia, the birthday of St. Sadoth, bishop, and one hundred twenty-eight others. On refusing to adore the sun, they obtained glorious crowns by their cruel death under Sapor, the Persian King.

On the island of Cyprus, the holy martyrs Potamius and Nemesius.

At Catania in Sicily, St. Leo, bishop, who was resplendent with virtues and miracles.

On the same day, St. Eucherius, Bishop of Orleans, who, the more he was harassed by calumny and envy, the more famous he became for his miracles.

At Tournai in Gaul, St. Eleutherius, bishop and confessor.

The Twenty-first Day of February

At Scythopolis in Palestine, St. Severian, bishop and martyr, who was slain by the Monophysites because he so energetically opposed them.

In Sicily, the birthday of seventy-nine martyrs, at the time of Diocletian. Undergoing different kinds of torments they obtained the crown by their profession of faith.

At Adrumetum in Africa, the holy martyrs Verulus, Secundinus, Syricius, Felix, Servulus, Saturninus, Fortunatus, and sixteen others. In the persecution by the Vandals, they were crowned with martyrdom for their confession of the Catholic faith.

At Damascus, St. Peter Mavimenus. To some Arabs who approached him when he was ill, he declared: "Everyone who does not belong to the Catholic Christian faith is lost, even as your false prophet Mohammed," whereupon the Arabs killed him.

At Metz in Gaul, St. Felix, bishop.

At Brescia (in Italy), St. Paterius, bishop. ✠

The Twenty-second Day of February

At Antioch, the Chair of St. Peter the Apostle. It was at Antioch that the disciples (of Christ) were first called Christians. *A totum duplex feast.*

At Faenza in Emilia (Italy), the birthday of St. Peter Damian, Cardinal Bishop of Ostia, and confessor, of the Camaldolese Order. He was celebrated for his learning and holiness, and Pope Leo XII declared him a Doctor of the Universal Church. His feast is observed February 23.

At Salamis in Cyprus, St. Aristio. Papias (the next to be mentioned) states that he was one of the seventy-two disciples of Christ.

At Hieropolis in Phrygia, St. Papias, bishop of that city. He was a disciple of St. John the Elder; moreover, he was also a companion of St. Polycarp.

In Arabia, the commemoration of many holy martyrs, who were inhumanly slaughtered under the Emperor Galerius Maximian.

At Alexandria, St. Abilius, bishop. He was the second bishop of that city succeeding St. Mark, and he discharged his office with eminent piety.

At Vienne in Gaul, St. Paschasius, bishop, famous for learning and holiness of life.

At Ravenna, St. Maximian, bishop and confessor.

At Cortona in Tuscany, St. Margaret, of the Third Order of St. Francis. She unceasingly wiped away the stains of her previous life by admirable penance and abundant tears. Her body has remained miraculously incorrupt and it gives forth a sweet odor; it is credited with many miracles, and at Cortona is held in high honor.

The Twenty-third Day of February

(*In Leap Year the announcement* The Vigil of St. Matthias the Apostle *is omitted, for it is transferred to the following day, namely the 24th.*)

The Vigil of St. Matthias the apostle.

St. Peter Damian, a Camaldolese monk, Cardinal Bishop of Ostia, confessor, and Doctor of the Church, who departed this life on February 22. *A duplex feast.*

At Smyrna, the birthday of St. Polycarp, a disciple of Blessed John the Apostle, by whom he was ordained bishop of that city and made primate of all Asia. At the time of Marcus Antonius and Lucius Aurelius Commodus, when the proconsul and all the people assembled in the amphitheatre cried out against Polycarp, he was delivered to the flames. Since they in no way hurt him, he received the crown of martyrdom by the sword. Twelve others, who had come with him from Philadelphia, were also martyred in the same city of Smyrna. The feast of St. Polycarp is celebrated on January 26.

At Sirmium, Blessed Sirenus, monk and martyr. He was arrested by order of the Emperor Maximian and, when he declared himself to be a Christian, was beheaded.

Also at Sirmium, the birthday of seventy-two holy martyrs, who suffered martyrdom in the aforesaid city and received everlasting life.

In the city of Astorga in Spain, St. Martha, virgin and martyr. In the reign of the Emperor Decius, under the proconsul Paternus, she was cruelly tortured for the faith of Christ and finally slain by the sword.

At Constantinople, St. Lazarus, monk. By command of the Iconoclast Emperor Theophilus, he was severely tortured because he painted sacred pictures. His hand was burnt with a red-hot iron, but he was miraculously healed, and repainted the holy pictures that had been destroyed. He ended his life in peace.

At Brescia, St. Felix, bishop.

At Rome, St. Polycarp, priest, who in company with St. Sebastian converted many to the faith of Christ, and by his exhortation led them to the glory of martyrdom.

At Seville in Spain, St. Florentius, confessor.

At Todi in Umbria, St. Romana, virgin. She was baptized by Pope St. Silvester, led a life of holiness in grottos and caves, and was renowned for the glory of her miracles.

In England, St. Milburga, virgin, the daughter of a King of Mercia. ✠

In Leap Year on February 24 is read only the following:
The Vigil of St. Matthias the Apostle.
Likewise the commemoration of many holy martyrs, confessors, and holy virgins.
R. Thanks be to God.

The Twenty-fourth Day of February
(In Leap Year the twenty-fifth Day of February)

In Judaea, the birthday of St. Matthias the Apostle. After the Lord's Ascension, he was chosen by lot by the Apostles to fill the place of Judas the traitor. He suffered martyrdom for preaching the Gospel. *A totum duplex feast of the second class.*

At Rome, St. Primitiva, martyr.

At Rouen, the suffering of St. Praetextatus, bishop and martyr.

At Caesarea in Cappadocia, St. Sergius, martyr. The inspiring Acts (of his life and death) are still extant.

In Africa, the holy martyrs Montanus, Lucius, Julian, Victorious, Flavian, and their companions. They were disciples of St. Cyprian, and suffered martyrdom under the Emperor Valerian.

At Treves, St. Modestus, bishop and confessor.

At Stilo in Calabria, St. John, called Theristus,[4] noted for holiness and his love of monastic life.

In England, St. Ethelbert, King of Kent, whom St. Augustine, Bishop of England, converted to the faith of Christ.

At Jerusalem, the first finding of the head of St. John the Baptist, the Precursor of the Lord.

The Twenty-fifth Day of February
(In Leap Year the Twenty-sixth Day of February)

At Ascoli-Piceno (in Italy), Blessed Constantius of Fabriano (confessor), of the Order of Preachers. He was greatly distinguished by the austerity of his life united with the gift of prayer. His body is piously preserved at Ascoli and his head at Fabriano. *A semi-duplex feast.*

In Egypt, the birthday of the holy martyrs Victorinus, Victor, Nicephorus, Claudian, Dioscorus, Serapion, and Papias, in the reign of the Emperor Numerian. The first two, after firmly enduring extreme tortures, were beheaded for professing the faith. Nicephorus was cut to

---

[4] "Theristus"—mower. He received this name because he helped some mowers to finish miraculously a large field in a short time.

pieces, limb from limb, after enduring red-hot gridirons and fire. Claudian and Dioscorus were burned to death, while Serapion and Papias were slain with the sword.

In Africa, the holy martyrs Donatus, Justus, Herena, and their companions.

At Constantinople, St. Tharasius, bishop, distinguished for learning and piety. There is still extant a letter of Pope Hadrian I to him, defending (the veneration of) the holy images.

At Nazianzum in Cappadocia, St. Caesarius, who was the son of Blessed Nonna and the brother of St. Gregory the Theologian and St. Gorgonia. St. Gregory declares that he saw Caesarius among the multitude of the blessed (in Heaven).

In the monastery of Heidenheim, in the Diocese of Eichstadt in Germany, St. Walburga, virgin. She was the daughter of St. Richard, King of England, and sister of St. Willebald, Bishop of Eichstadt.

The Twenty-sixth Day of February
(In Leap Year the Twenty-seventh Day of February)

At Perga in Pamphylia, the birthday of Blessed Nestor, bishop. Unremitting in his prayer day and night that the flock of Christ might be protected, he was seized in the persecution of Decius. Confessing the name of the Lord with wonderful zeal and readiness, he was most cruelly tortured on the rack by order of Pollio the governor. At last, when he firmly declared that he would always remain loyal to Christ, he was crucified and thus passed as victor to Heaven.

In the same place, the suffering of SS. Papias, Diodorus, Conon, and Claudian; they preceded St. Nestor in martyrdom.

Likewise the holy martyrs Fortunatus, Felix, and twenty-seven others.

At Alexandria, St. Alexander, a glorious old man.[5] He was one of the successors of Blessed Peter as bishop of that see. It was he who cast out of the Church the priest Arius when he had become tainted with heresy and convicted by divine truth. He afterwards was one of the three hundred and eighteen Fathers who condemned Arius in the Council of Nicaea.

At Bologna, St. Faustinian, bishop. By his preaching of the Word of God, he strengthened and increased the Church when it was being persecuted in the reign of Diocletian.

At Gaza in Palestine, St. Porphyrius, bishop who, in the time of the

[5] When he became bishop of Constantinople (in 313 or 317), he was seventy-three years old. With astonishing vigor he fought the enemies of the Church to the day of his death—twenty-three years later.

Emperor Arcadius, overthrew the idol Marna and its temple. After enduring many sufferings, he died a peaceful death in the Lord.

At Florence, St. Andrew, bishop and confessor.

In the province of Champagne in Gaul, St. Victor, confessor, whose eulogy was written by St. Bernard. ✠

The Twenty-seventh Day of February
(In Leap Year the Twenty-eighth Day of February)

At Rome, the birthday of the holy martyrs, Alexander, Abundius, Antigonus, and Fortunatus.

At Alexandria, the suffering of St. Julian, martyr. Though so crippled with gout that he could neither walk nor stand, he was brought to the judge, together with two servants of his who bore him in his chair. One of these denied the faith, but the other, named Eunus, persevered with his master in confessing Christ. They were placed upon camels, led about the whole city, and cut to ribbons with scourges. Finally, in the presence of a great throng they were burned to death.

In the same place, St. Besas, soldier. He had rebuked the people who insulted the aforesaid martyrs. Brought before the judge, he unwaveringly confessed the faith and was beheaded.

At Seville in Spain, the birthday of St. Leander, bishop of that city, brother of the Bishop St. Isidore, and of St. Florentina, virgin. By his preaching and zeal the Visigothic people, with the help of their King Recared, were converted from the Arian heresy to the Catholic faith.

At Constantinople, the holy confessors Basil and Procopius, who fought strenuously in the time of the Emperor Leo in behalf of the veneration of holy images.

At Lyons in Gaul, the subdeacon St. Baldomer, a man devoted to God. His tomb is noted for frequent miracles.

At Isola in the Abruzzi, St. Gabriel of the Seven Dolours, confessor and cleric of the Congregation of the Cross and Passion of our Lord. He was renowned for his great merits in his short life, and for his miracles after his death. Pope Benedict XV inscribed him in the canon of the saints.

The Twenty-eighth Day of February
(In Leap Year the Twenty-ninth Day of February)

At Florence, Blessed Villana (de'Botti), widow, who joined the Third Order of St. Dominic. She became noted for her love of the Crucified

Saviour, for her admirable patience, self-denial, contempt of worldly things, and for other virtues. *A semi-duplex feast.*

At Rome, the birthday of the holy martyrs Macarius, Rufinus, Justus, and Theophilus.

At Alexandria, the suffering of SS. Caerealis, Pupulus, Caius, and Serapion.

Likewise the commemoration of the holy priests, deacons, and many others in the time of the Emperor Valerian. A most deadly pestilence was raging, but they willingly met their death while ministering to the sick. The religious faith of pious persons has honored them as martyrs.

At Rome, St. Hilary, pope and confessor.

In the territory of Lyons in the Jura Mountains, the death of St. Romanus, abbot. He first led an eremitical life there, and afterward, being renowned for many miracles and virtues, was the spiritual father of many monks.

At Pavia, the transferal of the body of St. Augustine, bishop, confessor and Doctor of the Church. Through the care of Luitprand, King of the Lombards, it was removed from the island of Sardinia (to Pavia).

march

The First Day of March

At Taggia (in Italy), Blessed Christopher of Milan, confessor, of the Order of Preachers. He was the founder of the monastery and church at Taggia. By his preaching he converted many to Christ. *A semi-duplex feast.*

At Rome, two hundred and sixty holy martyrs, condemned for the name of Christ. Claudius first ordered them to dig sand outside the Salarian gate, and afterward to be slain in the amphitheatre by the arrows of the soldiers.

Likewise the birthday of the holy martyrs Leo, Donatus, Abundantius, Nicephorus, and nine others.

At Marseilles in Gaul, the holy martyrs Hermes and Hadrian.

At Heliopolis in Lebanon, St. Eudocia, martyr. She was baptized by the Bishop Theodotus, and fortified for the strife. By order of the governor Vincent, in Trajan's persecution, she was put to the sword, and thus received the crown of martyrdom.

On the same day, St. Antonina, martyr. In Diocletian's persecution, she mocked at the gods of the heathen, and after various tortures was sealed up in a cask and drowned in a marsh near the city of Caea.[1]

At Rome, the birthday of Pope St. Felix III, who was an ancestor of St. Gregory the Great. The latter relates of him that he appeared to his niece St. Tharsilla and called her to Heaven.

At the city of Kaiserswerth, St. Swithbert, bishop, who in the time of Pope Sergius I preached the Gospel among the Frisians, Batavians, and other peoples of Germany.

At Angers in Gaul, St. Albinus, bishop and confessor, a man of most remarkable virtue and holiness. *A memory.*

At Le Mans in Gaul, St. Siviard, abbot.

At Perugia, the transferal of the remains of St. Herculanus, bishop and martyr, who had been beheaded by order of Totila, King of the Goths. Pope St. Gregory in his writings declares that, forty days after his head

[1] "Caea" is due to the error of a mediaeval scribe; it should read Nicaea (in Bithynia).

43

had been cut off, it was found to have been re-united to the body, just as if the sword had never touched it. ✠

The Second Day of March

At Ulm, in Germany, Blessed Henry Suso of Swabia, confessor, of our Order. He was celebrated for observance of the rules of religious life, for the holiness of his life, and the reputation for miracles. He died January 25, but his feast is observed today. *A semi-duplex feast.*

At Rome, on the Via Latina, the holy martyrs Jovinus and Basileus, who suffered under the Emperors Valerian and Gallienus.

Likewise at Rome, many holy martyrs, who underwent prolonged torture under the Emperor Alexander and Ulpian the prefect, and at last were condemned to capital punishment.

At Caesarea in Cappadocia, the holy martyrs Lucius, bishop, Absalon, and Lorgius.

At Portus Romanus (near Ostia), the holy martyrs, Paul, Heraclius, Secundilla, and Januaria.

In Campania, the commemoration of eighty holy martyrs. When they refused to eat meat sacrificed to idols or to adore the head of a goat, they were put to death in a most cruel manner by the Lombards.

At Lichfield in England, St. Chad, Bishop of Mercia and Lindisfarne, whose outstanding virtues St. Bede the Venerable commemorates.

The Third Day of March

At Caesarea in Palestine, the holy martyrs Marinus, soldier, and Asterius, senator, in the persecution of Valerian. The first was accused by his fellow-soldiers of being a Christian, and when questioned by the judge, testified with a very clear voice that he was a Christian. He was beheaded and thus obtained the crown of martyrdom. Asterius took up the headless body of the martyr and bore it on his shoulders with his own garment placed beneath it. Without delay, he himself received as a martyr the honor which he had offered to a martyr.

At Calahorra in Spain, the birthday of the holy martyrs Hemiterius and Cheledonius, who were brothers. They were performing military service at Leon, a city of Galicia, when the storm of persecution broke out. They travelled as far as Calahorra to confess the name of Christ; there they suffered many tortures and were crowned with martyrdom.

On the same day, the suffering of SS. Felix, Luciolus, Fortunatus, Marcia, and their companions.

Likewise, the holy soldiers Cleonicus, Eutropius, and Basiliscus. In the persecution of Maximian, under the governor Asclepias, they happily triumphed over the torture of crucifixion.

At Brescia, St. Titian, bishop and confessor.

At Bamberg, St. Cunegund the Empress, who was married to Emperor Henry I, but preserved her virginity with his consent. Rich in the merit of good works, she died a holy death and thereafter was famous for her miracles. ✠

The Fourth Day of March

At Vilna in Lithuania, the confessor Blessed Casimir, son of King Casimir. The Sovereign Pontiff, Leo X, inscribed him in the number of the saints. *A simplex feast.*

At Rome, on the Appian Way, the birthday of St. Lucius I, pope and martyr. He was sent into exile for the faith of Christ in the persecution of Valerian, and afterward by the will of God was permitted to return to his Church. When he had labored much against the Novatians, he obtained his martyrdom by being beheaded. St. Cyprian highly praised him.

At Nicomedia, St. Hadrian, martyr, with twenty-three others. All gained martyrdom under the Emperor Diocletian, by having their legs broken. Their relics were taken to Byzantium by the Christians, and buried there with reverence and honor. The body of St. Hadrian was afterward transferred to Rome on September 8, on which day his feast is commemorated.

At Rome, on the Appian Way, nine hundred holy martyrs, who were buried in the cemetery of St. Cecilia.

In the Chersonese, the suffering of the holy Bishops Basil, Eugene, Agathodorus, Elpidius, Aetherius, Capito, Ephrem, Nestor, and Arcadius.

On the same day, St. Caius Palatinus. He and twenty-seven others were drowned in the sea.

Likewise, the suffering of SS. Archelaus, Cyril, and Photius.

The Fifth Day of March

At Antioch, the birthday of St. Phocas, martyr. After suffering many outrages for the name of the Redeemer, he triumphed over the Old Serpent. His victory over him is manifested to the people of today by reason of this miracle, that if one is bitten by a serpent and in faith touches the door of the martyr's basilica, forthwith the power of the poison ceases, and he is instantly healed.

At Caesarea in Palestine, St. Hadrian, martyr. In the persecution of Diocletian, he was first cast to a lion for the faith of Christ, at the command of the governor Firmilian. Afterward, slain by the sword, he received the crown of martyrdom.

On the same day, the suffering of St. Eusebius Palatinus, and nine other martyrs.

At Caesarea in Palestine, St. Theophilus, bishop. Under the Emperor Severus, he was remarkable for his wisdom and holiness of life.

Also in Palestine, on the banks of the Jordan, St. Gerasimus, hermit and abbot, who flourished in the time of the Emperor Zeno.

At Naples in Campania, the death of St. John-Joseph of the Cross, priest, of the Order of Friars Minor, and confessor. By zealously imitating St. Francis of Assisi and St. Peter of Alcantara, he added great glory to the Seraphic Order. Pope Gregory XVI enrolled him in the canon of the saints.

The Sixth Day of March

At Pisa, Blessed Jordan (of Pisa), confessor, of our Order. He was famous for his teaching, preaching, virtues, and miracles. *A semi-duplex feast.*

SS. Perpetua and Felicitas, who, on March 7, received from the Lord the glorious crown of martyrdom.

At Tortona (in Italy), St. Marcian, bishop and martyr. While Trajan was emperor, he was slain for the sake of Christ and thus received his crown.

At Nicomedia, the birthday of the holy martyrs Victor and Victorinus, who, together with Claudian and his wife Bassa, for three years were kept in prison and subjected to many tortures. They died while in prison.

In Cyprus, St. Conon, martyr. In the reign of the Emperor Decius, his feet were pierced with nails; then he was forced to run before a chariot until, falling to his knees, he died while praying.

In Syria, the suffering of forty-two holy martyrs who were arrested at Amorium (in Phrygia). They were conducted to Syria where, after a glorious combat, they received the palm of martyrdom as victors.

At Constantinople, St. Evagrius who, in the time of Valens, was chosen bishop by the Catholics. Sent by the (Arian) Emperor into exile, he died in the Lord.

At Bologna, St. Basil, bishop, who was ordained by Pope St. Silvester. He governed the Church entrusted to him in the greatest holiness both by word and example.

At Barcelona in Spain, Blessed Ollegar, at first a canon and later Bishop of Barcelona, and Archbishop of Tarragona.

At Viterbo, St. Rose, virgin, of the Third Order of St. Francis.

At Ghent in Flanders, St. Colette, virgin. At first she followed the rule of the Third Order of St. Francis. Then, guided by the Spirit of God, she restored many monasteries of nuns of the Second Order to their ancient discipline. Adorned with divine virtues and renowned for innumerable miracles, she was inscribed by the Sovereign Pontiff, Pius VII, in the roll of the saints.

The Seventh Day of March

In the monastery of Fossa Nuova, near Terracina, St. Thomas Aquinas of the Order of Preachers, confessor and Doctor of the Church. He was most illustrious for nobility of birth, holiness of life, and knowledge of theology. He preserved until death the grace of virginity. On account of the extraordinary superiority of his learning, he rightly earned the title of "Angelic Doctor." His writings, remarkable for the solidity of doctrine and approved by our Lord Himself, marvellously illuminate as dazzling lights the Catholic Church and every school of the orthodox world. Leo XIII declared him to be the celestial patron of all Catholic schools. *A totum duplex feast of the first class.*

At Carthage, the birthday of the holy martyrs Perpetua and Felicitas. Felicitas, who was with child, was granted a respite, in accordance with the law, until she was delivered. St. Augustine observes that when she was in labor she had sorrow, but when she was thrown to wild beasts she was glad. Together with Perpetua and Felicitas, during the reign of Severus, there suffered Revocatus, Saturninus, and Secundulus. Secundulus died in prison but all the others were killed by the wild beasts. The feast of Perpetua and Felicitas is kept March 6.

At Casearea in Palestine, the suffering of St. Eubulus. He was a companion of St. Hadrian. Two days after the latter's death, he was mangled by the lions and killed by the sword. He was the last one to receive the crown of martyrdom in that city.

At Nicomedia, St. Theophilus, bishop who, because of his veneration of holy images, was driven into exile where he died.

At Pelusium in Egypt, St. Paul, bishop and confessor. He too died in exile and for the same reason as St. Theophilus.

At Brescia (in Italy), St. Gaudiosus, bishop and confessor.

In the Thebaid, St. Paul, called the Simple.[2]

---

[2] He was so called because of his childlike disposition and his humility.

The Eighth Day of March

At Granada in Spain, St. John of God, confessor and founder of the Order of Brothers Hospitallers of the Sick. He was noted for mercy to the poor and contempt of himself. The Sovereign Pontiff, Leo XIII, declared him heavenly patron of the sick and of all hospitals. *A duplex feast.*

At Nicomedia, St. Quinctilis, bishop and martyr.

In Africa, SS. Cyril, bishop, Rogatus, Felix, another Rogatus, Beata, Herenia, Felicitas, Urban, Silvanus, and Mamillus.

At Antinoë, a city in Egypt, the birthday of the holy martyrs Apollonius, deacon, and Philemon. They were arrested and brought before the judge; when they firmly refused to sacrifice to the idols, their heels were bored through, and they were dragged in a horrible way about the city. Finally, they fulfilled their martyrdom by being put to the sword.

In the same place, the suffering of SS. Arian, governor, Theoticus, and three others. The judge put them to death by drowning them in the sea; their bodies were brought to the shore by dolphins.

At Carthage, St. Pontius, deacon of St. Cyprian the Bishop. Up to the day of Cyprian's death, he underwent exile with him, and left an excellent volume on the bishop's life and sufferings. In his own sufferings he constantly glorified the Lord and so merited the crown of life.

At Toledo in Spain, the death of Blessed Julian, bishop and confessor, most renowned for holiness and learning.

In England, St. Felix, bishop, who converted the East Angles to the faith.

The Ninth Day of March

At Rome, St. Frances, widow, distinguished for her noble birth, her holy life, and the gift of miracles. *A duplex feast.*

At Sebaste in Armenia, the birthday of the Forty Holy Soldiers of Cappadocia. At the time of the Emperor Licinius, while Agricolaus was governor, the forty soldiers were chained and cast into foul dungeons; their faces were beaten with rocks. Then they were condemned to spend the night naked in the open air on a frozen pond in the very depth of winter; their bodies frozen by the cold were congealed, and their martyrdom was completed by having their legs broken. Among them the most noteworthy were Cyrion and Candidus. St. Basil and other Fathers have celebrated in their writings the illustrious glory of these martyrs. Their feast is observed March 10.

At Nyssa, the death of St. Gregory, bishop. He was the son of SS.

Basil and Emmelia, and the brother of SS. Basil the Great, bishop, Peter, Bishop of Sebaste, and Macrina, virgin. He was most famous for his life and learning. In the reign of the Arian Emperor Valens, he was driven out of the city for his defence of the Catholic faith.

At Barcelona in Spain, St. Pacian, bishop, remarkable both for his life and for his preaching. He died at an advanced old age during the reign of the Emperor Theodosius.

At Bologna, St. Catherine, virgin of the Second Order of St. Francis, noted for holiness of life. Her body is held in great honor in that city. ✠

The Tenth Day of March

At Palermo in Sicily, Blessed Peter of Jeremia, confessor, of the Order of Preachers. Encouraged in his missionary labors by St. Vincent Ferrer, he devoted himself entirely to the salvation of souls. *A semi-duplex feast.*

The Forty Holy Martyrs whose birthday is commemorated March 9.

At Apamea in Phrygia, the birthday of the saintly martyrs Caius and Alexander. They were crowned with a glorious martyrdom in the persecution of Marcus Antoninus and Lucius Verus. Appollinaris, Bishop of Hieropolis, in his book against the Cataphrygian heretics, relates their martyrdom.

In Persia, the suffering of forty-two holy martyrs.

At Corinth, the holy martyrs Codratus, Dionysius, Cyprian, Anectus, Paul, and Crescens. In the persecution of Decius and Valerian, they were slain with the sword under the governor Jason.

In Africa, St. Victor, martyr, on whose feast St. Augustine delivered a panegyric on him to the people.

At Rome, St. Simplicius, pope and confessor.

At Jerusalem, St. Macarius, bishop and confessor. It was at his exhortation that Constantine the Great and St. Helena his mother cleansed the holy places and built sacred basilicas.

At Paris, the death of Abbot Blessed Droctoveus, a disciple of Bishop St. Germanus.

In the monastery of Bobbio, St. Attala, abbot, famed for his miracles.

The Eleventh Day of March

At Sardis (in West Asia Minor), St. Euthymius, bishop who, because of his veneration of the holy images, was sent into exile by the Iconoclast Emperor Michael. Later on, during the reign of Theophilus, he suffered martyrdom by an inhuman beating with scourges made of cow-hide.

At Cordoba in Spain, St. Eulogius, priest and martyr. During the Saracen persecution he deserved to be joined with the martyrs of that city, for by his writings he had emulated their contests in behalf of the faith. On account of his fearless and outstanding confession of Christ, he was scourged, beaten, and finally beheaded.

At Carthage, the holy martyrs Heraclius and Zosimus.

At Alexandria, the suffering of SS. Candidus, Piperion, and twenty others.

At Laodicea in Syria, the holy martyrs Trophimus and Thalus. In the persecution of Diocletian, they obtained crowns of glory, after (enduring) many savage torments.

At Antioch, the commemoration of many holy martyrs. At the command of the Emperor Maximian, some were placed upon red-hot gridirons, and condemned, not to death, but to continued torture. The rest of them attained the palm of martyrdom by being subjected to other torments of a most inhuman nature.

Likewise, the holy martyrs SS. Gorgonius and Firmus.

At Jerusalem, St. Sophronius, bishop.

At Milan, St. Benedict, bishop.

In the district of Amiens, St. Firminus, abbot.

At Carthage, St. Constantine, confessor.

At Babuco in the Hernican mountains (Italy), St. Peter, confessor, famous for the glory of his miracles.

The Twelfth Day of March

At Rome, Pope St. Gregory I, confessor and eminent Doctor of the Church. For the famous things he did and for the conversion of the English to the faith, he is surnamed the Great, and is called the Apostle of the English. *A duplex feast.*

In the same place, the death of St. Innocent I, pope and confessor; his feast is observed on July 28.

Likewise at Rome, St. Mamilian, martyr.

At Nicomedia, St. Egdunus, priest, and seven others. They were suffocated one by one on successive days, so that fear might be struck in those who remained.

Also the suffering of St. Peter, martyr, who was a chamberlain of the Emperor Diocletian. As he protested freely concerning the extreme tortures of the martyrs, at the command of the Emperor he was led forth, and, having been hung up, was flogged for a long time. Then salt and vinegar were poured over him, and he was roasted on a gridiron over a slow fire. Thus, indeed, did he become an inheritor both of Peter's faith and name.

At Constantinople, St. Theophanes who, from being a very rich man, became a poor monk. He was kept in prison for two years by the impious Leo the Armenian, for his veneration of holy images. Then he was exiled to Thrace where, weighed down with miseries, he died. He was famous for many miracles.

At Capua, St. Bernard, bishop and confessor.

The Thirteenth Day of March

At Cordoba in Spain, the holy martyrs, Ruderic, priest, and Solomon.

At Nicomedia, the birthday of the holy martyrs Macedonius, Patricia his wife, and their daughter Modesta.

At Nicaea in Bithynia, the holy martyrs Theusetas and Horres his son, Theodora, Nymphodora, Mark, and Arabia, who were all cast into the flames for Christ.

At Hermopolis in Egypt, St. Sabinus, martyr, who underwent many sufferings and finally was martyred by being thrown into the river.

In Persia, St. Christina, virgin and martyr.

At Camerino, St. Ansovinus, bishop and confessor.

In the Thebaid, the death of St. Euphrasia, virgin.

At Constantinople, the transferal (of the body) of St. Nicephorus, bishop of that city and confessor. His body was brought to Constantinople from the island of Propontis in the Proconnesus, where he had died on June 2 while in exile because of his veneration of the holy images. He was given an honorable burial by the Bishop of Constantinople, St. Methodius, in the church of the Holy Apostles on this, the very day on which Nicephorus had been driven into exile.

The Fourteenth Day of March

At Rome, in the field of Veranus,[3] St. Leo, bishop and martyr.

Also at Rome, the birthday of forth-seven holy martyrs, during the reign of Nero. They were baptized by St. Peter the Apostle while he and St. Paul his co-Apostle were prisoners in the Mamertine prison. After nine

[3] A mile outside of Rome, on the Via Tiburtina, was a tract of land known as the *Ager Veranus*. It was owned by a noble Christian widow, Cyriaca, who gave it to the Church. It was used by the Church as a cemetery and renamed the Cemetery of Cyriaca. The present Basilica of St. Lawrence-outside-the-Walls marks its location.—Ferretto, *Note Storico-Bibliografiche di Archeologia Cristiana*, p. 119.

months of imprisonment, all forty-seven Christians were put to the sword because of their most devout confession of the faith.

In the province of Valeria, two saintly monks. Although the Lombards killed them by hanging them from a tree, even after they died their executioners heard them continuing their hymn.

Also in that persecution, a deacon of the Church of the Marsi [4] was beheaded for confessing the faith.

In Africa, the holy martyrs Peter and Aphrodisius, who received the crown of martyrdom in the Vandal persecution.

At Carrhae in Mesopotamia, the patrician St. Eutychius and his companions, who were slain by Evelid, a caliph of Arabia, for their confession of the faith.

At Halberstadt in Germany, the death of Blessed Queen Matilda, mother of Emperor Otto I. She was noted for humility and patience.

The Fifteenth Day of March

At Caesarea in Cappadocia, the suffering of St. Longinus, a soldier. He is believed to have been the one who pierced the Lord's side with a spear.

On the same day, the birthday of St. Aristobulus who was a disciple of the Apostles. He was martyred after a life spent in preaching the Gospel.

In the Hellespont, St. Menignus, a fuller, who suffered under the Emperor Decius.

In Egypt, St. Nicander, martyr. At the time of the Emperor Diocletian, he zealously sought out the relics of the holy martyrs, and so merited himself to become a martyr.

At Cordoba in Spain, St. Leocritia, virgin and martyr. In the Arabian persecution she was subjected to various tortures and then beheaded for the faith of Christ.

At Thessalonica, St. Matrona, the handmaid of a certain Jewess. She privately worshipped Christ and went daily to the church for secret prayer. She was discovered by her mistress and tortured in many ways. At last she was beaten to death with heavy clubs. Thus, having confessed Christ, she surrendered her pure soul to God.

At Rieti, St. Probus, bishop. At his death, the martyrs Juvenal and Eleutherius appeared to him.

At Vienna in Austria, St. Clement-Mary Hofbauer, priest of the Congregation of the Most Holy Redeemer. He was famous for his extraordinary labors in promoting the glory of God and the salvation of souls,

[4] The Marsi were a tribe living around Lake Fucino. Theirs was one of the few dioceses named after a tribe instead of after a city.

as well as in extending his Congregation. Distinguished for miracles and virtues, he was canonized by the Sovereign Pontiff, Pius X.

At Capua, St. Speciosus, monk. Pope St. Gregory relates that his brother saw the soul of Speciosus being borne to Heaven.

The Sixteenth Day of March

At Rome, the suffering of St. Cyriacus, deacon. After wasting away for a long time in prison, melted pitch was poured over him. He was stretched out on a platform, bound with leather thongs, and beaten with clubs. Finally, at the command of Maximian, he was beheaded in company with Largus, Smaragdus, and twenty others. Their feast is observed on August 8 because that was the day on which the bodies of these twenty-three martyrs were exhumed by Pope St. Marcellus and given honorable burial.

At Aquileia, the birthday of Bishop St. Hilary and the deacon Tatian. At the time of Emperor Numerian and the governor Beronius, they were subjected to the rack and to other tortures. They completed their martyrdom, together with Felix, Largus and Dionysius.

In Lycaonia, St. Papas, martyr. For his Christian faith, he was beaten, torn with iron hooks, and commanded to walk in shoes filled with nails; then, while roped to a tree, his soul ascended to the Lord. (After his death) this same tree, which had been barren, became fruitful.

At Anazabus in Cilicia, St. Julian, martyr. He was tortured for a long time by Marcian the governor, and was finally tied in a sack containing serpents and drowned in the sea.

At Ravenna, St. Agapitus, bishop and confessor.

At Cologne, St. Heribert, bishop, famed for holiness.

In Auvergne in Gaul, the death of St. Patrick, bishop.

In Syria, St. Abraham, hermit, whose deeds St. Ephrem the deacon committed to writing. ✠

The Seventeenth Day of March

At Downpatrick in Ireland, the birthday of St. Patrick, bishop and confessor. He was the first to preach Christ in those parts, and acquired great renown for miracles and virtues. *A duplex feast.*

At Jerusalem, St. Joseph of Arimathea, "a noble councillor." [5] He was that disciple of the Lord, who took down His Body from the Cross and buried It in his own new tomb.

[5] He is so called in the Bible; See Mark, 15:43.

At Rome, SS. Alexander and Theodore, martyrs.

At Alexandria, the commemoration of many holy martyrs. In the reign of the Emperor Theodosius, they were seized by idolators of Serapis. As the Christians firmly refused to worship the idol, they were savagely slaughtered. Soon after, the Emperor issued a rescript ordering the temple of Serapis to be destroyed.

At Constantinople, St. Paul, martyr, who was burned to death under Constantine Copronymus for defending the veneration of holy images.

At Chalons in Gaul, St. Agricola, bishop.

At Nivelles in Brabant, St. Gertrude, virgin. Though of noble birth, she despised the world and spent all her life in the performance of holy works; thus she merited to obtain Christ for her Bridegroom in Heaven.

The Eighteenth Day of March

At Jerusalem, St. Cyril, bishop, confessor, and Doctor of the Church. He suffered many injuries at the hands of the Arians for the sake of the faith, and was often driven from his diocese. At last he died in peace, crowned with the glory of holiness. The First Oecumenical Council of Constantinople, in a letter to Pope St. Damasus, gave excellent testimony of his fearless faith. *A duplex feast.*

At Caesarea in Palestine, the birthday of St. Alexander, bishop. Leaving his own city in Cappadocia where he was bishop, he came to Jerusalem to visit the holy places. The Bishop of Jerusalem at that time was Narcissus, an extremely old man. Alexander, directed by a revelation of God, took over the government of that see. However, later, at the time of the persecution of Decius, when he himself was now venerable by reason of his advanced age, he was led to Caesarea and imprisoned. There he completed his martyrdom for confessing Christ.

At Augsburg, St. Narcissus, bishop. He first preached the Gospel in Rhaetia; then he went to Spain, and at Gerona converted many to the faith of Christ. Here, together with the deacon Felix, he obtained the crown of martyrdom in the persecution of Diocletian.

At Nicomedia, ten thousand holy martyrs, who were slain by the sword for confessing Christ.

In the same place, the holy martyrs Trophimus and Eucarpius.

In Britain, King St. Edward, who was murdered through the treachery of his stepmother. He was renowned for many miracles.

At Lucca in Tuscany, the birthday of St. Frigidian, bishop, famed for his power of miracles.

At Mantua, St. Anselm, Bishop of Lucca, and confessor,

The Nineteenth Day of March

In Judea, the birthday of St. Joseph, husband of the Blessed Virgin Mary, and confessor. The Sovereign Pontiff, Pius IX, acquiescing in the wishes and prayers of the whole Catholic world, declared him to be the Patron of the Universal Church. *A totum duplex feast of the first class.*

At Sorrento, the holy martyrs Quinctus, Quinctilla, Quartilla, Mark, and nine others.

At Nicomedia, St. Pancharius, a Roman. To win the favor of Diocletian who was then emperor, he abjured Christ for vain gods. However, by the persuasion of his mother and sister, he soon returned to the true faith. As he remained firm in it, he was flogged with thongs and beheaded, thus gaining the crown of a martyr.

On the same day, SS. Apollonius and Leontius, bishops.

At Ghent in Flanders, SS. Landoald, a Roman priest, and Amantius, deacon. Pope St. Martin sent them to preach the Gospel, and they faithfully performed this apostolic commission. After their deaths, both were renowned for their miracles.

At Pinna, the birthday of St. John, a man of great holiness. He came from Syria to Italy and built a monastery there. For forty-four years he was the spiritual father of many servants of God and, noted for his virtues, rested in peace.

The Twentieth Day of March

At Siena, in Tuscany, Blessed Ambrose (Sansedoni) of the Order of Friars Preachers. He was remarkable for his sanctity, preaching, and miracles. Clement VIII ordered his name to be inscribed in the Roman Martyrology. *A duplex feast.*

In Judea, St. Joachim, the father of the Blessed Virgin Mary, Mother of God. His feast is kept on August 16.

In Asia, the birthday of Blessed Archippus, a fellow-worker of St. Paul the Apostle. He is mentioned by St. Paul in the Epistle to Philemon and in the Epistle to the Colossians.[6]

In Syria, the holy martyrs Paul, Cyril, Eugene, and four others.

On the same day, SS. Photina, a Samaritan woman, her sons Joseph and Victor, Sebastian, a military officer, Anatolius, Photius, Photides, and two sisters, Parasceves and Cyriaca. They all confessed Christ and obtained martyrdom.

At Amisus in Paphlagonia, the seven holy women, Alexandra, Claudia,

[6] Philemon, 5:2; Colossians, 4:17.

Euphrasia, Matrona, Juliana, Euphemia, and Theodosia. They were killed for confessing the faith. They were followed in death by Derphuta and her sister.

At Apollonia (in Albania), St. Nicetas, bishop. Because he venerated the holy images, he was driven into exile and there died.

In the monastery of Fontanelle in Gaul, St. Wulfran, Bishop of Sens, who resigned the bishopric and, renowned for miracles, departed this life.

In Britain, the death of St. Cuthbert, Bishop of Lindisfarne, who from childhood till death shone forth by holy works and remarkable miracles.

The Twenty-first Day of March

At Monte Cassino, the birthday of St. Benedict, abbot, who restored and wonderfully propagated monastic discipline which had almost perished in the West. His life, which was glorious for virtue and miracles, was written by Pope St. Gregory. *A totum duplex feast.*

At Catania in Sicily, St. Birillus, who was ordained bishop by St. Peter. After he had converted many Gentiles in Sicily to the faith, he died peacefully in extreme old age.

At Alexandria, the commemoration of the holy martyrs. At the time of the Emperor Constantius and Philagrius the prefect, they were slaughtered when the Arians and heathens stormed the churches on Good Friday.

On the same day, the holy martyrs Philemon and Domninus.

At Alexandria, blessed Serapion, hermit and Bishop of Thmuis. A man of great virtues, he was driven by the fury of the Arians into exile where he died, a confessor of the Lord.

In the territory of Lyons, St. Lupicinus, abbot, whose life was noted for the glory of holiness and miracles.

The Twenty-second Day of March

At Pavia (in Italy), Blessed Isnard (of Chiampo), confessor. He was received into the Order of Friars Preachers by the Patriarch St. Dominic. He fervently fulfilled the office of preaching, and became distinguished by his virtues and miracles. *A semi-duplex feast.*

At Narbonne in Gaul, the birthday of Blessed Paul, bishop and disciple of the Apostles. He is said to have been the proconsul Sergius Paulus who was baptized by the Apostle St. Paul. When the latter went to Spain, he remained at Narbonne where he was made bishop. He zealously performed his duties and, famous for his miracles, he departed for heaven.

At Terracina in Campania, St. Epaphroditus, disciple of the Apostles. He was named bishop of that city by St. Peter the Apostle.

At Ancyra in Galatia, St. Basil, priest and martyr who, afflicted with the most agonizing tortures under Julian the Apostate, gave up his soul to God.

At Carthage, the archdeacon St. Octavian and many thousands of martyrs who, on account of their Catholic faith, were killed by the Vandals.

In Africa, the holy martyrs Saturninus and nine others.

In Galatia, the birthday of the holy martyrs Callinica and Basilissa.

At Rome, the birthday of Pope St. Zachary, who governed the Church of God with the greatest vigilance and, renowned for his merits, died a peaceful death.

At Carthage, St. Deogratias, bishop of that city. He redeemed many captives brought from Rome by the Vandals. Celebrated for many other good deeds, he went to his rest in the Lord.

At Osimo in Piceno (Italy), St. Benvenuto, bishop.

At Rome, St. Lea, widow, whose virtues and death are described by St. Jerome.

The Twenty-third Day of March

At Pavia, Blessed Sybillina, virgin, of the Order of Preachers. At the age of twelve she became afflicted with total blindness. As a result, she was better able to contemplate the mysteries of the Passion of our Lord, the lessons of which she strove to imitate in her own actions as far as possible. *A semi-duplex feast.*

In Africa, the holy martyrs Victorian, proconsul of Carthage, and two brothers from Aquaregia. Likewise, Frumentius, and another Frumentius, both merchants. The African Bishop Victor relates that, for their constancy in confessing the Catholic faith, they were tortured with the most frightful atrocity in the persecution by the Vandals under the Arian King Hunneric. All received noble crowns.

Likewise in Africa, St. Fidelis, martyr.

In the same place, St. Felix and twenty other martyrs.

At Caesarea in Palestine, the saintly martyrs Nicon and ninety-nine others.

Likewise the crowning of the holy martyrs Domitius, Pelagia, Aquila, Eparchius, and Theodosia.

At Lima in Peru, St. Turibius, archbishop, through whose virtue, faith and ecclesiastical discipline were spread throughout (South) America.

At Antioch, St. Theodulus, priest.

At Barcelona in Spain, St. Joseph Oriol, priest, rector of the church of St. Mary of the Kings. He was famous for every virtue; especially for mortification of the body, love of poverty, and compassion for the needy and sick. Glorious both in life and after death for his miracles, Pope Pius X inscribed him among the number of the saints.

At Caesarea, St. Julian, confessor.

In Campania, St. Benedict, monk, who was shut up in a heated oven by the Goths, and the next day found unhurt.

The Twenty-fourth Day of March

The Feast of St. Gabriel the Archangel, who was sent by God to declare the mystery of the Incarnation of the Divine Word. *A totum duplex feast.*

At Rome, St. Epigmenius, priest who, in the persecution of Diocletian, under the judge Turpius, was slain with the sword and so gained his martyrdom.

Also at Rome, at the time of Julian the Apostate, the suffering of Blessed Pigmenius, priest. Because of his faith in Christ, he was cast into the Tiber and drowned.

At Rome, the holy martyrs Mark and Timothy, who were crowned with martyrdom under the Emperor Antoninus.

At Caesarea in Palestine, the birthday of the holy martyrs Timolaus, Dionysius, Pausides, Romulus, Alexander, another Alexander, Agapius, and a second Dionysius. In the persecution of Diocletian under the governor Urban, they were beheaded, thus earning crowns of (eternal) life.

In Morocco, the birthday of SS. Romulus and Secundus, brothers, who suffered for the faith of Christ.

At Trent, the suffering of the boy St. Simeon, who was most cruelly murdered by Jews, and afterward glorified with many miracles.

At Synnada in Phrygia, St. Agapitus, bishop.

At Brescia, St. Latinus, bishop.

In Syria, St. Seleucus, confessor.

In Sweden, St. Catherine, virgin, who was the daughter of St. Bridget.

The Twenty-fifth Day of March

The Annunciation of the Blessed Virgin Mary, Mother of God. *A totum duplex feast of the first class.*

At Jerusalem, the commemoration of the Good Thief who confessed

Christ upon the Cross, and deserved to hear from Him the words: "This day shalt thou be with Me in Paradise." [7]

At Rome, St. Quirinus, martyr. Under the Emperor Claudius, he was deprived of his possessions, confined in a filthy prison, subjected to many beatings, and was executed by the sword. His body was cast into the Tiber, but the Christians afterward found it on the island of Lycaonia, later called St. Bartholomew's. He was buried in the cemetery of Pontian.

In the same place, two hundred and sixty-two holy martyrs.

At Sirmium, the suffering of St. Irenaeus, bishop and martyr. In the time of the Emperor Maximian, under the governor Probus, he was afflicted first with most severe tortures. Then he underwent many more days of excruciating torments in prison, and finally was martyred by having his head cut off.

At Nicomedia, St. Dula, the servant of a soldier. She merited the crown of martyrdom, being slain for preserving her chastity.

At Laodicea in Lebanon, St. Pelagius, bishop, who suffered exile and other afflictions for the Catholic faith under Valens and, at last, restored to his see, died peacefully in the Lord.

At Aindre, an island in the Loire river, St. Hermeland, abbot, whose glorious life was approved by the remarkable testimony of his miracles.

At Pistoia in Tuscany, the holy confessors Barontius and Desiderius.

The Twenty-sixth Day of March

At Rome on the Via Lavicana, St. Castulus, martyr. He was a chamberlain of the palace and gave asylum to the Christians. Three times he was suspended (by his thumbs) and three times interrogated by the judges. As he persevered in confessing the Lord, he was flung into a pit and received his crown of martyrdom after great masses of sand buried him alive.

Also at Rome, the crowning of the holy martyrs Peter, Marcian, Jovinus, Thecla, Cassian, and others.

At Pentapolis in Libya, the birthday of the holy martyrs Theodore, bishop, Irenaeus, deacon, Serapion and Ammonius, lectors.

At Sirmium, the holy martyrs Montanus, priest, and Maxima. Because of their Christian faith they were drowned in a river.

Likewise, the holy martyrs Quadratus, Theodosius, Emmanuel, and forty others.

At Alexandria, the holy martyrs Eutychius and others. In the time of

[7] Luke, 23:43.

Constantius, under the Arian Bishop George, they were put to the sword for their Catholic faith.

On the same day, St. Ludger, Bishop of Munster, who preached the Gospel to the Saxons.

At Saragossa in Spain, St. Braulius, bishop and confessor.

At Treves, St. Felix, bishop.

The Twenty-seventh Day of March

St. John Damascene, priest, confessor, and Doctor of the Church, whose birthday is commemorated on May 6. *A duplex feast.*

At Drizipara in Hungary, St. Alexander, a soldier. Under the Emperor Maximian, after he had endured many sufferings for Christ, and had performed numerous miracles, he completed his martyrdom by being beheaded.

In Illyria, SS. Philetus, a senator, his wife Lydia, and his sons Macedo and Theoprepius; also Amphilochius, a captain, and Chronides, a notary. After they had undergone many tortures for confessing Christ, they gained the crown of glory.

In Persia, the birthday of the holy martyrs Zanitas, Lazarus, Marotas, Narses, and five others. They were savagely cut to pieces in the reign of Sapor, King of the Persians, and so merited the palm of martyrdom.

At Salzburg in Austria, St. Rupert, bishop and confessor, who spread the Gospel in a wonderful manner among the Bavarians and Austrians.

In Egypt, the hermit St. John, a man of great sanctity. Among other evidences of his virtue was the gift of prophecy by which he foretold to the Emperor Theodosius his victories over the tyrants Maximus and Eugene.

The Twenty-eighth Day of March

St. John of Capistrano, priest and confessor, of the Order of Friars Minor, of whom mention is made on October 23.

At Caesarea in Palestine, the birthday of the holy martyrs Priscus, Malchus, and Alexander. At the time of Valerian's persecution, all three dwelt on a little farm in the suburbs of Caesarea. When heavenly crowns of martyrdom were being offered in Caesarea, the three Christians were inflamed with the divine fire of faith. They presented themselves to the judge, and demanded why he raged so much for the blood of holy men. The judge at once had them delivered to the beasts to be devoured for the name of Christ.

At Tarsus in Cilicia, the holy martyrs Castor and Dorotheus.

In Africa, the holy martyrs Rogatus, Successus, and sixteen others.

At Norcia (in Italy), St. Spes, abbot, a man of wondrous patience. Pope St. Gregory relates that when he departed this life, his soul was seen by all the brethren ascending to Heaven in the form of a dove.

At Chalons in Gaul, the death of St. Guntram, King of the Franks. He so devoted himself to spiritual things that, leaving the pomps of the world, he bestowed his treasures on churches and the poor.

The Twenty-ninth Day of March

At Heliopolis in Lebanon, St. Cyril, deacon and martyr, at the time of Julian the Apostate. His body was ripped open and his liver plucked out by Gentiles who, like wild beasts, devoured it.

In Persia, the holy monks and martyrs Jonas and Barachisius, who were brothers. In the reign of Sapor, King of Persia, Jonas was squeezed in a vise until his bones were broken; then he was cut in two. Barachisius was choked to death by having boiling pitch poured down his throat.

At Nicomedia, the suffering of the holy martyrs Pastor, Victorinus, and their companions.

In Africa, the holy confessors Armogastes, a count, Masculas, an actor, and Saturus, procurator of the king's household. At the time of the Vandal persecution under Genseric the Arian King, they suffered many severe tortures and insults for the confession of the truth, and thus completed the course of their glorious strife.

In the city of Asti (in Italy), St. Secundus, martyr.

In the monastery of Luxeuil in Gaul, the death of the Abbot St. Eustasius, a disciple of St. Columban. He was the spiritual father of almost six hundred monks. Noteworthy for holiness of life, he was distinguished by his miracles.

The Thirtieth Day of March

At Rome, on the Appian Way, the suffering of blessed Quirinus, a tribune, who was the father of the virgin St. Balbina. He, with all his household, was baptized by Pope St. Alexander who was in his custody. When, in the reign of the Emperor Hadrian, this unconquerable soldier of Christ was handed over to the judge Aurelian and remained firm in the confession of his faith, his tongue was cut out; he was stretched on the rack, his hands and feet were cut off, and at last he won the fight for martyrdom, by the sword.

At Thessalonica, the birthday of the holy martyrs Domninus, Victor, and their companions.

At Constantinople, the commemoration of many holy martyrs of the Catholic faith in the time of Constantius. They were killed by Macedonius the heresiarch who subjected them to unheard-of kinds of torture. Among other cruelties, he mutilated faithful women by pressing them between the heavy lids of chests, and burning them with red-hot irons.

In the town of Senlis in Gaul, the death of St. Regulus, Bishop of Arles.

At Orleans in Gaul, St. Pastor, bishop.

At Syracuse in Sicily, St. Zosimus, bishop and confessor.

On Mount Sinai, St. John Climacus, abbot.

At Aquileria in Spain, St. Peter Regalatus, priest and confessor, of the Order of Friars Minor, born in Valladolid. He restored regular discipline in the Spanish monasteries. The Sovereign Pontiff, Benedict XIV, added his name to the list of the saints.

At Aquino, St. Clinius, confessor.

The Thirty-first Day of March

At Thecua in Palestine, St. Amos the Prophet. The priest Amasius repeatedly flogged him, and the priest's son Ozias drove an iron spike through his temples. Half dead, the prophet was carried back to his own land where he died and was buried with his forefathers.

In Persia, St. Benjamin, deacon. As he would not cease to preach the Word of God, he was tortured under King Yezdegerd by having sharp reeds forced under his nails, and a thorny stake driven through his abdomen, thus completing his martyrdom.

In Africa, the martyrs Theodulus, Anesius, Felix, Cornelia, and their companions.

At Rome, St. Balbina, virgin, daughter of St. Quirinus the martyr. She was baptized by Pope St. Alexander, and chose Christ as her Spouse in her virginity. Having completed her trial in this world, she was buried near her father on the Appian Way.

april

The First Day of April

The Commemoration of the Imprinting of the Stigmata of St. Catherine of Siena, virgin of the Order of Preachers. *A duplex feast.*

At Rome, the suffering of St. Theodora, the sister of the illustrious martyr Hermes. In the time of the Emperor Hadrian, and at the command of the judge Aurelius, she suffered martyrdom, and was buried near her brother on the Via Salaria, not far from the city.

On the same day, St. Venantius, bishop and martyr.

In Egypt, the holy martyrs Victor and Stephen.

In Armenia, the holy martyrs Quinctian and Irenaeus.

At Constantinople, St. Macarius, confessor, who under the Emperor Leo died in exile for defending (the veneration of) holy images.

At Ard-Patrick in Munster, a province of Ireland, St. Celsus, bishop, who preceded Blessed Malachy in the bishopric.

At Grenoble in Gaul, St. Hugh, bishop. He passed his life in solitude for many years, and departed to the Lord, illustrious for the glory of miracles.

At Amiens in Gaul, St. Valéry, abbot, whose sepulchre is noted for frequent miracles.

The Second Day of April

At Tours in Gaul, St. Francis of Paola, confessor, founder of the Order of Minims. Renowned for virtues and miracles, he was inscribed among the number of the saints by Pope Leo X. *A duplex feast.*

At Caesarea in Palestine, the birthday of St. Apphian, who was martyred ahead of his brother Aedesius, during the persecution of Galerius Maximian. He censured the governor Urban for sacrificing to idols. For this, he was savagely mangled. Then his feet were wrapped in cloths dipped in oil and set on fire. Having undergone the most excruciating sufferings, he was finally flung into the sea. Thus, passing through fire and water, he was brought to a place of (eternal) rest.

In the same place and in the same persecution, the suffering of St,

Theodosia, a virgin from Tyre. She publicly greeted the holy confessors as they were standing before the tribunal and begged them to remember her when they had reached the Lord. She was seized by the soldiers and taken to the governor Urban. By his orders, her flesh was torn off her breast and sides to the bone. At last, she was hurled into the sea.

At Langres in Gaul, St. Urban, bishop.

At Como, St. Abundius, bishop and confessor.

At Capua, St. Victor, bishop, noted for his learning and holiness.

At Lyons in Gaul, St. Nicetius, bishop of that city, renowned for his life and miracles.

In Palestine, the death of St. Mary of Egypt, who was called the Sinner.

The Third Day of April

At Rome, the birthday of blessed Sixtus I, pope and martyr. He ruled the Church with the greatest distinction in the reign of the Emperor Hadrian. Then, in the reign of Antoninus Pius, he willingly suffered a temporal death that he might gain Christ.

At Taormina in Sicily, St. Pancras, bishop. He sealed with his blood the Gospel of Christ which St. Peter the Apostle had sent him there to preach.

At Tomis in Scythia, the birthday of the holy martyrs Evagrius and Benignus.

At Tyre in Phoenicia, St. Vulpian, martyr. In the persecution of Maximian Galerius, he was sewn up in a sack containing a serpent and a dog, and cast into the sea.

At Thessalonica, the suffering of the holy virgins Agape and Chionia, at the time of the Emperor Diocletian. Under the same Emperor, their sister the holy virgin Irene was later to be put to death. Upon Agape and Chionia refusing to deny Christ, they were first starved in prison and afterward cast into the fire. Although the flames did not injure them, they gave up their souls to God as they were praying to Him.

In the monastery of Medicion in Bithynia, the death of St. Nicetas, abbot. On account of his veneration of holy images, he suffered greatly under Leo the Armenian. Finally, the confessor died in peace near Constantinople.

In England, St. Richard, Bishop of Chichester, remarkable for holiness and the renown of his miracles.

At Farmoutiers, near Meaux, St. Burgundofara, abbess and virgin. She is also called St. Fara.

The Fourth Day of April

At Seville in Spain, St. Isidore, bishop, confessor, and Doctor of the Church, a man remarkable for sanctity and learning. He enlightened Spain by his zeal for the Catholic faith and his observance of ecclesiastical discipline. *A duplex feast.*

At Milan, the death of St. Ambrose, bishop, confessor, and Doctor of the Church. In addition to his gifts of learning and miracles was the zeal by which he converted to the Catholic faith nearly all Italy at the time of the Arian heresy. His feast is celebrated on December 7, the day on which he was consecrated Bishop of Milan.

At Thessalonica, the holy martyrs Agathopodes, deacon, and Theodulus, lector. Under the Emperor Maximian and the governor Faustinus, they confessed the Christian faith; (for this reason) stones were tied to their necks, and they were cast into the sea.

At Constantinople, St. Plato, monk, who fought with dauntless spirit for many years against the heretical destroyers of holy images.

In Palestine, St. Zosimus, the hermit who buried St. Mary of Egypt.

At Palermo, St Benedict of San Fradello, confessor, of the Order of Friars Minor. He was called the Black, on account of the color of his skin. He died famous for his virtues and miracles, and was enrolled among the saints by the Sovereign Pontiff, Pius VII.

The Fifth Day of April

At Vannes in Brittany, St. Vincent Ferrer, confessor, of the Order of Preachers. He was an apostle powerful in deed and in word who converted many thousands of unbelievers to Christ. Although he preached in his own native tongue to people who spoke different languages, yet, because of his celebrated and extraordinary gift of tongues, he was clearly understood by everybody. Outstanding for his virginity and for his gift of prophecy, he went to heaven to receive the crown for his many great virtues. *A totum duplex feast of the second class.*

In Africa, the suffering of the holy martyrs who, in the persecution of Genseric, the Arian king, were slain in church on Easter Day. Among them was a lector who, while he was singing the Alleluia in the pulpit, was pierced through the throat by an arrow.

On the same day, St. Zeno, martyr. He was covered with pitch and cast into a fire. While in the midst of the flames, he was pierced with a spear, thus completing his martyrdom.

On the island of Lesbos, the suffering of five holy virgins, who were killed by the sword.

At Thessalonica, St. Irene, virgin, who hid the sacred books despite Diocletian's edict. After enduring imprisonment, she was pierced with an arrow and burned to death by order of the governor, Dulcetius. Her sisters, Agape and Chionia, had previously been put to death by the same governor.

The Sixth Day of April

At Milan, the suffering of St. Peter, martyr, of the Order of Preachers, who was slain by the heretics on account of his Catholic faith. His feast is celebrated on April 29.

At Welehrad, in Moravia, the birthday of St. Methodius, bishop and confessor. With his brother, St. Cyril, also a bishop, whose birthday falls on February 14, he converted many of the Slav races and their kings to the faith of Christ. Their festival is, however, observed on July 7.

In Macedonia, SS. Timothy and Diogenes, martyrs.

In Persia, one hundred and twenty holy martyrs.

In Ascalon in Palestine, the suffering of SS. Platonides and two other martyrs.

At Carthage, St. Marcellinus, martyr, who was slain by the heretics for his defense of the Catholic faith.

In Denmark, St. William, abbot, famous for his life and miracles.

The Seventh Day of April

At Rouen, the birthday of St. John Baptist de la Salle, priest and confessor. He excelled in the teaching of the young, particularly of those that were poor, and deserved well of religion and of civil society. He founded the Society of the Brothers of the Christian schools. His festival, however, is observed on May 15.

In Africa, the birthday of the holy martyrs, Epiphanius the bishop, Donatus, Rufinus, and thirteen others.

At Alexandria, St. Peleusius, priest and martyr.

At Sinope in Pontus, two hundred holy martyrs.

In Cilicia, St. Calliopus, martyr. Under the governor Maximian, he endured many tortures. He was finally crucified with his head downward, and received the noble crown of martyrdom.

At Nicomedia, St. Cyriacus and ten other martyrs.

At Verona, St. Saturninus, bishop and confessor.

At Rome, St. Hegesippus, who lived shortly after apostolic times. He came to Rome to visit Pope Anicetus and remained there until the reign of Eleutherius. He composed a history of the Church from the Passion of the Lord to his own time in simple language, so as to express by his narrative the character of those whose life he imitated.

In Syria, St. Aphraates, hermit, who by the power of his miracles defended the Catholic faith against the Arians in the reign of Valens.

The Eighth Day of April

The commemoration of SS. Herodion, Asyncritus, and Phlegon, whom St. Paul the apostle mentions in his Epistle to the Romans.[1]

At Alexandria, St. Aedesius, martyr, brother of St. Apphian. At the time of the Emperor Maximian Galerius, the saint publicly rebuked a wicked judge because he delivered to procurers virgins consecrated to God. For this, he was seized by the soldiers, subjected to the most atrocious tortures and then drowned in the sea for the sake of Christ our Lord.

In Africa, the holy martyrs Januarius, Maxima, and Macaria.

At Carthage, St. Concessa, martyr.

At Corinth, blessed Dionysius, bishop. By the learning and unction with which he explained the Word of God, he instructed not only the people of his own city and province, but also, by his letters, the bishops of other provinces and cities. His veneration for the Roman Pontiffs was such that he was wont to read their letters publicly in the church on Sundays. He flourished in the times of Marcus Antoninus Verus and Lucius Aurelius Commodus.

At Tours in Gaul, St. Perpetuus, bishop, a man of admirable holiness.

At Ferentino in the Hernican mountains, St. Redemptus, bishop, whom Pope St. Gregory mentions.

At Como, St. Amantius, bishop and confessor. ✠

The Ninth Day of April

At Bricherasio, near the Alps, the birthday of Blessed Anthony Pavoni of Savigliano, of our Order. After a life spent in a holy and useful fight for the Catholic faith, he was slain by heretics on the first Sunday after Easter and thus was happily joined to the white-robed band of martyrs. *A semi-duplex feast.*

In Judea, St. Mary Cleophas, whom St. John the Evangelist calls the "sister" of Blessed Virgin Mary, Mother of God, and relates that she stood beside her beneath the cross of Jesus.[2]

---

[1] Romans, 16:11 and 14.
[2] John, 19:25.

At Antioch, St. Prochorus, who was one of the first seven deacons.[3] Noted for his faith and miracles, he was crowned with martyrdom.

At Rome, the birthday of the holy martyrs Demetrius, Concessus, Hilary, and their companions.

At Caesarea in Cappadocia, St. Eupsychius, martyr, who obtained martyrdom under Julian the Apostate for having helped to destroy the Temple of Fortuna.

In Africa, the holy martyrs of Massylita, on whose birthday St. Augustine delivered a discourse (concerning them).

At Sirmium, the suffering of seven holy virgins and martyrs, who together purchased eternal life, at the price of their blood.

At Amida in Mesopotamia, St. Acatius, bishop. He melted down and sold the sacred vessels of the church in order to redeem captives.

At Rouen, St. Hugh, bishop and confessor.

In the city of Die in Gaul, St. Marcellus, bishop, famed for miracles.

At Mons in Hainaut, Blessed Waldetrudis (widow), wondrous for sanctity of life and miracles.

At Rome, the transferal of the body of St. Monica, mother of the Bishop Blessed Augustine. Under Pope Martin V, it was brought from Ostia and honorably laid to rest in the church of the same Blessed Augustine.

The Tenth Day of April

At Tunis in Africa, Blessed Anthony Neyrot, of our Order. He fell away from the faith, but a short time after he gloriously affirmed that faith with his blood. His body was transferred to Rivoli. *A semi-duplex feast.*

At Babylon, the holy Prophet Ezechiel. He was slain by a judge of the people of Israel because he rebuked him for the worship of idols. He was buried in the sepulchre of Sem and Arphaxad, ancestors of Abraham, at which place many people were wont to gather for prayer.

At Rome, the birthday of many holy martyrs, whom Pope St. Alexander baptized while he was kept in prison. Aurelian the prefect ordered them all to be put on board an old ship, taken out into the deep sea, and there to be drowned with stones tied to their necks.

At Alexandria, the holy martyrs Apollonius, priest, and five others, who were drowned in the sea during Maximian's persecution. In Africa, the holy martyrs Terence, Africanus, Pompey, and their companions. They were beaten with rods, stretched on the rack, and tortured with

[3] Acts, 6:5.

other punishments, under the Emperor Decius and the prefect Fortunian. At last they completed their martyrdom by being beheaded.

At Ghent in Flanders, St. Macarius, Bishop of Antioch, renowned for virtues and miracles.

At Valladolid in Spain, St. Michael de Sanctis, confessor, of the Order of Discalced Trinitarians for the Redemption of Captives. He was remarkable for innocence of life, admirable penitence, and love of God. The Supreme Pontiff Pius IX inscribed his name in the roll of the saints.

The Eleventh Day of April

At Rome, St. Leo I, surnamed the Great. He was pope, confessor, and Doctor of the Church. His birthday is recalled on November 10. *A duplex feast.*

At Pergamum in Asia, St. Antipas, "the faithful witness," of whom St. John in the Apocalypse makes mention.[4] Under the Emperor Domitian he was shut in a red-hot brazen bull, and thus suffered martyrdom.

At Salona in Dalmatia, the holy martyrs Bishop Domnio and eight soldiers.

At Gortyna in Crete, St. Philip, bishop, famous for his life and doctrine. He ruled the church entrusted to him in the reigns of Marcus Antoninus Verus and Lucius Aurelius Commodus, and preserved it from the rage of the heathens and the intrigues of heretics.

At Nicomedia, St. Eustorgius, priest.

At Spoleto, St. Isaac, monk and confessor, whose virtues are commemorated by Pope St. Gregory.

At Gaza in Palestine, St. Barsanuphius, hermit, at the time of the Emperor Justinian.

The Twelfth Day of April

At Verona, the suffering of St. Zeno, bishop. He governed that diocese with wondrous constancy amid the storms of persecution, and was crowned with martyrdom in the time of Gallienus.

In Cappadocia, St. Sabas the Goth. Under the Emperor Valens, when King Athanaric of the Goths was persecuting the Christians, Sabas was severely tortured and then cast into a river. It was at the same time, as St. Augustine relates, that many orthodox Goths were adorned with the crown of martyrdom.

[4] St. John calls him "my faithful witness, who was slain among you." (Apoc., 2:13).

At Braga in Portugal, St. Victor, martyr. While still a catechumen, he refused to worship an idol and confessed Christ Jesus with great firmness. After enduring many torments, he was beheaded, thus meriting to be baptized in his own blood.

At Fermo in Piceno (Italy), St. Vissia, virgin and martyr.

At Rome, on the Via Aurelia, the birthday of Pope St. Julius I, who labored greatly for the Catholic faith against the Arians, and after many illustrious deeds rested in peace, famed for his sanctity.

At Gap in Gaul, St. Constantine, bishop and confessor.

At Pavia, St. Damian, bishop. ✠

The Thirteenth Day of April

In the town of Metola, of the diocese of Tiphernum, Blessed Margaret, virgin.[5] Although she was born blind, she was illuminated by God to a marvellous degree, and at His inspiration she became a member of the Third Order of our holy Father Dominic. *A semi-duplex feast.*

At Seville in Spain, St. Hermengild, martyr. He was the son of Leovigild, the Arian King of the Visigoths (in Spain). He was imprisoned for his profession of the Catholic faith. When he refused to receive Holy Communion from an Arian Bishop on Easterday, by the command of his treacherous father his head was split in two with an axe. As a king and martyr he entered a heavenly kingdom in exchange for an earthly one.

At Rome, in the persecution of Marcus Antoninus Verus and Lucius Aurelius Commodus, St. Justin, philosopher and martyr. He addressed to the aforesaid emperors his second *Apologia* in defence of our religion. He was strenuously spreading the faith by his disputations, when he was denounced as being a Christian at the instigation of Crescens the Cynic, whose manner of living and evil practices he had condemned. As a reward of his faithful preaching, he received the crown of martyrdom. His feast is observed on April 14.

At Pergamos in Asia, in the same persecution, the birthday of the holy martyrs Carpus, Bishop of Thyatira, Papylus, deacon, his sister Agathonica, a most holy woman, Agathodorus their servant, and many others. After various torments, they were crowned with martyrdom for their joyful confessions (of faith).

[5] This entry contains a number of errors. 1) There is no town of Metola in this part of Italy. Metola was an isolated castle in the Apennines. 2) Margaret did not die there but at Città di Castello (Tiphernum). 3) In Margaret's time, Metola was not part of the Diocese of Tiphernum.

The entry should read: In the town and Diocese of Città di Castello . . .

At Dorostis in Lower Mysia, the suffering of SS. Maximus, Quinctilian, and Dadas, in the persecution of Diocletian.

At Ravenna, St. Ursus, bishop and confessor.

The Fourteenth Day of April

At Túy in Spain, Blessed Peter Gonzales, called St. Telmo, confessor, of the Order of Preachers. *A semi-duplex feast.*

St. Justin, philosopher and martyr, whose commemoration is noted on April 13.

At Rome, on the Appian Way, the birthday of the holy martyrs Tiburtius, Valerian, and Maximus, in the reign of the Emperor Aurelian and the prefect Almachius. Tibertius and Valerian had been converted to Christ by the exhortations of St. Cecilia and baptized by Pope St. Urban. Later, because of their confession of faith, they were beaten with clubs and then beheaded. Maximus, chamberlain of the prefect, moved by their constancy and encouraged by the vision of an angel, believed in Christ. He was flogged with whips tipped with lead until he expired. *A memory.*

At Teramo, St. Proculus, bishop and martyr.

On the same day, St. Ardalion, an actor. He was mocking in the theatre the sacred rites of the Christians, when, being suddenly converted, he approved them not only by words, but by the testimony of his blood.

At Teramo, St. Domnina, virgin and martyr, crowned with her virgin companions.

At Alexandria, St. Thomais, martyr. She was struck by the sword and cut asunder from head to foot by her father-in-law, because she refused to consent to his evil desires.

At Lyons in Gaul, St. Lambert, bishop and confessor.

At Alexandria, St. Fronto, abbot, whose life was renowned for holiness and miracles.

At Rome, St. Abundius, sacristan of the church of St. Peter.

The Fifteenth Day of April

At Rome, SS. Basilissa and Anastasia. These noble women were disciples of the Apostles, and they remained constant in the confession of the faith. Under the Emperor Nero their tongues were removed and their feet cut off; they finally obtained the crown of martyrdom by being beheaded.

On the same day, the holy martyrs Maro, Eutyches, and Victorinus.

They were first exiled with Blessed Flavia Domitilla to the island of Pontia for confessing Christ, but afterward they were set at liberty under the Emperor Nerva. When they had converted many to the faith, they were ordered by the judge Valerian, during the persecution of Trajan, to be put to death in different ways.

In Persia, the holy martyrs Maximus and Olympias. In the reign of the Emperor Decius, they were beaten with rods and whips tipped with lead. Finally, they were struck over the head with clubs until they died.

At Ferentino in the Hernican mountains, St. Eutychius, martyr.

At Myra in Lycia, St. Crescens, who completed his martyrdom by fire.

In Thrace, the holy martyrs Theodore and Pausilippus, who suffered under the Emperor Hadrian.

The Sixteenth Day of April

At Corinth, the birthday of the holy martyrs Callistus and Charisius, with seven others who, after enduring many tortures, were all drowned in the sea.

At Saragossa in Spain, the birthday of eighteen holy martyrs: Optatus, Lupercus, Successus, Martial, Urban, Julia, Quinctilian, Publius, Fronto, Felix, Cecilian, Eventius, Primitivus, Apodemius, and four others all said to have been called Saturninus. All were tortured and slain together under Dacian, governor of Spain. Prudentius has set forth in verse their illustrious martyrdom.

In the same city, SS. Caius and Crementius. For a second time they confessed their faith in Christ and as they persevered in that confession, they drank the chalice of martyrdom.

In the same place, St. Lambert, martyr.

Also at Saragossa, St. Encratis, virgin and martyr. Her body was mangled; she was then mutilated, and her liver torn out. As she still survived, she was cast into prison until her body, covered with wounds, rotted away.

At Palentia, St. Turibius, Bishop of Astorga. By the help of Pope St. Leo, he drove the Priscillian heresy entirely from Spain. Renowned for his miracles, he died in peace.

At Braga in Portugal, St. Fructuosus, bishop.

At Scicy, in the district of Coutances in Gaul, the death of St. Paternus, Bishop of Avranches and confessor.

At Rome, the birthday of St. Benedict Joseph Labre, confessor. He was famous for his contempt of himself and for his praise of extreme voluntary poverty.

At Valenciennes in Gaul, St. Drogo, confessor.

At Siena in Tuscany, Blessed Joachim, of the Order of Servants of the Blessed Virgin Mary.

The Seventeenth Day of April

At Pisa in Italy, Blessed Clara Gambacorta, (widow), of the Order of Preachers. She was foundress of the monastery of St. Dominic in the same city. The Sovereign Pontiff, Pius VIII, confirmed her immemorable cultus. *A semi-duplex feast.*

At Rome, St. Anicetus, pope and martyr, who received the palm of martyrdom in the persecution of Marcus Aurelius Antoninus and Lucius Verus.

At Cordoba in Spain, the holy martyrs Elias, priest, and the monks Paul and Isidore. They were slain in the Arab persecution because of their profession of the Christian faith.

At Antioch, the holy martyrs Peter, deacon, and Hermogenes, who was Peter's servant.

In Africa, the birthday of Blessed Mappalicus, martyr who, as St. Cyprian tells in his Epistle to Martyrs and Confessors, was crowned with martyrdom, together with many others.

In the same place, the holy martyrs Fortunatus and Marcian.

At Vienne in Gaul, St. Pantagathus, bishop.

At Tortona (in Italy), St. Innocent, bishop and confessor.

At Citeaux in Gaul, St. Stephen, abbot. He was the first to dwell in the wilderness of Citeaux, and he gladly received St. Bernard and his companions when they came to him.

In the monastery of Chaise-Dieu in the Diocese of Clermont in Gaul, St. Robert, confessor, builder and first Abbot of that monastery.

The Eighteenth Day of April

At Mount Senario in Etruria, St. Amideo, confessor, one of the seven founders of the Servants of the Blessed Virgin Mary. He was famous for his burning love towards God. His feast, together with that of his companions, is kept on February 12.

At Rome, Blessed Apollonius, a senator. At the time of the Emperor Commodus and the prefect Perennius, he was revealed by one of his slaves as being a Christian. Being commanded to give an account of his faith, he composed an admirable treatise which he read in the Senate; notwithstanding, by order of the Senate, he was beheaded for Christ.

At Messina in Sicily, the birthday of the holy martyrs Eleutherius, Bishop of Illyria, and Anthia his mother. He was famed for holiness of life and the power of miracles. Under the Emperor Hadrian, he endured a red-hot iron bed, a gridiron, and a pan filled with boiling oil, pitch, and resin. Then he was cast to the lions, but he was in no wise harmed by them. Finally, his throat was cut. His mother underwent the same death.

At Cordoba in Spain, St. Perfectus, priest and martyr, who was put to the sword by the Moors for disputing against the Mohammedan religion.

At Messina in Sicily, St. Corebus, a prefect, who was converted to the faith by St. Eleutherius. He was slain with the sword.

At Brescia, St. Calocerus, martyr, who was converted to Christ by SS. Faustinus and Jovita. He fulfilled the glorious contest of his confession of faith under the Emperor Hadrian.

At Milan, St. Galdinus, cardinal bishop of that city, who, after completing a sermon against heretics, rendered up his spirit to God.

The Nineteenth Day of April

At Corinth, the birthday of St. Timon, one of the seven first deacons (of Jerusalem).[6] He first took up his abode as a teacher at Berea; spreading the word of the Lord from there, he came to Corinth. There, he is said to have been cast into the flames by the Jews and Greeks, but was in no wise hurt. He at last completed his martyrdom by crucifixion.

At Canterbury in England, St. Elphege, bishop and martyr.

At Melitine in Armenia, the holy martyrs Hermogenes, Caius, Expeditus, Aristonicus, Rufus, and Galata, who were all crowned on the same day.

At Collioure in the Spanish (Archdiocese of) Tarragona,[7] the suffering of St. Vincent, martyr.

On the same day, the holy martyrs Socrates and Dionysius, who were pierced with lances.

At Jerusalem, St. Paphnutius, martyr.

At Rome, Pope St. Leo IX, noted for his virtues and miracles.

At Antioch in Pisidia, St. George, bishop, who for his veneration of holy images died in exile.

In the monastery of Lobbes in Belgium, St. Ursmar, bishop.

At Florence, St. Crescentius, confessor, who was a disciple of Bishop St. Zenobius.

[6] Acts, 6:5.

[7] Actually, Collioure is on the French side of the Pyrenees; but long ago, the Diocese of Perpignan (to which it belongs) was a suffragan of Tarragona; hence the rather confusing reference in the Martyrology.

The Twentieth Day of April

At Montepulciano, St. Agnes, virgin, of the Order of our holy Father Dominic. She was illustrious for her great virtues and her miracles. She merited to be adorned with divine gifts by Christ her Spouse. St. Catherine of Siena learned in a vision that she and Agnes would share equal glory in Heaven. *A totum duplex feast of the second class.*

At Rome, the holy martyrs Sulpicius and Cervilian, who were converted to the Christian faith by the discourses and miracles of the virgin St. Domitilla. In the persecution of Trajan, they refused to sacrifice to idols, and both were beheaded by Anian, prefect of the city.

At Nicomedia, the holy martyrs Victor, Zoticus, Zeno, Acindynus, Caesareus, Severian, Chrysophorus, Theonas, and Antoninus. In the reign of the Emperor Diocletian, they were converted to Christ by the suffering and miracles of St. George. Because of their fearless confession of the faith, they were tortured in various ways and so fulfilled their martyrdom.

At Tomis in Scythia, St. Theotimus, bishop, who was revered even by barbarous infidels for his remarkable sanctity and miracles.

At Embrun in Gaul, St. Marcellinus, who was the first bishop of that city. He came from Africa at divine command, together with his holy comrades, Vincent and Domninus. He converted to the Christian faith most of the people of the Maritime Alps by his preaching, and by miracles for which he is noted even to the present day.

At Auxerre, St. Marcian, priest.

At Constantinople, St. Theodore, confessor, surnamed Trichinas from the rough habit of sackcloth he wore. He was noteworthy for many miracles, especially against demons. From his body there issues forth an unguent which gives health to the sick.

The Twenty-first Day of April

At Canterbury in England, St. Anselm, bishop, confessor, and Doctor of the Church, remarkable for holiness and learning. *A duplex feast.*

In Persia, the birthday of St. Simeon, Bishop of Seleucia and Ctesiphon. He was arrested by order of Sapor, King of Persia, loaded with chains and brought before wicked tribunals. As he refused to adore the sun but freely and unfalteringly bore testimony to Jesus Christ, he was first starved for a long time in prison together with a hundred others; some of these were bishops, others priests, and others clerics of various orders. He recalled to repentance Usthazanes, the King's tutor, who had fallen away from the faith, but who now bravely underwent martyrdom. On the following day, which was the anniversary of the Lord's Passion, all the others were beheaded in the presence of Simeon, who earnestly encouraged every one of them. At last, he himself was beheaded. There also suffered with him men of renown, Abdechalas and Ananias, who were his priests. Pusicius, the overseer of the King's workmen, because he had encouraged Ananias when he was wavering, underwent a cruel death: his neck was perforated and through the opening his tongue was plucked out. After him, his daughter, who was a consecrated virgin, was subjected to many cruel tortures and finally beheaded with a sword.

At Alexandria, the holy martyrs, Arator, priest, Fortunatus, Felix, Silvius, and Vitalis; all died in prison.

At Nicomedia, the holy martyrs Apollo, Isacius, and Codratus. In the reign of the Emperor Diocletian, Codratus was slain by blows on the head. Not many days later, the two others died from starvation in prison and they also merited the crown of martyrdom.

At Antioch, St. Anastasius of Sinai, bishop. ✠

The Twenty-second Day of April

At Piedmont (Italy), the birthday of the Dominican Blessed Bartholomew of Cervere, who was born at Savigliano. He was famous for his learning and by his reputation for holiness. He labored extremely hard to eradicate heresy from the Northern Italian provinces. Finally, he was killed by the heretics and so entered the heavenly kingdom a glorious martyr. *A semi-duplex feast.*

At Rome, on the Appian Way, the birthday of St. Soter, pope and martyr.

Also at Rome, St. Caius, pope and martyr, who was crowned with martyrdom under the Emperor Diocletian.

At Smyrna, SS. Apelles and Lucius, from among the first disciples of Christ.

On the same day, many holy martyrs throughout all Persia. The year after the death of Simeon and on the anniversary of Good Friday, King Sapor ordered them to be slain because of their belief in Christ. In this conflict for the faith there suffered the eunuch Azades, who was much beloved by the King; Milles, bishop, famed for his holiness and the gift of miracles; Acepsimes, bishop, with his priest James; Aithalas and Joseph, priests; Azadas and Abdiesus, deacons, and many other clerics. The Bishops Mareas and Bicor likewise suffered, together with twenty other bishops, about two hundred and fifty clerics, many monks, and many consecrated virgins, among whom was a sister of Bishop St. Simeon, named Tarbula, and her servant; these two were bound to stakes and then put to an atrocious death by being sawed in two.

Likewise in Persia, SS. Parmenius, Helimenes, and Chrysotelus, priests, Luke and Mucius, deacons, whose triumph of martyrdom is noted in the Acts of SS. Abdon and Sennen.

At Alexandria, the birthday of St. Leonides, martyr, who suffered under Severus.

At Lyons in Gaul, St. Epipodius, who was arrested in the persecution of Antoninus Verus together with his colleague Alexander. After cruel torments his martyrdom was completed by his being beheaded.

At Constantinople, Pope St. Agapitus I, whose holiness is mentioned by St. Gregory the Great; his body was later removed to Rome, where it lies buried in the Vatican.

At Sens, St. Leo, bishop and confessor.

At Anastasiopolis in Galatia, St. Theodore, bishop, renowned for miracles.

The Twenty-third Day of April

The birthday of St. George, martyr, whose illustrious martyrdom the Church of God holds in reverence among the crowns of the martyrs. *A simplex feast.*

At the village Tenkitten on the Vistula Lagoon, in Prussia, the birthday of St. Adalbert, Bishop of Prague and martyr, who preached the Gospel to the Hungarians and Poles.

At Valence in Gaul, the suffering of the holy martyrs Felix, priest, Fortunatus and Achilleus, deacons. They were sent by St. Irenaeus, Bishop of Lyons, to preach the Word of God. They had converted the greater part of Valence to the faith of Christ, when they were thrown into prison by Cornelius, an army officer. There they were scourged for a long time and their legs were broken. They were bound to revolving wheels and while being stretched on the rack were forced to inhale smoke; at last they gained their crown by the sword.

At Milan, St. Marolus, bishop and confessor.

At Toul in Gaul, St. Gerard, bishop of that city.

The Twenty-fourth Day of April

The Commemoration of the most holy Crown of Thorns of our Lord. *A totum duplex feast.*

At Seewis in Switzerland, St. Fidelis of Sigmaringen, priest and martyr. He was a Capuchin friar who was sent there to preach the Catholic faith, and, being slain by the heretics, obtained the crown of martyrdom. The

Sovereign Pontiff, Benedict XIV, numbered him among the holy martyrs.

At Rome, St. Sabas, an army officer, who was accused of visiting the Christians in prison. He freely admitted to the judge that he was a follower of Christ. He was burnt with torches and cast into a cauldron of boiling pitch, but he emerged unharmed, and by this miracle converted seventy souls to Christ. All these converts, remaining constant in the profession of the faith, were slain by the sword. Sabas was drowned in the river, thus completing his martyrdom.

At Lyons in Gaul, the birthday of St. Alexander, martyr. In the persecution of Antoninus Verus, after being kept in prison, he was flogged with such cruelty by the executioners that the flesh over his ribs was ripped away, his bowls were lacerated, and the insides of his body became visible. He was then crucified, but having become utterly exhausted, gave up his blessed spirit. There suffered with him also thirty-four others, whose memory is kept on other days.

At Nicomedia, the holy martyrs Eusebius, Neon, Leontine, Longinus, and four others, who, after intense sufferings, were slain by the sword in the persecution of Diocletian.

In England, the death of Bishop St. Mellitus. He was sent into England by St. Gregory, and converted to the faith the East Saxons and their king.

At Elvira in Spain, St. Gregory, bishop and confessor.

At Brescia, St. Honorius, bishop.

On Iona, an island of Scotland, St. Egbert, priest and monk, a man of admirable humility and chastity.

At Rheims in Gaul, the holy virgins Bova and Doda.

At Milan, the Conversion of St. Augustine, bishop, confessor, and Doctor of the Church. The Bishop St. Ambrose instructed him in the Catholic faith and baptized him on this very day.

The Twenty-fifth Day of April

At Rome, the Greater Litanies at St. Peter's.

At Alexandria, the birthday of St. Mark the Evangelist. He was the disciple and interpreter of St. Peter the Apostle. At the request of the brethren at Rome, he wrote a Gospel which he took with him to Egypt. At Alexandria he was the first to preach Christ and to found there a Church. Later on he was arrested for the faith, bound with cords, and grievously tortured by being dragged over rocks. After this he was kept in prison, and there he was strengthened first by a visit of an angel and later by an apparition of our Lord. He was called to the kingdom of Heaven in the eighth year of the reign of Nero. *A totum duplex feast of the second class.*

Likewise, at Alexandria, the Bishop St. Anianus, a disciple of St. Mark and his successor in the bishopric. He died peacefully in the Lord, renowned for his virtues.

At Antioch, St. Stephen, bishop and martyr; he suffered much at the hands of the heretics who opposed the Council of Chalcedon. He was cast into the river Orontes in the reign of the Emperor Zeno.

At Syracuse in Sicily, the holy martyrs Evodius, Hermogenes, and Callista.

At Lobbes in Belgium, the birthday of St. Ermin, bishop and confessor.

At Antioch, the holy deacons Philo and Agathopodes. St. Ignatius, bishop and martyr, praises them in his letters.

The Twenty-sixth Day of April

At Besians in the kingdom of Aragon, Blessed Dominic and Gregory, of our Order. While journeying during their missionary labors they were overtaken by a severe tempest; they took refuge under a rock which fell and buried them beneath it. The natives found the bodies in a miraculous way and began venerating them as saints. *A semi-duplex feast.*

At Rome, the birthday of St. Cletus, pope and martyr. He succeeded the Apostle Peter as head of the Church, and was crowned with martyrdom in Domitian's persecution.

(Likewise at Rome,) St. Marcellinus, pope and martyr; his birthday is kept on October 25.

At Amasea in Pontus, St. Basileus, bishop and martyr. He gained an illustrious martyrdom under the Emperor Licinius. His body was thrown into the sea and, on being found by Elpidiphorus, through the direction of an angel, was honorably buried.

At Braga in Portugal, the martyr St. Peter, who was the first bishop of that city.

At Vienne in Gaul, St. Clarence, bishop and confessor.

At Verona, St. Lucidius, bishop.

In the monastery of Centola in Gaul, St. Richarius, priest and confessor.

At Troyes in Gaul, St. Exuperantia, virgin.

The Twenty-seventh Day of April

At Cattaro in Montenegro, Blessed Osanna, virgin, of the Third Order of St. Dominic. She was outstanding by reason of her virtues and was endowed with the gift of prophecy. *A semi-duplex feast.*

At Nicomedia, the birthday of St. Anthimus, bishop and martyr, who obtained in the persecution of Diocletian a glorious martyrdom by being beheaded for confessing Christ. Almost the whole multitude of his flock followed him, some of whom the judge commanded to be beheaded by the sword, others to be burned alive, others to be placed on ships and drowned in the sea.

At Tarsus in Cilicia, SS. Castor and Stephen, martyrs.

At Bologna, St. Tertullian, bishop and confessor.

At Brescia, St. Theophilus, bishop.

In Egypt, St. Theodore, abbot, who was a disciple of St. Pachomius.

At Constantinople, St. John, abbot, who strove valiantly in defense of the veneration of holy images under Leo the Isaurian.

At Tarragona in Spain, Blessed Peter Armengol, of the Order of Blessed Mary of Mercy for the Redemption of Captives.[8] He suffered much for the ransoming of the faithful in Africa, and at last died a holy death in the convent of Saint Mary of the Meadows.

In Lucca in Tuscany, Blessed Zita, virgin, noteworthy for the fame of her virtues and miracles.

The Twenty-eighth Day of April

At the town of St. Laurent-sur-Sèvres, in the Diocese of Luçon, St. Louis-Marie Grignon de Montfort, confessor, of the Third Order of Penance of St. Dominic. He was the founder of both the Congregation of the Missionary Priests of Mary, and of the Sisters of Divine Wisdom. Illustrious for his virtues and miracles, Leo XIII added his name to the roll of the Blessed. *A duplex feast.*

St. Paul of the Cross, priest and confessor, founder of the Congregation of the Cross and Passion of our Lord Jesus Christ. He died in the Lord on October 18. *A memory.*

At Ravenna, the birthday of St. Vitalis, martyr, the husband of St. Valeria, and father of SS. Gervase and Protase. He buried with due honor the body of Blessed Ursicinus which he had found. He was arrested by Paulinus the governor, who subjected him to the rack, and afterward commanded that he be cast into a deep pit and covered with earth and stones; by such a martyrdom he passed to Christ. *A memory.*

At Atino in Campania, St. Mark, who was ordained bishop by the Blessed Apostle Peter, and first preached the Gospel to the Equicoli. He received the crown of martyrdom in Domitian's persecution, under the governor Maximus.

[8] This religious Order is more commonly called the Order of Our Lady of Mercy (or of Ransom).

At Prusa in Bithynia, the holy martyrs Patrick, bishop, Acatius, Menander, and Polyaenus.

On the same day, SS. Aphrodisius, Caralippus, Agapius, and Eusebius, martyrs.

In Hungary, St. Pollio, martyr, under the Emperor Diocletian.

At Milan, St. Valeria, martyr, wife of St. Vitalis, and the mother of SS. Gervase and Protase.

At Alexandria, the suffering of St. Theodora, virgin. When she refused to sacrifice to the idols, she was consigned to a house of ill-fame; but through the admirable care of God, one of the Christians named Didymus changed clothing with her and thus saved her. Later, during the persecution of Diocletian, under the governor Eustratius, Didymus was beheaded with Theodora and together they received their crown.

At Tarazona in Spain, St. Prudentius, bishop and confessor.

At Corfinium among the Pelignians, St. Pamphilus, Bishop of Valva.[9] He was noted for charity towards the poor, and the grace of miracles. His body is buried at Sulmona.

The Twenty-ninth Day of April

At Milan, St. Peter Martyr, of the Order of Preachers. To the very end of his life he preserved the dazzling jewel of virginity. With great energy he fought against the heretics by his preaching and teaching. When he was fatally stabbed by the heretics and lay dying on the ground, he wrote with his own blood the Catholic doctrine he had so staunchly defended in life. He died April 6. *A totum duplex feast of the second class.*

At Rome, the birthday of St. Catherine of Siena, virgin, of the Third Order of St. Dominic. She was renowned for her life and miracles, and the Sovereign Pontiff, Pius II, included her name among those of the holy virgins. Her festival, however, is kept on April 30.

At Paphos on Cyprus, St. Tychicus, a disciple of the Apostle St. Paul. The same Apostle, in his Epistles, calls him: "Dearest brother and faithful minister and fellow servant in the Lord."[10]

At Pisa in Tuscany, St. Torpes, martyr. He was a man of high standing in the household of Nero, and one of those whom the Apostle St. Paul mentioned when he wrote from Rome to the Philippians: "All the saints salute you, but especially they who are of Caesar's household.[11] Afterward, at the command of Satellicus, Torpes was beaten, savagely

---

[9] The Pelignians were an ancient Sabine tribe. Their chief town, Corfinium, no longer exists; near its ruins is the city of Valva.

[10] Ephesians, 6:21; Colossians, 4:7.

[11] Philippians, 4:22.

scourged and delivered to the beasts to devour. As he was uninjured by them, his martyrdom was ended by his being beheaded.

At Cirta in Numidia, the birthday of the holy martyrs Agapius and Secundinus, both bishops. They had been exiles at Cirta for a long time when the persecution of Valerian began, a persecution in which the rage of the heathens sorely tested the faith of Christians. Agapius and Secundinus were transformed from exemplary priests to glorious martyrs. In their company, there also suffered a soldier named Aemilian, two consecrated virgins, Tertulla and Antonia, and a certain woman with her twin children.

On the island of Corcyra, seven repentant thieves who were converted to Christ by St. Jason and obtained by martyrdom life everlasting.

At Naples in Campania, St. Severus, bishop. One of his remarkable deeds was to raise a dead man from the grave for a short time so that he might convict of falsehood the lying creditor of a widow and her children.

At Brescia, St. Paulinus, bishop and confessor.

In the monastery of Cluny in Gaul, St. Hugh, abbot.

In the monastery of Molesmes in Gaul, St. Robert, who was the first Abbot of Citeaux.

The Thirtieth Day of April

At Rome, St. Catherine of Siena, virgin, of the Order of our Father St. Dominic. While hardly more than an infant, she consecrated her virginity to Christ and preserved it unsullied until death. She was famed for her innumerable halos of virtue, and excelled in a remarkable innocence of life. Strengthened by Christ her Spouse in frequent sweet conversations, she merited to become a sharer in His sufferings and wounds. Lastly, she was distinguished by the gift of prophecy, by miracles, and by doctrine. Having frequently conquered and triumphed over Satan, she ascended to heaven to the happy embraces of her Spouse on April 29. She was buried in the Church of Santa Maria sopra Minerva, and Pius II inscribed her in the number of the holy virgins. *A totum duplex feast of the first class.*

At Saintes in Gaul, Blessed Eutropius, bishop and martyr. St. Clement consecrated him bishop, and sent him into Gaul. There he long performed the office of a preacher; finally, because of his testimony for Christ, his skull was crushed and he died a victor.

At Cordoba in Spain, the holy martyrs Amator, priest, Peter, monk, and Louis.

At Novara, the martyrs St. Laurence, priest, and some children whom he had received to educate.

At Alexandria, the holy martyrs Aphrodisius, priest, and thirty others.

At Lambesa in Numidia, the holy martyrs Marian, lector, and James, deacon. The first, in his confession of Christ, had overcome the trials of the persecution of Decius. He was again taken with his renowned companion, and both were wonderfully confirmed by divine revelations after cruel and exquisite torments. At last, with many other Christians, they were martyred by the sword.

At Ephesus, St. Maximus, martyr, who was crowned in the persecution of Decius.

At Fermo in Piceno (Italy), St. Sophia, virgin and martyr.

At Evora in Epirus, St. Donatus, bishop, who shone with remarkable holiness in the time of the Emperor Theodosius.

At Naples in Campania, St. Pomponius, bishop.

At London in England, St. Erconwald, bishop, who was noted for many miracles.

may

The First Day of May

The birthday of the holy Apostles Philip and James. Philip, after he had converted almost all Scythia to the Christian faith, was crucified and stoned at Hierapolis, a city in Asia, so that he went to his eternal rest by a glorious death. James, (also called "the brother of the Lord"), was the first Bishop of Jerusalem. He was cast headlong from a pinnacle of the temple, and his legs were broken by the fall. He died when his brains were scattered by a blow from a fuller's club. He was buried not far from the temple. *A totum duplex feast of the second class.*

At Rome, St. Pius V, of the Order of Preachers, pope and confessor. He restored ecclesiastical discipline, eradicated heresies, and applied himself strenuously and successfully to combating the enemies of Christ. He governed the Catholic Church in holiness of life and legislation. His feast is celebrated on May 5.

In Egypt, St. Jeremias, prophet. Stoned by the people, he died at Taphnas, where he was buried. St. Epiphanius relates that the faithful were wont to make their supplications at his tomb, and that by dust taken from it the bites of serpents were healed.

In the region of Viviers in Gaul, Blessed Andeolus, subdeacon. St. Polycarp, Bishop of Smyrna, sent him from the East to Gaul, together with others, to preach the Word of God. Here, he was beaten with thorny clubs under the Emperor Severus. He at last completed his martyrdom when his head was split crosswise into four parts with a wooden sword.

At Huesca in Spain, the martyrs SS. Orentius and Patience.

In the village of Columna, in the province of Orleans in Gaul, the suffering of St. Sigismund, King of Burgundy. He died by being drowned in a well and after his death was renowned for his miracles. His sacred body was finally recovered from the well and taken to the monastery of St. Maurice in the Diocese of Sion, and there honorably enshrined.

At Auxerre, St. Amator, bishop and confessor.

At Auch in Gaul, St. Orientius, bishop.

At Llanelwy in England, St. Asaph, bishop, in whose memory the episcopal city was later named St. Asaph's.

At Forli (in Italy), St. Peregrinus, of the Order of the Servants of Mary.

At Bergamo, St. Grata, widow.

The Second Day of May

At Alexandria, the birthday of St. Athanasius, bishop of that city, confessor, and Doctor of the Church. Although famous for his sanctity and learning, almost the whole world conspired to persecute him. Notwithstanding, he courageously fought in defence of the Catholic Church against emperors, governors, and numerous Arian bishops, from the reign of Constantine down to that of Valens. He steadfastly endured persecutions and was forced to be a wanderer on the face of the earth where no place remained where he might live in safety. At long last, he was restored to his see, whence, after many afflictions and numerous trials of patience, he departed for heaven in the forty-sixth year of his priesthood, at the time when Valentinian and Valens were Emperors. *A duplex feast.*

At Florence, St. Antoninus, bishop and confessor, of the Order of Preachers, famed for holiness and learning. His feast is celebrated May 10.

At Rome, the holy martyrs Saturninus, Neopolus, Germanus, and Celestine. They suffered many tortures and then were cast into prison, where they died in the Lord.

On the same day, St. Vindemialis, bishop and martyr. Together with the holy Bishops Eugene and Longinus, he strove against the Arians by his teaching and miracles. After he had undergone many tortures, he was beheaded by command of King Hunneric.

At Seville in Spain, St. Felix, deacon and martyr.

At Attalia in Pamphylia, the holy martyrs Exuperius, his wife Zoë, and their sons Cyriacus and Theodulus. At the time of the Emperor Hadrian, they were slaves of a man named Paganus. Because of their fearless profession of the Christian faith, their master commanded them to be flogged and severely tortured in other ways. Then they were thrown into a raging furnace, thus surrendering their souls to God. ✠

The Third Day of May

At Jerusalem, the Finding of the most Holy Cross of the Lord, in the reign of the Emperor Constantine. *A totum duplex feast of the second class.*

At Rome, on the Via Nomentana, the suffering of the holy martyrs Alexander I, pope, Eventius and Theodulus, priests. At the time of the

Emperor Hadrian and the judge Aurelian, Alexander suffered chains, imprisonment, the rack, torture by iron hooks, and then fire. Finally he was pierced with many sharp points in all his limbs, and slain. Eventius and Theodulus, after long imprisonment, were tortured by fire, and at last beheaded. *A memory.*

At Narni (in Italy), St. Juvenal, bishop and confessor.

At Mt. Senario in Etruria, SS. Sosthenes and (Hugo) Uguccio, confessors, two of the seven founders of the Order of Servants of Mary. Having been forewarned from Heaven, they passed out of this life at the same day and hour while reciting the Angelic Salutation. Their feast, together with that of their companions, is kept on February 12.

At Constantinople, the holy martyrs SS. Alexander, soldier, and Antonina, virgin. In the persecution of Maximian, she was condemned to a house of ill fame by Festus, the governor, but she was secretly delivered by Alexander, who changed garments with her and remained there in her place. She was afterward put to the torture with him, and both were cast into the flames together, with their hands cut off. In this way they were crowned, after ending gloriously the contest.

In the Thebaid, the holy martyrs Timothy and Maura, his wife. After they had suffered many torments, the prefect Arian ordered them to be crucified. They hung there alive for nine days, encouraging each other in the faith; thus they completed their martyrdom.

At Aphrodisia in Caria, the holy martyrs Diodorus and Rhodopian, who were stoned to death by their fellow-citizens in Diocletian's persecution.

The Fourth Day of May

At Ostia, St. Monica, the mother of St. Augustine, whose excellent life her son has left recorded in the ninth book of his Confessions. *A duplex feast.*

At the copper mines near Phûnon in Palestine, the birthday of Blessed Silvanus of Gaza, bishop. In the persecution of Diocletian, by command of Galerius Maximian, he was crowned with martyrdom, together with many of his clergy.

At Jerusalem, St. Cyriacus, bishop who, when he visited the holy places, was there slain by Julian the Apostate.

At Camerino (in Italy), St. Porphyrius, priest and martyr. In the reign of the Emperor Decius and the governorship of Antiochus, he converted many to the faith, among whom was Venantius; for this reason he was beheaded.

Likewise in the mines of Phûnon, thirty-nine holy martyrs, who were condemned to the mines. After being burnt with hot irons and suffering other torments, they were beheaded together.

At Lorch in Austria, St. Florian, martyr. In the reign of the Emperor Diocletian, and at the command of the governor Aquilinus, he was cast into the river Enns with a stone tied to his neck.

At Cologne, St. Paulinus, martyr.

At Tarsus in Cilicia, St. Pelagia, virgin and martyr. She was roasted to death in a red-hot brazen bull and thus gained martyrdom.

At Nicomedia, the birthday of St. Antonia, martyr. She was tortured with various sufferings to an exceptional degree; among them, she was suspended (from a beam) by one arm for three days. She was kept in prison for two years, and finally, under the governor Priscillian, was burned to death for her profession of faith.

At Milan, St. Venerius, bishop, whose virtues St. John Chrysostom recorded in an epistle written to him.

In the district of Perigueux, St. Sacerdos, Bishop of Limoges.

At Hildesheim in Saxony, St. Godehard, bishop and confessor, who was ranked among the saints by Innocent II.

At Auxerre, St. Curcodomus, deacon.

The Fifth Day of May

At Rome, St. Pius V, pope and confessor, of the Order of Preachers. He zealously reformed the morals of the clergy and the laity, everywhere suppressed heresies, and by his prayers obtained from God a naval victory for the Christians at Lepanto. He fulfilled every duty of a good pastor and died May 1. *A totum duplex feast of the second class.*

At Rome, St. Silvanus, martyr.

Also at Rome, St. Crescentiana, martyr.

At Leocata, in Sicily, St. Angelus, priest and martyr, of the Order of Carmelites, who was slain by heretics for his defence of the Catholic faith.

At Alexandria, St. Euthymius, deacon, who died while imprisoned for the faith of Christ.

At Auxerre, the suffering of St. Jovinian, lector.

At Thessalonica, the birthday of the holy martyrs Irenaeus, Peregrinus, and Irene. They were burned to death, thus receiving the palm of martyrdom.

At Jerusalem, St. Maximus, bishop. Caesar Maximian Galerius condemned him to the metal mines after one of his eyes was dug out (with a dagger) and one leg lamed by a red-hot iron. Later, he was allowed to leave there a free man. While he was ruling his church at Jerusalem, he died in peace, renowned as a glorious confessor.

At Edessa in Syria, St. Eulogius, bishop and confessor.

At Arles in Gaul, St. Hilary, bishop, remarkable for his learning and holiness.

At Vienne in Gaul, St. Nicetus, bishop, a man venerable for his sanctity.

At Bologna, St. Theodore, bishop, renowned for his merits.

At Milan, St. Geruntius, bishop.

On the same day, St. Sacerdos, Bishop of Sagunto (in Spain).

The Sixth Day of May

At Rome, the Apostle and Evangelist St. John, before the Latin Gate. By order of Domitian, he was brought in chains from Ephesus to Rome, and by decree of the Senate was cast into a cauldron of boiling oil before the Latin Gate. He came forth from it more healthy and more vigorous than when he had entered it. *A totum duplex feast.*

At Damascus, the birthday of St. John Damascene, priest, confessor, and Doctor of the Church. He was celebrated for his learning and holiness. By means of his writings and preaching, he powerfully defended the veneration of the holy images against Leo the Isaurian. Because of the calumnies of the Emperor, the Saracen calif ordered the saint's right hand to be cut off. When St. Damascene commended himself to the Blessed Virgin Mary, whose images he had defended, his hand was instantly restored to him, entire and sound. His festival is observed on March 27.

At Cyrene in Libya, St. Lucius, bishop. St. Luke mentions him in the Acts of the Apostles.[1]

At Antioch, St. Evodius. St. Ignatius, writing to the people of Antioch, says that Evodius was ordained the first Bishop of Antioch by the Apostle St. Peter and ended his life there by a glorious martyrdom.

In Africa, the holy martyrs Heliodorus, Venustus, and seventy-five others.

In Cyprus, St. Theodotus, Bishop of Cyrinia. In the reign of the Emperor Licinius, he suffered many grievous trials; but when peace had been restored to the Church, he gave up his soul to God.

At Carrhae in Mesopotamia, St. Protogenes, bishop and confessor.

In England, St. Eadbert, Bishop of Lindisfarne, famous for his learning and holiness.

[1] Acts, 13:1.

At Rome, St. Benedicta, virgin.

At Salerno, the transferal of the body of St. Matthew, Apostle and Evangelist. His holy body had been borne from Ethiopia into various lands, and at last was taken to Salerno where it was buried with great honor in the church dedicated to his name. ✠

The Seventh Day of May *

St. Stanislaus, Bishop of Cracow and martyr, who suffered martyrdom on May 8. *A duplex feast.*

At Terracina in Campania, the birthday of Blessed Flavia Domitilla, virgin and martyr. She was the daughter of St. Plautilla, the sister of St. Flavius Clemens, consul, and was given the holy veil by St. Clement. In the persecution of Domitian, she was exiled to the island of Pontia with many others for confessing Christ, and there she endured prolonged suffering. At last she was brought back to Terracina, where, by her teaching and miracles, she converted many to the faith of Christ. At the command of the judge, the room in which she lived with her two maids, Euphrosina and Theodora, was set on fire, and thus she completed the course of a resplendent martyrdom. Her feast is kept, together with that of the holy martyrs Nereus, Achilleus, and Pancras, on May 12.

On the same day, St. Juvenal, martyr.

At Nicomedia, the holy martyrs Flavius, Augustus, and Augustine, brothers.

In the same place, St. Quadratus, martyr, who, in the persecution of the Emperor Decius, was again and again called upon to undergo torments, and at last gained martyrdom by being beheaded.

At York in England, St. John, bishop, renowned for his life and miracles.

At Pavia, St. Peter, bishop.

At Rome, the transferal of the body of St. Stephen, the Proto-martyr. It was brought to that city from Constantinople under Pope Pelagius I, and placed in the tomb of St. Laurence the Martyr in the field of Veranus, where it is honored with great reverence by the faithful.

The Eighth Day of May

On Monte Gargano, the Appearance of St. Michael the Archangel. *A totum duplex feast.*

* In the Third Order, the reading for today begins: The octave of St. Catherine of Siena, of the Order of Preachers. *A solemn octave.*

At Cracow in Poland, the birthday of St. Stanislaus, bishop and martyr, who was slain by the wicked King Boleslaus. His festival, however, is observed on May 7.

At Milan, the birthday of St. Victor, martyr. He was by nationality a Moor, but was a Christian from his early years. While he was a soldier in the imperial camp, he was required by Maximian to sacrifice to the idols, but remained steadfast in the faith. For that reason, he was first severely beaten with clubs, but through the protection of God he received no injury; molten lead was then poured over him, and again he suffered no harm; at last, he completed a glorious martyrdom by being beheaded.

At Constantinople, St. Agathus, centurion. He was denounced as a Christian by Firmus, the tribune, in the persecution of Diocletian and Maximian. He was most cruelly tortured by Bibianus the judge at Perinthos; then at Byzantium he was condemned to death by Flaccinus the proconsul. His body was afterward impelled miraculously to the shore of Squillace in Calabria, and is there preserved in honor.

At Rome, Pope St. Boniface IV, who dedicated the Pantheon in honor of our Lady and the martyrs.

Likewise at Rome, St. Benedict II, pope and confessor.

At Vienne in Gaul, St. Dionysius, bishop and confessor.

At Auxerre, St. Helladius, bishop.

In the monastery of Bonnevaux, in the district of Besançon, St. Peter, a Cistercian monk, who later became Bishop of Tarantaise in Savoy.

At Roermond in Gelderland, St. Wiro, a bishop from Scotland.

The Ninth Day of May

At Nazianzus in Cappadocia, the birthday of St. Gregory, bishop, confessor, and Doctor of the Church. He is called the Theologian by reason of his extraordinary knowledge of divine things. He fulfilled his office as bishop of that city by restoring the Catholic religion which had become weakened, and by repressing heresies and the enemies of the Church. *A duplex feast.*

At Rome, St. Hermas, whom the Apostle Paul mentions in the Epistle to the Romans.[2] He made a worthy sacrifice of himself; being made an acceptable offering to God, and renowned for his virtues, he gained the heavenly kingdom.

At Cagli on the Via Flaminia, the suffering of St. Gerontius, Bishop of Cervia.

In Persia, three hundred and ten holy martyrs.

[2] Romans, 16:14.

In Egypt, St. Pachomius, abbot. He built many monasteries in that land and wrote a rule for monks, which he had learned from the dictation of an angel.

In the village of Vendôme in Gaul, the death of St. Beatus, confessor.

At Bologna, Blessed Nicholas Albergati, a Carthusian monk, bishop of that city and cardinal of the Holy Roman Church. He was renowned for his holiness and for his negotiations as Apostolic Legate. His body was buried at Florence in the Carthusian monastery.

At Constantinople, the transferal from Achaia of the bodies of the Apostle St. Andrew and the Evangelist St. Luke; and of Timothy, the disciple of the Apostle St. Paul, from Ephesus. The body of St. Andrew was long afterward taken to Amalfi, and is honored there by the pious concourse of the faithful. From his tomb there issues continually a liquid that heals the sick.

At Rome, the transferal of the body of St. Jerome, priest, confessor, and Doctor of the Church, from Bethlehem of Judea to the Basilica of St. Mary Major's at-the-Crib.

Also, at Bari in Apulia, the transferal of the body of St. Nicholas, bishop and confessor, from Myra, a city of Lycia.

The Tenth Day of May

At Florence, St. Antoninus, archbishop of the same city and a member of the Order of Preachers. On account of the excellence of his doctrine and his holiness, he was compelled to become bishop, although he was unwilling. He was illustrious for his mercy and his piety. He likewise excelled to a remarkable degree in sacerdotal zeal. He was so celebrated for his prudence and good counsel, that he was justly called "Antoninus the Counsellor." Famous for his virtues and his miracles, he departed for Heaven in the seventieth year of his life, on May 2. He lies buried in the Church of San Marco where he is held in high veneration by the people. *A totum duplex feast of the second class.*

At Rome, on the Via Latina, the birthday of the holy martyrs Gordian and Epimachus. In the time of Julian the Apostate, Gordian was long beaten with whips loaded with lead for confessing Christ's name, and at last beheaded. He was buried at night by the Christians on the same road in a crypt to which the relics of Blessed Epimachus the Martyr had been transferred a short while before from Alexandria, where he had suffered martyrdom for the Christian faith on December 12. *A memory.*

In the land of Hus, holy Job the Prophet, a man of admirable patience.

At Rome, Blessed Calepodius, priest and martyr. The Emperor Alexander caused him to be slain with the sword, and his body to be dragged through the city and cast into the Tiber. After it had been recovered, Pope Callistus buried it. Palmatius the consul was also beheaded with his wife and children, and forty-two others of his household, of both sexes; likewise the senator Simplicius with his wife and sixty-eight of his household; and also Felix with Blanda, his wife. Their heads were hung at various gates of the city as a warning to the Christians.

Likewise at Rome, on the Via Latina at Centum Aulae, the birthday of the holy martyrs Quartus and Quinctius, whose bodies were taken to Capua.

At Leutini in Sicily, the holy martyrs Alphius, Philadelphus, and Cyrinus.

At Smyrna, St. Dioscorides, martyr.

At Taranto, St. Cataldus, bishop, renowned for miracles.

At Madrid, St. Isidore the Ploughman. He is famous for his miracles, and Gregory XV inscribed him in the number of the saints, together with SS. Ignatius, Francis Xavier, Teresa, and Philip Neri.

At Milan, the finding of the bodies of the holy martyrs Nazarius and Celsus. St. Ambrose, the bishop, found the body of St. Nazarius still sprinkled with fresh blood, and bore it to the Basilica of the Apostles, together with the body of Blessed Celsus, a youth whom he had reared. During the persecution of Nero, Anolinus had commanded both to be slain by the sword on July 28, on which day the celebration of their martyrdom is observed.

The Eleventh Day of May

At Cremona, Blessed Albert of Valle d'Ogna near Bergamo, a tertiary of our Order, who was renowned for his miracles. He died on May 7. *A semi-duplex feast.*

At Rome, on the Via Salaria, the birthday of Blessed Anthimus, priest. After marvels of virtue and preaching, he was thrown into the Tiber in Diocletian's persecution, rescued by an angel, and restored to his own oratory. Then he was beheaded and passed as a victor to heaven.

In the same city, St. Evellius, martyr, of the household of Nero. Witnessing the martyrdom of St. Torpes, he also believed in Christ; for this reason he also was beheaded.

Likewise at Rome, the holy martyrs Maximus, Bassus, and Fabius, who were slain on the Via Salaria, under Diocletian.

At Osimo in Piceno, the holy martyrs Sisinius, deacon, Diocletius and Florentius, disciples of the priest St. Anthimus. They fulfilled their martyrdom by being stoned to death in the reign of Diocletian.

At Camerino, the holy martyrs Anastasius and his companions. They were slain in the persecution of Decius under the governor Antiochus.

At Varennes in Gaul, St. Gangulphus, martyr.

At Vienne in Gaul, St. Mamertus, bishop. To avert an imminent slaughter, he instituted in the city Solemn Litanies for three days before the Lord's Ascension. This rite the Universal Church afterward approved by adopting it.

At Souvigny in Gaul, the death of St. Majolus, Abbot of Cluny, whose life was remarkable for holy merits.

At Naples in Campania, St. Francis of Jerome, confessor and priest, of the Society of Jesus. He was born in the town of Grottaglie in the Diocese of Taranto. He showed a wonderful charity and patience in looking after the salvation of souls, and Pope Gregory XVI inscribed him in the list of the saints.

At San Severino in Piceno, St. Illuminatus, confessor.

The Twelfth Day of May

In the Dominican monastery of Aveiro, the birthday of the virgin, Blessed Joan, Infanta of Portugal, daughter of King Alphonse V. Pope Innocent XII took counsel with the Cardinals of the Sacred Congregation of Rites and, because of Blessed Joan's singular merits, granted permission to all Portugal and the whole Dominican Order to celebrate her feast. The office for it was to be taken from the Common of a Virgin not a Martyr. *A semi-duplex feast.*

At Rome, on the Via Ardeatina, the holy martyrs Nereus and Achilleus, brothers; together with Domitilla, whose slaves they were. They first endured a long exile on the island of Pontia because of their faith. Later, they were subjected to a most brutal flogging. Then, when the ex-consul Minutius Rufus was trying by the use of the rack and of fire, to force them to sacrifice to the gods, the brothers answered that they had been baptized by the Apostle St. Peter himself and that under no condition would they offer sacrifice. Whereupon they were beheaded. By the command of Pope Clement VIII their sacred relics, together with those of Flavia Domitilla, were on the eve of this day solemnly transferred from the deaconry [3] of St. Hadrian to the old church which bears their name and which was now restored. It was here that they had formerly been buried. The Pope also ordered that the feast of Domitilla the virgin,

[3] The deaconry (*diaconia*) originally was the place where food and alms were distributed to the poor by one of the seven deacons of Rome. Each *diaconia* consisted of a hall and a chapel.

whose martyrdom was mentioned on May 7, should be observed on this day. *A memory*.

Likewise at Rome, on the Via Aurelia, St. Pancras, martyr. When he was fourteen years old he was martyred under Diocletian by being beheaded. *A memory*.

At Salamina in Cyprus, St. Epiphanius, bishop. He excelled in many branches of learning and the knowledge of sacred letters, and stood forth remarkable for holiness of life, zeal for the Catholic faith, generosity towards the poor, and the power of working miracles.

At Constantinople, St. Germanus, bishop, famous for virtue and learning. He opposed Leo the Isaurian with great firmness when an edict was published against the veneration of holy images.

At Treves, St. Modoald, bishop.

At Rome, St. Dionysius, uncle of the martyr St. Pancras.

At Agirone in Sicily, St. Philip, priest. He was sent to that island by the Roman Pontiff, and converted a great part thereof to Christ. His holiness was chiefly manifested in freeing those possessed with devils.

In the city of Calzada, in Spain, St. Dominic, confessor.

The Thirteenth Day of May

At Bologna, a commemoration of the precious death of Blessed Imelda, virgin, of the Order of Preachers. After receiving the sacrament of the Most Holy Eucharist, which she most ardently desired, she could not sustain the most intense fire of love. Her journey in life ended, she happily entered heaven to reign as a victim of love. *A duplex feast*.

At Rome, the dedication of the church of St. Mary of the Martyrs. In the reign of the Emperor Phocas, Pope St. Boniface IV purified the Pantheon, the ancient temple of all the gods, and consecrated it in honor of our Lady and all the holy martyrs. But later, the Sovereign Pontiff, Gregory IV, decreed that the annual solemnity, now extended to honor all saints, should be observed by the Universal Church on November 1.

At Constantinople, Blessed Mucius, priest and martyr. At the time of the Emperor Diocletian and the proconsul Laudicius, he was subjected to many penalties and tortures because of his faith. He was first tortured at Amphipolis in Macedonia; then he was taken to Constantinople where he was beheaded.

At Alexandria, the commemoration of many holy martyrs, who were slain by the Arians in the church at Theonas on account of their Catholic faith.

At Heraclea in Thrace, St. Glyceria, a Roman martyr. She suffered many grievous torments from the hands of the governor Sabinus in the reign of the Emperor Antoninus; but she escaped unharmed from them all by the help of God. At length she was cast to the wild beasts; when one of them had bitten her, she gave up her soul to God.

At Utrecht, St. Servatius, Bishop of the Church of Tongres. His merits were made plain to all men by the fact that, in winter, when snow covered all the earth round about, it never fell upon his tomb, until by the zeal of the citizens a basilica was built thereon. His feast is observed May 22.

In Palestine, St. John the Silent. He resigned the see of Colonia in Armenia, retired to the laura [4] of St. Sabbas, and finally departed this life by a holy death.

The Fourteenth Day of May

At Santarem in Portugal, the death of Blessed Giles of Vouzella, of our Order. He was renowned for his penance and for the power of working miracles. *A semi-duplex feast.*

At Tarsus in Cilicia, the birthday of St. Boniface, martyr, who suffered under Diocletian and Maximian. His body was afterward removed to Rome and buried on the Via Latina.

In Gaul, St. Pontus, martyr. His earnest teaching converted to the faith of Christ two Caesars: Philip and his son of the same name. Later, during the reign of the Caesars Valerian and Gallienus, Pontus received the crown of martyrdom.

In Syria, the holy martyrs Victor and Corona, under the Emperor Antoninus. Victor was subjected to various terrible torments by the judge Sebastian. Corona, the wife of a soldier, began to declare him blessed for his constancy in martyrdom, and she saw two crowns descend from heaven, one sent for Victor and one for herself. When she had testified to this publicly, she herself was put to death by being torn apart between two trees; Victor, however, was beheaded.

In Sardinia, the holy martyrs Justa, Justina, and Henedina.

At Ferentino in Tuscany, St. Boniface, bishop. As Pope St. Gregory relates, he was known from childhood for holiness and the gift of miracles.

The Fifteenth Day of May

St. John Baptist de la Salle, priest and confessor, who founded the

---

[4] A *laura* was a monastery where the monks lived in separate huts or cells around the church.

Brothers of the Christian Schools and who died on April 7. *A duplex feast.*

In Spain, SS. Torquatus, Ctesiphon, Secundus, Indaletius, Caecilius, Hesychius, and Euphrasius. They were ordained bishops at Rome by the holy Apostles and sent to preach the Word of God in Spain. They evangelized various cities and brought the faith of Christ to innumerable multitudes. They were martyred in different places in that country: Torquatus at Guadix, Ctesiphon at Verga, Secundus at Avila, Indaletius at Urci, Caecilius at Granada, Hesychius at Gibraltar, Euphrasius at Andujar.

At Faustina in Sardinia, St. Simplicius, bishop and martyr. He gained martyrdom by being pierced with a spear, at the time of the Emperor Diocletian, and the governor Barbarus.

At Evora in Portugal, St. Mancius, martyr.

On the island of Chios, the birthday of Blessed Isidore, martyr. In his basilica, there is a well into which he is said to have been hurled. Oftentimes the sick who drink some of the water of this well are healed.

At Lampsacus in the Hellespont, the suffering of SS. Peter, Andrew, Paul, and Dionysia.

In Auvergne in Gaul, the holy martyrs Cassius, Victorinus, Maximus, and their companions.

At Gheel in Brabant, St. Dympna, virgin and martyr, daughter of a king of Ireland. She was beheaded at the command of her father because she refused to give up her faith and her virginity.

The Sixteenth Day of May

At Prague in Bohemia, St. John Nepomucen, a canon of the metropolitan church. Urged in vain to break the seal of the confessional, he merited the palm of martyrdom by being thrown into the River Moldau. *A duplex feast.*

At Gubbio, St. Ubald, bishop and confessor, noted for miracles.

At Auxerre, the suffering of St. Peregrinus, the first bishop of that city. In company with other clerics, he was sent by Pope Sixtus II into Gaul, where he fulfilled his duty of preaching the Gospel. For this, he was condemned to death and thus gained a glorious martyrdom.

In Persia, the holy martyrs Adus, bishop, seven priests, nine deacons, and seven virgins. They were subjected to various kinds of tortures under King Yezdegerd, and so fulfilled a glorious martyrdom.

In Isauria, the birthday of the holy martyrs Aquilinus and Victorian.

At Uzala in Africa, the holy martyrs Felix and Gennadius.

In Palestine, the suffering of the holy monks in the laura of St. Sabbas who were put to death by the Saracens.

At Amiens in Gaul, St. Honoratus, bishop.

At LeMans in Gaul, St. Domnolus, bishop.

At Mirandola in Emilia, St. Possidius, Bishop of Calama in Numidia, a disciple of St. Augustine, and his biographer.

In the monastery of Enachduin in Ireland, the passing of St. Brendan, Abbot of Clonfort.

At Treves in Gaul, St. Fidolus, confessor.

At Fréjus in Gaul, St. Maxima, virgin, who died peacefully, renowned for many virtues. ✠

The Seventeenth Day of May

At Aix in Provence, Blessed Andrew Abellon, confessor, of the Order of Preachers. Outstanding for his preaching of the divine Word and for his zeal in restoring regular observance, he became more famous by the miracles performed through his intercession after death. *A semi-duplex feast.*

At Villareal in Spain, St. Paschal, confessor, of the Order of Friars Minor. He was a man of wondrous innocence and penitence, whom Leo XIII declared celestial patron of all Eucharistic Congresses and societies of the Most Holy Eucharist.

At Noyon in Gaul, the holy martyrs Heradius, Paul, and Aquilinus, with two others.

At Chalcedon, the holy martyrs Solochan and his fellow-soldiers under the Emperor Maximian.

At Alexandria, the holy martyrs Adrion, Victor, and Basilla.

On the same day, St. Restituta, virgin and martyr. In the reign of Valerian, she was tortured in various ways by Proculus the judge in Africa; then she was placed in a boat filled with pitch and tow, so that she might be burned alive at sea. When fire was lighted, the flames turned against her persecutors, and she gave up her spirit in prayer to God. The boat with her body, by the will of God, was borne to Ischia, an island near Naples in Campania, where it was received by the Christians with great reverence. Afterward Constantine the Great erected a basilica at Naples in her honor.

The Eighteenth Day of May

At Camerino (Italy) St. Venantius, martyr. He was only fifteen years old, at the time of the Emperor Decius and the governor Antiochus, when, with ten companions, he completed the course of a glorious contest by being beheaded. *A duplex feast.*

At Ravenna, the birthday of St. John I, pope and martyr. He was lured there by Theodoric, the Arian King of Italy, and because of his orthodox faith was cast into prison where he was ill-treated until his death. His festival is, however, observed on May 27, on which day his blessed body was taken to Rome and buried in the Basilica of St. Peter, the Prince of the Apostles.

At Spoleto, St. Felix, bishop, who gained the palm of martyrdom under the Emperor Maximian.

At Heraclea in Egypt, St. Potamion, bishop, who was a confessor under Maximian Galerius. Afterward, he was crowned with martyrdom under the Emperor Constantius and the Arian governor Philagrius. The holy Fathers of the Church, Athanasius and Epiphanius, have sung the praises of this blessed man.

In Egypt, St. Dioscorus, lector. The governor inflicted many different tortures on him, such as pulling out his nails and burning his sides with torches. But they who were torturing him fell down, terrified by the shining of a light from heaven. At last, burned with red-hot metal plates, he completed his martyrdom.

At Ancyra in Galatia, St. Theodotus, martyr, and seven holy virgins, SS. Thecussa his aunt, Alexandra, Claudia, Faina, Euphrasia, Matrona, and Julitta. They were first sent to a place of infamy by the governor, but by God's power were preserved. Stones were then fastened to their necks, and they were cast into a marsh. Their relics were gathered up by Theodotus and honorably buried, whereupon he himself was arrested by the governor and grievously mangled. At last, being put to the sword, he obtained the crown of martyrdom.

At Upsala in Sweden, St. Eric, king and martyr.

At Rome, St. Felix, confessor, of the Order of Friars Minor Capuchin, famous for his evangelical simplicity and charity. Clement XI, the Sovereign Pontiff, inscribed him in the roll of the saints.

The Nineteenth Day of May

The birthday of St. Peter di Morrone, confessor. After being a hermit, he was created Supreme Pontiff and named Celestine V. He abdicated the papacy and led a religious life in solitude. Famous for virtues and miracles, he passed to the Lord. *A duplex feast.*

At Rome, St. Pudentiana, virgin. She underwent innumerable trials. After caring reverently for the burial of many destitute martyrs, and distributing all her goods to the poor, she at length passed from earth to heaven. *A memory.*

In the same city, St. Pudens, senator, father of the aforesaid St. Pudentiana and of St. Praxedes, virgin. He was adorned for Christ in baptism by the Apostles, and he guarded his robe of innocence without stain until (he received) the crown of life.

Likewise in Rome, on the Appian Way, the birthday of SS. Calocerus and Parthenius, eunuchs. The former was chamberlain to the wife of the Emperor Decius, and the other chief officer of another office. They refused to offer sacrifice to idols and were tortured in various cruel ways. At last, after their necks had been broken with a red-hot bar, they gave up their souls to God.

At Nicomedia, St. Philoterus, martyr, son of the proconsul Pacian. He suffered much under the Emperor Diocletian, and received the crown of martyrdom.

In the same city, six holy virgins and martyrs, of whom the most famous was Cyriaca. She boldly rebuked the wickedness of Maximian. She was grievously beaten and mangled, and at last was burned to death, thus gaining martyrdom.

At Canterbury in England, St. Dustan, bishop.

At Lovannec in Brittany, St. Ivo, priest and confessor who, for the love of Christ, defended the cause of the orphan, the widow, and the poor.

The Twentieth Day of May

At Perugia, Blessed Colomba of Rieti, virgin, of the Order of our Father St. Dominic. She was renowned for her purity, patience, and abstinence. *A semi-duplex feast.*

At Aquila, among the Vestinians,[5] St. Bernadine of Siena, priest and confessor, of the Order of Friars Minor, who enlightened Italy by word and example.

At Rome, St. Plautilla, the wife of a consul. She was the sister of the consul Flavius Clemens and the mother of the holy virgin Flavia Domitilla, both of whom were holy martyrs. She was baptized by the Apostle St. Peter and died a peaceful death, being noted for her virtues.

Likewise at Rome on the Via Salaria, the birthday of St. Basilla, virgin. She was of royal birth and had been betrothed to a noble of high rank. When she refused to marry, he denounced her as being a Christian. Gallienus Augustus decreed that she should either accept her betrothed or

[5] The Vestinians were an ancient branch of the Sabines, who settled on the highlands of Rieti.

die by the sword. Upon hearing this, she replied that she had espoused herself to the King of Kings. She was pierced with a sword.

At Nîmes in Gaul, St. Baudelius, martyr. Having been seized by the pagans, he refused to offer sacrifice. He remained unmoved in the faith of Christ despite scourging and tortures, and so received by his precious death the crown of martyrdom.

At Edessa, near Aegea, in Cilicia, the holy martyrs Thalalaeus, Asterius, Alexander, and their companions, who suffered under the Emperor Numerian.

In the Thebaid, St. Aquila, martyr, who was torn with iron combs for (his belief in) Christ.

At Bourges in Aquitaine, St. Austregisilus, bishop and confessor.

At Brescia, St. Anastasius, bishop.

At Pavia, St. Theodore, bishop.

The Twenty-first Day of May

St. Valens, bishop, who was slain with three children.

At Alexandria, the commemoration of the holy martyrs Secundus, priest, and others. In the reign of the Emperor Constantius, the Arian Bishop George ordered them to be killed in a most savage way on the holy day of Pentecost.

In Morocco, the birthday of the holy martyrs Timothy, Polius, and Eutychius, deacons. They spread abroad the Word of God in that region, and merited to be crowned together.

At Caesarea in Cappadocia, the birthday of the holy martyrs Polyeuctus, Victorius, and Donatus.

At Cordoba in Spain, St. Secundinus, martyr.

On the same day, the holy martyrs Synesius and Theopompus.

At Caesarea Philippi, the birthday of the holy martyrs Nicostratus and Antiochus, tribunes, with other soldiers.

At Alexandria, the commemoration of the holy bishops and priests who were sent into exile by the Arians, and merited to be joined to the holy confessors.

At Nice near the Var river, St. Hospitius, confessor, remarkable for the virtue of abstinence and the spirit of prophecy.

The Twenty-second Day of May

(At Utrecht), St. Servatius, Bishop of the Church of Tongres, whose birthday was May 13. *A duplex feast.*

At Rome, the holy martyrs Faustinus, Timothy, and Venustus.

In Africa, the holy martyrs Castus and Emilius. They completed their martyrdom by the torture of fire. St. Cyprian wrote that, although these men had yielded when first tortured, yet in the second contest the Lord made them victorious so that they became stronger than the flames to which they had first yielded.

At Comana in Pontus, St. Basiliscus, martyr. Under the Emperor Maximian and the governor Agrippa, he was shod with iron shoes which were fastened to his feet by red-hot nails. He also suffered many other tortures, and was at last beheaded and cast into a river, thereby obtaining the glory of martyrdom.

In Corsica, St. Julia, virgin, who was crowned by the punishment of the cross.

In Spain, St. Quiteria, virgin and martyr.

At Ravenna, St. Marcian, bishop and confessor.

At Pistoia in Tuscany, Blessed Attho, of the Order of Vallombrosa.

In the district of Auxerre, Blessed Romanus, abbot, who provided food for St. Benedict in the cave. Going forth thence into Gaul, he built a monastery, and having placed many followers in the path of sanctity, died in the Lord.

At Aquino, St. Fulk, confessor.

At Auxerre, St. Helen, virgin.

At Cascia in Umbria, St. Rita, widow and nun of the Order of the Hermits of St. Augustine. After worldly espousals, she loved Christ alone, the eternal Spouse.

The Twenty-third Day of May

At Langres in Gaul, the suffering of St. Desiderius, bishop. Seeing his people harried by an army of the Vandals, he went to their king to make supplication on behalf of his flock. The king ordered his throat to be cut at once and the bishop cheerfully presented his neck to the executioner that he might die for the sheep entrusted to his care. Thus with the stroke of a sword he went to Heaven. There suffered with him many of his flock, all of whom were buried in the same city.

In Spain, the holy martyrs Epitacius, bishop, and Basileus.

In the district of Lyons, St. Desiderius, Bishop of Vienne, who was stoned to death by command of King Theoderic, and so crowned with martyrdom.

In Africa, the holy martyrs Quinctian, Lucius, and Julian, who suffered in the Vandal persecution and merited eternal crowns.

In Cappadocia, the commemoration of the holy martyrs who were slain in the persecution of Maximian Galerius. They were killed by having their legs broken. Others at the same time in Mesopotamia were hung up by their feet, head downward, stifled with smoke, and burned by a slow fire, thus fulfilling their martyrdom.

At Synnada in Phrygia, St. Michael, bishop.

On the same day, St. Mercurialis, bishop.

At Naples in Campania, St. Euphebius, bishop.

At Rome, St. John Baptist de Rossi, priest and confessor, wondrous for patience and for his charity in preaching the Gospel to the poor.

At Norcia, the holy monks Eutychius and Florentius, who are mentioned by Pope St. Gregory.

The Twenty-fourth Day of May

At Bologna, the transferal of the body of our Father St. Dominic. At the time of Pope Gregory IX, his sacred body was transferred to a worthier place. In addition to the other miracles which occurred, his body gave forth an aroma of such great fragrance that all who were present were filled with a wonderful joy. Thus did God beautifully indicate how pleasing to Him was the excelling sanctity of His apostle. *A totum duplex feast.*

At Antioch, the birthday of St. Manahen, foster-brother of Herod the Tetrach.[6] Under the influence of the New Testament, he became a "doctor and a prophet." He lies buried in that city.

Likewise Blessed Joanna the wife of Chuza, Herod's steward, whom Luke the evangelist mentions.[7]

At Portus Romanus, the birthday of St. Vincent, martyr.

At Nantes in Brittany, the blessed martyrs Donatian and Rogatian, brothers. At the time of the Emperor Diocletian, they were cast into prison for their constancy in the faith. They were stretched on the rack and mangled; then they were pierced by a lance. Finally their heads were cut off.

In Istria, the holy martyrs Zoellus, Servilius, Felix, Silvanus, and Diocles.

On the same day, the holy martyrs Meletius, an army general, and his two hundred and fifty-two companions, who suffered martyrdom by various kinds of deaths.

Likewise, the holy martyrs Susanna, Marciana, and Palladia, wives of the aforesaid soldiers. They were slain together with their children.

[6] Acts, 13:2.
[7] Luke, 8:3.

At Milan, St. Robustian, martyr.

At Brescia, St. Afra, martyr, who suffered under the Emperor Hadrian.

In the monastery of Lerins in Gaul, St. Vincent, priest, remarkable for learning and holiness.

In Morocco in Africa, the suffering of Blessed John of Prado, priest and martyr, of the Order of Friars Minor. For preaching the Gospel, he was punished by chains, imprisonment, scourging, and many other tortures which he bore bravely for Christ. He completed his martyrdom by fire.

The Twenty-fifth Day of May

At Rome, on the Via Nomentana, the birthday of Blessed Urban I, pope and martyr. By his exhortation and teaching many persons, including Tiburtius and Valerian, received the faith of Christ and suffered martyrdom. He himself suffered much for God's Church in the persecution of Alexander Severus, and at length was crowned with martyrdom by being beheaded. *Three lessons.*

At Salerno, the death of Blessed Gregory VII, pope and confessor, the upholder and valiant defender of the liberty of the Church.

At Jarrow in England, the birthday of St. Bede the Venerable, priest, confessor and Doctor of the Church. He was celebrated for his holiness and learning. His festival is observed on May 27.

At Florence, the birthday of St. Mary Magdalen de'Pazzi, virgin of the Carmelite Order, who was noted for her holy life. Her festival is observed on May 29.

At Silistria in Bulgaria, the birthday of the holy martyrs Pasicrates, Valention and two others who were crowned with them.

At Milan, St. Dionysius, bishop. He was exiled to Cappadocia by the Arian Emperor Constantius on account of his Catholic faith. There, more a martyr than a confessor, he gave up his soul to God. His holy body was sent by Bishop Aurelius to St. Ambrose, bishop of Milan, in which pious work St. Basil the Great is also said to have had a share.

At Florence, the birthday of St. Zenobius, bishop of that city, who is well known because of his holy life and miracles.

In Britain, St. Aldhelm Bishop of Sherborne.

In the territory of Troyes, St. Leo, confessor.

At Veroli in the Hernican mountains, the transferal of the body of St. Mary, the mother of James. Her holy body is honored by many miracles.

At Assisi in Umbria, the transferal of the body of St. Francis, confessor, at the time of the pontificate of Pope Gregory IX. ✠

The Twenty-sixth Day of May

At Rome, St. Philip Neri, priest and confessor, founder of the Congregation of the Oratory. He is famous for his virginity, his gifts of prophecy, and miracles. *A duplex feast.*

Likewise at Rome, St. Eleutherius, pope and martyr. He brought many Roman nobles to the faith of Christ, and sent SS. Damian and Fugatius to Britian where they baptized King Lucius, together with his wife and almost all his people.

At Canterbury in England, St. Augustine, bishop and confessor. He was sent there with others by Pope St. Gregory, and preached Christ's Holy Gospel to the English folk. He died there, glorious for virtues and miracles. His feast is kept on May 28.

At Athens, the birthday of Blessed Quadratus, a disciple of the Apostles. In the persecution of Hadrian, by his faith and zeal, he gathered together the (faithful of his) Church who had been scattered in great terror. In the defence of the Christian religion, he offered to the Emperor a most useful book, one worthy of the teaching of the Apostles.

At Rome, the holy martyrs Simitrius, priest, and twenty companions, who suffered in the reign of Antoninus Pius.

At Vienne in Gaul, St. Zacharias, bishop and martyr, who suffered under Trajan.

In Africa, St. Quadratus, martyr, on whose anniversary St. Augustine delivered a panegyric.

At Todi in Umbria, the birthday of the holy martyrs Felicissimus, Heraclius, and Paulinus.

In the district of Auxerre, the suffering of St. Priscus, martyr. He was beheaded together with a great number of fellow Christians.

The Twenty-seventh Day of May

St. Bede the Venerable, priest, confessor and Doctor of the Church, who departed to heaven on May 25. *A duplex feast.*

St. John I, pope and martyr. His birthday is mentioned on May 18, but his festival is observed today on account of the transferal of his sacred body.

At Silistria in Bulgaria, the suffering of Blessed Julius. He was a veteran and a soldier of note in the reign of the Emperor Alexander, yet he was arrested and brought before the governor Maximus. In his presence, Julius anathematized the idols and confessed the name of Christ with the utmost firmness; for this, he was put to death.

In the district of Arras, St. Ranulphus, martyr.

At Sora, St. Restituta, virgin and martyr. In the reign of the Emperor Aurelius and under the proconsul Agathius, she was tried for the faith. She overcame the onslaughts of demons, the entreaties of parents, and savage tortures. Finally she was beheaded together with other Christians, thus obtaining the crown of martyrdom.

At Grange in Gaul, St. Eutropius, bishop, illustrious for his virtues and miracles.

At Würzburg in Germany, St. Bruno, bishop and confessor.

The Twenty-eighth Day of May

At Florence, Blessed Mary-Bartholomew Bagnesi, virgin, of the Third Order of St. Dominic. Tried daily by various sufferings, she merited to be conformed to her Crucified Spouse. *A semi-duplex feast.*

St. Augustine, Bishop of Canterbury and confessor, whose birthday is mentioned on May 26.

In Sardinia, the holy martyrs Emilius, Felix, Priam, and Lucian, who fought for Christ and were gloriously crowned.

At Chartres in Gaul, St. Caraunus, martyr who, under the Emperor Domitian, received martyrdom by beheading.

Likewise, the suffering of SS. Crescens, Dioscorides, Paul, and Helladius.

At Thecua in Palestine, the holy martyred monks, who were slain by the Saracens in the time of the younger Theodosius. The inhabitants of the place gathered together their holy relics, and preserved them with great reverence.

At Corinth, St. Heliconis, martyr, in the time of the Emperor Gordian. When Perenius was governor, she was first subjected to numerous tortures. Then, under his successor Justin, she was again tortured, but was set free by angels. Next, she was mutilated, exposed to wild beasts, and even tried by fire. Finally, she completed her martyrdom by being beheaded.

At Paris, St. Germanus, bishop and confessor. How great was his sanctity, how numerous his merits, and the miracles by which his fame was enhanced, all this was committed to writing by Fortunatus, the bishop.

At Milan, St. Senator, bishop, famed for his virtues and learning.

At Urgel in Spain, St. Justus, bishop.

At Florence, St. Podius, bishop and confessor.

At Novara, St. Bernard of Mentone, confessor. He built a famous monastery and hospice in the Alps on Mons Jovis.[8]

[8] Mons Jovis is now called after the saint—Mount St. Bernard.

The Twenty-ninth Day of May

At Avignonet in Gaul, Blessed William (of the Order of Preachers) and his companions. Zealously carrying out the duties of inquisitors in the diocese of Toulouse, they were treacherously seized by Albigensian heretics and put to the sword. By their glorious death they gained heaven. *A semi-duplex feast.*

St. Mary Magdalen de'Pazzi, virgin, of the Carmelite Order, whose birthday is mentioned on May 25.

At Rome, on the Via Aurelia, the birthday of St. Restitutus, martyr.

At Iconium in Lycaonia, the suffering of SS. Conon and his twelve-year-old son. In the reign of the Emperor Aurelian, they were placed on a red-hot gridiron over burning coals on which oil had been poured. They suffered this torture with the utmost constancy. Then they were stretched on the rack and endured burning with fire. Finally, they died after their hands had been broken with a wooden mallet.

In the neighborhood of Trent, the birthday of the holy martyrs Sisinius, Martyrius, and Alexander. Paulinus, in his life of St. Ambrose, states that they were persecuted by the heathens in the district of Anaunia during the reign of the emperor Honorius, and obtained the crown of martyrdom.

At Camerino, the suffering of one thousand five hundred and twenty-five holy martyrs.

At Caesarea Philippi, the holy martyrs Theodosia, who was the mother of the martyr St. Procopius, and twelve other noble matrons. They were beheaded in the persecution of Diocletian.

At Treves, blessed Maximinus, bishop and confessor. To his honor, he protected the bishop St. Athanasius, when the latter was in exile during the Arian persecution.

At Verona, St. Maximus, bishop.

At Arcano in Latium (Italy), St. Eleutherius, confessor.

The Thirtieth Day of May

At Pistoia, Blessed Andrew Franchi, of the Order of Preachers, bishop and confessor. Aflame with apostolic zeal, he gained innumerable souls for Christ. He died in the love of Christ in the year 1401. *A semi-duplex feast.*

St. Felix I, pope and martyr, whose birthday is commemorated on December 30.

At Terres in Sardinia, the holy martyrs Gabinus and Crispulus.

At Antioch, SS. Sycus and Palatine, who suffered many tortures for Christ.

At Ravenna, St. Exuperantius, bishop and confessor.

At Pavia (in Italy), St. Anastasius, bishop.

At Caesarea in Cappadocia, SS. Basil and Emmelia his wife, the parents of SS. Basil the Great, the Bishops Gregory of Nyssa, and Peter of Sebaste, and St. Macrina, virgin. These holy spouses were exiled in the time of Galerius Maximian and dwelt in the deserts of Pontus. They died after the persecution, leaving their children heirs of their virtues.

At Seville in Spain, St. Ferdinand III, King of Castile and Leon. On account of the excellence of his virtues, he was called "The Saint." He was renowned for his zeal in propagating the faith. After overcoming the Moors, he left his earthly kingdom and entered an eternal one.

At Rouen, the virgin St. Joan of Arc, called the Maid of Orleans. After fighting bravely for her fatherland, she was at length delivered into the power of her enemies, condemned by a wicked judge and burned at the stake. Benedict XV, the Supreme Pontiff, inscribed her on the roll of the saints.

The Thirty-first Day of May

The Feast of the Blessed Virgin Mary, Mediatrix of all Graces. *A totum duplex feast.*

St. Angela Merici, virgin, of the Third Order of St. Francis. She was the Foundress of the Nuns of St. Ursula, and was called by her heavenly Spouse to receive an incorruptible crown on January 27. *A memory.*

At Rome, the virgin St. Petronilla, a spiritual daughter of the apostle St. Peter. She refused to wed Flaccus, a nobleman. Accepting three days' delay for deliberation, she spent them in fasting and prayer, and on the third day, after receiving the Sacrament of Christ, gave up the ghost. *A memory.*

At Aquileia, the holy martyrs Cantius, Cantian, and Cantianilla, brothers and sister. They came from the famous race of the Anicii. Together with Protus their instructor, they were beheaded under Diocletian and Maximian for their constancy in the faith of Christ.

At Torres in Sardinia, St. Crescentian, martyr.

At Comana in Pontus, St. Hermias, soldier. Under the Emperor Antoninus, he was delivered by the help of God from numberless savage tortures. He converted the executioner to Christ and made him a partaker of the same crown of martyrdom, which he himself first received, being beheaded by the sword.

At Verona, St. Lupicinus, bishop.

At Rome, St. Paschasius, deacon and confessor, whom Pope St. Gregory mentions.

JUNE

The First Day of June

At Rome, St. Juventius, martyr.

At Autun, SS. Reverian, bishop, and Paul, priest, with ten others, who were crowned with martyrdom under the Emperor Aurelian.

At Caesarea in Palestine, St. Pamphilus, priest and martyr, a man of admirable holiness, learning, and bounty to the poor. In the persecution of Galerius Maximian, under the governor Urban, Pamphilus was tortured and cast into prison because of his Christian religion. Under Firmilian, he was again subjected to torture, and in company with others suffered martyrdom. At that time, there suffered also Valens, deacon, Paul, and nine others, but their remembrance is kept on other days.

In Cappadocia, St. Thespesius, martyr. Under the Emperor Alexander and the prefect Simplicius, he was tortured and then beheaded.

In Egypt, the holy martyrs Isychrion, an army general, and five other soldiers. They were slain for their faith by different kinds of death in the reign of the Emperor Diocletian.

Likewise, St. Firmus, martyr. In the persecution of Maximian, he was subjected to a most vicious scourging, struck with stones, and at last beheaded.

At Perugia, the holy martyrs Felinus and Gratinian, soldiers. They were subjected to various tortures under Decius, and obtained by a glorious death the palm of martyrdom.

At Bologna, St. Proculus, martyr, who suffered under the Emperor Maximian.

At Amelia in Umbria, St. Secundus, martyr who, at the time of Diocletian, was cast into the Tiber, and so suffered martyrdom.

At Tifernum in Umbria, St. Crescentian, a Roman soldier, crowned with martyrdom under the same Emperor.

In the monastery of Lerins in Gaul, St. Caprasius, abbot.

In the monastery of Onia at Burgos in Spain, St. Eneco, a Benedictine abbot, noted for holiness and the glory of miracles.

At Montefalco in Umbria, St. Fortunatus, priest, famed for virtue and miracles.

At Treves, St. Simeon, monk, who was numbered among the saints by Pope Benedict IX.

The Second Day of June

At Sandomir, the suffering of forty-nine martyrs of the Order of Preachers. They were warned by these selfsame words (miraculously) inserted in the martyrology the day before, and while they were in the church singing to the Mother of God, the infidels put them all to death at the same time. *A semi-duplex feast.*

At Rome, the birthday of the holy martyrs, Marcellinus, priest, and Peter, exorcist. At the time of Diocletian, the judge Serenus cast them into prison where they converted many to the faith. After suffering from the cruel chains and many other torments, they were beheaded at a place called the Black Forest. Later, the place was renamed the White Forest in honor of the saints. Their bodies were buried in a crypt near St. Tiburtius. Pope St. Damasus afterward adorned their sepulchre with verses. *A memory.*

In Campania, St. Erasmus, bishop and martyr. In the reign of the Emperor Diocletian, he was first scourged with leaded whips, and then severely beaten with clubs. Though molten resin, sulphur, lead, pitch, wax, and oil were poured over him, he remained uninjured. Then, at Formia under Maximian, he was again subjected to various inhuman tortures, but God preserved him for the strengthening of others. At last, the Lord called him and, famed for his martyrdom, he met a holy death. His body was later transferred to Gaeta.

At Lyons in Gaul, the holy martyrs Pothinus, bishop, Sanctus, deacon, Vetius Epagathus, Maturus, Ponticus, Biblis, Attalus, Alexander, and Blandina, with many others. Their mighty and repeated contests are confirmed by a letter written from the Church of Lyons to the Churches of Asia and Phrygia, in the reign of Marcus Aurelius Antoninus and Lucius Verus. Among these martyrs was St. Blandina, who though weaker because of her sex, more feeble in body, and less spirited because of her servile state, underwent more prolonged and sharper trials. However, her courage did not fail, and when her throat was cut, she followed (to Heaven) the other martyrs whom she had encouraged to victory.

On the island of Proconnesus in the Sea of Marmora, St. Nicephorus, Bishop of Constantinople. He was a most zealous fighter for the traditions of the Fathers and constantly opposed Leo the Armenian, the Iconoclast emperor, in regard to the veneration of the sacred images. On this account he was exiled by him and, after a long martyrdom of fourteen years, departed to the Lord.

At Rome, St. Eugenius I, pope and confessor.

At Trani in Apulia, St. Nicholas Peregrinus, confessor, whose miracles were recited in a Roman Council over which Pope St. Urban II presided.

The Third Day of June

In the province of Fukien, in a city of the Chinese Empire, five blessed martyrs of the Order of Preachers: Peter Sanz, Bishop of Mauricastro and Vicar Apostolic of Fukien, Francis Serrano, Bishop-elect of Tipasa, John Alcobar, Joachim Royo, and Francis Diaz. They undertook extraordinary labors to propagate and protect the faith. After prolonged imprisonment and countless horrible tortures, Blessed Peter was beheaded; the rest were suffocated or strangled. Thus all gained the palm of triumph. *A duplex feast.*

At Arezzo in Tuscany, the holy martyrs Pergentinus and Laurentinus, brothers. In the persecution of Decius, under the governor Tiburtius, although the brothers were yet boys, they endured fearful torments and performed great miracles. They were slain by the sword.

At Constantinople, the holy martyrs Lucillian and four boys: Claudius, Hypatius, Paul, and Dionysius. Lucillian had been a pagan priest before becoming a Christian. After they had undergone various torments by order of the governor Silvanus, they were thrust into a furnace, but a shower of rain put out the fire and they all came forth uninjured. Finally, Lucillian was crucified while the boys were beheaded.

At Cordoba in Spain, Blessed Isaac, monk, who was slain with the sword for the faith of Christ.

At Constantinople, St. Paula, virgin and martyr. While gathering up the blood of the martyrs Lucillian and his companions, she was arrested, beaten with rods, and cast into the fire. As she came forth uninjured, she was beheaded in the same place where St. Lucillian had been crucified.

At Carthage, St. Cecilius, priest, who converted St. Cyprian to the faith of Christ.

In the territory of Orleans, St. Liphard, priest and confessor.

At Anagni, St. Olive, virgin.

At Paris, St. Clotilde, queen, by whose prayers her husband Clovis, King of the Franks, received the faith of Christ.

The Fourth Day of June

At Agnone in the Abruzzi, the confessor St. Francis, of the noble Caracciolo family of Naples. He was founder of the Congregation of

Minor Clerks Regular. He burned with a wondrous love for God and his neighbor and with a most ardent zeal for the propagation of the cult of the Holy Eucharist. He was inscribed in the canon of the saints by the Sovereign Pontiff, Pius VII. The body of the saint was removed to Naples where it is religiously venerated. *A duplex feast.*

At Rome, the holy martyrs Aretius and Dacian.

At Sisak in Illyria, St. Quirinus, bishop. Under the governor Galerius, as Prudentius writes, he was cast for his faith into a river with a millstone tied to his neck. But the stone floated, and he exhorted the surrounding Christians at great length that they should not be terrified at his torture nor shaken in the faith. That he might attain the glory of martyrdom, he obtained from God by his prayers that he might be drowned.

At Milan, St. Clateus, Bishop of Brescia and martyr. By order of the prefect of that city, in the reign of the Emperor Nero, he was arrested and, because he would not renounce Christ, he was severely scourged and beheaded.

In Hungary, the holy martyrs Rutilus and his companions.

At Tivoli, St. Quirinus, martyr.

At Arras in Gaul, St. Saturnina, virgin and martyr.

At Constantinople, St. Metrophanes, a famous bishop and confessor.

At Milevi in Numidia, St. Optatus, bishop, noteworthy for learning and holiness. The holy Fathers of the Church, Augustine and Fulgentius, sang his praises.

At Verona, St. Alexander, bishop.

The Fifth Day of June

At Venice, Blessed James Salomoni of the Order of Preachers. Desiring to imitate in all things the example of our Father St. Dominic, he unceasingly cultivated virginity, humility, and charity toward God and his neighbor. God endowed him with the gift of prophecy and made him renowned for his power of working miracles. His feast was first sanctioned by several popes for Forli and Venice; then Gregory XV extended it to the whole Order of Preachers. *A semi-duplex feast.*

In Friesland, St. Boniface, Bishop of Mainz and martyr. He came from England to Rome, and was sent by Pope Gregory II into Germany to preach the faith of Christ to those nations. He brought a great multitude of them, particularly of the Frisians, under the yoke of the Christian religion, and merited to be called the Apostle of the Germans. Finally, he was slain by the sword in Friesland, at the hands of enraged heathens;

he suffered martyrdom together with Eoban his fellow-bishop, and certain other servants of God.

At Tyre, in Phoenicia, St. Dorotheus, priest, who suffered much under Diocletian, but survived until the time of Julian. During the latter's reign, Dorotheus, now one hundred and seven years old, dignified his venerable old age with martyrdom.

In Egypt, the birthday of the holy martyrs Marcian, Nicanor, Apollonius, and others, who completed an illustrious martyrdom in the persecution of Galerius Maximian.

At Perugia, the holy martyrs Florentius, Julian, Cyriacus, Marcellinus, and Faustinus, who were beheaded in the persecution of Decius.

At Cordoba in Spain, Blessed Sancho, a young man. Although this youth had been brought up at the royal court, he did not hesitate during a Moslem persecution to undergo martyrdom for the Christian faith.

At Caesarea in Palestine, the suffering of SS. Zenais, Cyria, Valeria, and Marcia, who through many torments joyfully attained martyrdom.

The Sixth Day of June

At Magdeburg, St. Norbert, bishop of that city, confessor, and founder of the Premonstratensian Order. *A duplex feast.*

At Caesarea in Palestine, the birthday of blessed Philip, who was one of the first seven deacons (of the Church of Jerusalem).[1] He was renowned for miracles and prodigies. He converted Samaria to the faith of Christ, baptized the eunuch of Candace, Queen of the Ethiopians, and then died at Caesarea. Near him lie buried three of his daughters, virgins and prophetesses; a fourth daughter, who was endowed with the gifts of the Holy Ghost to a high degree, died at Ephesus.

At Rome, St. Artemius, with his wife Candida and his daughter Paulina. Artemius, at the preaching and miracles of St. Peter the Exorcist, believed in Christ, and was baptized with all his household by St. Marcellinus, priest. At the command of the governor Serenus, he was flogged with leaden-tipped whips and then slain by the sword. His wife and daughter were driven into a crypt which was then filled with stones and rubble.

In the country of Bologna, St. Alexander, martyr and Bishop of Fiesole. He was on his way back from the town of Pavia, where he had claimed, in the presence of the King of the Lombards, the goods of his church against those who had usurped them, when he was seized by these same usurpers, who cast him into the Rhine river and drowned him.

[1] Acts, 6:5.

At Tarsus in Cilicia, twenty holy martyrs. In the reign of Diocletian and Maximian, under Simplicius the judge, they glorified God in their bodies by various torments.

At Noyon in Gaul, the holy martyrs Amantius, Alexander, and their companions.

At Milan, the death of St. Eustorgius II, bishop and confessor.

At Verona, the Bishop St. John.

At Besançon in Gaul, St. Claudius, bishop.

The Seventh Day of June

At Constantinople, the birthday of St. Paul, bishop of that city. He was often driven from his see by the Arians on account of his Catholic faith; he was restored to it by St. Julius I, the Roman Pontiff. Finally, he was exiled by the Arian Emperor Constantius to Cucusus, a little town in Cappadocia, and there passed to Heaven, being cruelly strangled as a result of the plots of the Arians. His body was transferred to Constantinople with great honor in the reign of Theodosius.

At Cordoba in Spain, the holy martyr monks, Peter, priest, Wallabonsus, deacon, Sabinianus, Wistremund, Habentius, and Jeremias. Because of their Christian faith, their throats were cut in the Arab persecution.

At Hermopolis in Egypt, St. Licarion, martyr. He was mangled, beaten with red-hot iron bars and subjected to other inhuman cruelties. Finally, he was put to the sword.

In England, St. Robert, abbot, of the Cistercian Order. ✠

The Eighth Day of June

At Aix in Gaul, St. Maximin, who was the first bishop of that city, and was believed to have been a disciple of the Lord.

On the same day, St. Calliopa, martyr. For her faith, she received the palm of martyrdom. She was mutilated, her flesh was burned, and then she was rolled on sherds. Finally, she gained the palm of martyrdom by being beheaded.

At York in England, St. William, bishop and confessor. Among other miracles that were manifested at his tomb was the raising of three men from the dead. He was placed on the roll of the saints by Honorius III.

At Soissons in Gaul, the birthday of St. Medard, Bishop of Noyon, whose life and death were approved by glorious miracles. *A memory.*

At Rouen, St. Gildard, bishop, twin brother of the same St. Medard.

Not only was he born on the same day, but he was consecrated bishop on the same day, and on the same day was withdrawn from this life, so that together they entered Heaven.

At Sens, St. Heraclius, bishop.

At Metz in Gaul, St. Clodulph, bishop.

In Piceno (in Italy), St. Severinus, Bishop of San Severino.

In Sardinia, St. Sallustian, confessor.

At Camerino, St. Victorinus, confessor, who was the brother of the aforesaid St. Severinus, Bishop of San Severino.

The Ninth Day of June

At Bologna in Aemilia (Italy), Blessed Diana d'Andalo, virgin, of the Order of Preachers. While yet living in the world, she made, in the presence of St. Dominic, a vow of virginity, and also one of entering the religious life. After his death, she courageously overcame the determined opposition of her relatives and founded, in the same city, the monastery of St. Agnes. Here she lived a most holy life for thirteen years, and after her death was noted for her miracles.

Likewise at Bologna, the Blessed Cecilia and Amata, virgins, of the Order of Preachers. They received the habit from St. Dominic himself and made their profession to him in the monastery of St. Sixtus at Rome. Later they were sent by Pope Honorius III to Bologna that they might be companions to Blessed Diana in the monastery of St. Agnes and assist her in carrying out the correct and holy practices of religious life. In death, they rest in glory with her in the same tomb. *A semi-duplex feast.*

At Nomento in the Sabine Hills, the birthday of the holy martyrs Primus and Felician, brothers, in the reign of the Emperors Diocletian and Maximian. These glorious martyrs passed a long life in the service of the Lord. After enduring severe tortures, sometimes alike for them both, at other times different, they at length completed the course of their happy warfare, for they were beheaded by Promotus, governor of Nomento. The bodies of these martyrs were afterward removed to Rome and honorably buried in the church of St. Stephen the Protomartyr on the Coelian Hill. *A memory.*

At Agen in Gaul, the suffering of St. Vincent, deacon and martyr. He was most cruelly beaten for the faith of Christ and then beheaded.

At Antioch, St. Pelagia, virgin and martyr, whom SS. Ambrose and John Chrysostom highly praised.

At Syracuse in Sicily, St. Maximian, bishop, whom Pope St. Gregory often mentions.

At Andria in Apulia, St. Richard, who was the first bishop of that city, and was famous for miracles.

On the isle of Iona, Scotland, St. Columba, priest and abbot.

At Edessa in Syria, St. Julian, monk, whose famous deeds the deacon St. Ephrem has described.

The Tenth Day of June

At Buda (in Hungary), the birthday of Blessed John Dominici, Archbishop of Ragusa and cardinal of the Holy Roman Church. He labored greatly to abolish schism and he illumined the Church of God by the sanctity of his morals. *A semi-duplex feast.*

St. Margaret, widow, Queen of Scotland, who died on November 16.

At Rome on the Via Salaria, the suffering of Blessed Getulius, a man of prominence and learning. He and his wife Symphorosa were the parents of seven brothers, all of them martyrs. Martyred with him were his companions Caerealis, Amantius, and Primitivus. At the command of the Emperor Hadrian, the consul Licinius had them stretched upon the ground and flogged; they were then thrown into prison. Later, they were cast into the flames, but, as they suffered no harm from the fire, they were beaten over the head with clubs, thus completing their martyrdom. Symphorosa, the wife of Getulius, took their bodies and gave them honorable burial in a sandpit on her farm.

Likewise at Rome, on the Via Aurelia, the birthday of SS. Basilides, Tripos, Mandal, and twenty other martyrs, under the Emperor Aurelian and Plato, prefect of the city.

At Naples in Campania, St. Maximus, bishop and martyr. For his strenuous confession of the Nicene faith, he was punished by the Emperor Constantius by being sent into exile. He died there, exhausted by his hardships.

At Prusiada in Bithynia, St. Timothy, bishop and martyr. Under Julian the Apostate, and by his orders, Timothy was beheaded because he refused to deny Christ.

At Cologne, St. Maurinus, abbot and martyr.

At Nicomedia, St. Zacharias, martyr.

In Spain, the holy martyrs Crispulus and Restitutus.

In Africa, the holy martyrs Aresius, Rogatus, and fifteen others.

At Petra in Africa, St. Asterius, bishop. He suffered greatly for the Catholic faith at the hands of the Arians, and was sent into exile in Africa by the Emperor Constantius. He was finally restored to his church, and died a glorious confessor.

At Auxerre, St. Censurius, bishop.

The Eleventh Day of June

At Salamina in Cyprus, the birthday of St. Barnabas the Apostle. A Cyprian by birth, he was ordained with Paul as an Apostle of the Gentiles, and with him he travelled through many regions, exercising the office that had been imposed on him to preach the Gospel. Afterward he went to Cyprus, and there adorned his apostolate with a glorious martyrdom. In the reign of the Emperor Zeno, his body was found through his own revelation, together with a codex of the Gospel of St. Matthew, written by his own hand. *A totum duplex feast.*

At Salamanca in Spain, the birthday of St. John of Sahagun, confessor, of the Order of Hermits of St. Augustine. He was renowned for his zeal for the faith, holiness of life, and miracles. His festival is, however, celebrated on the day following.

At Aquileia, the suffering of SS. Felix and Fortunatus, brothers, who were tortured on the rack in the persecution of Diocletian and Maximian. Lighted torches were applied to their sides, but by the power of God they were extinguished. Then boiling oil was poured into their bodies through the intestines. Since they persisted in confessing Christ, they were at last beheaded.

At Bremen, the birthday of St. Rembert, Bishop of Hamburg and Bremen.

At Treviso, St. Parisius, a citizen of Bologna, confessor and monk of the Camaldolese Order.

At Rome, the transferal of the body of St. Gregory Nazianzen, bishop, confessor, and Doctor of the Church. His holy body had formerly been brought to Rome from Constantinople, and long kept there in the Church of the Mother of God, in the Campus Martius. Pope Gregory XIII transferred it with great honor to a chapel magnificently adorned by him, in the Basilica of St. Peter, and on the day following buried it with due honor beneath the altar. ✠

The Twelfth Day of June

At Saluzzo in Piedmont, the birthday of Blessed Stephen Bandelli, confessor, of our Order. He was renowned for personal holiness, learning, preaching the Word of God, and for miracles. *A semi-duplex feast.*

St. John of Sahagun, confessor, of the Order of Hermits of St. Augustine, who passed away on June 11.

At Rome, on the Via Aurelia, the birthday of the holy martyrs Basilides, Cyrinus, Nabor, and Nazarius, soldiers. Because they confessed the name of Christ, they were cast into prison in the persecution of Diocletian and

Maximian, under the prefect Aurelius. After their bodies had been torn to ribbons by the scorpions [2] (of the executioners), they were beheaded. *A memory.*

At Nicaea in Bithynia, St. Antonina, martyr. Priscillian, the governor in the same persecution, commanded her to be beaten with clubs, stretched on the rack, her sides to be mangled and burned with fire. At length he ordered her to be slain with the sword.

At Rome, in the Vatican Basilica, Pope St. Leo III. His eyes and his tongue were torn out by wicked men, but God wonderfully restored them.

In Thrace, St. Olympius, bishop, who was driven from his see by the Arians, and died a confessor.

In Cilicia, St. Amphion, bishop, who was an excellent confessor in the time of Galerius Maximian.

In Egypt, St. Onuphrius, hermit. For sixty years he lived a religious life in the vast desert, and, famous for great virtues and merits, passed into heaven. His outstanding deeds were recorded by the Abbot Paphnutius.

The Thirteenth Day of June

At Padua, St. Anthony, a Portuguese priest, of the Order of Friars Minor, confessor and Doctor of the Church. He was illustrious for his life, miracles, and preaching. Pope Gregory IX placed him in the list of the saints less than one year after his death. *A duplex feast.*

At Rome, on the Via Ardeatina, the birthday of St. Felicula, virgin and martyr. Since she refused either to wed Flaccus or to offer sacrifice to idols, she was handed over to a certain judge. When he saw that she was firm in confessing Christ, he starved her in a dark prison, and then had her tortured on the rack for so long a time that she died. Her body was taken down and cast into a sewer. St. Nicomedes, a priest, recovered the body and buried it on the Via Ardeatina.

Among the Pelignians,[3] St. Peregrinus, bishop and martyr. Because of his Catholic faith, he was cast into the river Aterno by the Lombards.

At Cordoba in Spain, St. Fandilas, priest and monk, who underwent martyrdom for Christ's faith in the Moslem persecution by being beheaded.

[2] The scorpion was an instrument of torture consisting of a number of equal lengths of chain; at the end of each length was an iron hook, or a ball of lead, or a piece of pointed iron. Scorpions were not often used on the martyrs as they brought on death too quickly.

[3] See note April 28.

In Africa, the holy martyrs Fortunatus and Lucian.

At Byblos in Phoenicia, St. Aquilina, virgin and martyr. In the time of the Emperor Diocletian and the judge Volusianus, this twelve-year old girl, because of her faith, was buffeted and whipped. Red-hot awls were thrust into her. Finally, she consecrated her virginity by martyrdom, being killed with a sword.

In Cyprus, St. Triphyllius, bishop. ✠

The Fourteenth Day of June

St. Basil the Great, confessor and Doctor of the Church. He died on January 1, but his festival is observed today, since he was ordained Bishop of Caesarea in Cappadocia on this day. *A duplex feast.*

At Samaria in Palestine, St. Eliseus the Prophet, at whose sepulchre, as St. Jerome writes, devils are affrighted; Abdias the Prophet is also buried there.

At Syracuse in Sicily, St. Marcian, bishop, who was ordained bishop by the Apostle St. Peter, and after preaching the Gospel was slain by the Jews.

At Cordoba in Spain, the holy martyrs Anastasius, priest, Felix, monk, and Digna, virgin.

At Soissons in Gaul, St. Valerius and Rufinus, martyrs, in the persecution of Diocletian. After many torments they were ordered by the governor Rictiovarus to be beheaded.

At Constantinople, St. Methodius, bishop.

At Vienne in Gaul, St. Aetherius, bishop.

At Rodez in Gaul, St. Quinctianus, bishop.

The Fifteenth Day of June

Near the river Sele in Lucania (Italy), the birthday of the holy martyrs Vitus, Modestus, and Crescentia. They were brought there from Sicily at the time of the Emperor Diocletian. They were placed in a cauldron of boiling lead, exposed to beasts, and tortured on the rack, but by the power of God they died victorious at the end of a glorious test. *A feast of three lessons.*

At Silistria in Bulgaria, St. Hesychius, soldier. At the time of Maximus, he was arrested together with Blessed Julius, and he was crowned with martyrdom after him.

At Zephyrium in Cilicia, St. Dulas, martyr. Under the governor Maximus, he was scourged with rods because of his faith in Christ, placed upon a gridiron, and scalded with boiling oil. After suffering other tortures, as a victor he received the palm of martyrdom.

At Cordoba in Spain, St. Benildis, martyr.

At Sibapolis in Mesopotamia, the holy virgins and martyrs Lybe and Leonis, sisters, and Eutropia, a girl twelve years of age. By various tortures, they gained the crown of martyrdom.

At Valenciennes in Gaul, the death of St. Landelin, abbot.

In Auvergne in Gaul, St. Abraham, confessor, illustrious for holiness and miracles.

At Pibrac in the diocese of Toulouse, St. Germaine Cousin, virgin. She was a shepherdess who lived in humility and poverty. After enduring patiently numerous trials, she went to her heavenly Spouse. After her death she became famed for many miracles, and was enrolled by the Sovereign Pontiff, Pius IX, among the number of holy virgins.

The Sixteenth Day of June

At Mainz, the suffering of SS. Aureus, Justina his sister, and other martyrs. While they were in church at Mass, they were slain by the Huns, who were then devastating Germany.

At Besançon in Gaul, the holy martyrs Ferreolus, priest, and Ferrutio, deacon. They were sent by Bishop St. Irenaeus to preach the Word of God. Afterward, under Claudius the judge, they were tortured with various punishments and died by the sword.

At Tarsus in Cilicia, the holy martyrs Quiricus and his mother Julitta, in the reign of the Emperor Diocletian. Quiricus, a boy of three years, seeing his mother being horribly flogged with thongs in the presence of the governor Alexander, cried with inconsolable grief. For this reason, he was hurled down the steps of the tribunal and killed. Julitta, after an inhuman beating and other severe tortures, completed the course of her martyrdom by being beheaded. *A memory*.

At Amathus in Cyprus, St. Tycon, bishop, at the time of the younger Theodosius.

At Lyons in Gaul, the death of Blessed Aurelian, Bishop of Arles.

At Nantes in Brittany, St. Similian, bishop and confessor.

At Meissen in Germany, St. Benno, bishop.

In Brabant, in the convent of Aywieres, St. Lutgard, virgin. ✠

The Seventeenth Day of June

At Rome, the birthday of two hundred and sixty-two holy martyrs. They were slain for the faith in the persecution of Diocletian, and were buried on the old Via Salaria at Cucumer Hill.

At Besançon in Gaul, St. Antidius, bishop and martyr, who was slain by the Vandals for his faith in Christ.

At Apollonia in Macedonia, the holy Athenian martyrs Isaurus, deacon, Innocent, Felix, Jeremias, and Peregrinus. They were tortured in various ways by the tribune Tripontius, and were then beheaded.

At Terracina in Campania, St. Montanus, soldier. In the reign of the Emperor Hadrian and the governor Leontius, he received the crown of martyrdom after having endured many tortures.

At Venafro in Campania, the holy martyrs Nicander and Marcian, who were beheaded in the persecution of Maximian.

At Chalcedon, the holy martyrs Manuel, Sabel, and Ismael. They were sent to Julian the Apostate by the King of Persia as legates to obtain peace. The emperor himself ordered them to worship the idols. When they firmly refused, he had them put to the sword.

At Amelia in Umbria, St. Hymerius, bishop, whose body was transferred to Cremona in Insubria.

Near Bourges, St. Gundulph, bishop.

At Orleans in Gaul, St. Avitus, priest and confessor.

In Phrygia, St. Hypatius, confessor.

Likewise, St. Bessarion, hermit.

At Pisa in Tuscany, St. Rainerius, confessor.

The Eighteenth Day of June

At Edessa in Mesopotamia, St. Ephrem, deacon of the church of Edessa, and confessor. He labored much for the Christian faith and was outstanding both for his doctrine and his holiness. He died during the time Valens was emperor and was declared a Doctor of the Universal Church by Pope Benedict XV. *A duplex feast.*

At Rome, on the Via Ardeatina, the birthday of the holy martyrs Mark and Marcellian, brothers. During Diocletian's persecution, at the command of the judge Fabian, they were bound to a stake and sharp spikes were driven through their feet. As the brothers would not cease praising Christ, their sides were pierced with spears and they passed with the glory of martyrdom to heavenly kingdoms. *A memory.*

At Malaga in Spain, the holy martyrs Cyriacus and Paula, virgin. Stoned to death, they gave back their souls to God.

At Tripoli in Phoenicia, St. Leontius, soldier. Under the governor Hadrian, he obtained the crown of martyrdom through savage tortures, together with Hypatius, a tribune, and Theodulus, whom he had converted to Christ.

On the same day, St. Aetherius, martyr. In the persecution of Diocletian, after he had endured fire and other tortures, he was put to the sword.

At Alexandria, the suffering of St. Marina, virgin.

At Bordeaux, St. Amandus, bishop and confessor.

At Sciacca in Sicily, St. Calogerus, hermit, whose holiness shone forth brightly in liberating those possessed by devils.

At Schönau in Germany, St. Elizabeth, virgin, famous for the observance of the monastic life.

The Nineteenth Day of June

At Milan, the holy brothers Gervase and Portase. The judge Astasius ordered Gervase to be flogged to death with whips tipped with lead, while his brother was condemned to be beaten with clubs and beheaded. Guided by a vision, St. Ambrose found their bodies as incorrupt as if they had just been killed; they were still covered with blood. During the transferal of the bodies (to a new tomb) a blind man touched the bier and received his sight, and many persons who were possessed by demons were delivered. *A feast of three lessons.*

At Florence, St. Juliana Falconieri, virgin, who founded the Sisters of the Order of the Servants of Mary. Clement XII, the Sovereign Pontiff, placed her name in the list of the saints.

In the monastery of Val di Castro in Piceno (Italy), the birthday of St. Romuald, a native of Ravenna, hermit, and founder of the Camaldolese monks. He reformed the lax discipline of the hermits of Italy, and spread his reform abroad to a marvellous degree. His festival is observed on February 7, on which day his sacred relics were transferred to Fabriano.

At Arezzo in Tuscany (Italy), the holy martyrs Gaudentius, bishop, and Culmatius, deacon. They were slain in the time of Valentinian by the fury of the heathens.

On the same day, St. Boniface, bishop and martyr. He was a disciple of St. Romuald. He was sent into Russia by the Roman Pontiff, Gregory V, to preach the Gospel, and, after passing unhurt through fire, baptized both the king and his people. He was slain by the enraged brother of the king, and thus obtained the crown of martyrdom he desired.

At Ravenna, St. Ursicinus, martyr. Under the judge Paulinus, he remained immovable in the confession of the Lord despite many tortures. He completed his martyrdom by being beheaded.

At Sozopolis in Bulgaria, St. Zosimus, martyr. In the persecution of Trajan under the governor Domitian, he was subjected to inhuman tortures, after which his head was cut off; thus he went to the Lord as a victor.

The Twentieth Day of June

At Mantua (in Italy), Blessed Osanna, virgin, of the Third Order of our Father St. Dominic. When only seven years old, she consecrated her virginity to God and preserved it unsullied until death by fasting, wearing hairshirts, scourgings, and other bodily penances. *A semi-duplex feast.*

On the island of Palmaria, the birthday of St. Silverius, pope and martyr. He refused to restore the heretical Bishop Anthimus, who had been deposed by his predecessor Agapitus. At the instigation of the wicked Empress Theodora, he was driven into exile by Belisarius and, exhausted by many hardships, died for the Catholic faith.

At Rome, the death of St. Novatus. He was the son of St. Pudens, and the brother of the holy priest Timothy as well as of the holy virgins Pudentiana and Praxedis. All were instructed in the faith by the Apostles (Peter and Paul). Their house was turned into a church and was called the "Title of the Shepherd." [4]

At Tomis in Pontus, the holy martyrs Paul and Cyriacus.

At Petra in Palestine, St. Macarius, bishop. He suffered much at the hands of the Arians and, being exiled to Africa, died in the Lord.

At Seville in Spain, the virgin St. Florentina, sister of the two bishops, SS. Leander and Isidore. ✠

The Twenty-first Day of June

At Rome, St. Aloysius Gonzaga, cleric and confessor of the Society of Jesus. He was renowned for his contempt of a princely rank and for his innocence of life.

Likewise at Rome, St. Demetria, virgin. She was the daughter of the martyrs Flavian and Dafrosa, and the sister of St. Bibiana, virgin and martyr. St. Demetria herself was crowned with martyrdom in the reign of Julian the Apostate.

On the same day, St. Eusebius, Bishop of Samosata (in Syria). In the reign of the Arian Emperor Constantius, he went about among the churches of God, disguised in a military uniform, to strengthen the people in the Catholic faith. Afterward, under Valens, he was exiled to Thrace. But when peace returned to the Church in the time of Theo-

---

[4] Before the Roman Church gained freedom of worship, the Christians referred to their houses of worship by the legal term "title," so as to invoke the protection granted by Roman law to private ownership.

In ancient documents there is some confusion regarding the "title" of this particular house; it is variously called *titulus Pudentis, titulus Pudentianae,* and *titulus Pastoris.* See Schuster, *Liber Sacramentorum* VIII, pp. 69–70.

dosius, he was recalled from exile and again visited the churches. A tile, cast down upon him from a height by an Arian woman, fractured his skull, so that he died a martyr.

At Iconium in Lycaonia, St. Terence, bishop and martyr.

At Syracuse in Sicily, the birthday of the holy martyrs Rufinus and Martia.

In Africa, the holy martyrs Cyriacus and Apollinaris.

At Mainz, St. Alban, martyr, who after long labors and hard struggles for the faith was made worthy of the crown of life.

At Pavia (in Italy), St. Urciscenus, bishop and confessor.

At Tongres (in Brabant), St. Martin, bishop.

Near Evreaux (in Gaul), St. Leutfrid, abbot.

The Twenty-second Day of June

At Rome, Blessed Innocent V, pope. Previously he had been known as Friar Peter of Tarantaise, of the Order of Preachers. He excelled in both learning and sanctity. He was made Archbishop of Lyons and later Cardinal Bishop of Ostia; finally, he was elected pope. He labored with suave prudence to protect the liberty of the Church and to promote concord among Christians. His fame was spread by many miracles both in life and after death. *A duplex feast.*

At Nola, in Campania (Italy), the birthday of Blessed Paulinus, bishop and confessor. Though a man of wealth and nobility, he became poor and humble for our Lord. What was more, he even gave himself up into slavery to redeem a widow's son, whom the Vandals had taken captive into Africa after the devastation of Campania. He was renowned, not only for learning and for extreme holiness of life, but also for his power against demons. SS. Ambrose, Jerome, Augustine, and Pope Gregory set forth his praise in their writings. His body was transferred to Benevento, and from there to Rome, but it was restored to Nola by command of the Sovereign Pontiff, Pius X.

At Mount Ararat, the suffering of ten thousand holy martyrs who were crucified.

At Old Verulam in Britain, St. Alban, martyr. In the reign of Diocletian, he received a cleric into his house as a guest and was instructed by him in the faith; he changed clothes with his guest and gave himself up in his place. For this reason he was scourged, grievously tortured, and then beheaded. In his company there suffered also one of the soldiers, who was converted to Christ while he was leading St. Alban to death; the soldier was slain by the sword, being found worthy to be baptized in his own blood. St. Bede the Venerable has left an account of the noble contest endured for God by St. Alban and his companion.

At Samaria in Palestine, one thousand four hundred and eighty holy martyrs who were slain for Christ by Chosroes, King of the Persians.

On the same day, St. Nicetas, Bishop of Remesiana, renowned for learning and holy conversation.

At Naples in Campania, St. John, bishop, whom blessed Paulinus, Bishop of Nola, called to heaven.

In the monastery of Cluny in Gaul, the death of St. Consortia, virgin.

At Rome, the transferal of the relics of St. Flavius Clemens, a man of consular rank and martyr. He was the brother of St. Plautilla and the uncle of St. Flavia Domitilla, virgin and martyr. He was slain for the faith by the Emperor Domitian, with whom he had been consul. His body was found in the basilica of Pope St. Clement, and buried there again with solemn honors.

The Twenty-third Day of June

The Vigil of the Nativity of St. John the Baptist.

At Rome, a holy priest named John. At the time of Julian the Apostate, he was beheaded before the idol of the sun-god on the old Via Salaria. His body was buried at the Council of the Martyrs [5] by the priest St. Concordius.

Likewise at Rome, St. Agrippina, virgin and martyr. She completed her martyrdom under the Emperor Valerian. Her body was removed to Sicily and buried at Mineo where it gained renown through many miracles.

At Sutri in Tuscany, St. Felix, priest. By the command of the prefect Tuscius, his face was pounded with a rock until he died.

At Nicomedia, the commemoration of many holy martyrs, who hid in mountains and caves in the time of Diocletian, but willingly underwent martyrdom for the name of Christ.

At Philadelphia in Arabia, the holy martyrs Zeno and Zenas, his slave. The latter kissed the chains of his master, and begged that he would think him worthy to be his associate in his tortures. He was arrested by the soldiers and, together with his master, received the crown of martyrdom.

In Britain, in the monastery of Ely, St. Audrey, queen and virgin. Renowned for holiness and miracles, she departed for Heaven. Her body after eleven years was found incorrupt.

[5] By the phrase *Martyrum Concilia,* the martyrologist is referring to the ancient cemetery "ad septem palumbas" on the old Via Salaria.

The Twenty-fourth Day of June

The Nativity of St. John Baptist, the Precursor of the Lord, the son of Zachary and Elizabeth. He was filled with the Holy Ghost while yet in the womb of his mother. *A totum duplex feast of the first class with a simple octave.*

At Rome, the commemoration of many holy martyrs who were falsely charged by the Emperor Nero with the burning of the city. They were sentenced to be slain by various kinds of cruel deaths. Some were covered with the skins of wild beasts and cast to the dogs to be torn, others were crucified, others were set aside to be burned and when night fell were used as torches. All these were disciples of the Apostles, and the first martyrs whom the Holy Roman Church, that fruitful field of martyrs, sent to their Lord before the Apostles themselves died.

Also at Rome, the holy martyrs Faustus and twenty-three others.

At Mechlin in Brabant, the suffering of St. Rumbold, Bishop of Dublin and martyr. He was the son of a Scottish king.

At Satalis in Armenia, the seven holy brothers, martyrs: Orentius, Heros, Pharnacius, Firminus, Firmus, Cyriacus, and Longinus, all soldiers. The Emperor Maximian expelled them from the army for being Christians. They were separated, taken to different places, and martyred, after they had undergone great sufferings and hardships.

At Creteil near Paris, the suffering of the holy martyrs Agoard and Aglibert, together with many others of both sexes.

At Autun (in Gaul), the death of St. Simplicius, bishop and confessor.

At Lobbes in Belgium, St. Theodulph, bishop.

The Twenty-fifth Day of June

At Guglietto, near Nusco (in Italy), St. William, confessor, founder of the Hermits of Monte Vergine.

At Beroea (in Syria), the birthday of St. Sosipater, who was a disciple of the Apostle St. Paul.

At Rome, St. Lucy, virgin and martyr, (put to death) with twenty-two other persons.

At Alexandria, St. Gallicanus, martyr. He was a man of consular rank who had received triumphal honors, and was dear to the Emperor Constantine. He was converted to the Christian faith by SS. John and Paul. After becoming a Christian, he went to Ostia with St. Hilarinus, and devoted himself to the relief of the poor and to the service of the sick. The report of this went abroad into all the world. Many came there from all parts to see a man who had once been a patrician and a consul now washing the feet of the poor, preparing their table, pouring water over their hands, ministering carefully to the sick, and performing other works of piety. He was afterward driven into exile by Julian the Apostate, and returned to Alexandria. There he was ordered by the judge Rautianus to offer sacrifice; when he refused to do so, he was put to the sword and became a martyr to Christ.

At Sibapolis in Mesopotamia, St. Febronia, virgin and martyr. In the persecution of Diocletian and while Lysimachus was governor, Febronia, for defending her faith and chastity, was first beaten with rods. She was then tortured on the rack, her body mangled with iron combs and burned with fire. Her teeth were knocked out, her feet were cut off and she was otherwise mutilated; finally, her head was cut off. Thus, adorned by the jewels of many sufferings, she left this world for her heavenly Spouse.

At Reggio, St. Prosper of Aquitaine, bishop of that city. He was famous for learning and piety, and strove mightily against the Pelagians in defence of the Catholic faith.

At Turin, the birthday of St. Maximus, bishop and confessor, renowned for learning and holiness.

In Holland, St. Adalbert, confessor, who was a disciple of the Bishop St. Willibrord. ✠

The Twenty-sixth Day of June

At Rome, on the Coelian Hill, the holy martyrs John and Paul, brothers. The former was the steward, and the latter the major domo of the virgin Constantia, daughter of the Emperor Constantine. Under Julian the Apostate, both obtained the palm of martyrdom, dying by the sword. *A duplex feast.*

At Trent, St. Vigilius, bishop. While trying to uproot completely the last traces of idolatry, he was stoned to death by wild and barbarous men, and thus fulfilled his martyrdom.

At Valenciennes in Gaul, SS. Salvius, Bishop of Angoulême, and Superius, martyrs.

At Cordoba in Spain, the birthday of St. Pelagius, a young boy. At the command of Abd-er-Rahman, caliph of the Saracens, Pelagius, because of his profession of faith, was torn limb from limb by iron pincers and thus gained his glorious martyrdom.

At Belley in Gaul, St. Anthelm, the prior of the Grande Chartreuse, who became bishop of that city.

In the country of Poitiers, St. Maxentius, priest and confessor, who was illustrious for miracles.

At Thessalonica, St. David, hermit.

On the same day, St. Perseveranda, virgin.

The Twenty-seventh Day of June

In Galatia, St. Crescens, who was a disciple of St. Paul the Apostle. He made a journey through Gaul where, by his preaching, he converted many to the Christian faith. He then returned to the Galatians for whom he had specifically been made bishop, and to the end of his life he strengthened them in their religion. At last, in the time of Trajan, he obtained martyrdom.

At Cordoba in Spain, the holy martyrs Zoilus and nineteen others.

At Caesarea in Palestine, St. Anectus, martyr. In the persecution of Diocletian, under Urban the governor, he exhorted others to martyrdom and caused idols to fall down by his prayers. He was ordered to be scourged by ten soldiers; then his hands and feet were cut off, and being beheaded, he received the crown of martyrdom.

At Constantinople, St. Sampson, priest, who gave shelter to the poor.

In the village of Chinon in Gaul, St. John, priest and confessor.

At Oradea in Hungary, St. Ladislaus, king, who even to this day is glorious for miracles of great renown.

The Twenty-eighth Day of June

The Vigil of the holy Apostles Peter and Paul.

At Lyons in Gaul, St. Irenaeus, bishop and martyr. As St. Jerome writes, he was a disciple of St. Polycarp, Bishop of Smyrna, and lived near the time of the Apostles. He fought much against the heretics both by word and writing. At length, in the persecution of Severus, he was crowned with a glorious martyrdom, together with almost all the Christians of his city. *A duplex feast.*

At Utrecht, St. Benignus, bishop and martyr.

At Alexandria, in the persecution of Severus, the holy martyrs Plutarch, Serenus, Heraclides, a catechumen, Heron, a neophyte, a second Serenus, Rhais, a catechumen, Potamiana, and Marcella her mother. Of these the most famous was the virgin Potamiana. First, in defense of her virginity, she underwent great and innumerable sufferings; then in defense of her faith she endured exquisite and unheard-of pains. At last, together with her mother, she was burned alive.

On the same day, St. Papius, martyr. In the persecution of Diocletian, he was scourged with whips, and cast into a cauldron full of oil and blazing fat. After suffering other terrible torments, he was at last crowned with martyrdom by beheading.

At Cordoba in Spain, St. Argymirus, monk and martyr, who, in the Arab persecution, was stretched on the rack and then put to the sword for the faith.

At Rome, St. Paul I, pope and confessor.

The Twenty-ninth Day of June

At Rome, the birthday of the holy Apostles Peter and Paul, who suffered in the same year and on the same day, under the Emperor Nero. St. Peter was crucified in that city, with his head downward, and was buried in the Vatican near the Triumphal Way; there he is honored with the veneration of the whole world. St. Paul was slain with the sword, and buried with like honor on the Via Ostiensis. *A totum duplex feast of the first class with a solemn octave.*

In Cyprus, St. Mary, mother of John who was surnamed Mark.[6]

In Argenton in Gaul, St. Marcellus, martyr, who was beheaded for the faith together with Anastasius, soldier.

At Genoa, the birthday of St. Syrus, bishop.

At Narni (in Italy), St. Cassius, bishop of that city. Hardly any day of his life passed, as St. Gregory relates, on which he did not offer up to the Omnipotent God the holy Sacrifice of Propitiation.[7] His life well accorded with the Sacrifice, for everything he possessed he had bestowed in alms. During the hour of the Holy Sacrifice he shed abundant tears. It was his custom to come to Rome every year for the Feast of the Apostles. It was on that feast day, after he had celebrated Solemn Mass and had given Communion and the Pax to all, that he departed for Heaven.

Near Sens (in Gaul), St. Benedicta, virgin.

The Thirtieth Day of June

The Commemoration of St. Paul the Apostle. *A totum duplex feast.*

At Rome, St. Lucina, a disciple of the Apostles. She disposed of her goods for the needs of the saints, visited the Christians in prison, and took care of the burial of the martyrs. She was buried in a tomb she herself had built near their graves.

Also at Rome, St. Emiliana, martyr.

[6] "He came to the house of Mary the mother of John, who was surnamed Mark." Acts, 12:12.

[7] Daily celebration of the Holy Sacrifice was not usual until modern times.

On the same day, the holy martyrs Caius, priest, and Leo, subdeacon.

At Alexandria, the suffering of St. Basilides, under the Emperor Severus. As Basilides led the virgin St. Potamiana to her execution, he protected her from the offensive conduct of lewd men. He received from her the reward of his reverential action; three days later, she appeared to him and placed a crown on his forehead. Not only did she convert him to Christ, but later, as he underwent a short combat for Christ, by her prayers she made him a glorious martyr.

At Limoges in Aquitaine, St. Martial, bishop, with the two priests Alpinian and Austriclinian. Their lives shone brightly with miracles.

At Viviers (in Gaul), St. Ostian, priest and confessor.

At Salanigo, in the district of Vicenza (Italy), St. Theobald, priest and hermit. He had been Count of Champagne in Gaul. On account of his renowned holiness and miracles, Pope Alexander III inscribed him on the list of saints.

July

The First Day of July

The Octave of the Nativity of St. John the Baptist. *A memory.*

The Feast of the most Precious Blood of our Lord Jesus Christ. *A totum duplex feast of the first class.*

On Mount Hor, the death of St. Aaron, the first priest of the Levitical order.

At Vienne in Gaul, St. Martin, bishop, a disciple of the Apostles.

At Sinuessa in Campania (Italy), the holy martyrs Castus and Secundinus, bishops.

In Britain, the holy martyrs Julius and Aaron. They suffered after St. Alban in Diocletian's persecution. At the same place and time, very many were tortured in various ways and savagely wounded, who thus attained by their struggle to the joys of the heavenly city.

In Auvergne in Gaul, St. Gal, bishop.

In the territory of Lyons, the death of St. Domitian, abbot. He first led the life of a hermit in that place. After gathering together many people there in the service of God, and being famous for great virtues and glorious miracles, he was gathered to his fathers at a ripe old age.

At Angoulême in Gaul, St. Eparchius, abbot.

In the territory of Rheims, the priest St. Theodoric, who was a disciple of Blessed Rémy, the bishop.

At Amesa in Phoenicia, St. Simeon, confessor, surnamed Salus.[1] He became a fool for Christ's sake, but his deep wisdom God manifested with great miracles.

The Second Day of July

The Visitation of Blessed Virgin Mary to Elizabeth. *A totum duplex feast of the second class.*

At Rome, on the Via Aurelia, the birthday of the holy martyrs Processus and Martinian. They were baptized by St. Peter the Apostle in the Mamertine prison. Under Nero, they suffered beating on the face, the

---

[1] The Martyrology evidently accepts the meaning of *Salus* in Syriac to be "mad." The saint deliberately acted as if he were lacking in sense.

rack, whipping, beating with clubs, fire, and scorpions. Finally, they were crowned with martyrdom, being slain with the sword. *A memory.*

Likewise at Rome, the suffering of three holy soldiers. They were converted to Christ at the martyrdom of St. Paul the Apostle, and merited to become with him partakers of heavenly glory.

On the same day, the holy martyrs Aristo, Crescentian, Eutychian, Urban, Vitalis, Justus, Felicissimus, Felix, Marcia, and Symphorosa. All were crowned with martyrdom in Campania, while the persecution of the Emperor Diocletian was raging.

At Winchester in England, St. Swithin, bishop, whose holiness was shown by his miracles.

At Bamberg, St. Otho, bishop, who preached the Gospel to the people of Pomerania and converted them to the faith.

At Tours in Gaul, the death of St. Monegund, a religious woman.

The Third Day of July

At Rome, the birthday of St. Leo II, pope and confessor, who died rich in merit in the first year of his pontificate. *A simplex feast.*

At Chiusi in Etruria, the holy martyrs Irenaeus, deacon, and Mustiola, a matron. In the reign of the Emperor Aurelian, they were tortured in various cruel ways, and merited the crown of martyrdom.

At Alexandria, the holy martyrs Trypho and twelve others.

At Constantinople, SS. Eulogius and his companions, martyrs.

At Caesarea in Cappadocia, St. Hyacinth, the chamberlain of Trajan the Emperor. He was accused of being a Christian, afflicted with various punishments, and cast into prison, where he was starved to death.

On the same day, the holy martyrs Mark and Mucian. They were slain with the sword for Christ. When a little boy warned them with a loud voice not to sacrifice to idols, the lad was ordered to be scourged. As he then confessed Christ more vehemently, he was slain, together with one Paul who also was encouraging the martyrs.

At Laodicea in Syria, St. Anatolius, bishop, who left writings which are admired not only by churchmen but also by (pagan) philosophers.

At Altino near Venice, St. Heliodorus, bishop, famed for learning and sanctity.

At Ravenna, St. Dathus, bishop and confessor.

At Edessa in Mesopotamia, the transferal from India (of the relics) of St. Thomas the Apostle; the relics were afterward removed to Ortona among the Frentani.[2]

---

[2] The Frentani were an ancient Italian tribe of Samnite origin, dwelling along the Adriatic coast northwest of Apulia.

The Fourth Day of July

At Estremoz in Portugal, the birthday of St. Elizabeth, widow, Queen of Portugal. The Sovereign Pontiff, Urban VIII, knowing her renown for virtues and miracles, placed her among the number of the saints. Pope Innocent XII directed that her feast be celebrated on July 8.

The holy Prophets Osee and Aggaeus.

In the territory of Bourges, St. Laurian, Bishop of Seville and martyr, whose head was taken to Seville in Spain.

In Africa, the birthday of St. Jucundian, martyr. On account of his religion, he was cast into the sea and drowned.

At Sirmium, the martyrs SS. Innocent and Sebastia, and thirty others.

At Madaura in Africa, St. Namphanion, martyr, and his companions, whom he strengthened for the fight and led forth to the crown (of victory).

At Cyrene in Libya, St. Theodore, bishop. In the persecution of Diocletian, under the governor Dignian, he was beaten with leaden tipped whips, and his tongue was cut out. However, later on he died a peaceful death as a confessor.

At Augsburg in Germany, St. Udalric, bishop, famed for the graces of wondrous abstinence, generosity, vigilance, and miracles.

At Tours in Gaul, the transferal of the relics of St. Martin, bishop and confessor, and the dedication of the basilica built in his name, on this same day on which many years before he had been consecrated bishop.

The Fifth Day of July

At Cremona in Insubria, St. Antony Maria Zaccaria, confessor, founder of the Clerks Regular of St. Paul and also of the Angelical Virgins. He was celebrated for all virtues and for miracles, and Leo XIII inscribed him among the number of the saints. His body is honored in the church of St. Barnabas at Milan. *A duplex feast.*

At Rome, St. Zoe, martyr, wife of the blessed martyr Nicostratus. While praying at the tomb of the Apostle St. Peter, she was arrested by the persecutors under the Emperor Diocletian, and cast into a totally dark prison. Then she was hanged from a tree by her neck and her hair and suffocated by a fetid smoke. She died professing her faith in Christ.

At Jerusalem, St. Athanasius, deacon. For defending the holy Synod of Chalcedon, he was seized by the heretics, and after experiencing all manner of tortures, was at last slain by the sword.

In Syria, the birthday of St. Domitius, martyr, who by his miracles bestows many benefits on the people there.

In Sicily, the holy martyrs Agatho and Triphina.

At Tomis in Scythia, the holy martyrs Marinus, Theodotus, and Sedopha.

At Cyrene in Libya, St. Cyrilla, martyr. In the persecution of Diocletian, she held in her hand for a long time burning coals and incense that had been placed there, lest by casting down the coals she might seem to offer incense. Lastly she was cruelly mangled and, adorned with her own blood, passed to her eternal Spouse.

At Treves, St. Numerian, bishop and confessor.

At Sanseverino in Piceno, St. Philomena, virgin.

The Sixth Day of July

The Octave of the holy Apostles Peter and Paul. *A solemn octave.*

At Jerusalem, St. Isaias the Prophet. Under King Manasses he was slain by being sawn asunder. He was buried under the oak of Rogel near the fountain.

At Fiesole in Tuscany, St. Romulus, bishop and martyr, a disciple of St. Peter the Apostle, who sent him to preach the Gospel. After he had announced Christ in many parts of Italy, he returned to Fiesole, and was crowned with martyrdom in the reign of Domitian, together with others who were his companions.

At Rome, the birthday of St. Tranquillinus, martyr, father of SS. Mark and Marcellian. He was converted to Christ by the preaching of St. Sebastian the martyr. He was baptized by the priest St. Polycarp, and ordained a priest by Pope St. Caius. In the reign of Diocletian he came to pray at the tomb of St. Paul on the octave day of the Apostles; he was seized by the heathens, and fulfilled his martyrdom by being stoned to death.

In Campania, St. Dominica, virgin and martyr. At the time of the Emperor Diocletian, she destroyed some idols; accordingly she was condemned to be thrown to the beasts. As they refused to harm her, she was beheaded and so went to the Lord. Her body is preserved with great honor at Tropea in Calabria.

On the same day, St. Lucy, martyr, who was a Campanian by birth. Arrested and severely tortured by Rixius Varus the acting-governor, she converted him to Christ. With her are remembered Antoninus, Severinus, Diodorus, Dion, and seventeen others, who were her companions in suffering and associates in her crown.

In the country of Treves, St. Goar, priest and confessor. ✠

The Seventh Day of July

At Perugia, Blessed Pope Benedict XI of Treviso, confessor, of the Order of Preachers. In the short space of his pontificate, he did much to promote peace for the Church, to restore discipline, and to increase religion to a wonderful degree. *A duplex feast.*

The holy Bishops Cyril and Methodius, whose birthdays are respectively February 14 and April 6.

At Rome, the holy martyrs Claudius, notary, Nicostratus, chief clerk and the husband of Blessed Zoe the martyr, Castorius, Victorinus, and Symphorian. St. Sebastian brought them to the faith of Christ, and the priest St. Polycarp baptized them. While they were occupied in recovering the bodies of the holy martyrs, the judge Fabian ordered them to be seized. After he had tried them for ten days with threats and flatteries and could not move them at all, he ordered them to be tortured on three (different) days and then cast headlong into the sea.

At Durazzo in Macedonia, the holy martyrs Peregrinus, Lucian, Pompey, Hesychius, Papius, Saturninus, and Germanus, natives of Italy. They fled to Durazzo in the persecution of Trajan, but seeing St. Astius the Bishop hanging there upon a cross for his faith, they openly confessed themselves Christians. At the governor's command they were arrested and drowned in the sea.

At Brescia, St. Apollonius, bishop and confessor.

At Eichstadt in Germany, St. Willibald, the first bishop of that city. He was the son of St. Richard the English King and the brother of St. Walburga, virgin. In company with St. Boniface he labored in preaching the Gospel and converted many tribes to Christ.

In Auvergne in Gaul, St. Illidius, bishop.

At Urgel in Aragon, St. Odo, bishop.

In England, St. Hedda, Bishop of the West Saxons.

At Alexandria, the birthday of St. Pantaenus, an apostolic man, and one adorned with all wisdom. He had such great zeal and love for the Word of God that, enkindled with the fire of faith and devotion, he went forth to preach Christ's Gospel even to the nations in the furthest corners of the East. Returning at last to Alexandria at the time of Antoninus Caracalla, he died in peace.

At Faremoutiers near Meaux, St. Ethelburga, abbess and virgin, daughter of an English king.[3]

---

[3] She was the daughter of Erconbert, King of the East Angles.

The Eighth Day of July

St. Elizabeth, widow, Queen of Portugal, who went to a heavenly kingdom on July 4.

In Asia Minor, SS. Aquila and Priscilla his wife, of whom mention is made in the Acts of the Apostles.[4]

At Würzburg in Germany, St. Chilian, bishop. He was sent by the Roman Pontiff to preach the Gospel. After he had led many there to Christ, he was slain together with his companions, Colman, priest, and Totnan, deacon.

At Portus Romanus, fifty holy soldiers, martyrs, who were brought to the faith by the martyrdom of St. Bonosa. After being baptized by Blessed Pope Felix I, they were slain in the persecution of the Emperor Aurelian.

At Caesarea in Palestine, St. Procopius, martyr. He was brought from Scythopolis to Caesarea under the Emperor Diocletian and, at the firmness of his very first replies, was beheaded by the judge Fabian.

At Constantinople, the suffering of the holy Abrahamite monks who defended the veneration of holy images against the Emperor Theophilus, and so underwent martyrdom.

At Spina Lamberti in Emilia, Pope St. Hadrian III. He was famous for his zeal in reconciling the Easterns to the Roman Church, and wondrous for his miracles. His body was brought to the monastery of Nonantola, and buried with honor in the church of St. Silvester.

At Treves, St. Auspicius, bishop and confessor.

At Rome, Blessed Eugene III, pope. After ruling the monastery of SS. Vincent and Anastasius at Tre Fontane with great and praiseworthy holiness and prudence, he was elected Sovereign Pontiff and governed the Universal Church in great sanctity. Pope Pius IX ratified and confirmed the cultus given to him from time immemorial.

The Ninth Day of July

At Briel in Holland, St. John of Cologne, of the Order of Preachers, and his companions of Gorcum. They suffered martyrdom because of their belief in the primacy of the Roman Church and in the presence of Christ in the Eucharist. *A totum duplex feast of the second class.*

At Rome, at the Ever-flowing Spring,[5] the birthday of the holy martyrs Zeno and ten thousand two hundred and three other Christians.

[4] Acts, 18:18, 26.
[5] Now called Tre Fontane.

At Gortyna in Crete, St. Cyril, bishop, who was cast into the flames under the governor Lucius in Diocletian's persecution. He escaped unharmed although the ropes binding him took fire. He was dismissed by the judge, who was overcome with amazement at so great a miracle. But later, by reason of his continued and vigorous preaching of Christ, he was again arrested and beheaded by the same judge.

At Thora near Lake Velino, the suffering of SS. Anatolia and Audax, under the Emperor Decius. After Anatolia, a virgin of Christ, had cured throughout the province of Piceno many who were laboring under various sicknesses, and had caused them to believe in Christ, she was subjected to various tortures by the command of the judge Faustinian. When she had been freed from a serpent that was set upon her, and converted Audax to the faith, at last, praying with outstretched hands, she was transfixed with a sword. Audax also was given into custody, and without delay was crowned by a capital punishment.

At Alexandria, the holy martyrs Patermuthius, Copres, and Alexander, who were slain under Julian the Apostate.

At Martula in Umbria, St. Brictius, bishop. He suffered much under the judge Marcian for confessing the Lord. Later on, after he had converted a great multitude of people to the faith, he died peacefully as a confessor.

At Tifernum in Umbria, St. Veronica Guilani, virgin. She was born in the town of Mercatello in the Diocese of Urbano, and became a nun of the Order of St. Francis, and Abbess of the convent of Tifernum. She was noted for her zeal for suffering and other virtues and for her heavenly gifts. She was inscribed in the list of holy virgins by Pope Gregory XVI. ✠

The Tenth Day of July

At Rome, the suffering of the seven martyred brothers, the sons of St. Felicitas, also a martyr, namely: Januarius, Felix, Philip, Silvanus, Alexander, Vitalis, and Martial. In the time of the Emperor Antoninus, under Publius, prefect of the city, Januarius, after being scourged with rods and imprisoned, was beaten to death with whips tipped with lead; Felix and Philip were beaten to death with clubs. Silvanus was thrown over a precipice; Alexander, Vitalis, and Martial were beheaded. *A simplex feast.*

Likewise at Rome, the holy virgins and martyrs Rufina and Secunda, sisters. They were subjected to torture in the persecution of Valerian and Gallienus, and at last went to Heaven, the one being beheaded by the sword and the other's throat being cut. Their bodies are preserved with due honor in the Lateran basilica, near the baptistery.

In Africa, the holy martyrs Januarius, Marinus, Nabor, and Felix, who were beheaded.

At Nicopolis in Armenia, the holy martyrs Leontius, Maurice, Daniel, and their companions. They were tortured in various ways under the Emperor Licinius and the governor Lysias. At last, cast into the fire, they finished their course of martyrdom.

At Pisidia, the holy martyrs Bianor and Silvanus, who suffered most savage tortures for Christ. At length they were beheaded, receiving thus the crown of life.

At Iconium in Lycaonia, St. Apollonius, martyr, who gained an illustrious martyrdom on the cross.

At Ghent in Flanders, St. Amelberga, virgin.

The Eleventh Day of July

In Eastern Tonkin (Indo-China), the blessed martyrs Ignatius, Delgado, Dominic, and Henares, all bishops of the Order of Preachers. During the persecution of the tyrant Minh-ming, Blessed Ignatius was sentenced to be beheaded, but before the sentence was carried out he died, weakened by illness and exposure. There suffered in the same persecution twenty-four other martyrs of whom nine were Friars Preachers and eight were members of the Third Order of St. Dominic. *A duplex feast.*

At Rome, St. Pius I, pope and martyr. He was crowned with martyrdom in the persecution of Marcus Aurelius Antoninus.

At Bergamo (in Italy), St. John, bishop, who was slain by the Arians for defending the Catholic faith.

At Sida in Pamphylia, St. Cindeus, priest. At the time of Diocletian the Emperor and Stratonicus the governor, he was cast into the fire after many torments, but was unharmed (by the flames). At last, while in prayer, he gave up his soul to God.

At Cordoba in Spain, St. Abundius, priest, who was crowned with martyrdom in the Arab persecution for preaching against Mohammedanism.

At Nicopolis in Armenia, the birthday of the holy martyrs Januarius and Pelagia. They were tortured for four days by the rack, iron claws, and potsherds, and thus gained martyrdom.

In the territory of Sens (in Gaul), St. Sidronius, martyr.

At Iconium in Lycaonia, St. Marcian, martyr, who passed through many torments to victory, under Perennius the governor.

At Brescia, the holy martyrs Savinus and Cyprian.

In the territory of Poitiers, St. Sabinus, confessor.

The Twelfth Day of July

In the monastery of Passignano, near Florence, St. John Gualbert, abbot, founder of the Order of Vallombrosa. *A duplex feast.*

At Lodi in Insubria, the holy martyrs Nabor and Felix. In the persecution of Maximian, they suffered martyrdom by being beheaded after various tortures. Their bodies were brought to Milan by Blessed Savina, and honorably buried there.

At Cyprus, Blessed Jason, an early disciple of Christ.

At Lucca in Tuscany, St. Paulinus, who was ordained the first bishop of that city by the Apostle St. Peter. Under Nero, he gained martyrdom with other companions, after many sufferings, at the foot of Mount Pisa.

At Aquileia, the birthday of St. Hermagoras, who was a disciple of St. Mark the Evangelist, and the first bishop of that city. Between performing miracles of healing, being diligent in preaching, and effecting the conversion of the people, he experienced many kinds of torture. Finally, with his deacon Fortunatus, he merited to obtain an unending triumph by undergoing capital punishment.

On the same day, the suffering of SS. Proclus and Hilarion. In the reign of the Emperor Trajan and the governor Maximus, he suffered the most atrocious torments to gain the palm of martyrdom.

At Toledo in Spain, St. Marciana, virgin and martyr, who was cast to the beasts for the faith and, being torn limb from limb by a bull, was crowned with martyrdom.

At Lentini in Sicily, St. Epiphana, who under the Emperor Diocletian and the governor Tertyllus suffered mutilation and gave up her soul to God.

At Lyons in Gaul, St. Viventiolus, bishop.

At Bologna, St. Paternian, bishop. ✠ *An Anniversary.*

The Thirteenth Day of July

At Genoa (in Italy), Blessed James, of the Order of Preachers, Archbishop of Genoa. He became illustrious by reason of his learning, preachin, holiness, and the miracles he performed. *A semi-duplex feast.*

At Rome, St. Anacletus, pope and martyr, who ruled the Church of God after St. Clement, and adorned it with his glorious martyrdom.

At Bamberg, the birthday of St. Henry I, Emperor of the Romans, and confessor. He led a life of perpetual virginity with his wife St. Cune-gund, and caused St. Stephen, King of Hungary, and almost all of his people to embrace the faith of Christ. His festival is, however, observed on July 15.

In Palestine, SS. Joel and Esdras, Prophets.

In Macedonia, Blessed Silas, who was one of the first converts. He was sent by the Apostles to the churches of the Gentiles together with Paul and Barnabas. Full of the grace of God, he readily carried out the office of preaching and, glorifying Christ in his sufferings, afterward died in peace.

Likewise, St. Serapion, martyr, who under Severus the Emperor and Aquila the governor, passed through fire to the crown of martyrdom.

In the island of Chios, St. Myrope, martyr. At the time of the Emperor Decius and the governor Numerian, she was beaten to death with iron bars and so went to the Lord.

In Africa, the holy confessors Eugene, Bishop of Carthage, glorious for faith and virtues, and all the clergy of that Church, to the number of five hundred or more. They were destroyed by slaughter and famine in the Vandal persecution under the Arian king Hunneric. Rejoicing in the Lord, they were sent far away into cruel exile. Many among them were young children who performed the office of lectors. There were also among them two most noble persons, an archdeacon named Salutaris, and Muritta, second in the ministry. For the third time, these men professed the faith; they made themselves illustrious by their glorious perseverance in the faith of Christ.

In Brittany, St. Turian, bishop and confessor, a man of wondrous simplicity and innocence.

The Fourteenth Day of July

St. Bonaventure, of the Order of Friars Minor, cardinal and Bishop of Alba, confessor and Doctor of the Church. He passed to the Lord on July 15. *A duplex feast.*

At Rome, the birthday of St. Camillus of Lellis, priest and confessor, and founder of the Clerks Regular for Ministering to the Sick. Famed for his miracles and virtues, the Sovereign Pontiff, Benedict XIV, canonized him, while Leo XIII declared him to be the heavenly patron of hospitals and the sick. His festival is, however, observed on July 18.

Also at Rome, St. Justus, a soldier under the tribune Claudius. When the cross miraculously appeared to him, he believed in Christ, was soon baptized, and bestowed all his goods on the poor. He was then arrested by Magnetius the prefect and ordered to be beaten with sinews, then to have a red-hot metal helmet placed on his head and to be cast upon a pyre. Although he was uninjured by the flames, he expired confessing the Lord.

At Sinope in Pontus, St. Phocas, martyr, bishop of that city. Under the Emperor Trajan he overcame for Christ imprisonment, chains, sword, and fire, and departed victorious to Heaven. His relics were taken to Vienne in Gaul, and buried in the Basilica of the Holy Apostles.

At Alexandria, St. Heracles, bishop. He enjoyed so lofty a reputation that Africanus the historian relates he hastened to Alexandria to see him.

At Carthage, St. Cyrus, bishop, on whose feast day St. Augustine delivered a panegyric on him to the people.

At Como, St. Felix, who was the first bishop of that city.

At Brescia, St. Optatian, bishop.

At Deventer in Belgium, St. Marcellinus, priest and confessor.

At Lima in Peru, St. Francis Solano, priest, of the Order of Friars Minor, and confessor. He died in the West Indies, illustrious for his preaching, miracles, and virtues. He was numbered among the saints by the Sovereign Pontiff, Benedict XIII. ✠

The Fifteenth Day of July

St. Henry I, Emperor of the Romans and confessor, whose birthday is noted on July 13. *A simplex feast.*

At Lyons in Gaul, the death of St. Bonaventure, cardinal and Bishop of Alba, confessor and Doctor of the Church, of the Order of Friars Minor. He is well known because of his learning and holiness of life. His festival is, however, observed July 14.

At Pavia, St. Felix, bishop and martyr.

At Portus Romanus, the birthday of the holy martyrs Eutropius, and the sisters Zosima and Bonosa.

At Carthage, Blessed Catulinus, deacon, in the praise of whom St. Augustine delivered a panegyric to the faithful; also SS. Januarius, Florentius, Julia, and Justa, martyrs, who were buried in the Basilica of Faustus.

At Alexandria, the holy martyrs Philip, Zeno, Narseus, and ten children.

On the island of Tenedos, St. Abudemius, martyr, who suffered under Diocletian.

At Sebaste in Armenia, St. Antiochus, a doctor, who was beheaded under the governor Hadrian. When milk flowed forth from him in place of blood,[6] Cyriacus his executioner was converted to Christ, and suffered martyrdom himself.

At Nisibis in Mesopotamia, the birthday of St. James, bishop of that city, a man of great holiness. He was famous for miracles and learning, and was one of the confessors under Galerius Maximian, who in the Nicene Synod condemned the heresy of Arius in opposing the (doctrine of) Homoousian.[7] By his prayers and those of Bishop Alexander, Arius received at Constantinople the reward of his iniquity, for he died a miserable death.

At Naples in Campania, St. Athanasius, bishop of that city, who suffered much at the hands of his wicked nephew Sergius, and was driven from his see. Exhausted by his privations, he passed to Heaven at Veroli in the Hernican mountains in the time of Charles the Bald.

At Palermo, the finding of the body of St. Rosalie, a virgin of Palermo. It was found by divine revelation in the pontificate of Urban VIII and delivered Sicily from pestilence in the year of Jubilee.

The Sixteenth Day of July

The Feast of the Blessed Virgin Mary of Mount Carmel. *A totum duplex feast.*

At Sebaste in Armenia, the holy martyrs Athenogenes, bishop, and his ten disciples, under the Emperor Diocletian.

At Treves, St. Valentine, bishop and martyr.

At Cordoba in Spain, St. Sisenand, cleric and martyr, whose throat was cut by the Saracens because of his faith.

On the same day, the birthday of St. Faustus, martyr. He was crucified in the reign of the Emperor Decius and lingered for five days. At last he was pierced through with arrows, and passed into Heaven.

At Saintes in Gaul, the holy martyrs Reineldis, virgin, and her companions, who were slain by the barbarians because of their faith.

At Bergamo, St. Domnio, martyr.

At Antioch, the birthday of Blessed Eustace, bishop and confessor, famous for learning and holiness. Under the Arian Emperor Constantius, he was exiled for his defense of the Catholic faith to Trajanopolis in Thrace, and there died in the Lord.

At Capua, St. Vitalian, bishop and confessor.

[6] This absurd statement is taken from the so-called "Acts" of the saint; they are worthless from the standpoint of historical accuracy.

[7] Homoousian is the word used by the Fathers of Nicaea to express the truth that the Son is one God with the Father. This doctrine is against the heresy of Arius.

At Ostia, the transferal of the body of St. Hilarinus, monk. He was arrested, together with St. Donatus, in the persecution of Julian, and since he would not sacrifice, was beaten with clubs. He underwent this martyrdom at Arezzo in Tuscany, on August 7.

The Seventeenth Day of July

At Wratislaw (in Poland), Blessed Ceslaus, confessor, of the Order of our Father St. Dominic. While at Rome, he received the religious habit from St. Dominic and strove to imitate his virtues. Aflame with zeal for the salvation of souls, he journeyed through all of Silesia on foot and, by his preaching and example, converted many from their errors to the true faith and led many sinners to repentance. *A semi-duplex feast.*

At Rome, St. Alexis, confessor, son of the Senator Euphemian. On the night of his nuptials, leaving his bride a virgin, he departed from his house. After long wandering, he returned to the city and remained unknown for seventeen years, dwelling in poverty in his father's house as a stranger, and so escaping the world by a new artifice. After his death he was made known both by a voice which was heard in the churches of the city, and by his writing.[8] In the reign of the Sovereign Pontiff, Innocent I, his body was borne with great honor to the Church of St. Boniface, where he is famous for many miracles.

At Carthage, the birthday of the holy martyrs of Scillium, Speratus, Narzal, Cythinus, Veturius, Felix, Acyllinus, Laetantius, Januaria, Generosa, Vestina, Donata, and Secunda. By command of the prefect Saturninus, after their first confession of Christ, they were cast into prison, then placed in stocks, and afterward beheaded by the sword. The relics of Speratus, together with the bones of St. Cyprian and the head of St. Pantaleon the martyr, were taken from Africa to Gaul, and honorably buried at Lyons in the Basilica of St. John the Baptist.

At Amastris in Paphlagonia, St. Hyacinth, martyr, who suffered much under the prefect Castritius, and died in prison.

At Tivoli, St. Generosus, martyr.

At Constantinople, St. Theodota, martyr, under Leo the Iconoclast.

At Rome, the death of St. Leo IV, pope.

At Pavia, St. Ennodius, confessor and bishop.

At Auxerre, St. Theodosius, bishop.

At Milan, St. Marcellina, virgin, sister of St. Ambrose, bishop. She re-

[8] This fanciful story rests on no solid foundations. There was a St. Alexis who lived and died at Edessa; no further details are known of him.

ceived the veil of consecration at Rome from Pope Liberius in the Basilica of St. Peter. St. Ambrose in his writings also bore witness to her holiness.

At Venice, the transferal of the body of St. Marina, virgin.

The Eighteenth Day of July

St. Camillus de Lellis, priest and confessor, founder of the Clerks Regular Ministering to the Sick, the heavenly patron of hospitals and the sick, whose birthday is commemorated on July 14. *A duplex feast.*

At Tivoli, St. Symphorosa, wife of St. Getulius, martyr, together with her seven sons, Crescens, Julian, Nemesius, Primitivus, Justin, Stacteus, and Eugene. In the reign of the Emperor Hadrian, because of her insuperable constancy, the mother was scourged for a long time by stems of palm trees, then hung by the hair, and at last bound to a stone and cast into the river. Her sons were fixed to stakes and stretched by pulleys; they completed their martyrdom by various kinds of deaths. Their bodies were afterward taken to Rome, and in the pontificate of Pius IV were discovered in the deaconry of St. Angelo in Pescheria.

At Utrecht, St. Frederick, bishop and martyr.

At Silistria in Bulgaria, St. Emilian, martyr, who was cast into a furnace in the time of Julian the Apostate, under the governor Capitolinus, and received the palm of martyrdom.

At Carthage, St. Gundenes, virgin. Because she confessed Christ, she was tortured on four separate occasions by being stretched on the rack and by being terribly torn with hooks, by command of the proconsul Rufinus. She endured the filth of imprisonment for a long time, and at last was slain with the sword.

In Galicia in Spain, St. Marina, virgin and martyr.

At Milan, St. Maternus, bishop. In the reign of the Emperor Maximian, he was thrust down into (the lower) prison and frequently scourged for the faith and the Church committed to him. At length, renowned for his frequent witness to the truth, he died in the Lord.

At Brescia, the birthday of St. Philastrius, bishop of that city. He fought strongly by word and writing against the heretics, particularly the Arians, at whose hands he greatly suffered. At last, renowned for his miracles, he died a peaceful death, as a confessor.

At Metz in Gaul, St. Arnulf, bishop, who was famous for holiness and miracles, and after leading the life of a hermit, died a blessed death.

At Segni (in Italy), St. Bruno, bishop and confessor.

At Forlimpopoli in Emilia, St. Ruffillus, bishop of that city.

The Nineteenth Day of July

St. Vincent de Paul, priest and confessor, the founder of the Priests of the Congregation of the Mission and the Sisters of Charity. He is heavenly patron of all charitable organizations. He died in the Lord on September 27. *A duplex feast.*

At Colossae in Phrygia, the birthday of St. Epaphras, whom St. Paul the Apostle calls his fellow-captive.[9] He was ordained Bishop of Colossae by that Apostle and, renowned for his merits, gained the palm of martyrdom for courageously defending the sheep committed to him. His body is buried at Rome in the Basilica of St. Mary Major.

At Treves, St. Martin, bishop and martyr.

At Seville in Spain, the suffering of the holy virgins Justa and Rufina. For confessing the Lord, they were seized by Diogenian the prefect, and were first tortured by the rack and torn with hooks. Afterward they were afflicted with imprisonment, starvation, and various torments. At last Justa died in prison, while Rufina was strangled.

At Cordoba in Spain, St. Aura, virgin, the sister of the holy martyrs Adulphus and John. For a while she apostatised through the persuasion of a Mohammedan judge, but quickly repenting of what she had done, she overcame the enemy in a second contest by the shedding of her blood.

At Rome, St. Symmachus, pope, who, worn out at length by schismatical factions, passed to the Lord, remarkable for holiness.

At Verona, St. Felix, bishop.

At Skete, a mountain in Egypt, St. Arsenius, a deacon of the Roman Church. In the reign of Theodosius, he retired to the desert; there he died after having been enriched with the gift of tears and every virtue.

In Cappadocia, St. Macrina, virgin. She was the daughter of SS. Basil and Emmelia, and the sister of the holy Bishops, SS. Basil the Great, Gregory of Nyssa, and Peter of Sebaste.

The Twentieth Day of July

St. Jerome Emiliani, confessor, founder of the Congregation of Somascha. He died in the Lord on February 8. *A duplex feast.*

An Antioch, the suffering of St. Margaret, virgin and martyr. *A memory.*

On Mount Carmel, the blessed Prophet Elias.

In Judaea, the birthday of Blessed Joseph, called the Just. The Apostles appointed him, together with Blessed Matthias, to fill the place of the traitor Judas in the apostolate. Although the lot fell on Matthias, never-

[9] Colossians, 1:7, 4:12; Philemon, 5:23.

theless Joseph gave himself up to the office of preaching and holiness, and sustained much persecution from the Jews for the faith of Christ, until his life came to a victorious end. It is related of him that he drank poison, and by reason of his faith in the Lord suffered no harm.

At Cordoba in Spain, St. Paul, deacon and martyr. He rebuked the heathen princes for Mohammedan impiety and cruelty and constantly preached Christ. By their command he was slain, thus passing to his reward in Heaven.

At Damascus, the holy martyrs Sabinus, Julian, Maximus, Macrobius, Cassia, and Paula, with ten others.

In Portugal, St. Wilgeforts, virgin and martyr, who defended her faith and her chastity, and thus merited to obtain a glorious triumph on the cross.

On the same day, the birthday of St. Flavian II, Bishop of Antioch, and St. Elias, Bishop of Jerusalem. They were driven into exile by the Emperor Anastasius for their defense of the Council of Chalcedon, and there as victors went to the Lord.

Near Boulogne in Gaul, St. Wulmar, abbot, a man of admirable sanctity.

At Treves, St. Severa, virgin. ✠

The Twenty-first Day of July

At Rome, St. Praxedes, virgin. She was brought up in all chastity and knowledge of the law of God. She passed her life devoted to vigils, prayer, and fasting, and gained eternal rest in Christ. She was buried near her sister Pudentiana on the Via Salaria. *A feast of three lessons.*

At Babylon, St. Daniel the Prophet.

At Comana in Armenia, St. Zoticus, bishop and martyr, who was crowned under Severus.

At Marseilles in Gaul, the birthday of St. Victor, soldier. He refused to perform military service or to offer sacrifice to idols, and was at first cast into prison, where he was visited by an angel; afterward he was punished with various tortures, and at last completed his martyrdom by being crushed by a millstone. There suffered also with him three other soldiers, Alexander, Felician, and Longinus.

At Troyes in Gaul, the suffering of SS. Claudius, Justus, Jucundinus, and five companions, under the Emperor Aurelian.

In the same place, St. Julia, virgin and martyr.

At Strasbourg, St. Arbogast, bishop, noted for miracles.

In Syria, the monk St. John, who was a companion of St. Simeon.

The Twenty-second Day of July

At Marseilles in Gaul, the birthday of St. Mary Magdalene, out of whom the Lord cast seven devils. She merited to be the first who should see the Saviour Himself risen from the dead. *A totum duplex feast of the second class.*

At Philippi in Macedonia, St. Syntyche, whom St. Paul the Apostle mentions.[10]

At Ancyra in Galatia, the birthday of St. Plato, martyr. In the reign of Agrippinus Vicarius, he was scourged, torn with iron hooks, and tortured in other most savage ways. At last, his head being cut off, he rendered up his unconquered soul to God. The Acts of the Second Nicene Synod bear witness to his miracles in helping captives.

In Cyprus, St. Theophilus the praetor. He was seized by the Arabs; as he could not be influenced either by gifts or by threats to deny Christ, he was slain with the sword.

At Antioch, St. Cyril, bishop, a man remarkable for learning and holiness.

At Menat near Auvergne, St. Meneleus, abbot.

In the monastery of Fontanelle in Gaul, St. Wandrille, abbot. He was noted for his miracles. His body was later taken to the monastery of Blandin, in Flanders.

At Lisbon in Portugal, St. Laurence of Brindisi, priest and confessor, minister-general of the Order of Friars Minor Capuchin of St. Francis. Renowned for his preaching of the divine Word and his zealous deeds for God's glory, he was inscribed by the Sovereign Pontiff, Leo XIII, in the number of the saints.

At Scythopolis in Palestine, Count St. Joseph.

The Twenty-third Day of July

At Orvieto in Etruria (in Italy), Blessed Joan, commonly called Vanna, virgin, of the Third Order of St. Dominic. She was illustrious for her singular innocence, her meditation on divine truth, and an abundance of heavenly gifts. *A semi-duplex feast.*

At Ravenna, the birthday of St. Apollinaris, bishop. He was ordained at Rome by St. Peter the Apostle and sent to Ravenna. He suffered varied and manifold punishments for the faith of Christ; afterward he preached the Gospel in Emilia and recalled many persons from idolatry. At last he returned to Ravenna, and under Vespasian Caesar gained a glorious martyrdom. *A memory.*

[10] Mark, 16:9; Philippians, 4:2.

At Le Mans in Gaul, St. Liborius, bishop and confessor.

At Rome, the birthday of St. Bridget, widow. After many pilgrimages to the holy places, she died filled with the spirit of God. Her feast is kept on October 8.

At the same place, St. Rasyphus, martyr.

Also at Rome, the suffering of St. Primitiva, virgin and martyr.

Likewise, the holy martyrs Apollonius and Eugene.

On the same day, the birthday of the holy martyrs Trophimus and Theophilus. In the reign of the Emperor Diocletian, they were stoned and tortured with fire. At last, put to the sword, they were crowned with martyrdom.

In Bulgaria, many holy martyrs. The wicked Emperor Nicephorus, who laid waste the churches of God, caused them to be slain by various kinds of deaths: by the sword, by the rope, by arrows, by long imprisonment, and by starvation.

At Rome, the holy virgins Romula, Redempta, and Herundo, of whom Pope St. Gregory has written.

The Twenty-fourth Day of July

The Vigil of St. James the Apostle.

At Piedmont (Italy), Blessed Augustine of Biella, confessor, of our Order. He was outstanding by the admirable sanctity of his life and by his exhausting labors in the work of the ministry. With the praise of the Lord lovingly on his lips, he expired at Venice. *A semi-duplex feast.*

At Tyro on Lake Bolsena in Tuscany, St. Christina, virgin and martyr. This virgin, believing in Christ, broke the gold and silver idols of her father and gave the pieces to the poor. At her father's command, she was torn with scourges, subjected to other cruel tortures, and cast into the lake with a huge stone fastened to her. However, she was rescued by an angel. Under another judge, who succeeded her father, she courageously underwent even more atrocious tortures. Finally, after she had been shut up by the governor Julian for five days in a burning furnace without any injury, and after being protected by the power of Christ from the sting of serpents, she ended her martyrdom by having her tongue cut out and by being pierced with arrows. *A memory.*

At Rome, on the Via Tiburtina, St. Vincent, martyr.

At Amiterno, among the Vestinians,[11] the suffering of eighty-three holy soldiers.

At Merida in Spain, St. Victor, soldier. In the persecution of Diocletian,

[11] See note for May 20.

he gained martyrdom by means of various tortures with his two brothers Stercatius and Antinogenes.

Likewise, the holy martyrs Meneus and Capiton.

In Lycia, the holy martyrs Niceta and Aquilina. They were converted to Christ by the preaching of blessed Christopher, martyr, and obtained the palm of martyrdom by being beheaded.

At Sens (in Gaul), St. Ursicinus, bishop and confessor.

The Twenty-fifth Day of July

St. James the Apostle, who was the brother of Blessed John the Evangelist. He was beheaded by Herod Agrippa about Easter time, being the first of the Apostles to receive the crown of martyrdom. His holy bones were taken on this day from Jerusalem to Spain, and buried in the remotest part of that country, in Galicia. There they are religiously venerated with great honor by the people and by the great concourse of Christians who go there to perform their religious duties and vows. *A totum duplex feast of the second class.*

In Lycia, St. Christopher, martyr. In the reign of Decius, he was beaten with iron rods and was preserved by the power of Christ from being burned in raging flames. At last, pierced through with arrow-wounds, he was beheaded, thus completing his martyrdom. *A memory.*

At Barcelona in Spain, the birthday of blessed Cucuphas, martyr. In the persecution of Diocletian under the governor Dacian, he overcame many torments and at last passed victoriously to Heaven by being beheaded. *A memory.*

In Palestine, St. Paul, martyr. Under the governor Firmilian, in the persecution of Maximian Galerius, he was condemned to death. Asking a little time for prayer, he besought God with all his heart for his fellow-sufferers, then for the Jews and Gentiles, that they might know the true faith, for the multitude that stood around, and lastly for the judge who had condemned him and the executioner who was to slay him. Then he was beheaded and so received the crown of martyrdom.

At Forcino among the Vestinians, the holy martyrs Florentius and Felix, both of Siponte.

At Cordoba in Spain, St. Theodemir, monk and martyr.

In Palestine, St. Valentina, virgin. When she was brought to an altar to offer sacrifice, she overturned it with her feet. She was terribly tortured and, being cast into the fire together with another virgin, her companion, hastened to her heavenly Spouse.

At Treves, St. Magnericus, bishop and confessor.

The Twenty-sixth Day of July

The death of St. Anne, mother of the Immaculate Virgin Mary, the Mother of God. *A totum duplex feast of the second class.*

At Philippi in Macedonia, the birthday of St. Erastus, who was left there as bishop by St. Paul the Apostle, and there crowned with martyrdom.

At Rome, on the Via Latina, the holy martyrs Symphronius, Olympius, Theodulus, and Exuperia, who, as is read in the Acts of Pope St. Stephen, were burned alive and so obtained the martyr's palm.

At Portus Romanus, the holy martyr Hyacinth. He was first cast into the fire and then into a river, but escaped unharmed. Afterward, Leontius, who had been consul under the Emperor Trajan, ordered him beheaded, and so ended his life. The matron Julia buried his body on her farm near Rome.

At Verona, St. Valens, bishop and confessor.

At Rome, St. Pastor, a priest in whose name a legal title is extant at St. Pudentiana's on the Viminal Hill.[12]

In the monastery of St. Benedict in the country of Mantua, St. Simeon, monk and hermit, who, famed for many miracles, died at a good old age.

The Twenty-seventh Day of July

In the kingdom of Tonkin, the blessed martyrs Joseph Maria Sanjurjo and Melchior Sampedro, both bishops; and their twenty-three companions. Although they died in different years, all endured many tortures for the faith of Christ, and all received the glorious palm of martyrdom. *A duplex feast.*

At Bisceglia in Apulia (Italy), the holy martyrs Maurus, bishop, Pantaleon, and Sergius, who suffered under Trajan.

At Nicomedia, St. Hermolaus, priest, by whose teaching Blessed Pantaleon was converted to the faith. Also SS. Hermippus and Hermocrates, brothers. After many tortures inflicted on them by the same Maximian for their confession of Christ, they were put to death.

At Cordoba in Spain, the holy martyrs, George, deacon, Aurelius and his wife Natalia, Felix and his wife Liliosa, in the Arab persecution.

At Nola in Campania (Italy), the martyrs SS. Felix, Julia, and Jucunda.

Among the Homerites in Arabia,[13] the commemoration of the holy

---

[12] See note for June 20.

[13] They are usually called Himyarites. They lived in southwestern Arabia and are said to have been named after a king called Himyar.

martyrs who because of their Christian faith were delivered to the fire under the tyrant Dunaan.

At Ephesus, the birthday of the Seven Sleepers, SS. Maximian, Malchus, Martinian, Dionysius, John, Serapion, and Constantine.

At Rome, Pope St. Celestine I, who condemned Nestorius, Bishop of Constantinople, and put Pelagius to flight. By his command the holy Universal Council of Ephesus was held to condemn the same Nestorius.

At Auxerre, the death of blessed Aetherius, bishop and confessor.

At Constantinople, blessed Anthusa, virgin, who was scourged under Constantine Copronymus for her veneration of holy images. Being sent into exile, she died in the Lord. ✠

The Twenty-eighth Day of July

In the town of San Germano of the diocese of Vercelli (Italy), Blessed Anthony della Chiesa, of the Order of Preachers, a man distinguished for his holiness, character, devotion, and knowledge. *A semi-duplex feast.*

At Nicomedia, the suffering of St. Pantaleon, a physician. Because of his Christian faith, he was imprisoned by the Emperor Maximian and tortured by the punishment of the rack and by burning with torches. Amidst these sufferings he was refreshed by the Lord appearing to him. At last, his martyrdom was ended by the sword.

At Milan, the birthday of SS. Nazarius and the boy Celsus, martyrs. Anolinus, in the raging persecution aroused by Nero, ordered them to be maltreated and afflicted for a long time in prison, and then slain with the sword. *A memory.*

At Rome, the suffering of St. Victor I, pope and martyr.

(Likewise at Rome), St. Innocent I, pope and confessor, who died in the Lord on March 12.

In the Thebaid in Egypt, the commemoration of many holy martyrs who suffered in the persecution of Decius and Valerian. The crafty enemy, seeing that the Christians desired to be slain with the sword for Christ, devised for them punishments which would ensure a slow death, being desirous rather of slaying their souls than their bodies. Among the number (of Christians) was one who, after he had endured the rack, burning torches and gridirons, was bound with his hands behind his back, anointed with honey, and exposed in the hot sun to the torture of ants and flies. Another was fastened in a wanton position among flowers, but when a shameless woman approached him to lure him to sin, he bit through his tongue and spat it forth in her face.

At Ancyra in Galatia, St. Eustathius, martyr. He was subjected to various kinds of torments and cast into a river, from which he was delivered by an angel. Then a dove came to him from heaven to call him to everlasting rewards.

At Miletus in Armenia, St. Achatius, martyr, who under the Emperor Licinius, after various punishments, was cast into a furnace. Being preserved unhurt by God's help, he fulfilled his martyrdom by being beheaded.

In Brittany, St. Sampson, bishop and confessor.

At Lyons in Gaul, St. Peregrinus, priest, whose blessedness is declared by glorious miracles.

The Twenty-ninth Day of July

At Tarascon, in the province of Narbonne in Gaul, St. Martha, virgin, the hostess of our Saviour, and the sister of SS. Mary Magdalene and Lazarus. *A simple feast.*

At Rome, on the Via Aurelia, St. Felix II, pope and martyr. He was removed from his see by the Arian Emperor Constantius for his defense of the Catholic faith, and secretly put to the sword at Cera in Tuscany, meeting with a glorious death. His body was taken thence by the clergy, and buried on the Via Aurelia. Afterward it was removed to the Church of SS. Cosmas and Damian. There it was found under the altar by the Sovereign Pontiff, Gregory XIII, together with the relics of the holy martyrs, Mark, Marcellian, and Tranquillinus. It was again buried in the same place, together with the other relics, on July 31. In that altar were found also the bodies of SS. Abundius, priest, and Abundantius, deacon, both martyrs. Not long after, these were removed to the Church of the Jesuits on the day before their birthday.

Likewise at Rome, on the Via Portuensis, the holy martyrs Simplicius, Faustinus, and Beatrice, in the time of the Emperor Diocletian. The two former, after many and varied tortures, were ordered to undergo capital punishment; Beatrice, their sister, was strangled in prison for confessing Christ. *A memory.*

At Rome likewise, the holy martyrs Lucilla and Flora, virgins, Eugene, Antoninus, Theodore, and eighteen of their companions, who suffered martyrdom under the Emperor Gallienus.

Also at Rome, St. Serapia, virgin. In the reign of Emperor Hadrian, she was handed over to two evil young men. She could not be corrupted by them, nor could she afterward be injured by flaming torches. By command of the judge Derillus she was scourged and then beheaded with the sword. Her body was buried by St. Sabina in her own tomb near the Vindician field, but the memory of her martyrdom is kept more especially on September 3, on which day their common tomb was finished, adorned, and consecrated as a fitting place of prayer.

At Gangra in Paphlagonia, St. Callinicus, martyr. He was scourged with iron rods and subjected to other tortures. Last of all, when cast into a furnace, he rendered up his spirit to God.

In Norway, St. Olaf, king and martyr.

At Troyes in Gaul, St. Lupus, bishop and confessor, who went forth with St. Germanus to combat the Pelagian heresy in Britain. By his fervent prayer he defended the town of Troyes from the fury of Attila, when he was laying waste to all Gaul. At last, after fulfilling worthily the office of the priesthood for fifty-two years, he died in peace.

In the city of St. Brieuc in Gaul, St. William, bishop and confessor.

Likewise, the death of Blessed Prosper, Bishop of Orleans.

At Todi in Umbria, St. Faustinus, confessor.

In the city of Mamia, St. Seraphina.

At Rome, Blessed Urban II, pope, who followed the policy of St. Gregory VII. He was resplendent for his zeal for learning and religion. He aroused the faithful to be crusaders and recover the holy places of Palestine from the power of the infidels. The Sovereign Pontiff, Leo XIII, ratified and confirmed the cult given him from time immemorial. ✠

The Thirtieth Day of July

At Calaruega in Spain, Blessed Mannes, brother of our Father St. Dominic. He possessed sincerity and simplicity to a high degree, and was devoted to contemplation. Rich in merit and renowned for his miracles, he died a holy death in the Cistercian monastery of St. Peter at Gamiel. *A duplex feast.*

At Rome, the holy martyrs Abdon and Sennen, Persians. Under the Emperor Decius, they were brought to Rome bound in chains, and for the Christian faith were first scourged with leaden tipped whips and then slain with the sword. *A memory.*

At Assisi in Umbria, St. Rufinus, martyr.

At Tuburbe in Africa, the holy virgins and martyrs Maxima, Donatilla, and Secunda. In the persecution of Valerian and Gallienus, Maxima and Donatilla were forced to drink vinegar and gall and were then severely beaten. They were tortured on the rack, burnt on gridirons, and then rubbed with lime. Afterward, they were thrown to the beasts, along with Secunda, a girl of twelve years of age. As the beasts did not harm them, all three were slain by the sword.

At Caesarea in Cappadocia, St. Julitta, martyr. She went to law to recover her goods from an influential man who had defrauded her. He maintained that since she was a Christian she ought not to be heard. She was immediately ordered by the judge to offer incense to idols, so that she might present her case. She firmly refused. Being cast into the flames, she rendered up her soul to God, but her body remained unhurt by the fire. St. Basil the Great has celebrated the excellence of her glory in a beautiful eulogy.

At Auxerre, St. Ursus, bishop and confessor.

The Thirty-first Day of July

At Rome, the birthday of St. Ignatius, priest and confessor, founder of the Society of Jesus, famous for holiness and miracles, and most zealous for the propagation everywhere of the Catholic religion. *A duplex feast.*

At Milan, St. Calimerius, bishop and martyr. He was seized in the persecution of Antonius, repeatedly stabbed, and his neck was run through with a sword. Flung headlong into a well, he completed the course of his martyrdom.

At Caesarea in Mauretania, the suffering of Blessed Fabius, martyr. He refused to carry the pagan ensign of the governor, and was cast into prison for some days. On being interrogated several times, he remained unmoved in confessing Christ, and was condemned by the judge to capital punishment.

At Synnada in Phrygia, the holy martyrs Democritus, Secundus and Dionysius.

In Syria, three hundred and fifty holy martyrs, monks, who, because they defended the Synod of Chalcedon, were slain by heretics.

At Ravenna, the passing of St. Germanus, Bishop of Auxerre. He was noble in birth, faith, learning, and glorious miracles, and he completely freed Britain from the heresy of the Pelagians. *A memory.*

At Tegaste in Africa, St. Firmus, bishop, celebrated for his glorious confession of faith.

At Siena in Tuscany, the birthday of Blessed John of Colombino, founder of the Congregation of the Jesuates, and famous for his holiness and miracles.

august

The First Day of August

At Rome, on the Esquiline Hill, the Dedication of the Church of St. Peter in Chains. *A totum duplex feast.*

At Antioch, the suffering of the seven holy brothers, the Machabees, with their mother, who suffered under King Antiochus Epiphanes. Their relics were taken to Rome and buried in the aforesaid Church of St. Peter in Chains. *A memory.*

At Vercelli, the birthday of St. Eusebius, bishop and martyr. For his confession of the Catholic faith, he was sent into exile by the Emperor Constantius to Scythopolis in Palestine, and from there to Cappadocia. He afterward returned to his Church and suffered martyrdom at the hands of the persecuting Arians. His memory is more especially honored on December 15, on which day he was ordained bishop. His feast is kept on December 16.

At Nocera de'Pagani in Campania (Italy), the birthday of St. Alphonsus Maria Liguori, founder of the Congregation of our most Holy Redeemer, bishop of Sant' Agata dei Goti, and confessor. He was noted for his zeal for souls, his writings and his example. The Sovereign Pontiff, Gregory XVI, canonized him, and Pius IX declared him to be a Doctor of the Universal Church. His festival, however, is observed on August 2.

At Rome, on the Via Latina, the holy martyrs Bonus, priest, Faustus and Maurus, with nine others, who are spoken of in the Acts of Pope St. Stephen.

Likewise at Rome, the suffering of the holy virgins Faith, Hope, and Charity, the children of St. Sophia. They obtained the crown of martyrdom under the Emperor Hadrian.

At Philadelphia in Arabia, the holy martyrs Cyril, Aquila, Peter, Domitian, Rufus, and Menander, crowned on the same day.

At Perge in Pamphylia, the holy martyrs Leontius, Attius, Alexander, and six other peasants, who were beheaded under the governor Flavian in Diocletian's persecution.

At Gerona in Spain, the birthday of St. Felix, martyr. After various kinds of tortures, he was ordered by Dacian to be mangled until he rendered up his unconquered spirit to Christ.

In the territory of Paris, St. Justin, martyr.

At Vienne in Gaul, St. Verus, bishop.

At Winchester in England, St. Ethelwold, bishop.

In the country of Lisieux in Gaul, St. Nemesius, confessor. ✠

The Second Day of August

St. Alphonsus Maria Liguori, founder of the Congregation of our Most Holy Redeemer, bishop of Sant' Agata dei Goti, confessor and Doctor of the Church, who died in the Lord on August 1. *A duplex feast.*

At Rome, in the cemetery of St. Callistus, the birthday of St. Stephen I, pope and martyr. In the persecution of Valerian, he was celebrating Mass when the soldiers arrived to arrest him. He remained at the altar, intrepid and unmoved, and finished the Sacred Mysteries he had begun. He was beheaded while he was sitting on his throne. *A memory.*

At Nicaea in Bithynia, the suffering of St. Theodota and her three sons. Nicetius the consul of Bithynia, seeing that Evodius the eldest confidently confessed Christ, ordered him to be beaten with clubs; then he commanded that the mother and all her sons should be burned alive.

In Africa, St. Rutilius, martyr. To escape persecution, he often fled from one place to another and sometimes even bought himself out of danger. He was unexpectedly arrested and brought to the governor. He was subjected to many tortures and finally, being delivered to the flames, he received the crown of an admirable martyrdom.

At Padua, St. Maximus, bishop of that city, who, famed for his miracles, died a blessed death.

The Third Day of August

At Lucera (in Italy), Blessed Augustine, bishop and confessor, of the Order of our Father St. Dominic. He was distinguished by his humility, patience, and kindness toward the poor. By his prayer, preaching, and the sanctity of his life, he completely reformed the diocese of Lucera which had been infected with the errors of the Saracens. *A semi-duplex feast.*

At Jerusalem, the finding of the relics of Blessed Stephen the Protomartyr, and SS. Gamaliel, Nicodemus and Abibo. Their location was divinely revealed to the priest Lucian, in the time of the Emperor Honorius. *A memory.*

At Philippi in Macedonia, St. Lydia, a seller of dyed cloth. In the Acts of the Apostles, St. Luke related that when St. Paul the apostle preached in that place, she was the first of all (his listeners) to believe in the Gospel.[1]

At Naples in Campania, St. Aspren, bishop, who was cured of an infirmity by St. Peter the Apostle. After his baptism, he was ordained bishop of that city.

At Constantinople, the birthday of St. Hermellus, martyr.

In India, near the Persian border, the suffering of certain holy monks and other Christians. King Abenner, persecuting the Church of God, commanded them to be punished with various tortures and slain.

At Autun, the death of St. Euphronius, bishop and confessor.

At Anagni, St. Peter, bishop. Renowned first for his monastic observance, and afterward for vigilance over his flock, he died in the Lord.

At Beroea in Syria, the holy women Marana and Cyra. ✠

The Fourth Day of August

At Bologna, our most holy Father St. Dominic, confessor and founder of the Order of Friars Preachers. He was most illustrious, being distinguished by nobility of birth, sanctity and learning. Until death he preserved without stain his virginity and by the singular grace of his merits he raised three persons from the dead. By his preaching he curbed heresies and established many persons in a religious and godly manner of life. On August 6, his soul soared to heaven, there to receive a reward commensurate with his extraordinary works. His feast, however, is celebrated on this day, by an ordinance of Pope Paul IV. *A totum duplex feast of the first class with a solemn octave.*

At Thessalonica, the birthday of St. Aristarchus, disciple and inseparable companion of St. Paul the Apostle. The latter wrote to the Corinthians: "Aristarchus my fellow-prisoner salutes you." [2] He was ordained Bishop of Thessalonica by the same Apostle and, after long trials under Nero, died and was crowned by Christ.

At Rome, St. Perpetua, who was baptized by St. Peter the Apostle. She converted her son Nazarius and her husband Africanus to the Christian faith and buried the bodies of a great number of martyrs. At length, rich in merit, she went to the Lord.

Likewise at Rome on the Via Latina, the suffering of Blessed Tertullinus, priest and martyr. At the time of the Emperor Valerian he suffered a cruel beating with clubs, the burning of his sides with fire, the

[1] Acts, 16:14–15.
[2] Philippians, 4:10.

breaking of his jaw, stretching on the rack, and the severing of his tendons. He completed his martyrdom by being beheaded.

At Constantinople, St. Eleutherius, martyr. Of senatorial rank, he was slain with the sword, in the persecution of Maximian, for the faith of Christ.

In Persia, the holy martyrs Ia and her companions, who, together with nine thousand Christian captives, suffered martyrdom under King Sapor after enduring various punishments.

At Verona, St. Agabius, bishop and confessor.

At Tours in Gaul, St. Euphronius, bishop.

At Cologne, the commemoration of St. Portase, martyr. In company with his brother Gervase, he suffered at Milan on June 19. ✠

The Fifth Day of August

At Rome, on the Esquiline Hill, the Dedication of the Basilica of Our Lady of the Snows. *A totum duplex feast.*

At Châlons-sur-Marne in Gaul, St. Memmius, a Roman citizen. He was consecrated bishop of that city by St. Peter the Apostle and converted to the Gospel the people assigned to his care.

At Rome, the suffering of twenty-three holy martyrs who, in the persecution of Diocletian, were beheaded on the old Via Salaria, and buried in the same place at Cucumer Hill.

At Ascoli in Piceno, St. Emidius, bishop and martyr. He was ordained bishop by Pope St. Marcellus, and sent there to preach the Gospel. He received the crown of martyrdom under the Emperor Diocletian for confessing Christ.

At Antioch, St. Eusignius, soldier. He was in his one hundred and tenth year when he rebuked Julian the Apostate for having given up the faith of Constantine the Great under whom he had fought. He charged Julian with having deserted the faith of his fathers. For this the Emperor ordered him to be beheaded.

Likewise the holy martyrs Cantidius, Cantidian, and Sobel, all Egyptians.

At Augsburg, the birthday of St. Afra, martyr. She was converted from paganism to Christ by the teaching of St. Narcissus, bishop. After being baptized with all her household, she was burned alive for confessing Christ. Seven days afterwards, her mother Hilaria and three handmaids were also crowned by enduring the same kind of suffering.

At Autun, Blessed Cassian, bishop.

At Teano in Campania (Italy), St. Paris, bishop.

In England, King St. Oswald, whose deeds St. Bede the Venerable commemorates.

On the same day, St. Nonna, mother of SS. Gregory Nazianzen, Caesarius, and Gorgonia.

The Sixth Day of August

On Mount Thabor, the Transfiguration of our Lord Jesus Christ. *A totum duplex feast of the second class.*

At Rome, on the Appian Way, in the cemetery of Callistus, the birthday of Blessed Sixtus II, pope and martyr. He was put to the sword in the persecution of Valerian, and received the crown of martyrdom.

Likewise at Rome, SS. Felicissimus and Agapitus, martyrs, deacons of the same St. Sixtus, and the subdeacons Januarius, Magnus, Vincent and Stephen. All were beheaded together with Sixtus and buried in the cemetery of Praetextatus. Blessed Quartus suffered also with them, as St. Cyprian declares. *A memory.*

At Bologna, the birthday of St. Dominic, confessor and founder of the Order of Friars Preachers. He was a man of great renown for holiness and learning. Until death he preserved without stain his virginity, and by the singular grace of his merits raised three dead men to life. By his preaching he curbed heresies, and established many persons in a religious and godly manner of life. He died on this day, but his festival, by an ordinance of Pope Paul IV, is celebrated on August 4.

At Burgos in Spain, in the Benedictine monastery of St. Peter of Cardegna, the suffering of two hundred monks and their abbot Stephen. They were slain by the Saracens for the faith, and buried there in the cloister by the Christians.

At Alcalá de Henares in Spain, the holy martyrs Justus and Pastor, brothers. The two boys were still learning the elements in school, when they threw aside their books and of their own accord hurried to gain martyrdom. Soon they were seized by the governor Dacian and beaten with clubs. As they firmly exhorted each other to constancy, they were taken outside the city by the executioner and strangled.

At Rome, St. Hormisdas, pope and confessor.

At Amida in Mesopotamia, St. James, hermit, renowned for miracles.

The Seventh Day of August

At Naples in Campania, St. Cajetan of Thienna, confessor, founder of the Clerks Regular. With remarkable confidence in God, he enjoined on his followers the primitive manner of life of the Apostles. Renowned for miracles, Pope Clement X enrolled him among the saints. *A duplex feast.*

At Arezzo in Tuscany, the birthday of St. Donatus, bishop and martyr. Among his other miraculous deeds, Pope St. Gregory narrates, he restored by his prayer a holy chalice broken by the heathens. In the persecution of Julian the Apostate, he was arrested by the imperial officer Quadratianus and, as he refused to offer sacrifice to idols, he gained martyrdom, being put to the sword. There suffered also with him blessed Hilarinus, a monk, whose memory is kept on July 16, when his body was taken to Ostia. *A memory.*

At Rome, the holy martyrs Peter and Julian, with eighteen others.

At Milan, St. Faustus, soldier, who after many trials obtained the palm of martyrdom under Aurelius Commodus.

At Como (in Italy), the suffering of the holy martyrs Carpophorus, Exanthus, Cassius, Severinus, Secundus, and Licinius, who were beheaded for confessing Christ.

At Nisibis in Mesopotamia, St. Dometius, a Persian monk, who with two disciples was stoned to death at the time of Julian the Apostate.

At Rouen, St. Victricius, bishop. While still a soldier, under the same Julian, he cast away his military insignia for the sake of Christ. He was subjected by his tribune to many tortures, and condemned to death, but the executioner sent to slay him was stricken with blindness and, his chains being loosed, he escaped. Afterwards he was made a bishop, and by the preaching of the Gospel led the unconquered tribes of the Morini and the Nervi to believe in Christ. He died a peaceful death.

At Châlons-sur-Marne in Gaul, St. Donatian, bishop.

At Messina in Sicily, St. Albert, a confessor of the Carmelite Order, noted for miracles. ✠

The Eighth Day of August

At Peñafiel in Spain, Blessed Joan de Aza, mother of the most Blessed Patriarch Dominic. Admirable for her virtue and beloved of God for her piety, she died at Calaruega in the love of the Lord. *A duplex feast.*

The holy martyrs Cyriacus, deacon, Largus, and Smaragdus, with twenty others, who suffered on March 16. Their bodies were buried on the Via Salaria by a priest named John, and on this day Pope St. Marcellus removed them to the garden of Lucina, on the Via Ostiensis. Afterward, they were brought into the city, and buried in the deaconry of St. Mary's *in Via Lata. A memory.*

At Anazarbus in Cilicia, St. Marinus, an old man. At the time of the Emperor Diocletian and the governor Lysias, he was flogged, then suspended (from a beam) and mangled. He was at last cast to the beasts, and died.

Likewise the holy martyrs Eleutherius and Leonides, who completed martyrdom by fire.

In Persia, St. Hormisdas, martyr, in the reign of King Sapor.

At Cyzicus in the Hellespont, St. Aemilian, bishop. At the hands of the Emperor Leo, he suffered much for his defending the veneration of holy images. His life was ended in exile.

In Crete, St. Myron, bishop, famed for miracles.

At Vienne in Gaul, St. Severus, priest and confessor. He undertook a wearisome journey from India in order to preach the Gospel, and coming to Vienne, he converted a huge multitude of heathens to the faith of Christ by his preaching and miracles. ✠

The Ninth Day of August

The Vigil of St. Laurence, martyr.

At Florence (in Italy), Blessed John of Salerno, confessor, of our Order. He received the religious habit from the holy Patriarch Dominic and emulated his virtues. Sent to propagate our Order in Etruria, he labored greatly for the faith at Florence, especially by his preaching against the heretical Patarines. *A semi-duplex feast.*

At Rome, St. Romanus, soldier and martyr. Moved by the confession of faith of St. Laurence, he begged to be baptized by him, and was forthwith seized, beaten with clubs, and at last beheaded.

In Tuscany, the birthday of the holy martyrs Secundian, Marcellian, and Verian. In the time of Decius, by order of Promotus the proconsul, they were first scourged, then stretched on the rack, and torn with iron hooks. Then fire was applied to their sides. They merited the triumphal palm of martyrdom by being beheaded.

At Verona, the holy martyrs Firmus and Rusticus. At the time of the Emperor Maximian, under the judge Anolinus, they refused to sacrifice to idols and remained firm in confessing Christ. After they had endured many other tortures, they were beaten with clubs and beheaded.

In Africa, the commemoration of many holy martyrs. In the persecution of Valerian they were cast into the fire, and with Numidicus encouraging them obtained the palm of martyrdom. But Numidicus himself, although he was cast into the pyre with the others and then overwhelmed with stones, was dug out by his daughter who found he was still alive. He recovered, and afterward by reason of his virtues merited to be chosen for the office of the priesthood in the Church of Carthage by St. Cyprian.

At Constantinople, the holy martyrs Julian, Marcian, and eight others. Because they had set up an image of the Saviour at the Bronze Gate (of the city), all of them underwent many tortures by command of the Emperor Leo and then were slain by the sword.

At Châlons-sur-Marne in Gaul, St. Domitian, bishop and confessor. ✠

The Tenth Day of August

At Rome on the Via Tiburtina, the birthday of St. Laurence, archdeacon. In the persecution of Valerian, he endured the many tortures of the prison and beatings with clubs and leaded whips. Red-hot metal plates were applied to his body. At last, he was roasted on a gridiron and thus completed his martyrdom. His body was buried in the cemetery of Cyriaca in the Veranus field by St. Hippolytus and the priest Justin. *A totum duplex feast of the second class.*

In Spain, the apparition of the Blessed Virgin Mary of Mercy, foundress of the Order for the Redemption of Captives established in her name. Her festival is observed on September 24.

At Rome, the suffering of one hundred and sixty-five soldiers, martyrs, under Aurelian the Emperor.

At Alexandria, the commemoration of the holy martyrs who in the persecution of Valerian, under Emilian the governor, were long tormented with various and exquisite tortures; they obtained the crown of martyrdom by different kinds of death.

At Bergamo, St. Asteria, virgin and martyr, in the persecution of the Emperors Diocletian and Maximian.

At Carthage, the holy virgins and martyrs Bassa, Paula, and Agathonica.

At Rome, St. Deusdedit, confessor. What he had earned during the week by the labor of his hands, he gave on Saturday to the poor.

The Eleventh Day of August

The Octave day of our holy Father Dominic. *A solemn octave.*

At Rome, between the two laurel trees, the birthday of St. Tiburtius, martyr. In the persecution of Diocletian, under Fabian the judge, he was made to walk with bare feet on burning coals. As he confessed Christ all the more firmly, he was led to the third milestone from the city and killed by the sword. *A memory.*

Likewise at Rome, St. Susanna, virgin. She was born of a noble family, and was the niece of Pope St. Caius. She obtained the palm of martyrdom in the time of Diocletian by being beheaded.

At Assisi in Umbria, the birthday of St. Clare, virgin. She was the first of the Poor Ladies of the Order of Friars Minor. Renowned for her life and miracles, she was canonized by Pope Alexander IV. Her festival, however, is kept on August 12.

At Comana in Pontus, St. Alexander, bishop, surnamed the Charcoal-burner.[3] A learned philosopher, he became proficient in the eminent science of Christian humility, and was raised up by St. Gregory the Wonderworker to the throne of that Church. He was illustrious not only for his preaching, but also for his martyrdom by fire.

On the same day, the suffering of St. Rufinus, Bishop of the Marsi,[4] and his companions, under the Emperor Maximin.

At Evreux in Gaul, St. Taurinus, bishop. He was ordained bishop of that city by Pope St. Clement, and spread abroad the Christian faith by his preaching of the Gospel. After sustaining many labors in that work, he died in the Lord, noteworthy for glorious miracles.

At Cambrai in Gaul, St. Gaugericus, bishop and confessor.

In the province of Valeria (in Italy), St. Equitius, abbot, whose holiness is approved by the testimony of Pope St. Gregory.

At Todi in Umbria (Italy), St. Digna, virgin.

The Twelfth Day of August

(At Assisi), St. Clare, virgin, the first of the Poor Ladies of the Order of Friars Minor. She was called to the everlasting nuptials of the Lamb on August 11. *A duplex feast.*

On the same day, the holy martyrs Porcarius, Abbot of the monastery of Lerins, and five hundred monks. They were slain for the Catholic faith by the heathens, and so were crowned with martyrdom.

At Catania in Sicily, the birthday of St. Euplius, deacon. In the reign of the Emperors Diocletian and Maximian, he was tortured for a long time for confessing the Lord, and at last obtained the palm of martyrdom by the sword.

At Augsburg, St. Hilaria. Because of her faith in Christ, she was keeping a vigil at the grave of her daughter St. Afra. On that very spot, the persecutors burned her to death. With her there were martyred her maids, Digna, Euprepia, and Eunomia. Also on the same day and in the same city, there suffered Quiriacus, Largius, Crescentian, Nimmia, and Juliana, with twenty others.

---

[3] Alexander gave away his wealth and became a charcoal-burner in order to practise humility. Hence his nickname.

[4] See note for March 14.

In Syria, the holy martyrs Macarius and Julian.

At Nicomedia, the holy martyrs Count Anicetus and his brother Photinus, with many others, in the reign of the Emperor Diocletian.

At Faleria in Tuscany, the suffering of St. Gracilian and the virgin St. Felicissima. For their confessing the faith, their faces were pounded with rocks. Then they were slain by the sword and so obtained the palm of martyrdom they desired.

At Milan, the death of St. Eusebius, bishop and confessor.

At Brescia, St. Herculanus, bishop. ✠

The Thirteenth Day of August

At Rome, Blessed Hippolytus, martyr. So glorious was his confession of faith, in the reign of the Emperor Valerian, that after the usual torments had been inflicted, his feet were tied to the necks of wild horses. Then he was cruelly dragged through briars and brambles until he died, his whole body having been torn to shreds. On the same day, Blessed Concordia, his nurse also suffered. Flogged with lead-tipped whips, she died ahead of him. Also nineteen others of his household were beheaded outside the Tiburtine Gate. All were buried with Hippolytus in the Veranian field. *A feast of three lessons.*

At Imola (in Italy), the birthday of St. Cassian, martyr. Because he refused to worship idols, the persecutor summoned those pupils to whom he had become hateful while teaching them, and gave them permission to kill St. Cassian. Although their hands were weak, the agony of the martyrdom was all the greater, being so long drawn out.

At Todi in Umbria, St. Cassian, bishop and martyr, under the Emperor Diocletian.

At Burgos in Spain, SS. Centolla and Helen, martyrs.

At Constantinople, St. Maximus, abbot, famous for his learning and zeal for Catholic truth. He fought strenuously against the Monothelites, and for that reason his hands and tongue were cut off by the heretical Emperor Constans. He was exiled to the Chersonese, and died there, celebrated for his glorious profession of faith. At that time, two of his disciples, both named Anastasius, and many others, also suffered various tortures and bitter exile.

At Tritzlar in Germany, St. Wigbert, priest and confessor.

At Rome, the birthday of St. John Berchmans, a scholastic of the Society of Jesus, confessor. He was noted for his innocence of life and careful observance of religious discipline. He was canonized by the Sovereign Pontiff, Leo XIII.

At Poitiers in Gaul, St. Radegund, queen, whose life was resplendent with miracles and virtues.

The Fourteenth Day of August

The Vigil of the Assumption of the Blessed Virgin Mary.

At Rome, the birthday of Blessed Eusebius, priest and confessor. He was imprisoned in a small room of his house by the Arian Emperor Constantius, for defending the Catholic faith. Persevering continually in prayer, he remained there (a prisoner) for seven months until he died. Two priests, Gregory and Orosius, took his body and buried it in the cemetery of Callistus on the Appian Way. *A memory.*

At Apamea in Syria, St. Marcellus, bishop and martyr. He broke to pieces a shrine of Jupiter and was slain by the outraged heathens.

At Todi in Umbria, St. Callistus, bishop and martyr.

In Illyria, St. Ursicius, martyr. After many and various torments he was slain with the sword for Christ's name, under Maximian the Emperor and Aristides the governor.

In Africa, St. Demetrius, martyr.

On the island of Aegina, St. Athanasia, widow, famous for her observance of the monastic life and for the grace of miracles.

The Fifteenth Day of August

The Assumption of the Most Holy Virgin Mary, Mother of God. *A totum duplex feast of the first class with a solemn octave.*

At Cracow in Poland, the birthday of St. Hyacinth, confessor, of the Order of Preachers, whom the Sovereign Pontiff Clement VIII canonized. His feast is kept on August 17.

At Albareale in Hungary, St. Stephen, King of Hungary. He was adorned with divine virtues, and was the first to convert the Hungarians to the faith of Christ. He was received into heaven by the Virgin Mother of God on the very day of her Assumption. His feast is kept, by an ordinance of Pope Innocent XI, on September 2, on which day the strongly-fortified city of Buda, by the aid of the holy King, was recaptured by the Christian army.

At Rome, on the Appian Way, St. Tarsicius, acolyte. The heathens detected him bearing the Sacrament of the Body of Christ, and asked what it was that he carried. But he deemed it an unworthy thing to cast pearls before swine, and was therefore attacked by them for a long time with clubs and stones, until he died. When his body was searched, the sacrilegious assailants could find nothing of Christ's Sacrament in his hands or among his clothing. The Christians gathered up the body of the martyr, and buried it with honor in the cemetery of Callistus.

At Tagaste in Africa, St. Alipius, bishop. He had formerly been a disciple of St. Augustine, and afterwards his fellow-convert. He was also his colleague in the pastoral office, his zealous fellow-worker in his contest against the heretics, and lastly his associate in heavenly glory.

At Soissons in Gaul, St. Arnulf, bishop and confessor.

At Rome, the holy Polish confessor St. Stanislaus Kostka, a novice of the Society of Jesus. He was made perfect in a short time, and is everywhere renowned for his angelic innocence of life. He was numbered among the saints by the Sovereign Pontiff, Benedict XIII.

The Sixteenth Day of August

St. Joachim, father of the Most Blessed Virgin Mary, Mother of God. His birthday is noted on March 20. *A totum duplex feast of the second class.*

At Rome, St. Titus, deacon, who, when the city was occupied by the Goths, distributed his wealth to the poor, and was commanded by a heathen tribune to be slain.

At Nicaea in Bithynia, St. Diomede, physician, who, in the persecution of Diocletian was slain with the sword for the faith of Christ, and so fulfilled his martyrdom.

In Palestine, thirty-three holy martyrs.

At Ferentino in the Hernican mountains, St. Ambrose the centurion. He was tortured in various ways in the persecution of Diocletian. When he passed through the fire unhurt, he was finally drowned and thus reached eternal rest.

At Milan, the death of St. Simplician, bishop, made famous by the testimony of SS. Ambrose and Augustine.

At Auxerre (in Gaul), St. Eleutherius, bishop.

At Nicomedia, St. Arsacius, confessor. In the persecution of Licinius, he forsook the life of a soldier and lived as a solitary. He was adorned with so many virtues that he is said to have cast out demons and by prayer to have slain a huge snake. At last, after foretelling the future destruction of the city, he died while at prayer.

At Montpellier in Gaul, the death of St. Roch, confessor. He freed many towns of Italy from the plague by the sign of the cross. His body was later taken to Venice, and buried with great honor in the church consecrated under his name.

At Rome, St. Serena, once the wife of the Emperor Diocletian.

The Seventeenth Day of August

The Octave of St. Laurence, martyr. *A memory.*

At Cracow in Poland, St. Hyacinth, confessor, of the Order of Preachers. Having received the religious habit from the hands of our Father St. Dominic, he excelled in learning and in a life of admirable innocence. He was celebrated for the glory of his miracles, especially for walking dryshod across wide rivers. Thought deserving of sweet converse with the holy Mother of God, distinguished for his spotless life, and filled with the gifts of the Holy Ghost, he died at an advanced age. He was called to his eternal reward on the very feastday of the Assumption of the Blessed Virgin Mary. He was canonized by Pope Clement VIII. *A totum duplex feast of the second class.*

At Carthage in Africa, the holy martyrs Liberatus, abbot, Boniface, a deacon, Servus and Rusticus, subdeacons, Rogatus and Septimus, monks, and the boy Maximus. In the Vandal persecution under King Hunneric, they were subjected to various unheard-of tortures for confessing the Catholic faith and defending one baptism. Last of all, they were nailed to the planks with which they were to be burned. Although the fire was kindled again and again, every time it was miraculously extinguished. By the command of the King, they then were slain by being beaten with the handles of oars until their brains were dashed out. Thus, crowned by the Lord, they fulfilled the remarkable course of their trial.

In Achaia, St. Myron, priest and martyr, who was beheaded at Cyzicus after many tortures, at the time of the Emperor Decius and the governor Antipater.

At Caesarea in Cappadocia, the birthday of St. Mamas, martyr, the son of SS. Theodotus and Rufina, martyrs. Under the governor Alexander, at the command of Aurelian, he suffered a prolonged martyrdom from childhood to old age, and at length happily completed it. The holy fathers Basil and Gregory Nazianzen celebrated him with great praise.

At Nicomedia, the holy martyrs Strato, Philip, and Eutychian. They were condemned to the beasts, but, remaining unhurt, their martyrdom was finished by fire.

At Ptolemais in Palestine, the suffering of the holy martyrs Paul and his sister Juliana, virgin. In the reign of the Emperor Aurelian, they were both punished with various cruel tortures and finally beheaded for their constancy in confessing the name of Christ.

At Rome, St. Eusebius, pope.

At Teramo (in Italy), St. Anastasius, bishop and confessor.

At Montefalco in Umbria, the virgin St. Clare, nun of the Order of Hermits of St. Augustine. On her heart, which the faithful honor with great devotion, were renewed the mysteries of the Lord's passion. The

Sovereign Pontiff, Leo XIII solemnly inscribed her in the list of the holy virgins.

The Eighteenth Day of August

At Savigliano in Piedmont, Blessed Aimo Taparelli, confessor, of our Order. He was outstanding by the holiness of his life, his learning, and his prolonged and extraordinary labors for the preservation of the Catholic faith. He was taken to Heaven on the Feast of the Assumption of the Mother of God, for whom he had an extraordinary devotion. *A semi-duplex feast.*

At Palestrina (in Italy), St. Agapitus, martyr. He was only fifteen years old but already fervent in the love of God when he was arrested by order of the Emperor Aurelian. He was savagely flogged with raw sinews. Later, under the governor Antiochus, he underwent more grievous sufferings. Then, by command of the Emperor, he was thrown to the lions. When these did not harm him, he was put to the sword and thus gained his crown. *A memory.*

At Rome, blessed John and Crispus, priests. In the persecution of Diocletian, they dutifully buried the bodies of many saints. Later, they themselves shared with them the merit of martyrdom and thus procured for themselves the joys of life eternal.

Also at Rome, the holy martyrs Hermas, Serapion, and Polyaenus, who were dragged through narrow, rocky, and rough places until they rendered up their souls to God.

In Illyria, the holy martyrs Florus and Laurus, stone-cutters. When their masters Proculus and Maximus had met their deaths by martyrdom under the governor Lician, they themselves were, after many sufferings, drowned in a deep well.

At Myra in Lycia, the holy martyrs Leo and Juliana.

At Metz in Gaul, St. Firminus, bishop and confessor.

At Rome, on the Via Lavicana, St. Helen, the mother of that religious emperor, Constantine the Great. He was the first to show to other princes an excellent example of the manner in which the Church should be protected and multiplied.

The Nineteenth Day of August

At Vercelli (in Italy), the holy virgin Emily Bicchieri, a nun of our Order, who, living in prayer, was inflamed with the desire of experiencing the sufferings of Christ. *A semi-duplex feast.*

At Rome, St. Julius, senator and martyr. He was given over to the judge Vitellius, who cast him into prison. At the command of the Emperor Commodus, he was beaten with clubs until he died. His body is buried in the cemetery of Calepodius on the Via Aurelia.

At Anagni, St. Magnus, bishop and martyr, who was slain in the persecution of Decius.

In Cilicia, the birthday of the tribune St. Andrew, and his fellow-soldiers. When a victory had been obtained by divine power over the Persians, Andrew and his companions were converted to the faith of Christ. In the reign of the Emperor Maximian, having been accused of being Christians, they were slain in a pass of Mount Taurus by the army of the governor Seleucus.

In Palestine, St. Timothy, martyr. In the persecution of Diocletian, under the governor Urban, Timothy was burned alive after he had endured many tortures. Thecla and Agapius suffered at the same place. The former was exposed to the beasts and, torn by their teeth, passed to her heavenly Spouse; but Agapius, after suffering many tortures, was reserved for greater trials.[5]

At Rome, St. Sixtus III, pope and confessor.

In Provence, at the village of Brignoles, the death of St. Louis, Bishop of Toulouse, of the Order of Friars Minor. He was a man renowned for holiness of life and for his miracles. His body was taken to Marseilles and honorably buried in the Church of the Friars Minor; afterward it was taken to Valencia in Spain and enshrined in the cathedral.

Near Sisteron in Gaul, Blessed Donatus, priest and confessor. From his earliest years he was wondrously endowed with God's grace, and led for many years the life of a hermit. He went to Heaven renowned for glorious miracles.

In the neighborhood of Bourges, St. Marianus, confessor. St. Gregory, Bishop of Tours, highly praised his virtues and miracles.

At Mantua, St. Rufinus, confessor.

The Twentieth Day of August

In the country of Langres, the death of St. Bernard, first Abbot of Clairvaux, glorious in his life, teaching and miracles. The Sovereign Pontiff, Pius VIII, declared and confirmed that he was a Doctor of the Universal Church. *A duplex feast.*

At Monte Senario in Etruria, the birthday of St. Manettus, confessor, one of the seven founders of the Order of the Servants of the Blessed

[5] See his entry under November 20.

Virgin Mary. He died as he was repeating a hymn to her. His feast, with that of his companions, is kept on February 12.

In Judea, St. Samuel the Prophet, whose holy relics (as St. Jerome writes), Arcadius the Emperor transferred to Constantinople, and buried near Septimum.

On the island of Cyprus, St. Lucius, a senator. He was converted to the faith of Christ by seeing the constancy of Theodore, Bishop of Cyrene, in his martyrdom. He also led to the faith Dignian the governor, with whom he went to Cyprus, where he saw other Christians crowned for confessing the Lord. He willingly offered himself and merited the same crown of martyrdom by beheading.

In Thrace, thirty-seven holy martyrs who, under the governor Apellian, were cast into a burning furnace for the Christian faith, after their hands and feet had been cut off.

In the same place, the holy martyrs, Severus and Memnon the centurion, who obtained their martyrdom by a similar death, and went as victors to heaven.

At Cordoba in Spain, the holy martyrs Leovigild and Christopher, monks. They were cast into prison for their defense of the Christian faith during the persecution of the Arabs. After their necks were broken, they were burned alive and thus obtained the crown of martyrdom.

On the island of Her (off the coast of Poitou), St. Philibert, abbot.

At Rome, Blessed Porphyry, who was a man of God. He taught the martyr St. Agapitus the faith and doctrine of Christ.

In the village of Chinon in Gaul, St. Maximus, confessor, a disciple of the Blessed Bishop Martin.

The Twenty-first Day of August

St. Jane Frances Fremiot de Chantal, foundress of the Order of the Nuns of the Visitation of St. Mary, whose birthday is mentioned on December 13. *A duplex feast.*

At Rome, in the Veranus field, St. Cyriaca, widow and martyr. In the persecution of Valerian, she bestowed all her goods and her time in ministering to the saints. Then she freely gave her life also, undergoing martyrdom for the sake of Christ.

In the country of Gevaudan (in Gaul), St. Privatus, bishop and martyr, who suffered in the persecution of Valerian and Gallienus.

At Salona in Dalmatia, St. Anastasius, a law officer. Seeing Blessed Agapitus enduring his torments with constancy, he was converted to the faith. He was slain at the command of Aurelian the Emperor for confessing Christ's name, and passed to the Lord a martyr.

In Sardinia, the birthday of the holy martyrs Luxorius, Cisellus, and Camerinus, who were slain with the sword, under Delphius the governor, in the persecution of Diocletian.

On the same day, the holy martyrs Bonosus and Maximian.

At Fundi in Latium, St. Paternus, martyr. He had come from Alexandria to Rome to visit the tombs of the Apostles. Departing thence to Fundi, he was seized by the tribune for burying the bodies of the martyrs, and died in chains.

At Edessa in Syria, the holy martyrs Bassa and her three sons, Theogonius, Agapius, and Fidelis. In Maximian's persecution, their holy mother encouraged them and sent them before herself with their crowns of martyrdom. She herself was beheaded and joyfully followed them to the victory.

At Verona, St. Euprepius, bishop and confessor.

Likewise, St. Quadratus, bishop.

In Auvergne in Gaul, St. Sidonius, bishop, noteworthy for learning and holiness.

At Siena in Tuscany, Blessed Bernard Ptolomei, abbot, founder of the Congregation of Olivetans.

The Twenty-second Day of August

The Octave of the Assumption of the Blessed Virgin Mary. *A solemn octave.*

The Feast of the Immaculate Heart of the same Blessed Virgin Mary. *A totum duplex feast of the second class.*

At Rome, on the Via Ostia, the birthday of St. Timothy, martyr. He was arrested by Tarquin, prefect of the city, and suffered a long imprisonment because he refused to sacrifice to idols. He was scourged on three occasions and, after passing through the most painful tortures, was at last beheaded.

At Autun, St. Symphorian, martyr. In the reign of the Emperor Aurelian, he refused to offer sacrifice to idols; (for this) he was first beaten and then imprisoned. He at last completed his martyrdom by being beheaded. *A memory.*

At Portus Romanus, St. Hippolytus, bishop, a man of great renown for his learning. Under the Emperor Alexander, for his noble confession of the faith, his hands and feet were tied and he was thrown into a deep pit full of water, thus receiving the palm of martyrdom. His body was buried by the Christians at the same place.

At Todi in Umbria, the birthday of the Florentine St. Philip Benizi, confessor. He was a zealous promoter of the Order of the Servants of the

Blessed Virgin Mary, and was a man of great humility. The Sovereign Pontiff, Clement X, added his name to the list of the saints. His festival, however, is observed on August 23.

At Rome, St. Antoninus, martyr. He loudly declared himself to be a Christian, and was condemned by the judge Vitellius to capital punishment. He was buried on the Via Aurelia by Rufinus, a priest.

At Tarsus in Cilicia, the commemoration of the holy martyrs Athanasius, bishop, Anthusa, a noble lady whom he had baptized, and also her two servants Charisius and Neophytus. All of them suffered in the reign of the Emperor Valerian.

At Portus Romanus, the holy martyrs Martial, Saturninus, Epictetus, Maprilis, and Felix, with their companions.

At Nicomedia, the suffering of the holy martyrs Agathonicus, Zoticus, and their companions, under the Emperor Aurelian and the governor Eutholmius.

At Rheims in Gaul, the holy martyrs Maurus and his companions.

In Spain, the holy martyrs Fabrician and Philibert.

At Pavia (in Italy), St. Gunifort, martyr.

The Twenty-third Day of August

The Vigil of St. Bartholomew the Apostle.

At Mevania in Umbria, the birthday of the Blessed James, confessor, of the Order of Preachers. He put an end to the rebirth of the heresy of the Nicolaites in Umbria and he was renowned for many miracles. *A semiduplex feast.*

(At Todi), St. Philip Benizi, confessor, promoter of the Order of the Servants of Blessed Virgin Mary. He departed to the Lord on August 22.

At Ostia, the holy martyrs Quiriacus, bishop, Maximus, priest, Archelaus, deacon, and their companions, who suffered in the time of Alexander, under Ulpian the prefect.

At Antioch, the birthday of the holy martyrs Restitutus, Donatus, Valerian, and Fructuosa, with twelve others, who were crowned with the most noble honor of confessing the faith.

At Aegaea in Cilicia, the holy martyrs Claudius, Asterius, and Neon, brothers. They were accused of being Christians by their stepmother. At the time of the Emperor Diocletian and the governor Lysias, they were nailed to a cross, after severe tortures, and triumphed as victors with Christ. After them suffered Donvina and Theonilla.

At Rheims in Gaul, the birthday of SS. Timothy and Apollinaris, who, having completed their martyrdom there, merited a heavenly kingdom.

At Lyons in Gaul, the holy martyrs Minervus and Eleazar, with his eight sons.

Likewise, St. Luppus, martyr. Though he was a slave, he was endowed with the liberty of Christ, and was deemed worthy to the crown of martyrdom.

At Jerusalem, St. Zachaeus, bishop, who ruled the Church of Jerusalem; he was the fourth bishop (of that Church) after St. James the Apostle.

At Alexandria, St. Theonas, bishop and confessor.

At Utica in Africa, Blessed Victor, bishop.

At Autun (in Gaul), St. Flavian, bishop.

The Twenty-fourth Day of August

St. Bartholomew the Apostle, who preached the Gospel of Christ in India; he then went into Greater Armenia. When he had converted many people there to the faith, he was flayed alive by the barbarians, and by command of King Astyages he fulfilled his martyrdom by being beheaded. His holy body was taken first to the Isle of Lipari, then to Benevento, and lastly to Rome, to the island in the Tiber, where it is honored with pious veneration by the faithful. *A totum duplex feast of the second class.*

At Lima in Peru, the birthday of St. Rose of St. Mary, virgin, of the Third Order of St. Dominic. Her festival is observed on August 30.

At Nepi (in Italy), St. Ptolemy, bishop, disciple of St. Peter the Apostle, by whom he was sent into Tuscany to preach the Gospel. He died at Nepi, a glorious martyr for Christ.

On the same day, St. Eutychius, who was a disciple of St. John the Evangelist. For his preaching the Gospel in many countries, he endured imprisonment, scourging, and fire, but finally died a peaceful death.

At Nepi, St. Romanus, bishop of that city. He was both a disciple of St. Ptolemy and a companion in his suffering.

At Carthage, three hundred holy martyrs, at the time of Valerian and Gallienus. The governor ordered to be prepared—among other tortures —a crater of burning lime, and also, in his presence, some coals and incense (for offering sacrifice). Then he said to these magnanimous Christians: "Choose one of these two things: either offer incense on these coals to Jupiter, or be plunged into the lime." The Christians, armed by their faith and proclaiming their belief that Christ is the Son of God, were moved by a sudden impulse and cast themselves into the fiery mass. They were soon burned to ashes in the smoking lime. Hence, this white-robed army of blesseds merited to be called the White Mass (*Massa Candida*).[6]

[6] See note to St. Apollonia, February 9.

In Isauria, St. Tation, martyr, who received a crown of martyrdom, being slain with the sword in the persecution of Diocletian, under the governor Urban.

Likewise, St. George Limniota, monk, who reproved the wicked Emperor Leo for breaking the holy images and burning the relics of the saints. At the latter's command, his hands were cut off and his head burned; he thus went as a martyr to the Lord.

At Ostia, on the Tiber, St. Aurea, virgin and martyr, who was drowned in the sea with a stone tied to her neck. Blessed Nonnus buried her body when it was washed up on the shore.

At Rouen, St. Ouen, bishop and confessor.

At Nevers in Gaul, St. Patrick, abbot.

The Twenty-fifth Day of August

At Carthage, St. Louis IX, King of France and confessor, illustrious for holiness of life and glorious miracles. His bones were later taken to Paris. *A duplex feast.*

At Rome, the birthday of St. Joseph Calasanctius, priest and confessor, noteworthy for his holy life and miracles. He founded the Order of Poor Clerks Regular of the Mother of God of the Christian Schools. His festival is observed on August 27.

Also at Rome, the holy martyrs Eusbius, Pontian, Vincent, and Peregrinus. Under the Emperor Commodus, they were first placed on the rack and stretched with ropes. Then they were beaten with clubs and their sides burnt with fire. Since they faithfully continued to the end to praise Christ, they were beaten with leaden-tipped whips until they died.

Also at Rome, the birthday of Blessed Nemesius, deacon, and the virgin Lucilla, his daughter. They were beheaded by command of the Emperor Valerian because they could not be turned from the faith of Christ. Their bodies were buried by Pope St. Stephen, and later interred in a more fitting tomb by St. Sixtus II on the Appian Way, on October 31. Gregory V removed them to the deaconry of Santa Maria Novella, together with SS. Symphronius, Olympius the tribune, Exuperia his wife, and his son Theodolus. The last three were converted by the help of Symphronius, baptized by the same Pope Stephen, and crowned with martyrdom. The bodies of these saints were found there in the pontificate of Gregory XIII, and more honorably laid to rest under the altar of the said church on December 8.

Likewise at Rome, St. Genesius, martyr. At first he had been an actor while he was still a gentile. He was mocking the Christian mysteries in the theatre in the presence of the Emperor Diocletian when, suddenly, inspired by God, he was converted to the faith and baptized. Forthwith by the Emperor's command he was cruelly beaten with clubs, then stretched upon the rack, tortured by the long-continued tearing of his flesh with hooks, and lastly burned with torches. But he continued in the faith of Christ, saying: "There is no King but Christ, and though I be slain a thousand times for Him, yet you cannot take Him from my life or from my heart." Finally, he merited the palm of martyrdom by being beheaded.

At Arles in Gaul, another blessed Genesius. By profession he was a notary. He refused to transcribe the impious edicts whereby the Christians were ordered to be punished and, casting away his books, publicly proclaimed himself a Christian. He was arrested and beheaded, and received the glory of martyrdom, being baptized in his own blood.

In Syria, St. Julian, martyr.

At Tarragona in Spain, St. Maginus, martyr.

At Talco in Spain, St. Geruntius, bishop, who preached the Gospel in that province in the time of the Apostles, and after many labors died in prison.

At Constantinople, St. Mennas, bishop.

At Utrecht, St. Gregory, bishop.

At Monte Falisco in Etruria, St. Thomas, Bishop of the Church of Hereford in England, and confessor.

At Naples in Campania, St. Patricia, virgin.

The Twenty-sixth Day of August

At Rome, St. Zephyrinus, pope and martyr, whose birthday falls on December 20.

At Cardona in Spain, the birthday of St. Raymond Nonnatus, cardinal and confessor, of the Order of our Lady of Mercy for the Redemption of Captives. He was renowned for holiness of life and for miracles. His feast is kept on August 31.

At Rome, the holy martyrs Irenaeus and Abundius. During the persecution of Valerian, they had taken the body of St. Concordia from the sewer in which she had been cast. For doing this, they themselves were drowned in the same sewer. Their bodies were recovered by the priest Justin and buried in a crypt near St. Laurence.

At Ventimiglia, a city of Liguria, St. Secundus, martyr, a noteworthy man, and a commander of the Theban legion.

At Bergamo in Lombardy, St. Alexander, martyr, who was also a soldier of that legion. He confessed with great firmness the name of the Lord Jesus Christ, and fulfilled his martyrdom by being beheaded.

Among the Marsians (in Central Italy),[7] SS. Simplicius and his sons Constantius and Victorian. Under the Emperor Antoninus, they were first tortured in various ways; then, struck with an axe, they gained the crown of martyrdom.

At Nicomedia, the suffering of St. Hadrian, a son of the Emperor Probus. He had condemned the persecution inaugurated against the Christians by Licinius. For this, he was ordered by Licinius to be put to death. His uncle, Domitius, Bishop of Byzantium, buried his body in a suburb of the city called Argyropolis.

In Spain, St. Victor, martyr, who was slain by the Moors for the Christian faith, and thus given the crown of martyrdom.

At Capua, St. Rufinus, bishop and confessor.

At Pistoia in Tuscany, St. Felix, priest and confessor.

The Twenty-seventh Day of August

St. Joseph Calasanctius, priest and confessor. He founded the Order of Poor Clerks Regular of the Mother of God of the Christian Schools. He died in the Lord on August 25. *A duplex feast.*

At Potenza in Lucania, the suffering of SS. Arontius, Honoratus, Fortunatus, and Sabinian. They were the sons of SS. Boniface and Thecla, and were condemned to capital punishment by the judge Valerian in the reign of the Emperor Maximian. Their festival, together with that of the others of the twelve holy brethren, is observed on September 1.

At Bergamo, St. Narnus, who was baptized by Blessed Barnabas, and by him was ordained first bishop of that city.

At Capua, the birthday of St. Rufus, bishop and martyr. He was of patrician rank and was baptized, together with all his household, by Blessed Apollinaris, the disciple of St. Peter. *A memory.*

In the same city, the holy martyrs Rufus and Carpophorus, who suffered under Diocletian and Maximian.

At Tomis in Pontus, the holy martyrs Marcellinus the tribune, his wife Mannea, and their sons John, Serapion, and Peter.

At Lentini in Sicily, St. Euthalia, virgin. She was slain by the sword with her brother Sermilian for being a Christian, and passed to her heavenly Spouse.

On the same day, the suffering of St. Anthusa the Younger, who, drowned in a well for the Christian faith, obtained martyrdom.

At Arles in Gaul, St. Caesarius, bishop, a man of wondrous holiness and piety.

[7] See note under March 14.

At Autun, St. Syagrius, bishop and confessor.

At Pavia (in Italy), St. John, bishop.

At Lerida in Spain, St. Licerius, bishop.

In the Thebaid, St. Poemon, hermit.

Among the people of Sanseverino in Piceno, St. Margaret, widow. ✠

The Twenty-eighth Day of August

At Hippo in Africa, the birthday of St. Augustine, bishop, confessor, and eminent Doctor of the Church. He was converted to the Catholic faith and baptized through the zeal of Bishop St. Ambrose. He became a most stalwart defender of the faith against the Manichees and other heretics. After enduring many other labors for the Church of God, he passed to his reward in Heaven. Because (of the invasion) of the barbarians, his relics were taken from his own city first to Sardinia, and afterward by Luitprand, King of the Lombards, to Pavia, and honorably buried there. *A totum duplex feast of the second class.*

At Rome, the birthday of St. Hermes, an illustrious man. As may be read in the Acts of Blessed Pope Alexander, he was first delivered over to be kept in prison. Then, with many others, he was put to the sword, ending his martyrdom under the judge Aurelian.

At Venosa in Apulia, the suffering of SS. Septiminus, Januarius, and Felix. In the reign of the Emperor Maximian, the judge Valerian ordered these sons of SS. Boniface and Thecla to be beheaded. Their festival, however, is observed with that of the others of the twelve holy brethren on September 1.

At Brioude in Auvergne, the suffering of St. Julian, martyr, who was a companion of the tribune Blessed Ferreolus. He served Christ in secret while leading the life of a soldier; in the persecution of Diocletian he was seized by soldiers and put to a barbarous death by having his throat cut.

At Constance in Germany, St. Pelagius, martyr, who, being beheaded, received the crown of martyrdom under the Emperor Numerian and the judge Evilasius.

At Salerno, the holy martyrs Fortunatus, Caius, and Anthes, who were beheaded under the Emperor Diocletian and the proconsul Leontius.

At Constantinople, St. Alexander, bishop, a glorious old man.[8] It was by the power of his prayer that the body of Arius, who had been condemned by the judgment of God, burst in the middle and his entrails gushed forth.

At Saintes in Gaul, St. Vivian, bishop and confessor.

[8] See note under February 26.

Likewise, St. Moses, an Ethiopian. From being a notorious robber, he became a famous hermit, converted many others, and brought them with him to his monastery. ✠

The Twenty-ninth Day of August

The beheading of St. John the Baptist, whom Herod ordered to be beheaded on the Feast of the Passover. But his memory is solemnly kept on this day, when his venerated head was found for the second time. It was afterwards taken to Rome, and is preserved in the church of St. Silvester in the Campus Martius, with the great devotion of the faithful. *A totum duplex feast.*

At Rome, on the Aventine, the birthday of St. Sabina, martyr, who was put to the sword under the Emperor Hadrian and obtained a crown of martyrdom. *A memory.*

At Veliniano on the confines of Apulia, the suffering of SS. Vitalis, Sator, and Repositus. They were sons of SS. Boniface and Thecla, and were condemned to capital punishment by the judge Valerian in the reign of the Emperor Maximian. Their festival, with that of the others of the twelve holy brethren, is observed on September 1.

At Rome, St. Candida, virgin and martyr, whose body Pope St. Paschal I transferred to the church of St. Praxedes.

At Constantinople, the holy martyrs Hypatius, a bishop of Asia, and Andrew, priest. At the time of Leo the Isaurian, both these men, because they venerated the holy images, had their beards smeared with pitch and then set on fire. The skin was peeled off their heads and their throats were cut.

At Antioch, the birthday of the holy martyrs Nicaeas and Paul.

At Metz in Gaul, St. Adelf, bishop and confessor.

At Paris, the death of St. Mederic, priest.

At Perugia (in Italy), St. Euthymius, a Roman. With his wife and his son Crescentius, he fled to Perugia from the persecution of Diocletian. Later, he died there a peaceful death.

In England, St. Sebbe, King (of the East Saxons).

At Sirmium, the birthday of St. Basilla, virgin.

In the country of Troyes, St. Sabina, virgin, glorious for her virtues and miracles. ✠

The Thirtieth Day of August

At Lima in Peru, St. Rose, virgin, of the Third Order of our holy Father St. Dominic. The Roman Pontiff Clement IX called her "the first

flower from the Western World." At the age of five she took the vow of
virginity; later she was received by Christ in a miraculous way as His
spouse. She added the most severe penances to a life of purest innocence
and her fame spread because of her many miracles. She died on August
24. *A totum duplex feast of the second class.*

At Rome, on the Via Ostia, the suffering of Blessed Felix, priest, under
the Emperors Diocletian and Maximian. After he had been tortured on
the rack, and sentence had been pronounced, a certain Christian met him
as he was being led to his execution. When the stranger openly confessed
that he too was a Christian, he was then beheaded with St. Felix. As the
Christians did not know his name, they called him Adauctus,[9] because he
was added to St. Felix in attaining the crown. *A memory.*

Likewise at Rome, St. Gaudentia, virgin and martyr, with three other
persons.

At Sufetula in Africa, sixty blessed martyrs, who were slain by the fury
of the heathens.

At Bologna, St. Bononius, abbot.

At Rome, St. Pammachius, priest, who was noteworthy for learning
and sanctity.

At Adrumetum in Africa, SS. Boniface and Thecla, who were the
parents of twelve sons, all martyrs.

At Thessalonica, St. Fantinus, confessor. He suffered much at the hands
of the Saracens, and was driven from the monastery in which he had
lived in marvellous abstinence. After he had brought many to the way of
salvation, he died at a good old age.

In the country of Meaux, St. Fiacre, confessor.

At Trebia in Latium, St. Peter, confessor. He was distinguished for
many virtues and miracles. He died at Trebia and is held in great veneration there. ✠

The Thirty-first Day of August

St. Raymund Nonnatus, confessor and cardinal, of the Order of our
Lady of Mercy for the Redemption of Captives. His birthday is commemorated on August 26. *A duplex feast.*

At Monte Senario, in Etruria, the birthday of St. Bonajuncta, confessor,
one of the seven Founders of the Order of the Servants of the Blessed
Virgin Mary. While he was preaching to the brethren about the Lord's
Passion, he gave up his soul into the hands of the Lord. His festival with
that of his companions is kept on February 12.

[9] Adauctus—an addition.

At Treves, the birthday of St. Paulinus, bishop. In the time of the Arian heresy, he was exiled by the Arian Emperor Constantius on account of his Catholic faith. He was worn out by having to change constantly the place of his exile until the day of his death, in regions far beyond the Christian lands. He finally received from the Lord the crown of such blessed suffering, and died in Phrygia.

At Transaco, among the Marsi of Lake Fucino, the birthday of the holy martyrs Caesidius, priest, and his companions, who were crowned with martyrdom in the persecution of Maximin.

Likewise, SS. Robustian and Mark, martyrs.

At Caesarea in Cappadocia, SS. Theodotus, Rufina, and Ammia. Theodotus and Rufina were the parents of the martyr St. Mamas to whom Rufina gave birth in prison and whom Ammia educated.

At Auxerre, St. Optatus, bishop and confessor.

In England, St. Aidan, Bishop of Lindisfarne. When St. Cuthbert, who is mentioned on March 20, was yet a shepherd-boy, he saw the soul of St. Aidan being borne up into Heaven. He forthwith left his flock and became a monk.

At Nosco (in Italy), St. Amatus, bishop.

At Athens, St. Aristides, a man most noble in faith and wisdom. He offered to the Emperor Hadrian a book on the Christian religion, which set forth the grounds for our teaching, and, in the presence of the emperor himself, he eloquently maintained that Jesus Christ alone is God.

septembeR

The First Day of September

In the province of Narbonne, St. Giles, abbot and confessor. The town which later grew up in this place where he built his monastery and where he died was named after him.[1] *A feast of three lessons.*

At Sentianum in Apulia, the suffering of St. Donatus and of another St. Felix,[2] who were the sons of SS. Boniface and Thecla. On this day, in the reign of the Emperor Maximian, they were sentenced by the judge Valerian to be beheaded, they already having undergone various tortures. Also on this day is observed the feast of the rest of the twelve holy brothers, whose birthdays are each noted in their proper places. The bodies of the twelve brothers were later transferred to Benevento and honorably enshrined there.

In Palestine, SS. Josue and Gideon.

At Jerusalem, Blessed Anna the Prophetess, whose holiness the Gospel declares.[3]

At Capua on the Via Aquaria, St. Priscus, martyr, who was one of the first disciples of Christ.

At Todi in Umbria, St. Terentian, bishop and martyr. In the reign of the Emperor Hadrian, at the command of the proconsul Laetian, he was tortured by the rack and by scorpions. Finally, after his tongue had been cut out, he was condemned to death and so ended his martyrdom.

At Heraclea in Thrace, St. Ammon, deacon, and forty holy virgins whom he had instructed in the faith. At the time of the tyrant Licinius, he took them with him to the glory of martyrdom.

In Spain, the holy martyrs Vincent and Laetus.

In Populonia in Tuscany, St. Regulus, martyr. He came from Africa and gained martyrdom at Populonia at the time of Totila.

[1] Saint-Gilles-du-Gard, near Arles.
[2] The phrase "another Felix" refers to the entry on August 28: "At Venosa in Apulia, the suffering of SS. Septiminus, Januarius, and Felix . . . sons of SS. Boniface and Thecla." However, hagiographers question whether Donatus and Felix were the sons of Boniface and Thecla.
[3] Luke, 2:36-38.

At Capua, St. Priscus, bishop. In the persecution by the Vandals he was one of these priests who were persecuted in various ways because of their Catholic faith. Put aboard an old ship, they made their way from Africa to the shores of Campania. Here they separated and went to different cities where they were placed in charged of various churches and so wonderfully spread the Christian faith. The companions of St. Priscus were Castrensis, whose birthday is recalled on February 11, Tammarus, Rosius, Heraclius, Secundinus, Adjutor, Mark, Augustus, Elpidius, Canion, and Vindonius.

At Sens, Blessed Lupus, bishop and confessor. It is said of him that one day, while he stood at the altar in the presence of his clergy, a jewel fell from heaven into his sacred chalice.

At Rheims in Gaul, St. Sixtus, who was the first bishop of that city.

At Le Mans in Gaul, St. Victorius, bishop.

At Aquino, St. Constantius, bishop, famed for the gift of prophecy and for his many virtues.

At Zurzach, in the territory of Constance, Germany,[4] St. Verena, virgin. ✠

The Second Day of September

St. Stephen, King of Hungary and confessor, who died in the Lord on August 15. *A simplex feast.*

At Rome, St. Maxima, martyr. Together with St. Ansanus, she confessed Christ in the persecution of Diocletian, and was beaten to death with clubs.

At Pamiers in Gaul, St. Antoninus, martyr, whose relics are preserved with great veneration in a church in Palencia in Spain.

Also the holy martyrs Diomede, Julian, Philip, Eutychian, Hesychius, Leonides, Philadelphus, Menalippus, and Pantagapa. Some of these completed their martyrdom by fire, some by water, others by the sword or by the cross.

At Nicomedia, the holy martyrs Zeno and his sons Concordius and Theodore.

At Lyons in Gaul, St. Elpidius, bishop and confessor.

At Piceno (Italy), another St. Elpidius, abbot. A town which bears his name glories in the possession of his body.[5]

On Mount Soracte, St. Nonnosus, abbot, who moved a huge rock by his prayer and was famed for other miracles.

[4] Zurzach is now inside the northern border of Switzerland.
[5] Sant' Elpideo a Mare.

On the same day, the commemoration of the holy martyrs Evodius, Hermogenes, and Callista, brothers and sister, who underwent martyrdom at Syracuse, Sicily. They are also commemorated on April 25.

At Lyons in Gaul, the transferal of the relics of St. Justus, bishop and confessor, and of St. Viator who was his servant. Their birthdays occur respectively on October 14 and October 21.

The Third Day of September

At Bergamo (in Italy), Blessed Guala, confessor, of the Order of Preachers and Bishop of Brescia. After many exhausting labors for the good of the Church and of the state, he peacefully died in the Lord. *A semi-duplex feast.*

At Corinth, the birthday of St. Phoebe. The Apostle St. Paul mentions her in his Epistle to the Romans.[6]

At Capua, the holy martyrs Aristaeus, bishop, and a boy Antoninus.

On the same day, the birthday of the holy martyrs Aigulph, Abbot of Lerins, and his companion monks. After their tongues and eyes had been cut out, they were beheaded by the sword.

Likewise, the holy martyrs Zeno and Chariton. One was cast into a vessel of molten lead and the other was thrown into the fire.

At Cordoba in Spain, St. Sandal, martyr.

At Aquileia, the holy virgins and martyrs Euphemia, Dorothy, Thecla, and Erasma. After enduring many tortures, they were put to the sword at the time of the Emperor Nero and the governor Sebastus. They were buried by St. Hermagoras.

At Nicomedia, the suffering of St. Basilissa, virgin and martyr. During the persecution of the Emperor Diocletian, under the governor Alexander, St. Basilissa, although only nine years old, overcame by the power of God the flogging, the fire, and the wild beasts. By so doing, she converted the governor to the faith of Christ. Finally, while she was being led outside the city (for execution), she died while engaged in prayer.

At Toul in Gaul, St. Mansuetus, bishop and confessor.

At Milan, the death of St. Auxanus, bishop.

On the same day, St. Simon Stylites the Younger.

At Rome, the transferal of (the relics of) St. Serapia, virgin and martyr, who suffered on July 29.

Likewise at Rome, the raising to the Sovereign Pontificate of the in-

---

[6] Romans, xvi, 1-2,

comparable St. Gregory the Great. Constrained to assume that burden, from a loftier throne he shed upon the world even stronger rays of sanctity.

The Fourth Day of September

The Octave of St. Augustine, bishop. *A memory.*

In Piedmont (Italy), Blessed Catherine Racconigi, virgin, of the Third Order of St. Dominic. She was illustrious by reason of her extraordinary charity and abundance of divine gifts. *A semi-duplex feast.*

On Mount Nebo in the land of Moab, St. Moses, lawgiver and Prophet.

At Naples in Campania, the birthday of St. Candida, who was the first to meet St. Peter when he came to that city. She was baptized by him and afterwards died a holy death.

At Treves, St. Marcellus, bishop and martyr.

At Ancyra in Galatia, the birthday of the three holy children Rufinus, Silvanus, and Vitalicus, martyrs.

On the same day, the holy martyrs Magnus, Castus, and Maximus.

At Chalons in Gaul, St. Marcellus, martyr, at the time of the Emperor Antoninus. The saint was invited by the governor Priscus to an idolatrous banquet and, abhorring such sinful meats, boldly rebuked all who were present for worshipping idols. For this reason, the governor with un-heard-of cruelty had him buried in the ground up to his waist. He remained so buried for three days, during which he persevered in giving praise to God; he then surrendered his undefiled soul to his God. *A memory.*

On the same day but under the Emperor Hadrian, St. Thamel, who had formerly been a priest of the pagan idols; with him suffered his companions.

Likewise, the holy martyrs Theodore, Oceanus, Ammian, and Julian. In the reign of the Emperor Maximian, after their feet had been cut off, the martyrs completed their trial by being cast into the fire.

At Rome, St. Boniface I, pope and confessor.

At Rimini, St. Marinis, deacon.

At Palermo, the birthday of St. Rosalie, a virgin of Palermo. She came of the royal blood of Charlemagne, but for the love of Christ she fled from the court and kingdom of her father and led a supernatural life alone on the mountains and in caves.

At Viterbo, during the pontificate of Alexander IV, the transferal of the body of St. Rose, virgin, of the Third Order of St. Francis. ✠

The Fifth Day of September

St. Laurence Giustiniani, the first Patriarch of Venice and confessor, who on this day unwillingly ascended the pontifical throne. He died in the Lord on January 8.

In the suburbs of Rome, Blessed Victorinus, bishop and martyr. Noted for his holiness and miracles, he was elected Bishop of Amiterno by the unanimous choice of the people. Later, under Nerva Trajan, he was banished with other servants of God to Contigliano. Here, the judge Aurelian ordered him to be suspended with his head downward over fetid sulphur springs. For the sake of the Lord, Victorinus endured this torture for three days and then left this world in triumph, with a glorious crown. The Christians recovered his body and gave it honorable burial at Amiterno, in the land of the Vestinians.

At Constantinople, the holy martyrs Urban, Theodore, Menedemus, and their seventy-seven companions of ecclesiastical rank. Because of their Catholic faith, they were placed by the Emperor Valens on board a ship and ordered to be burned at sea.

At Portus Romanus, the birthday of St. Herculaneus, soldier, who was scourged and beheaded in the reign of the Emperor Gallus because of his Christian faith.

At Capua, the holy martyrs Quinctius, Arcontius, and Donatus.

On the same day, St. Romulus, who was an official of the court of Trajan. The saint denounced the cruelty of the Emperor toward the Christians; for this, he was beaten with rods and then beheaded.

At Melitine in Armenia, the suffering of the holy soldiers Eudoxius, Zeno, Macarius, and eleven hundred and four of their fellow-soldiers. They flung aside their military insignia in Diocletian's persecution and were slain for confessing Christ.

In the district of Therouanne, at the monastery of Sithiu, in Gaul, St. Bertinus, abbot.

At Toledo in Spain, St. Obdulia, virgin. ✠ *An Anniversary.*

The Sixth Day of September

In the town of Bosquet, in the Diocese of Valence in southern Gaul, Blessed Bertrand of Garriga, confessor, of the Order of Preachers. He was distinguished by the remarkable way in which he reflected in his own life the virtues of St. Dominic. After his death, he became renowned for his miracles. *A semi-duplex feast.*

In Palestine, St. Zachary the Prophet. When he was an old man, he returned from Chaldea to his native land and, dying there, was buried near the Prophet Aggaeus.

In the Hellespont, St. Onesiphorus, a disciple of the Apostles, whom St. Paul mentions in his Epistle to Timothy.[7] At the command of Hadrian the proconsul, Onesiphorus, together with St. Porphyrius, was severely scourged and then dragged by wild horses until he died.

In Africa, the holy Bishops Donatian, Praesidius, Mansuetus, Germanus, and Fusculus. For defending Catholic doctrine during the Vandal persecution, they were mercilessly beaten with clubs at the command of the Arian king, Hunneric. Then driven into exile (in the desert), they all perished. Among them was a bishop named Laetus, a zealous and learned man, who, after enduring for a long time the filth of a dungeon, was burned alive.

At Alexandria, the suffering of the holy martyrs Faustus, priest, Macarius, and ten others, who, in the time of the Emperor Decius and the governor Valerius, fulfilled their martyrdom for the name of Christ by being beheaded.

In Cappadocia, the holy martyrs Cottidus, deacon, Eugene, and their companions.

At Verona, St. Petronius, bishop and confessor.

At Rome, St. Eleutherius, abbot. This servant of God, as Pope St. Gregory relates, was instrumental by his prayers and tears in raising a dead man to life.

The Seventh Day of September

At Troyes in Gaul, St. Nemorius, deacon, and his companions, martyrs, whom Attila, King of the Huns, put to death.

In Nicomedia, the birthday of Blessed John, martyr. When he saw displayed in the forum the cruel edicts against the Christians, he was fired with zeal for the faith, and pulling down the edicts, tore them up with his own hands. When this was reported to the Emperors Diocletian and Maximian who were residing in that city, they commanded that every variety of torture should be inflicted on him. This noble man endured them with such readiness of demeanor and spirit that they did not appear to disturb him.

At Caesarea in Cappadocia, St. Eupsychius, martyr. In the reign of the Emperor Hadrian, he was accused of being a Christian and was cast into prison, but after a short time was set free. Without delay, he sold his inheritance and distributed part of it to the poor; the rest he gave to those

[7] 2 Timothy, 1:16, 4:19.

who had accused him, as if they were his benefactors. Arrested for a second time, he firmly refused to sacrifice to the idols, and he was mercilessly tortured by the judge Sapritius. He finished his martyrdom when he was pierced through with a sword.

At Pompeiopolis in Cilicia, St. Sozen, martyr. During the reign of the Emperor Maximian, he was thrown into the fire and so died.

At Aquileia, St. Anastasius, martyr.

At Alesia in the territory of Autun, St. Regina, virgin and martyr. At the time of the proconsul Olybrius, she endured tortures by imprisonment, the rack, and flaming torches. At last, sentenced to death, she went to her heavenly Spouse.

At Orleans in Gaul, the death of St. Evortius, bishop. He was at first a subdeacon of the Roman Church; later, he was divinely designated by means of a dove as bishop of Orleans.

In Gaul, St. Augustalis, bishop and confessor.

At Capua, St. Pamphilius, bishop.

In the neighborhood of Paris, St. Cloud, priest and confessor.

The Eighth Day of September

The Nativity of the Most Blessed Mary, ever Virgin, Mother of God. *A totum duplex feast of the second class.*

St. Hadrian, martyr, whose birthday is remembered on March 4; his festival, however, is observed today, because on this day his sacred body was transferred to Rome.

At Valencia in Spain, the birthday of St. Thomas of Villanova, bishop and confessor, of the Order of Hermits of St. Augustine. He was noted for his ardent charity toward the poor. Pope Alexander VII inscribed him among the saints. His feast is observed on the twenty-second day of this month.

At Alexandria, SS. Ammon, Theophilus, Neoterius, and twenty-two other martyrs.

At Antioch, SS. Timothy and Faustus, martyrs.

At Gaza in Palestine, the holy martyrs Eusebius, Nestabus, and Zeno, brothers. At the time of Julian the Apostate, a pagan mob rushed upon them and killed them by tearing them to pieces.

At the same place and under the same Julian, St. Nestor, martyr. He died after having been savagely tortured by the same group of enraged pagans.

At Rome, St. Sergius I, pope and confessor.

At Freising (in Germany), St. Corbinian, the first bishop of that city. He was ordained by Pope St. Gregory II and sent there to preach the

Gospel. After his words had brought abundant fruit in Gaul and Germany, he died a peaceful death, noted for his virtues and miracles.

At Cartagena in South America, St. Peter Claver, priest and confessor of the Society of Jesus. For more than forty years, he devoted himself to a life of remarkable self-denial and extraordinary charity for the Negroes who had been enslaved. With his own hand he baptized almost three hundred thousand of them. The Sovereign Pontiff, Leo XIII, added him to the list of saints and later declared him to be the heavenly patron of the missions to the Negro races.

The Ninth Day of September

At Nicomedia, the suffering of the holy martyrs Dorotheus and Gorgonius. They had received the greatest honors from the Emperor Diocletian, but when in his presence they denounced the persecution he was inflicting on the Christians, they were first condemned to be hung up and their entire bodies torn with lashes; after the skin had been torn from their bodies, vinegar and salt were poured on them and they were roasted on a gridiron. Finally, they were put to death by being strangled with a noose. Some time later, the body of Blessed Gorgonius was taken to Rome and buried on the Via Latina; from here, it was removed to the Basilica of St. Peter. *A feast of three lessons.*

In the Sabine mountains, at the thirtieth milestone from Rome, the holy martyrs Hyacinth, Alexander, and Tiburtius.

At Sebaste in Armenia, St. Severian. Though he was a soldier of the Emperor Licinius, he frequently visited the forty martyrs while they were in prison. Because of this, by orders of the governor Lysias, he was hung up with a large rock fastened to his feet; then he was flogged. He was torn by the whips to such an extent that he died during the torture.

On the same day, the suffering of St. Strato, who underwent martyrdom for Christ by being tied to two trees and torn asunder.

Likewise, the holy martyrs Rufinus and Rufinian, brothers.

In the country of Therouanne in Gaul, St. Omer, bishop.

In the monastery of Clonmacnois in Ireland, St. Kiernan, priest and abbot. ✠

The Tenth Day of September

In Japan, Blessed Alphonsus Navarette, and two hundred and four companions, (martyrs). More than half of that number belonged to the Order of Preachers. From 1617 until 1632, they strove energetically for the faith and merited to be crowned with a glorious martyrdom. *A duplex feast.*

At Tolentino in Ascoli Piceno (Italy), St. Nicholas, confessor of the Order of Hermits of St. Augustine. *A memory.*

In Africa, the birthday of the holy Bishops Nemesian, Felix, Lucius, another Felix, Litteus, Polyanus, Victor, Jader, Dativus, and others. In the furious persecution under Valerian and Gallienus, at their first firm confession of Christ, they were severely beaten with clubs. Then, loaded with chains, they were sent to the mines, where they finished their splendid contest in behalf of the faith.

At Liege in Belgium, St. Theodard, bishop and martyr. He laid down his life for his sheep and after death he became renowned for miracles.

At Chalcedon, the holy martyrs Sosthenes and Victor. In the persecution of Diocletian, under Priscus proconsul of Asia, these martyrs were chained and exposed to wild beasts. Surviving this ordeal, they were condemned to be burned alive. They saluted one another with a holy kiss, and, kneeling in prayer, gave up their souls to God.

Likewise, the holy martyrs Apellius, Luke, and Clement.

In Bithynia, the holy virgins Menodora, Metrodora, and Nymphadora, sisters. At the time of the Emperor Maximian and the governor Fronto, they were crowned with martyrdom, attaining the glory by their fearless confession of faith.

At Compostella, St. Peter, bishop, who was adorned with many virtues and noted for miracles.

At Albi in Gaul, St. Salvius, bishop and confessor.

At Novara (in Italy), St. Agapius, bishop.

At Constantinople, the Empress St. Pulcheria, virgin, who was famed for her religion and piety.

At Naples in Campania, St. Candida the Younger, noted for her miracles.

The Eleventh Day of September

At Rome, on the old Via Salaria, in the cemetery of Basilla, the birthday of the holy martyrs Protus and Hyacinth, brothers. They were eunuchs who belonged to St. Eugenia. During the reign of the Emperor Gallienus, they were arrested on the charge of being Christians and ordered to offer sacrifice. Upon their refusal, they first were beaten inhumanly and then beheaded. *A feast of three lessons.*

At Leon in Spain, St. Vincent, abbot and martyr.

At Laodicea in Syria, the suffering of SS. Diodorus, Diomede, and Didymus.

In Egypt, St. Paphnutius, bishop. At the time of the Emperor Gallienus, he was one of those confessors who, after having the right eye dug out (with a dagger) and the tendons of the left knee severed, was condemned to work in the mines. Later, (freed) under Constantine the Great, he strenuously defended the Catholic faith against the Arians. At last, enriched by many crowns, he went to his eternal rest.

At Lyons in Gaul, the death of St. Patiens, bishop.

At Vercelli, St. Aemilian, bishop.

At Alexandria, St. Theodora, (penitent). Through recklessness, she fell into sin; then, repenting of her deed, she persevered incognito in the religious life in wonderful self-denial and long-suffering until her death.

The Twelfth Day of September

The feast of the Most Holy Name of the Blessed Virgin Mary. The Sovereign Pontiff, Innocent XI, commanded this feast to be celebrated because of the brilliant victory obtained over the Turks at Vienna in Austria by the help of the Blessed Virgin. *A totum duplex feast.*

In Bithynia, St. Autonomus, bishop and martyr. He went there from Italy to avoid the persecution of Diocletian. After he had converted a great many people to the faith, one day while he was celebrating Mass, he was slain at the altar by enraged pagans, and thus became a sacrifice of Christ.

At Iconium in Lycaonia, St. Curonotus, bishop. He was beheaded at the time of the governor Perennius, thus receiving the palm of martyrdom.

At Alexandria, the birthday of the holy martyrs Hieronides, Leontius, Serapion, Silesius, Valerian, and Strato. In the reign of the Emperor Maximian, they were drowned in the sea for confessing the name of Christ.

At Meri in Phrygia, the holy martyrs Macedonius, Theodulus, and Tatian. At the time of Julian the Apostate, they underwent various torments at the hands of the governor Almachius, and then were placed on red-hot gridirons. Still rejoicing, they completed their martyrdom.

At Pavia, St. Juventius, bishop, of whom mention is made on February 8. St. Hermagores, a disciple of St. Mark the Evangelist, sent Juventius to Pavia along with the St. Syrus mentioned on December 9. Both these (missionaries) preached the Gospel of Christ at Pavia and distinguished themselves by their miracles and their great virtues. By their admirable deeds, they brought the faith even to the neighboring cities. Thus, with an honor befitting their pontifical dignity, their lives came to a glorious close.

At Lyons in Gaul, the death of St. Sacerdos, bishop.

At Verona, St. Silvinus, bishop.

At Anderlecht near Brussels in Brabant, St. Guy, confessor. ✠

The Thirteenth Day of September

At Alexandria, the birthday of Blessed Philip, the father of the virgin St. Eugenia. He resigned the office of prefect of Egypt and received the grace of Baptism. His successor, the prefect Terence, had Philip's throat cut with a sword while he was occupied in prayer.

Likewise, the holy martyrs Macrobius and Julian, who suffered under Licinius.

On the same day, St. Ligorius, martyr. He lived in the desert and was slain by the heathens for the faith of Christ.

At Alexandria, St. Eulogius, bishop, celebrated for his learning and holiness.

At Angers in Gaul, St. Maurilius, bishop, who was famed for innumerable miracles.

At Sens, St. Amatus, bishop and confessor.

In the monastery of Remiremont in Gaul, St. Amatus, priest and abbot. He was illustrious for the virtue of self-denial and the grace of miracles.

On the same day, St. Venerius, confessor, a man of admirable holiness, who lived the life of a hermit on the island of Palmaria.

The Fourteenth Day of September

The Exaltation of the Holy Cross, at the time when the Emperor Heraclius brought it back from Persia to Jerusalem after he had defeated King Chosroes. *A totum duplex feast.*

At Rome, on the Appian Way, the Blessed Cornelius, pope and martyr. In the persecution of Decius, he was first exiled; then he was beaten with leaden-tipped whips. He was beheaded with twenty-one other persons of both sexes. Also, Caerealis, soldier, with his wife Sallustia, whom the said Cornelius had instructed in the faith; both husband and wife were beheaded on the same day.

In Africa, the suffering of St. Cypian, Bishop of Carthage, a man most renowned for holiness and learning. During the reign of the Emperors Valerian and Gallienus, he suffered from a harsh exile and then completed his martyrdom by being beheaded on the seashore, at the sixth milestone from Carthage. The memory of these two saints, Cornelius and Cyprian, is kept on September 16.

At Comana in Pontus, the birthday of St. John, Bishop of Constantinople, confessor and Doctor of the Church. He was surnamed Chrysostom by reason of the golden stream of his eloquence. He was driven into exile by the machinations of his enemies, but was recalled by a decree of the Sovereign Pontiff, St. Innocent I. However, he suffered on the journey so much ill-treatment from the soldiers of his escort that he died. His feast is observed on January 27, the day on which his holy body was transferred to Constantinople by Theodosius the Younger. Pope Pius X declared and appointed this most glorious preacher of the divine Word to be the heavenly patron of all preachers of sacred truth.

At Treves, St. Maternus, bishop, a disciple of the Apostle St. Peter. He converted the inhabitants of Tongres, Cologne, Treves, and of other adjacent regions, to the faith of Christ.

At Rome, St. Crescentius, a boy, who was the son of St. Euthymius. In the persecution of Diocletian, under the judge Turpilius, he was put to death by the sword on the Via Salaria.

In Africa, the suffering of the holy martyrs Crescentian, Victor, Rosula, and Generalis.

The Fifteenth Day of September

The Octave of the Nativity of the Blessed Virgin Mary. *A memory.*

The feast of the Seven Dolours of the same Most Blessed Virgin Mary. *A totum duplex feast of the second class.*

At Rome on the Via Nomentana, the birthday of St. Nicomedes, priest and martyr. Upon his reply to those who sought to make him offer sacrifice: "I offer no sacrifice except to the Almighty God who reigns in Heaven," he was flogged with leaden-tipped whips until he expired. *A memory.*

At Cordoba in Spain, the holy martyrs Emilias, deacon, and Jeremias. During the persecution by the Arabs, they suffered a long imprisonment for the sake of Christ and completed their martyrdom by being beheaded.

In the country of Chalons, the holy martyr Valerian. The governor Priscus ordered him to be hung up and severely mangled by iron claws. When he saw that Valerian could not be shaken in his confession of Christ, but continued to praise the Lord with a joyful heart, he commanded him to be slain by the sword.

At Adrianople in Thrace, the holy martyrs Maximus, Theodore, and Asclepiodotus, who were crowned in the time of the Emperor Maximian.

Likewise, St. Porphyrus, a comedian. In the presence of the Emperor Julian the Apostate, he was being baptized in mockery. Suddenly, through the grace of God, he declared himself to be a Christian. At the command of the Emperor, he was beheaded, thus gaining his crown of martyrdom.

On the same day, St. Nicetas the Goth, whom King Athanaric ordered to be burned alive because of his Catholic faith.

At Marcianopolis in Thrace, St. Melitina, martyr. In the time of the Emperor Antoninus and the governor Antiochus, she was taken again and again to the temple; but every time the idols toppled over in her presence. She was therefore hung up and her body mangled. At last, her head was struck off.

At Toul in Gaul, St. Aper, bishop.

Also, St. Leobinus, Bishop of Chartres.

At Lyons in Gaul, St. Albinus, bishop.

On the same day, the death of St. Aichard, abbot.

In Gaul, St. Eutropia, widow.

At Genoa, St. Catherine, widow, famous for her contempt of the world and her love of God. ✠

The Sixteenth Day of September

The holy martyrs Pope Cornelius, and Cyprian, Bishop of Carthage, whose memory is recalled on September 14. *A simplex feast.*

At Chalcedon, the birthday of St. Euphemia, virgin and martyr. At the time of the Emperor Diocletian and the proconsul Priscus, she endured for the sake of Christ various tortures: imprisonment, blows, the punishment of the wheel, fire, the weight of heavy stones, wild beasts, floggings, sharp saws, and red-hot metal. When she was again brought back to the arena to be cast to the wild beasts, she prayed that (this time) God would take her soul to Him. Then, while most of the beasts licked her feet, one animal killed her. Thus she surrendered her unspotted soul to God. *A memory.*

At Rome, the holy martyrs Lucy, a noble matron, and Geminianus. In the reign of Diocletian the Emperor, their bodies were afflicted and twisted by the most unmerciful tortures. Finally, they were beheaded, after their praiseworthy victory of testimony for the faith.

The birthday of St. Martin I, pope and martyr. He summoned a council at Rome and condemned the heretics Sergius, Paul, and Pyrrhus. By order of the heretical Emperor Constantius, he was taken prisoner by trickery and brought to Constantinople. He was exiled to the Chersonese, where, adorned with many virtues, he died exhausted by his labors for the Catholic faith. He was famed for his many miracles. Later, his body was taken back to Rome and buried in the church of SS. Silvester and Martin. His feast is celebrated on November 12.

Also at Rome, the birthday of St. Cecilia, virgin and martyr. She converted her husband and his brother Tiburtius to the faith of Christ and later encouraged them to be martyrs. After their martydom, Almachius the prefect of the city had her arrested and, after she had endured amazing suffering and passed through fire unscathed, was slain by the sword. This occurred in the reign of the Emperor Marcus Aurelius Severus Alexander. Her feast is observed on November 22.

At Heraclea in Thrace, St. Sebastiana, martyr. She had been converted to the faith of Christ by the Apostle St. Paul. At the time of the Emperor Domitian and the governor Sergius, her faith was tested in many ways; finally, she was killed by the sword.

At Rome on the Via Flaminia, the holy martyrs Abundius, priest, and the deacon Abundantius. The Emperor Diocletian ordered them to be slain with the sword, at the tenth milestone from the city. With them died Marcian, an illustrious man, and his son John; both had been raised from the dead by Abundius and Abundantius.

At Cordoba in Spain, SS. Rogellus and Servideus, martyrs. Their hands and feet were cut off, and they were beheaded.

At Whithorn in Scotland, St. Ninian, bishop and confessor.

In England, St. Edith, the virgin daughter of the English King Edgar. She was dedicated to God in a monastery from her earliest years; hence it may be said that she did not forsake the world but rather that she never knew the world.

At Monte Cassino, the Blessed Pope Victor III. As the successor of Pope St. Gregory VII, he shed fresh lustre on the Apostolic See, and by the help of God gained a famous victory over the Saracens. The Sovereign Pontiff, Leo XIII, ratified and confirmed the cult accorded him from time immemorial.

The Seventeenth Day of September

On Mount Alvernia in Etruria, the commemoration of the Imprinting of the Sacred Stigmata, which God by a wonderful grace made in the hands, feet, and side of St. Francis, the founder of the Order of Friars Minor. *A duplex feast.*

At Rome, on the Via Tiburtina, the birthday of St. Justin, priest and martyr. He was famous for his glorious confession during the persecution of Valerian and Gallienus. He buried the bodies of Pope St. Sixtus II, Laurence, Hippolytus, and many other saints. Finally, he himself was martyred under Claudius.

Also at Rome, the holy martyrs Narcissus and Crescentio.

At Liege in Belgium, Blessed Lambert, Bishop of Maastricht. In his zeal for religion, he rebuked the royal family. Without just cause, he was slain by evil men and so entered the court of the heavenly kingdom as a victor forever. *A memory.*

At Saragossa in Spain, St. Peter de Arbues, the first inquisitor of the faith in the kingdom of Aragon. Some relapsed Jews brutally killed him because of the Catholic faith which he had zealously protected by virtue of his office. Pope Pius IX added him to the list of martyr saints.

In Britain, the holy martyrs Socrates and Stephen.

At Noyon in Gaul, the holy martyrs Valerian, Marinus, and Gordian.

At Autun, St. Flocellus, a boy. At the time of the Emperor Antoninus and the governor Valerian, he endured many tortures. Finally, torn to pieces by wild beasts, he gained the crown of martyrdom.

At Cordoba in Spain, St. Colomba, virgin and martyr.

In Phrygia, St. Ariadne, martyr, in the reign of the Emperor Hadrian.

On the same day, St. Agathoclia, (martyr). She was the servant-girl of a certain pagan woman, who for a long period subjected the girl to blows and other sufferings to make her deny Christ. Finally, she handed her over to a magistrate. Although the girl was savagely mangled, she persevered in her confession of the faith; then her tongue was cut out and she was flung into the flames.

At Milan, the death of St. Satyrus, confessor, whose outstanding merits have been commemorated by his brother, St. Ambrose.

At Bingen in the diocese of Mainz, St. Hildegard, virgin.

At Rome, St. Theodora, matron, who zealously ministered to the holy martyrs in the persecution of Diocletian. ✠

The Eighteenth Day of September

At Lima in South America, the Spaniard Blessed John Massias. Rejecting all worldly things, he became a lay-brother in the Order of Preachers. He was distinguished by the marvellous humility, patience, and integrity of his life, and he became famous for his miracles. *A duplex feast.*

At Osimo in Piceno, St. Joseph of Cupertino, confessor. He was a priest of the Order of Friars Minor Conventual. Pope Clement XIII enrolled him among the number of the saints.

At Chalcis in Greece, the birthday of St. Methodius (martyr). He was first Bishop of Olympus in Lycia and later Bishop of Tyre in Phoenicia. He was most renowned for the eloquence of his preaching and for his learning. He was crowned with martyrdom, as St. Jerome states, at the very end of the last persecution.

In the country of Vienne (Gaul), St. Ferreolus, martyr, who had the rank of tribune. He was arrested at the instance of the wicked governor

Crispin. First, he was mercilessly beaten; then, weighed down with the heavy load of many chains, he was thrust into a prison devoid of light. Through a miracle, the chains fell off and the prison gate opened. Ferreolus escaped but he was captured again by his pursuers. He gained the crown of martyrdom by being beheaded.

Also, the holy martyrs, Sophia and Irene.

At Milan, St. Eustorgius I, bishop of that city. He was made famous by the testimony of St. Ambrose (in his behalf).

At Gortyna in Crete, St. Eumenius, bishop and confessor.

The Nineteenth Day of September

At Pozzuoli in Campania (Italy), the holy martyrs Januarius, Bishop of the city of Benevento, Festus his deacon; Desiderius, lector, Sosius, a deacon of the church of Miseno, Proculus, a deacon of Pozzuoli, Eutychius, and Acutius. All these were chained, imprisoned, and then beheaded, in the persecution of the Emperor Diocletian. The body of St. Januarius was taken to Naples and honorably buried in the church. Here, the blood of the blessed martyr is still kept in a glass vessel, and when placed near his head is seen to liquefy and bubble up as if just shed. *A duplex feast.*

In Palestine, in the persecution of Diocletian, the holy martyrs Peleus, Nilus, and Elias, Bishops of Egypt. These, along with many others of the clergy, were burned to death for Christ.

At Nocera, the birthday of the holy martyrs Felix and Constantia, who suffered under Nero.

On the same day, the holy martyrs Trophimus, Sabbatius, and Dorymedon, in the reign of the Emperor Probus. By command of the governor Atticus at Antioch, Sabbatius was flogged so long that he died, but Trophimus was sent to the governor Perennius at Synnada. There, after many tortures, he gained martyrdom by being beheaded. With him was beheaded the senator, Dorymedon.

At Eleutheropolis in Palestine, St. Susanna, virgin and martyr. She was the daughter of Arthemius, a pagan priest, and of Martha, a Jewish woman. After the death of her parents, she was converted to the Christian faith. For this reason, she was tortured in various ways and cast into prison by the prefect Alexander. There she died while engaged in prayer.

At Cordoba in Spain, St. Pomposa, virgin and martyr. In the Arab persecution, because of her fearless confession of Christ, she was beheaded and so obtained the palm of martyrdom.

At Canterbury, St. Theodore, bishop. He was sent into England by Pope Vitalian, and was distinguished for his learning and holiness.

At Tours in Gaul, St. Eustochius, bishop, a man of great virtue.

In the country of Langres, St. Sequanus, priest and confessor.

At Barcelona in Spain, blessed Mary of Cervellione, virgin, of the Order of our Lady of Ransom for the redemption of captives. By reason of her prompt help to them that invoke her, she is commonly called Mary of Help.

The Twentieth Day of September

The Vigil of St. Matthew, Apostle and Evangelist.

At Cordoba in Spain, Blessed Francis Possadas (of the Order of Preachers). He was distinguished to an extraordinary degree by his apostolic preaching, his hearing of confessions, the austerity and innocence of his life. *A duplex feast.*

At Rome, the suffering of the holy martyrs Eustace, Theopistis his wife, and their two sons Agapitus and Theopistus. They were condemned to the beasts at the time of the Emperor Hadrian, but miraculously were not hurt by them. They were then enclosed in a red-hot brazen bull and so completed their martyrdom.

At Cyzicus in Propontis, the birthday of the holy martyrs Fausta, virgin, and Evilasius, in the reign of the Emperor Maximian. Evilasius was then a priest in the service of idols; he had Fausta's head shaved so that he might shame her. Then she was hung up and tortured. But when he wished to have her cut in two, the executioners were not able to harm her. Astounded by this, Evilasius became a Christian; then he too was severely tortured by order of the Emperor. Fausta had her head bored through and her whole body transfixed with spikes; she was then placed on a red-hot metal pan. At last, summoned by a voice from heaven, Fausta with Evilasius passed from earth to heaven.

In Phrygia, the holy martyrs Dionysius and Privatus.

Likewise, St. Priscus, martyr, who was repeatedly stabbed with daggers and then beheaded.

At Perga in Pamphylia, SS. Theodore, Philippa his mother, and their fellow-martyrs, in the reign of the Emperor Antoninus.

At Carthage, St. Candida, virgin and martyr. In the persecution of Diocletian, she gained martyrdom when her entire body had been ripped to shreds by blows.

At Milan, St. Clicerius, bishop and confessor.

At Rome, the removal of the body of St. Agapitus I, pope and confessor, from the city of Constantinople where he had died on April 22.

The Twenty-first Day of September

In Ethiopia, the birthday of St. Matthew, Apostle and Evangelist, who suffered martyrdom while preaching in that country. In the reign of the Emperor Zeno, the Gospel written by St. Matthew in the Hebrew tongue was found by his own revelation, together with the body of St. Barnabas, the Apostle. *A totum duplex feast of the second class.*

In the land of Saar, St. Jonas the Prophet, who was buried in Goth.

In Ethiopia, St. Iphigenia, virgin. She was baptized and consecrated to God by the Apostle St. Matthew. She ended her days in holiness.

At Rome, St. Pamphilus, martyr.

On the same day, on the Via Claudia, at the twentieth milestone from Rome, the suffering of St. Alexander, bishop. In the time of the Emperor Antoninus, he overcame for Christ chains, clubs, the rack, burning torches, tearing with hooks, beasts, and the flames of furnaces. At last, he was put to the sword and thus gained a glorious life. Pope St. Damasus later removed the body into the city on November 26.

In Cyprus, St. Isacius, bishop and martyr.

In Phoenicia, St. Eusebius, martyr. Of his own accord, he presented himself to the prefect and declared he was a Christian. He was subjected to numerous torments and then beheaded.

In Cyprus, St. Meletius, bishop and confessor. ✠

The Twenty-second Day of September

At Sitten in Gaul, at Saint-Maurice, the holy Theban martyrs Maurice, Exuperius, Candidus, Victor, Innocent, and Vitalis, with their companions of the same Legion. In the reign of Maximian, they were slain for Christ, thus enlightening the world by their martyrdom. *A feast of three lessons.*

St. Thomas of Villanova, confessor, of the Order of Hermits of St. Augustine, (Arch)bishop of Valencia. His birthday is remembered on September 8.

At Rome, the suffering of the holy virgins and martyrs Digna and Emerita, in the reign of Valerian and Gallienus. Their relics are preserved in the church of St. Marcellus.

At Ratisbon in Bavaria, St. Emmeram, bishop and martyr, who patiently suffered a most cruel death for Christ that he might set others free.

At Arpajon (in Gaul), St. Jonas, priest and martyr, who went to Gaul with St. Dionysius. By command of the prefect Julian, he was flogged and then gained martyrdom by being put to the sword.

At Antinopolis in Egypt, St. Irais, a virgin of Alexandria and her companion martyrs. They were on their way to draw water from a fountain when they saw a ship laden with (prisoners, all) confessors of Christ. Casting aside her water-jar, she joined them and was taken with them into the city. She was the first of all to be beheaded, but only after she had undergone many tortures. Then the rest, priests, deacons, and virgins, were put to the same kind of death.

At Rome, Pope St. Felix IV, who labored much for the Catholic faith.

At the city of Meaux, Blessed Sanctinus, bishop. He was a disciple of St. Dionysius the Areopagite, by whom he was consecrated bishop of that city and he was the first to preach the Gospel there.

In the country of Coutance in Gaul, St. Lauto, bishop.

On Mount Glonne near the Loire river in Gaul, St. Florentius, priest.

At Levroux in the territory of Bourges, St. Silvanus, confessor.

At Laon in Gaul, St. Salaberga, abbess. ✠

The Twenty-third Day of September

At Pesaro (in Italy), Blessed Mark of Modena, a confessor of our Order. He was remarkable for the sanctity of his life. Fired by zeal for the salvation of souls, he travelled over nearly all of Italy, preaching the Word of God and converting many to a Christian manner of life. *A semi-duplex feast.*

At Rome, St. Linus, pope and martyr. After the Apostle St. Peter, he was the first to govern the Roman Church. He gained the crown of martyrdom and was buried in the Vatican near the same Apostle.

At Iconium in Lycaonia, St. Thecla, virgin and martyr. She was converted to the faith by St. Paul. In the persecution of the Emperor Nero, she conquered the fire and the wild beasts in her confession of Christ. After numerous trials which she overcame for the instruction of many, she (escaped and) came to Seleucia; it was here that she died a peaceful death. The holy Fathers of the Church highly extolled her.

In Spain, the holy women Xantippe and Polyxena, who were disciples of the Apostles.

In Africa, the holy martyrs Andrew, John, Peter, and Anthony.

At Ancona, St. Constantius, sacristan of the church, who was remarkable for the gift of miracles.

In Campania, the commemoration of blessed Sosius, a deacon of Miseno. The holy Bishop Januarius saw a flame rise from the head of Sosius as he was reading the Gospel, and he prophesied that the deacon would soon be a martyr. Not many days after, Sosius, then about thirty years old, was martyred by being beheaded, together with St. Januarius.

At Scicy in the territory of Coutances in Gaul, the commemoration of

St. Paternus, confessor and Bishop of Avranches. His birthday is mentioned on April 16.

The Twenty-fourth Day of September

The feast of the Blessed Virgin Mary of Ransom, called under this name the foundress of the Order for the redemption of captives. The apparition of the same Blessed Virgin occurred on August 10. *A totum duplex feast.*

At Brescia, the death of St. Anathalon, bishop. He was a disciple of the Apostle St. Barnabas, and succeeded him as Bishop of the Church of Milan.

In Hungary, St. Gerard, Bishop of Csanad and martyr. He is called the Apostle of Hungary. By birth, he was a patrician of Venice. While on a journey from Csanad to Szekesfehervav, he was attacked by pagans near the Danube, stoned and then pierced with a lance. Thus, he was the first who adorned his (adopted) fatherland by a noble martyrdom.

At Autun, the birthday of the holy martyrs Androchius, priest, Thyrsus, deacon, and Felix. They were sent by St. Polycarp, Bishop of Smyrna, from the East to preach the Gospel in Gaul. There, they were scourged most severely; then, with their hands (twisted) behind them, they were hung up (by the wrists) all day long. Next, they were cast into the fire, but since they were not burned their necks were broken by heavy iron bars, and thus they were most gloriously crowned.

In Egypt, the suffering of SS. Paphnutius and his fellow-martyrs. He was dwelling in the wilderness when he learned that many Christians were being kept in chains. Aroused by the spirit of God, he offered himself of his own will to the perfect and freely confessed the Christian religion. He was first bound with iron chains and then tortured for a long time on the rack. Then, together with many others, he was sent to Diocletian, by whose command he was nailed to a palm tree. The rest of the Christians were slain by the sword.

At Chalcedon, forty-nine holy martyrs. In the reign of Diocletian, after the execution of St. Euphemia, they were condemned to the beasts. As they were miraculously delivered from them, they were at last slain by the sword, and thus passed to heaven.

At Auvergne in Gaul, the death of St. Rusticus, bishop and confessor.

At Flay in the territory of Beauvais, St. Germar, abbot.

At San Severino in Piceno, the death of St. Pacificus, priest and confessor of the Order of Friars Minor of St. Francis of Reformed Observance. Illustrious for his wonderful patience and love of solitude, he was placed in the canon of the saints by Pope Gregory XVI. ✠

The Twenty-fifth Day of September

The commemoration of our Father St. Dominic at Suriano. *A totum duplex feast.*

In the village of Emmaus, the birthday of Blessed Cleophas, who was a disciple of Christ. For confessing Christ, he is said to have been slain by the Jews in the same house in which he had made supper for the Lord. He was honorably buried there.

At Amiens in Gaul, Blessed Firminus, bishop. In the persecution of Diocletian, under the governor Rictiovarus, he underwent various tortures and gained martyrdom by being beheaded.

On the same day, on the Via Claudia, St. Herculanus, soldier and martyr. In the reign of the Emperor Antoninus, he was converted to Christ by the miracles which took place at the martyrdom of the Bishop St. Alexander. After he had suffered many tortures, he was put to death by the sword.

At Damascus, the holy martyrs Paul, Tatta his wife, and their sons Sabinian, Maximus, Rufus, and Eugene. They were accused of being Christians, and, tortured by floggings and other punishments, they gave up their souls to God.

In Asia, the suffering of SS. Bardomian, Eucarpus, and twenty-six other martyrs.

At Lyons in Gaul, the death of St. Lupus, a bishop who had formerly been a hermit.

At Auxerre, St. Anacharius, bishop and confessor.

At Blois in Gaul, St. Solemnius, Bishop of Chartres, famous for his miracles.

On the same day, St. Principius, who was Bishop of Soissons, and brother of Bishop Blessed Remigius.

At Anagni, the holy virgins Aurelia and Neomisia.

The Twenty-sixth Day of September

At Gerona (in Spain), Blessed Dalmatius Moner, confessor, of the Order of our Father St. Dominic. He was noteworthy for his severe austerity of life and his admirable abstinence from food and drink. On account of his intimacy with the angels, he was commonly referred to as "the brother who converses with the angels." *A semi-duplex feast.*

At Nicomedia, the birthday of the holy martyrs Cyprian and the virgin Justina. At the time of the Emperor Diocletian and the governor Eutholomius, she endured many sufferings for Christ. She converted to the faith the magician Cyprian who had endeavored to bewitch her by his magical arts. Later, she was martyred with him. Their bodies were flung to the beasts, but at night some Christian sailors removed the bodies and took them to Rome. Afterward, they were removed to the Constantine Basilica where they are buried near the baptistry.

At Rome, St. Callistratus, martyr, and forty-nine other soldiers. They were converted to Christ in the persecution of Diocletian, when Callistratus was sewn in a sack and cast into the sea but miraculously emerged unhurt. The forty-nine were martyred with him.

At Bologna, St. Eusebius, bishop and confessor.

At Brescia, St. Vigilius, bishop.

In the territory of Tusculum, Blessed Nilus, abbot, founder of the monastery of Grottaferrata, a man of great sanctity.

At Tifernum in Umbria, St. Amantius, priest, noted for the gift of miracles.

At Albanum, St. Senator.

The Twenty-seventh Day of September

At Aegeae (in Cilicia), the birthday of the holy martyrs and brothers Cosmas and Damian. In the persecution of Diocletian, after they had passed through many tortures, chains, imprisonment, the sea, fire, the cross, stoning, and arrows, but were miraculously unhurt, they were finally beheaded. It is said that their three brothers, Anthimus, Leontius, and Euprepius, were also martyred with them. *A simplex feast.*

At Paris, the birthday of St. Vincent de Paul, priest and confessor. He was the founder of the Congregation of the Mission, and of the Sisters of Charity. He was an apostolic man and a father to the poor. The Sovereign Pontiff, Leo XIII, appointed this saint as the heavenly patron before God of all charitable societies throughout the world which in any way were derived from him. His feast is observed on July 19.

At Byblus in Phoenicia, St. Mark, bishop. St. Luke calls him John (surnamed Mark).[8] He was the son of the St. Mary whose memory is recalled on June 29.

At Milan, St. Caius, bishop. He was a disciple of the Apostle St. Barnabas. After suffering much in the persecution of Nero, he finally died a peaceful death.

At Rome, St. Epicharis, the wife of a senator. In the persecution of Diocletian, she was beaten with leaden-tipped whips and then put to the sword.

[8] Acts, 12:12: "And considering, he (Peter) came to the house of Mary the mother of John, who was surnamed Mark." See also Acts, 15:37.

At Todi in Umbria, the holy martyrs Fidentius and Terence, who died under the same Diocletian.

At Cordoba in Spain, the holy martyrs Adulf and John, brothers, who were martyred for Christ in the Arab persecution. Their sister, the virgin St. Aurea, was inspired by their example to return to the faith. Later, she suffered martyrdom most bravely on July 19.

At Pseudon in Gaul, St. Florentinus, martyr. After his tongue had been torn out, he was slain by the sword together with St. Hilary.

At Ravenna, St. Aderitus, bishop and confessor.

At Paris, St. Elzear, Count (of Ariano).

In Hainault, St. Hiltrude, virgin. ✠

The Twenty-eighth Day of September

At Pistoia in Etruria, Blessed Laurence of Ripafratta, a confessor of our Order. Having "decided in his heart to rise ever higher" [9] **(in perfection), he soon shone with every religious virtue. St. Antoninus praised him highly, for he had had him as a novice-master and so knew well his holiness.** *A semi-duplex feast.*

At Stara Boleslav in Bohemia, St. Wenceslas, martyr, Duke of Bohemia. Famed for his holiness and miracles, he was slain by the treachery of his brother and thus achieved the palm of martyrdom.

At Rome, St. Privatus, martyr. He had been afflicted with ulcers but was healed by Pope St. Callistus. Afterward, in the reign of Emperor Alexander, he was beaten to death with leaden-tipped whips.

Also at Rome, St. Stacteus, martyr.

In Africa, the holy martyrs Martial, Laurence, and twenty others.

At Antioch in Pisidia, the shepherd St. Mark, martyr. Likewise, the commemoration of SS. Alphius, Alexander, and Zosimus, his brothers; also SS. Nicon, Neon, Heliodorus, and thirty soldiers. At the miracles of St. Mark they believed in Christ and were crowned with martyrdom in various ways and places.

On the same day, the suffering of St. Maximus, under the Emperor Decius.

At Toulouse, St. Exuperius, bishop and confessor. St. Jerome in a memorable passage told how this holy man was as sparing of his own needs as he was generous to those of others.

At Genoa, St. Salomon, bishop and confessor.

At Brescia, St. Silvinus, bishop.

In Bethlehem of Juda, St. Eustochium, virgin. With her mother St.

[9] Psalm 83:6.

Paula, she went from Rome to Palestine. There at Bethlehem, in company with other consecrated virgins, she was brought up in the ways of the spiritual life. She went to the Lord rich in unusual merits.

At Schornsheim near Mainz, St. Lioba, virgin, noted for her miracles.

The Twenty-ninth Day of September

On Mount Gargano (in Italy), the venerated memory of St. Michael the Archangel. Here, a church was consecrated in his name, built indeed on a humble plan but marked by heavenly power. *A totum duplex feast of the first class.*

At Auxerre, St. Fraternus, bishop and martyr.

In Thrace, the birthday of the holy martyrs Eutychius, Plautus, and Heracles.

In Persia, the holy martyrs Dadas, a kinsman of King Sapor, Casdoa his wife, and Gabdelas his son. They were stripped of their honors, mangled by various tortures and, after a long imprisonment, slain by the sword.

In Armenia, the holy virgins Ripsimis and her companion martyrs, under King Tiridates.

In Persia, St. Gudelia, martyr. In the reign of King Sapor, she converted many persons to Christ. Upon her refusal to adore the sun and fire she was subjected to many tortures; then the skin was torn from her head and she was nailed to a tree; thus she merited to gain her triumph.

At Pontecorvo near Aquino, St. Grimoald, priest and confessor.

In Palestine, St. Quiriacus, hermit.

The Thirtieth Day of September

In Bethlehem of Juda, the death of St. Jerome, priest, confessor, and Doctor of the Church. He eagerly studied all branches of learning and lived after the manner of monks of strict observance. With the sword of his doctrine, he destroyed many monsters of heresy. Finally, when he had lived to an extreme old age, he died peacefully, and was buried near the crib of our Lord (in Bethlehem). Later, his body was removed to Rome and buried in the Basilica of St. Mary Major. *A duplex feast.*

At Rome, the birthday of St. Francis Borgia, priest and confessor. He was general of the Society of Jesus, and is memorable for his mortification, gift of prayer, renunciation of the world, and refusal of ecclesiastical dignities. His feast is kept on October 10.

At Lisieux in France, St. Thérèse of the Child Jesus, a member of the

Order of Discalced Carmelites. She became most renowned by reason of the innocence of her life and her simplicity. The Sovereign Pontiff, Pius XI, canonized her and declared her to be the special patron of all missions. He also decreed that her feast should be observed on October 3.

Also at Rome, St. Leopardus, martyr, a member of the household of Julian the Apostate. He was beheaded and his body later removed to Aix.

At Solothurn in Gaul, the suffering of the holy martyrs Victor and Ursus, of the glorious Theban Legion. In the reign of Maximian, they were first punished with inhuman tortures but were delivered when a light from heaven shone upon them and their executioner fell to the ground. Afterward, they were cast into the fire, but they suffered no harm. Finally, they were killed by the sword.

At Piacenza, St. Antoninus, martyr, of the same Legion.

On the same day, St. Gregory, Bishop of Greater Armenia. He suffered much under Diocletian but finally, in the reign of the Emperor Constantine the Great, died a peaceful death.

At Canterbury in England, St. Honorius, bishop and confessor.

At Rome, St. Sophia, widow, mother of the holy virgins Faith, Hope and Charity.

OCTOBER

The First Day of October

St. Remigius, Bishop of Rheims and confessor. While he died in the Lord on January 13, he is especially commemorated on this day because of the transferal of his body (to the abbey at Rheims). *A feast of three lessons.*

At Rome, Blessed Aretas, martyr, and fifty-four others.

At Tournai in Gaul, St. Piato, priest and martyr. Together with St. Quinctinus and his companions, he left Rome for Gaul to preach the Gospel. Afterward, in the persecution of Maximian, he completed his martyrdom and so went to the Lord.

At Tomis in Pontus, the holy martyrs Priscus, Crescens, and Evagrius.

At Lisbon in Portugal, the holy martyrs Verissimus and Maxima and Julia, his sisters, who suffered in Diocletian's persecution.

At Thessalonica, St. Domninus, martyr, at the time of the Emperor Maximian.

At Orvieto, St. Severus, priest and confessor.

At the port of Ghent (Belgium), St. Bavo, confessor.

The Second Day of October

Feast of the Holy Guardian Angels. *A totum duplex feast.*

At Rome, the suffering of St. Modestus of Sardinia, deacon and martyr. He was tortured on the rack and then burned alive by the Emperor Diocletian. His sacred body was later removed to Benevento and buried in a church named after him.

In the region of Arras, the suffering of St. Leger, Bishop of Autun. Subjected to various injuries and tortures for upholding the truth, he was slain by Ebroin, major-domo of Theodoric. *A memory.*

At Nicomedia, St. Eleutherius, soldier and martyr, together with innumerable others. When Diocletian's palace was destroyed by fire, they were falsely accused of this deed and at the command of the same cruel Emperor were brutally slain in groups. Some of them were beheaded, some were burned alive, others were cast into the sea. But the most prominent of them, Eleutherius, was tortured for a long time. He became stronger through the torments as gold is tried in the fire, and completed his victory by martyrdom.

At Antioch, the holy martyrs Primus, Cyril, and Secundarius.

On the same day, St. Gerinus, martyr. He was the brother of St. Leger, Bishop of Autun, and, by order of the same Ebroin, he was stoned to death.

At Constantinople, St. Theophilus, monk. He was most inhumanly flogged by Leo the Isaurian for defending the (veneration of) holy images and was driven into exile where he died.

The Third Day of October

St. Thérèse of the Child Jesus, virgin, of the Order of Discalced Carmelites, special patron of all missions, whose birthday is September 30. *A duplex feast.*

At Rome, at the place called Ursus Pileatus, St. Candidus, martyr.

Among the ancient Saxons, two brothers both named Ewald, priests and martyrs. When these priests began to preach Christ to the pagans, they were seized and killed. Nightly over their bodies shone a bright light, visible for a long time, which revealed where they were and how great was their merit.

On the same day, the holy martyrs Dionysius, Faustus, Caius, Peter, Paul, and four others. They first underwent great sufferings in the reign of Decius; later, under Valerian, they were subjected to prolonged torture at the hands of the governor Emilian, and thus merited the palm of martyrdom.

In Africa, St. Maximian, Bishop of Bagaia. Again and again, he suffered the most merciless tortures at the hands of the Donatists, and was finally hurled from a high tower and left for dead. But afterward he was found (to be still alive) by persons who were passing by and recovered through their pious care. He did not stop defending the Catholic Church until, renowned for the glory of his testimony for the faith, he died a peaceful death in the Lord.

At Leon in Spain, St. Froilan, Bishop of that city. He was famed for his zeal in propagating the monastic life, generosity to the poor, and other virtues, as well as for his miracles.

In the diocese of Namur among the Belgians, St. Gerard, abbot.

In Palestine, St. Hesychius, confessor, who was a disciple of St. Hilarion and the companion of his journeys.

The Fourth Day of October

At Assisi in Umbria, the birthday of St. Francis, deacon and confessor. He was the founder of three Orders, namely: the Friars Minor, the Poor Clares, and the Brothers and Sisters of Penance. His life, replete with holiness and miracles, was written by St. Bonaventure. *A totum duplex feast of the first class.*

At Corinth, the birthday of SS. Crispus and Caius, whom the Apostle St. Paul mentions in his Epistle to the Corinthians.[1]

At Athens, St. Hierotheus, who was a disciple of the Apostle St. Paul.

At Damascus, St. Peter, bishop and martyr. He was accused before the ruler of the Agarenes of teaching the faith of Christ. His tongue, hands, and feet were cut off and he finished his martyrdom by crucifixion.

At Alexandria, the holy priests and deacons, Caius, Faustus, Eusebius, Chaeremon, Lucius, and their companions. Some were made martyrs in the persecution of Valerian, while others, by serving the martyrs, gained the rewards of martyrs.

In Egypt, the holy martyrs Mark and Marcian, brothers, and an almost countless multitude of other martyrs of both sexes and every age. Some (died) after being scourged, others endured horrible tortures of various kinds and were then flung into the flames. Some were drowned in the sea, others were beaten on the head (until they expired), many were starved to death. Finally, some were suspended by the feet from a gibbet and hung head downward (until they died). All merited a most blessed crown of martyrdom.

At Bologna, St. Petronius, bishop and confessor, who was resplendent for doctrine, miracles, and holiness.

At Paris, St. Aurea, a virgin.

The Fifth Day of October

At Nuremburg in Germany, Blessed Raymond of Capua. He became the confessor of St. Catherine of Siena, and later the master general of the Order. To the day of his death, he zealously devoted himself to the restoration of religious discipline in the Order and to the defense of the authority of the pope. *A duplex feast.*

At Messina in Sicily, the birthday of the holy martyrs Placidus, monk and disciple of St. Benedict the Abbot, his brothers, Eutychius and Victorinus, his sister the virgin Flavia; also Donatus, Firmatus, deacon, Faustus, and thirty other monks. All were killed for the faith of Christ by the pirate Manucha.

[1] Corinthians, 1:14.

At Smyrna, the birthday of Blessed Thraseas, Bishop of Eumenia, who suffered martyrdom.

At Auxerre, the death of St. Firmatus, deacon, and his sister Flaviana, virgin.

At Treves, the holy martyrs Palmatius and his companions, who were martyred by the governor Rictiovarus in the persecution of Diocletian.

On the same day, the suffering of St. Charitina, virgin. At the time of the Emperor Diocletian and under the proconsul Domitius, she was tortured by fire and then thrown into the sea. When she emerged from it unharmed, her teeth were torn out and her hands and feet were cut off. She died while in prayer.

At Ravenna, St. Marcellinus, bishop and confessor.

At Valence in Gaul, St. Apollinaris, bishop, whose life was illustrious for his virtues, and whose death was adorned with signs and wonders.

On the same day, St. Attilan, Bishop of Zamora, whom Pope Urban II placed in the number of saints.

At Rome, St. Galla, widow, daughter of Symmachus the consul. After the death of her husband, she remained for many years near the church of St. Peter, devoted to prayer, alms, fasting, and other good works. Her most happy death is described by Pope St. Gregory.

The Sixth Day of October

In the monastery of La Torre, in the diocese of Squillace in Calabria, St. Bruno, confessor and founder of the Carthusian Order. *A duplex feast.*

At Laodicea in Phrygia, Blessed Sagar, bishop and martyr. He was one of the first disciples of St. Paul the Apostle.

At Auxerre, St. Romanus, bishop and martyr.

At Capua, the birthday of the holy martyrs Marcellus, Castus, Emilius, and Saturninus.

At Treves, the commemoration of almost countless martyrs who, in the reign of Diocletian and under the governor Rictiovarus, were put to death in various ways because they had testified to the faith of Christ.

At Agen in Gaul, the birthday of St. Faith, virgin and martyr. By her example, Blessed Caprasius was encouraged to martyrdom and on October 20 completed happily his own trial.

Likewise, St. Erotis, martyr, who, aflame with the love of Christ, overcame the flames of the fire.

At Oderzo near Venice, St. Magnus, bishop, whose body is buried at Venice.

At Naples in Campania, the death of St. Mary Frances of the Five Wounds of our Lord Jesus Christ, virgin, of the Third Order of St. Francis. Being renowned for her virtues and miracles, she was canonized by Pope Pius IX.

The Seventh Day of October

At Vigevana in Insubria (Italy), Blessed Matthew Carreri of Mantua, confessor, of the Order of Preachers. *A semi-duplex feast.*

At Rome, on the Via Ardeatina, the burial of St. Mark, pope and confessor. *A memory.*

In the province called Resapha in Mesopotamia, the holy martyrs Sergius and Bacchus. They were noble Romans who lived at the time of the Emperor Maximian. Bacchus was flogged with whips of raw hide until his body was torn to shreds; he died, still confessing Christ. The feet of Sergius were forced into boots full of sharp nails; when he remained unshaken in his confession of faith, he was ordered to be beheaded. The place where he was buried was named "Sergiopolis" in his honor; Christians frequently gather there on account of the many miracles performed. *A memory.*

At Rome, the holy martyrs Marcellus and Apuleius. At first, they were followers of Simon Magus. But seeing the miracles performed by our Lord through the Apostle Peter, they left Simon Magus and embraced the teaching of the Apostle. After the death of the Apostles (Peter and Paul), they themselves gained the crown of martyrdom at the time of the consul Aurelian and were buried not far from the city.

Also at Resapha in Mesopotamia, St. Julia, virgin, who gained her martyrdom under the governor Marcian.

At Padua, St. Justina, virgin and martyr. She was baptized by Blessed Prosdocimus, a disciple of St. Peter. Since she remained unmoved in the faith of Christ, she was pierced with a sword at the command of Maximus the governor and so went to her Lord.

At Bourges in Aquitaine, St. Augustus, priest and confessor.

In the country of Rheims, St. Helanus, priest.

In Sweden, the removal of the body of St. Bridget, widow, (to Vadstena, Sweden).

The Eighth Day of October

St. Bridget, widow. Her birthday is celebrated on July 23 and the transferal of her holy body on October 7. *A duplex feast.*

On the same day, the birthday of Blessed Simeon. The Gospel related that when the Lord Jesus was presented in the temple, the old man took Him in his arms and prophesied concerning Him.[2]

At Laodicea in Phrygia, St. Artemon, priest, who received the crown of martyrdom by fire in the reign of Diocletian.

At Thessalonica, St. Demetrius, a proconsul. Because he had converted many persons to the faith of Christ, by the command of the Emperor Maximian, he was pierced with spears and so gained martyrdom.

In the same place, St. Nestor, martyr.

At Seville in Spain, St. Peter, martyr.

At Caesarea in Palestine, the suffering of St. Reparata, virgin and martyr. In the reign of the Emperor Decius, because she refused to sacrifice to idols, she was subjected to different kinds of torture, and was finally put to the sword. Her soul was seen in the form of a dove to leave her body and ascend to heaven.

In the territory of Laon, St. Benedicta, virgin and martyr.

At Ancona, SS. Palatias and Laurentia. During the persecution of Diocletian under the governor Dion, they were sent into exile where they died of labor and exhaustion.

At Rouen, St. Evodius, bishop and confessor.

At Jerusalem, St. Pelagia, called the Penitent.

The Ninth Day of October

At Paris, the birthday of the holy martyrs the Bishop Dionysius the Areopagite, the priest Rusticus, and the deacon Eleutherius. Dionysius was baptized by the Apostle Paul, and ordained first Bishop of Athens. Then, coming to Rome, he was sent into Gaul by the Roman Pontiff, St. Clement, to preach the Gospel. Arriving at Paris, he faithfully carried out for a number of years the work entrusted to him. At last, after being subjected to most severe tortures by the prefect Fescenninus, he underwent martyrdom, together with his companions, by being put to the sword. *A duplex feast.*

On the same day, the memory of St. Abraham, Patriarch and father of all believers.

At Monte Cassino, St. Deusdedit, abbot. He was cast into prison by the tyrant Sicardus and there died from labors and starvation.

At Julia, on the Via Claudia, in the province of Parma, St. Domninus, martyr. While he tried to avoid the fury of the persecution under the Emperor Maximian, yet when captured by his pursuers he met death bravely and died by the sword.

[2] Luke, 2:25 ff.

In Hainault, St. Gislenus, bishop and confessor. Resigning his bishopric, he led the life of a monk in the monastery he had built. He was distinguished for his many virtues.

At Valencia in Aragon, St. Louis Bertrand, confessor, of the Order of Preachers. He was of a noble and apostolic spirit and confirmed, both by the innocence of his life and by the numerous miracles he performed, the Gospel he preached to the American Indians. His feast is observed October 10.

At Jerusalem, SS. Andronicus and Athanasia his wife.

At Antioch, St. Publia, abbess. When Julian the Apostate was passing by her dwelling, she and the consecrated virgins living with her were singing the psalm of David: "The idols of the Gentiles are of gold and silver," and "they that make them are like unto them." By command of the Emperor, she was buffeted and grossly reviled.

At Rome, St. John Leonardi, confessor, and founder of the Congregation of Clerks Regular of the Mother of God. He was distinguished for his labors and miracles, and by his efforts missions were instituted for the propagation of the faith. ✠

The Tenth Day of October

At Valencia in Spain, St. Louis Bertrand, (confessor) of the Order of Preachers. He was sent to the West Indies, and although he could speak only the Spanish tongue—a language unknown to the Indians—he converted countless souls to the Christian religion. He was distinguished for his numerous miracles both in life and after death. He died October 9 and was beatified by Paul V. He was canonized by Clement X. *A totum duplex feast of the second class.*

St. Francis Borgia, priest of the Society of Jesus, and confessor, whose birthday is noted on September 30.

At Ceuta in Morocco, the suffering of the seven holy martyrs of the Order of Friars Minor, namely: Daniel, Samuel, Angelus, Leo, Nicholas, Ugolino, and Domnus. All were priests except Domnus. Because they preached the Gospel and put to silence the Mohammedan teachers, the Saracens reviled, chained, and scourged them. Finally, they were beheaded and thus gained the palm of martyrdom.

At Cologne, St. Gereon, martyr, who, in the persecution of Maximian, together with three hundred and eighteen others, patiently suffered beheading for the true religion.

In the neighborhood of the same city, SS. Victor and his companions, martyrs.

At Bonn in Germany, the holy martyrs Cassius and Florentius, with very many others.

At Nicomedia, the holy martyrs Eulampius and the virgin Eulampia, his sister. On hearing that her brother was being tortured for Christ, she broke through the crowd and, embracing her brother, joined him as another Christian. Both were cast into a vessel of boiling oil; when this failed to harm them in the slightest, they fulfilled their martyrdom by being beheaded. Two hundred spectators, who had been converted by the miracle and believed in Christ, were executed with them.

On the island of Crete, Blessed Pinytus, one of the most noble of bishops. He flourished as bishop in the city of Gnosia, under Marcus Antoninus Verus and Lucius Aurelius Commodus. In his writing, as in a mirror, he has left a living image of himself.

At York in England, St. Paulinus, bishop. He was a disciple of Pope St. Gregory, who sent him to England, together with others, to preach the Gospel. He converted King Edwin and his people to the Christian faith.

At Piombino in Tuscany, St. Cerbonius, bishop and confessor. As St. Gregory states, he was noteworthy for his miracles both in life and in death.

At Verona, (another) St. Cerbonius, bishop.

At Capua, St. Paulinus, bishop.

The Eleventh Day of October

At Bologna, Blessed James (of Ulm), a German lay-brother of the Order of Preachers. Remarkable in the exercise of heroic virtues and especially in humility, he made himself lovable to heaven and wonderful on earth. *A semi-duplex feast.*

At Tarsus in Cilicia, the holy women Zenais and Philonilla, sisters. They were kinsfolk of the Apostle St. Paul, and his disciples in the faith.

Near Vexin in Gaul, the sufferings of the holy martyrs Nicasius, Bishop of Rouen, the priest Quirinus, the deacon Scubiculus, and Pientia, virgin, under the governor Fescenninus.

At Besançon in Gaul, St. Germanus, bishop and martyr.

Likewise, the suffering of SS. Anathasius, priest, Placidus, Genesius, and their companions.

At Tarsus in Cilicia, the birthday of the holy martyrs, Tharacus, Probus, and Andronicus. In the persecution of Diocletian, they suffered detention for a long time in a filthy prison. On three occasions they were put to the torture in various ways; they finally obtained the crown of glory for their confessing Christ by being beheaded.

In the Thebaid, St. Sarmata, who was a disciple of Blessed Anthony the Abbot. He was slain for Christ by the Saracens.

At Uzès in Gaul, St. Firmin, bishop and confessor.

At Calozzo in the Diocese of Asti, formerly that of Pavia, St. Alexander Sauli, of the Clerks Regular of St. Paul, bishop and confessor. He was of noble birth and was renowned for his virtues, learning and miracles. He was canonized by Pius X, the Sovereign Pontiff.

In the monastery of Aghaboe in Ireland, St. Kenny, priest and abbot.

At Lier in Belgium, the death of St. Gummar, confessor.

At Rennes in Gaul, St. Emilian, confessor.

At Verona, St. Placidia, virgin.

The Twelfth Day of October

At Monte Cerignone in the Diocese of Montefeltro, Blessed Dominic Spadafora, (a confessor) of our Order. He was outstanding in his assiduous practice of prayer, of regular observance, and of preaching the Word of God. Pope Benedict XV ratified and confirmed his immemorial cult. *A semi-duplex feast.*

At Rome, the holy martyrs Evagrius, Priscian, and their companions.

In Africa, four thousand nine hundred and sixty-six confessors and martyrs in the Vandal persecution under the Arian King Hunneric. Some were bishops of the Churches of God, some were priests and deacons, while the rest were multitudes of the faithful. Because of their adherence to the Catholic religion, they were driven into a horrible desert. Many were cruelly treated by the Moors, by being compelled to run at spearpoint, and by being stoned. Others had their feet tied together and were dragged like corpses through rough and stony places until torn limb from limb. All, tortured in diverse ways, finally gained martyrdom. Chief among them were the noble priests of God, Bishop Felix and Bishop Cyprian.

At Ravenna, on the Via Laurentina, the birthday of St. Edistius, martyr.

In Lycia, St. Domnina, martyr, in the reign of the Emperor Diocletian.

At Celje in Hungary, St. Maximillian, Bishop of Lorach.

At York in England, St. Wilfrid, bishop and confessor.

At Milan, St. Monas, bishop. When the question of electing a bishop was being discussed, he was surrounded by a light from heaven and by that wondrous sign was received as the bishop of that church.

At Verona, St. Salvinus, bishop.

In Syria, St. Eustace, priest and confessor.

At Ascoli in Piceno (Italy), St. Seraphinus, confessor, of the Order of Friars Minor Capuchin. He was remarkable for his holy life and humility; he was canonized by the Sovereign Pontiff, Clement XIII.

The Thirteenth Day of October

In the town of Trino-Vercellese (in Italy), Blessed Magdalen Panattieri, virgin, of our Order. She joined innocence to patience and merited to be enriched with heavenly gifts. At last, abounding in merit and virtue, she received the crown set aside for her in heaven. *A semi-duplex feast.*

St. Edward, King of England and confessor. He died on January 5, but is preferably commemorated on this day when his body was transferred (to a shrine in the choir).

At Troas, a city in Asia Minor, the birthday of St. Carpus, who was a disciple of the Apostle St. Paul.

At Cordoba in Spain, the birthday of the holy martyrs Faustus, Januarius, and Martial. They were first tortured on the rack; then they eyelids were cut off, their teeth torn out, their ears and noses sliced off. Finally, they finished their martyrdom by fire.

At Thessalonica, St. Florentius, martyr, who after undergoing various tortures was burned alive.

At Stockerau in Austria, St. Coloman, martyr.

At Antioch, the holy Patriarch Theophilus. He was the sixth after St. Peter the Apostle to hold the bishopric of that Church.

At Tours in Gaul, St. Venantius, abbot and confessor.

At Subiaco in Latium (Italy), St. Chelidonia, virgin.

The Fourteenth Day of October

At Rome, on the Via Aurelia, the birthday of Blessed Callistus I, pope and martyr. At the command of the Emperor Alexander, he was tortured for a long time, starved in prison, and flogged daily. Then he was thrown from a window of the house where he had been imprisoned and drowned in a well; thus he merited the triumph of victory. *A duplex feast.*

At Rimini, St. Gaudentius, bishop and martyr.

At Caesarea in Palestine, SS. Carponius, Evaristus, and Priscian, brothers of St. Fortunata. Their throats were cut by the sword and together they won the palm of martyrdom.

Also, SS. Saturninus and Lupus.

At Caesarea in Palestine, St. Fortunata, virgin and martyr. She was the sister of the martyrs just mentioned—Carponius, Evaristus, and Priscian.

She surrendered her soul to God after she had endured the rack, fire, wild beasts, and other tortures in Diocletian's persecution. Her body was afterward transferred to Naples in Campania.

At Todi in Umbria, St. Fortunatus, bishop. As St. Gregory tells us, he was distinguished by an extraordinary gift of putting unclean spirits to flight.

At Würzburg in Germany, St. Burchard, who was the first bishop of that city.

At Bruges in Flanders, St. Donatian, Bishop of Rheims.

At Treves, St. Rusticus, bishop.

At Lyons in Gaul, St. Justus, bishop and confessor. He was a man of wonderful sanctity and endowed with the gift of prophecy. He resigned his bishopric and departed with his lector Viator into a desert of Egypt. For many years he led a life that was almost angelic and when the fitting end of his labors drew near, he went to the Lord to receive a crown of justice. His holy body, together with the remains of blessed Viator, his minister, were afterward transferred to Lyons on September 2.

On the same day, the death of blessed Dominic Loricatus.

At Arpino in Latium, St. Bernard, confessor.

The Fifteenth Day of October

At Avila in Spain, St. Teresa, virgin. She was the mother and mistress of the Brothers and Sisters of the Carmelite Order of Strict Observance. *A duplex feast.*

At Cracow in Poland, the birthday of St. Hedwig, widow, and a duchess of Poland. She devoted herself to the service of the poor and was, in addition, famous for her miracles. The Sovereign Pontiff, Clement IV, canonized her. Her feast is observed on October 17.

At Rome, on the Via Aurelia, St. Fortunatus, martyr.

In Prussia, St. Bruno, Bishop of the Ruthenians and martyr. While he was preaching the Gospel in that region, he was seized by wicked men who first cut off his hands and feet, and then beheaded him.

At Cologne, the birthday of three hundred holy martyrs who, in the persecution of Maximian, persevered to the end in their trial.

At Carthage, St. Agileus, martyr. On his anniversary, St. Augustine delivered a panegyric concerning him.

At Lyons in Gaul, St. Antiochius, bishop. He zealously administered the pontifical office to which he had been appointed and thus gained a heavenly kingdom.

At Treves, St. Severus, bishop and confessor.

At Strasbourg, St. Aurelia, virgin.

In Germany, St. Thecla, abbess and virgin. She had charge of the convents of Kitzingen and Ochsenfürt, and rich in merit departed for heaven. ✠

The Sixteenth Day of October

In the monastery of Moutier-en-Der in Gaul, St. Becharius, abbot and martyr.

In Africa, two hundred and seventy holy martyrs, crowned together.

In the same country, SS. Martinian and Saturian with their two brothers. In the Vandal persecution under the Arian King Genseric, they were the servants of a certain Vandal and were converted to the Catholic faith by their fellow-servant, St. Maxima, virgin. For their constancy in the Catholic faith, their master beat them with knobbed clubs even to the bones. They endured these beatings for many days but always appeared on the next day unhurt. They were then driven into exile where they converted many barbarians to the faith of Christ. They obtained from the Roman Pontiff a priest and other ministers to baptize them. Eventually, their feet were fastened to the back of chariots and they were dragged through thorny places in the woods until they died. Maxima, however, after triumphing in several contests, was delivered by a miracle, and ended her days quietly in a monastery where she was the spiritual mother of numerous consecrated virgins.

Also, SS. Saturninus, Nereus, and three hundred and sixty-five martyrs.

At Cologne, St. Eliphius, martyr, at the time of Julian the Apostate.

In the territory of Bourges, St. Ambrose, Bishop of Cahors.

At Mainz, St. Lullus, bishop and confessor.

At Treves, St. Florentinus, bishop.

Near Arbon in Germany, St. Gall, abbot, who was a disciple of Blessed Columban.

At Muro in Lucania (Italy), St. Gerard Majella, confessor and professed lay-brother of the Congregation of the Most Holy Redeemer. Renowned for miracles, he was added to the list of saints by the Sovereign Pontiff, Pius X.

The Seventeenth Day of October

St. Hedwig, widow, and a duchess of Poland, who died October 15.

At Antioch, the birthday of St. Heron, who was a disciple of Blessed Ignatius. He was made bishop after the latter and religiously followed his master's example, giving his life as a lover of Christ for the flock entrusted to him.

On the same day, the suffering of SS. Victor, Alexander, and Marianus.

In Persia, St. Mameltas, martyr. By the warning of an angel, he was converted to the faith from the worship of idols. He was stoned by the pagans and drowned in a deep lake.

At Orange in Gaul, St. Florentius, bishop. Rich in merit, he died a peaceful death.

At Paray in the Diocese of Autun, St. Margaret Mary Alacoque. She made her profession in the Order of the Visitation of Blessed Virgin Mary. She excelled by her merit in spreading devotion to the Most Sacred Heart of Jesus and in advancing its public cult. Pope Benedict XV canonized her.

The Eighteenth Day of October

In Bithynia, the birthday of St. Luke the Evangelist. He suffered greatly for the name of Christ and died filled with the Holy Ghost. His remains were transferred to Constantinople and from there were taken to Pavia. *A totum duplex feast of the second class.*

At Rome, the birthday of St. Paul of the Cross, priest, confessor, and founder of the Congregation of the Cross and Passion of our Lord Jesus Christ. He was a man remarkable for his innocence and penance, and was aflame with love for Christ crucified. Pope Pius IX canonized him and appointed April 28 as the date for the celebration of his feast.

At Arenas in Spain, the birthday of St. Peter of Alcantara, priest of the Order of Friars Minor and confessor. The Sovereign Pontiff, Clement IX, canonized him because of his remarkable penance and numerous miracles. His feast, however, is celebrated on October 19.

At Antioch, St. Asclepiades, bishop. He was one of that famous band of Martyrs who suffered so gloriously under Macrinus.

At Neocaesaria in Pontus, St. Athenodorus, bishop, who was the brother of the Wonder-Worker. Distinguished for his learning, he suffered martyrdom in the persecution of Aurelian.

At Louvres near Beauvais, St. Justus, martyr. He was still only a boy when he was beheaded in the persecution of Diocletian by the governor Rictiovarus.

At Rome, St. Tryphonia, widow of the Emperor Decius. She was the mother of the virgin martyr St. Cyrilla. Her body was buried in the crypt near that of St. Hippolytus.

Near Edessa in Mesopotamia, the commemoration of St. Julian, hermit, surnamed Sabas, who is also mentioned on January 17.

The Nineteenth Day of October

St. Peter of Alcantara, priest, of the Order of Friars Minor, and confessor, whose birthday is noted on October 18. *A duplex feast.*

At Rome, the birthday of the holy martyrs Ptolemy and Lucius, under Marcus Antoninus. As St. Justin relates, Ptolemy converted a certain sinful woman to the faith of Christ and taught her to prize chastity; for so doing, he was accused by a wicked man before the prefect Urbicius and forced to undergo for a long time a foul imprisonment. At last, when by a public confession he testified that Christ was his master, he was ordered to be led out for execution. Lucius, on protesting against the sentence of Urbicius and freely confessing that he himself was a Christian, received the same sentence. A third martyr was added to these; he was also condemned to the same punishment.

At Antioch, SS. Beronicus, Pelagia, virgin, and forty-nine others.

In Egypt, St. Varus, soldier. In the reign of the Emperor Maximian, he visited and encouraged seven holy monks who were imprisoned. When one of them died, he wished to be accepted in his place; after suffering with them the most inhuman tortures, he gained the palm of martyrdom.

At Evreux in Gaul, St. Aquilinus, bishop and confessor.

In the territory of Orleans, the death of St. Veranus, bishop.

Near Salerno, St. Eusterius, bishop.

In the monastery of Nectan Wood, in Ireland, St. Ethbin, abbot.

At Oxford in England, St. Frideswide, virgin.

The Twentieth Day of October

St. John Cantius, priest and confessor, who died in the Lord December 24.

At Avia near Aquila (Italy), among the Vestinians, the birthday of St. Maximus, deacon and martyr. Longing to suffer for Christ, he deliberately gave himself up to the executioners who were seeking him. After he had firmly answered all questions, he was suspended on the rack and tortured; then he was beaten with clubs. He died finally when he was hurled from a high place.

At Agen in Gaul, St. Caprasius, martyr. To escape the raging persecution, he hid in a cave. At length, after hearing how the virgin St. Faith had endured torture for Christ, he was drawn to follow her example. He asked God that, if He judged him worthy of the glory of martyrdom, a spring of clear water should flow from a rock in the cave. The Lord gave him this sign and he hastened, now sure of himself, to the place of the contest. By his courageous strife, he merited the palm of martyrdom, under Maximian.

At Antioch, St. Artemius. He was an imperial officer who occupied high positions in the army under Constantine the Great. He rebuked Julian the Apostate for his cruelty toward the Christians. For this, he was beaten with clubs, subjected to other tortures, and finally ordered to be beheaded.

At Constantinople, St. Andrew of Crete, monk. On account of his veneration of holy images during the reign of Constantine Copronymus, he was repeatedly scourged. Finally, after one foot had been cut off, he expired.

At Cologne, the suffering of the holy virgins Martha and Saula with many others.

At Tomar in Portugal, St. Irene, virgin and martyr. Her body was honorably buried at Scalabis and since then the town has been re-named Santarem after her.

At Aussonce near Rheims, St. Sindulphus, priest and confessor.

Near Minden in Germany, the transferal of (the relics of) St. Felician, Bishop of Foligno and martyr. A portion of his holy relics was placed in an urn and brought to Germany from the city of Foligno in Umbria, where he died on January 24.

At Paris, likewise the transferal from Cordoba in Spain, of (the relics of) the holy martyrs George, deacon, and Aurelius. They were martyred at Cordoba, together with three companions, on July 27.

The Twenty-first Day of October

At Cortona (in Italy), Blessed Peter Cappucci of Tiferno, confessor, of our Order. By constant meditation on death, he raised himself to heavenly things, and by his preaching he led many hardened sinners to virtue. *A semi-duplex feast.*

In Cyprus, the birthday of Blessed Hilarion, abbot. His life, which was written by St. Jerome, was rich in virtues and miracles.

At Cologne, the birthday of St. Ursula and her companions, martyrs. For the Christian religion and for their constancy in virginity, they were massacred by the Huns and so ended their lives by martyrdom. The bodies of many of them are buried at Cologne. *A memory.*

At Ostia, St. Asterius, priest and martyr. He suffered under Alexander the Emperor, as is written in the Acts of Pope St. Callistus.

At Nicomedia, the birthday of SS. Dasius, Zoticus, Caius, and twelve other soldiers, who, after various tortures, were drowned in the sea.

At Lyons in Gaul, St. Viator, a minister of St. Justus, Bishop of Lyons.

At Maronia in Syria, near Antioch, St. Malchus, monk.

In the town of Laon, St. Cilinia, mother of St. Remigius, Bishop of Rheims.

The Twenty-second Day of October

The Anniversary of the Dedication of our own Church. *A totum duplex feast of the first class.*

At Jerusalem, St. Mary Salome, the mother of the Apostles James and John. She is referred to in the Gospel as having cared for the burial of the Lord.[3]

Also at Jerusalem, Blessed Mark, bishop. A most noble and learned man, he was the first Gentile to receive the office of governing the Church of Jerusalem. Not long after, he merited to receive the palm of martyrdom under the Emperor Antoninus.

At Adrianople in Thrace, the birthday of the holy martyrs Philip, bishop, Severus, priest, Eusebius, and Hermes. In the time of Julian the Apostate, after they had been imprisoned and scourged, they were burned to death.

Likewise the holy martyrs Alexander, bishop, Heraclius, soldier, and their companions.

Near Fermo in Piceno, St. Philip, bishop and martyr.

Near Cologne, St. Cordula, who was one of the companions of St. Ursula. She hid herself, being terrified by the tortures and slaying of the others. But on the next day, repenting of her deed, she gave herself up to the Huns, and thus was the last of all to receive the crown of martyrdom.

At Huesca in Spain, the holy virgins Nunilo and Alodia, sisters. They were sentenced to death by the Saracens for confessing the faith, and so gained their martyrdom.

At Hieropolis in Phrygia, St. Abercius, bishop, who flourished in the time of the Emperor Marcus Antoninus.

At Rouen, St. Melanius, bishop. He was ordained by Pope St. Stephen and sent to Rouen to preach the Gospel.

In Tuscany, St. Donatus the Scot, Bishop of Fiesole.

At Verona, St. Verecundius, bishop and confessor.

The Twenty-third Day of October

At Vicenza (in Italy), Blessed Bartholomew Breganza, bishop and confessor, of the Order of our Father St. Dominic. He was first placed in charge of the see at Limassol (on the island of Cyprus); afterward, he

[3] Mark, 16:1.

was in charge of the see of Vicenza. Because of his outstanding piety and his labors for spreading the Catholic religion, he was most highly regarded by Pope Gregory IX (to whom he was an advisor), as well as by other Sovereign Pontiffs, and by St. Louis, King of France. *A semi-duplex feast.*

At Ilok in Hungary, the birthday of St. John of Capistrano, priest, of the Order of Friars Minor, and confessor. He was illustrious for holiness of life and zeal in extending the Catholic faith. By his prayers and miracles, he delivered from a siege the fortress of Zemun (a suburb of Belgrade), when it was beleaguered by a powerful Turkish army. His feast, however, is observed on March 28.

At Antioch, the birthday of St. Theodore, priest. He was arrested in the persecution of the wicked Julian. Despite the torment of the rack and other severe tortures, including the burning of his sides with torches, he persevered in his confession of Christ. He completed his martyrdom by being put to the sword.

At Osuma near Cadiz in Spain, the holy martyrs Servandus and Germanus. In the persecution of Diocletian, under the acting governor Viator, they were flogged, confined to a foul prison, subjected to hunger and thirst, and forced to endure the hardships of a long journey which they made loaded with chains. They eventually finished the course of their martyrdom by having their throats cut. Germanus was buried at Merida and Servandus at Seville.

At Constantinople, St. Ignatius, bishop. He rebuked Bardas Caesar for putting away his wife; for this reason, he was subjected to many sufferings by the Emperor and driven into exile. However, he was restored (to his see) by the Roman Pontiff St. Nicholas, and at last died a peaceful death.

At Bordeaux, St. Severinus, Bishop of Cologne, confessor.

At Rouen, St. Romanus, bishop.

At Salerno, St. Verus, bishop.

In the territory of Amiens, St. Domitius, priest.

In the country of Poitiers, St. Benedict, confessor.

At Mantua, Blessed John the Good, confessor, of the Order of the Hermits of St. Augustine, whose excellent life was written by St. Antoninus.

The Twenty-fourth Day of October

The feast of St. Raphael the Archangel. His dignity and his favors (to the human race) are set forth in the sacred book of Tobias. *A totum duplex feast.*

At Venosa in Apulia, the birthday of the holy martyrs Felix, an African bishop, Audactus and Januarius, priests, and the lectors Fortunatus and Septimus. In the reign of Diocletian, they all were punished by being heavily chained and imprisoned for a long time in Africa and in Sicily. Since Felix would not comply with the Emperor's edict and surrender the holy books, all the above-mentioned men were put to the sword.

At Tongres in Belgium, St. Evergislus, Bishop of Cologne and martyr. On account of the duties of his pastoral office, he journeyed to Tongres. That night, while on his way to pray alone in the monastic church of the Most Holy Mother of God, he was attacked by robbers and killed by an arrow.

At Nagran, among the Hymarites in Arabia,[4] the suffering of SS. Aretas and his three hundred and forty companions, at the time of the Emperor Justin, under the Jewish tyrant Dunaan. After they had been put to death, a Christian woman was thrown into the fire. Her five-year-old son lisped that he too was a Christian, and neither caresses nor threats could prevent him from flinging himself into the fire where his mother was dying.

At Constantinople, St. Proclus, bishop.

On the Isle of Jersey, St. Maglorious, bishop. After he had resigned his episcopal see, which he had filled for three years toward his scattered flock in Brittany, he built a monastery on the Isle of Jersey, where he spent the remainder of his life in holiness. His body was later transferred to Paris.

In the monastery of Durin in Gaul, St. Martin, deacon and abbot. His body was removed to the monastery of Vertou.

In Campania, St. Mark the Solitary, whose remarkable deeds are recorded by Pope St. Gregory.

The Twenty-fifth Day of October

At Rome, the holy martyrs Chrysanthus and his wife Daria. After many sufferings endured for Christ under the prefect Celerinus, they were sentenced by the Emperor Numerian to be placed in a sand-pit on the Via Salaria and to be buried alive with earth and stones.

Also, the birthday of Marcellinus, pope and martyr. In the reign of Maximian, he, together with Claudius, Cyrinus, and Antoninus, was beheaded for the faith of Christ. The persecution at that time was so great that in one month seventeen thousand Christians received the crown of

[4] See note under July 27.

martyrdom. The feast of St. Marcellinus, together with that of the pope and martyr St. Cletus, is observed on April 26.

At Perigueux in Gaul, St. Fronto, who was ordained bishop by the Apostle St. Peter. He converted a great multitude of that people to Christ with the assistance of a priest named George. Famed for his miracles, he died a peaceful death.

At Rome, the birthday of forty-six holy soldiers. They were all baptized together by Pope St. Dionysius, and shortly after, by command of the Emperor Claudius, they were beheaded and were buried on the Via Salaria. There also were buried one hundred and twenty-one other martyrs, among whom were the four soldiers of Christ, Theodosius, Lucius, Mark, and Peter.

At Porto Torres in Sardinia, the holy martyrs Protus, priest, and Januarius, deacon. They were sent to that island by Pope St. Caius and were martyred there in the reign of Diocletian under the governor Barbarus.

At Constantinople, the suffering of SS. Martyrius, subdeacon, and Marcian, a choir singer. They were slain by heretics in the reign of the emperor Constantius.

At Soissons in Gaul, the holy martyrs Crispin and Crispinian. In the persecution of Diocletian, under the governor Rictiovarus, these noble Romans, after enduring great torments, were butchered by the sword, thus obtaining the crown of martyrdom. Their bodies were afterward taken to Rome and buried with honors in the church of St. Laurence in Panisperna. *A memory.*

At Florence, the suffering of Blessed Minias, soldier. He fought bravely for the faith for Christ in the reign of the Emperor Decius, and was crowned with a noble martyrdom.

At Brescia, the birthday of St. Gaudentius, bishop. He was remarkable for his learning and sanctity.

At Gabali in Gaul, St. Hilary, bishop.

The Twenty-sixth Day of October

At Reggio Emilia (in Italy), Blessed Damian Furcherio of Finario, (confessor, of the Order of Preachers). To the subjection of the body, he joined integrity of life. Fired with zeal for preaching, he became a wonderful herald of Christ, and after death was noted for his miracles. *A semi-duplex feast.*

At Rome, St. Evaristus, pope and martyr. He enriched the Church of God with his blood at the time of the Emperor Hadrian.

In Africa, the holy martyrs Rogatian, priest, and Felicissimus. They were crowned with an illustrious martyrdom in the persecution of Valerian and Gallienus. St. Cyprian speaks of them in his Epistle to the Confessors.

At Nicomedia, the holy martyrs Lucian, Florius, and their companions.

At Narbonne in Gaul, St. Rusticus, bishop and confessor, who lived in the reigns of the Emperors Valentinian and Leo.

Near Salerno, St. Gaudiosus, bishop.

At Pavia, St. Fulk, bishop.

Also, St. Quadragesimus, subdeacon, who raised a dead man to life.

The Twenty-seventh Day of October

The Vigil of the holy Apostles Simon and Jude.

At Avila in Spain, the suffering of SS. Vincent, Sabina, and Christeta. They were first stretched on the rack until all the joints of their bodies were dislocated. Their heads were then placed upon stones and they were struck with heavy bars until their brains were beaten out. Thus, under the governor Dacian, they fulfilled their martyrdom.

At Thil-Châtel in Gaul, St. Florentius, martyr.

In Cappadocia, the holy martyrs Capitolina and Erotheis her maid; they suffered in the reign of Diocletian.

In the Indies, St. Frumentius, bishop. He was first a captive there, and after he was ordained bishop by St. Athanasius, he spread the Gospel in that region.

At Naples in Campania, St. Gaudiosus, an African bishop. Because of the Vandal persecution, he came to Campania and died a peaceful death in a monastery of that city.

In Ethiopia, St. Elesbaan, king. Having overcome the enemies of Christ at the time of the Emperor Justin, he sent his royal diadem to Jerusalem, led a monastic life, as he had vowed to do, and departed for his eternal reward.

The Twenty-eighth Day of October

In Persia, the birthday of the Blessed Apostles Simon the Canaanite, and Thaddeus, who is also called Jude. Simon preached the Gospel in Egypt, and Thaddeus in Mesopotamia. Then both went to Persia and there suffered martyrdom, after having won over a vast multitude to Christ. *A totum duplex feast of the second class.*

At Rome, the holy martyrs, Anastasia the Elder, virgin, and Cyril. In the persecution of Valerian, under the prefect Probus, Anastasia was loaded with chains, buffeted, and tortured by fire as well as by floggings. As she remained unshaken in her confession of Christ, she was then mutilated, her nails torn out, her hands and feet amputated, and finally her head cut off. Thus, enriched with the jewels of many sufferings, she went to her heavenly Spouse. She had begged for a cup of water (during her agony) and Cyril gave it to her; for his reward, he gained the crown of martyrdom.

Also at Rome, St. Cyrilla, the virgin daughter of St. Tryphonia. At the time of the Emperor Claudius, because she confessed Christ, her throat was cut.

Near Como, St. Fidelis, martyr, in the reign of the Emperor Maximian.

At Mainz, the martyr St. Ferrutius.

At Meux in Gaul, St. Faro, bishop and confessor.

At Vercelli, the bishop St. Honoratus. ✠

The Twenty-ninth Day of October

Octave of the Dedication of our own Church *A simplex octave.*

The holy bishops, Maximilian a martyr, and Valentine a confessor.

At Sidon in Phoenicia, St. Zenobius, priest. Throughout the fury of the last persecution, he encouraged others during their martyrdom, and he himself was found worthy of such a death.

In Lucania, the holy martyrs Hyacinth, Quinctius, Felician, and Lucius.

At Bergamo, St. Eusebia, virgin and martyr.

At Jerusalem, the birthday of Blessed Narcissus, bishop. He was a man praiseworthy for his holiness, patience, and faith. He died in the Lord when one hundred and sixteen years of age.

At Autun, St. John, bishop and confessor.

At Cassiope on the island of Corcyra, St. Donatus, bishop. He is mentioned by Pope St. Gregory.

At Vienne in Gaul, the death of Blessed Theodore, abbot.

The Thirtieth Day of October

At Cividale in Friuli (Italy), Blessed Benvenuta Bojani, virgin, of our Order, who blossomed by penance, prayer, and humility. *A semi-duplex feast.*

In Sardinia, the birthday of St. Pontianus, pope and martyr. He was exiled to Sardinia in company with Hippolytus, priest, by the Emperor Alexander. Here he gained martyrdom by being clubbed to death. His body was brought to Rome by Pope St. Fabian and buried in the cemetery of St. Callistus. His feast, however, is observed on November 19.

At Aeges in Cilicia, the sufferings of SS. Zenobius, bishop, and his sister Zenobia, under the governor Lysias, in the reign of the Emperor Diocletian.

At Altino near Venice, St. Theonestus, bishop and martyr, who was put to death by the Arians.

In Africa, the birthday of two hundred and twenty holy martyrs.

At Tangier in Mauretania, the suffering of St. Marcellus, a centurion. He was the father of the holy martyrs Claudius, Lupercus, and Victorius. He gained martyrdom by being beheaded under Agricolaus, who was acting as praetor in the place of Praefectus.

At Alexandria, thirteen holy martyrs. In company with SS. Julian, Eunus, and Macharius, they suffered under the emperor Decius.

At Cagliari in Sardinia, St. Saturninus, martyr. In the persecution of Diocletian, he was beheaded by the governor Barbarus.

At Apamea in Phrygia, St. Maximus, martyr, under the same Diocletian.

At Leon in Spain, the holy martyrs Claudius, Lupercus, and Victorius, the sons of the centurion St. Marcellus. In the persecution of Diocletian and Maximian, they were condemned to be beheaded by the governor Diogenian.

At Paris, St. Lucanus, martyr.

At Alexandria, St. Eutropia, martyr. She was arrested while visiting the martyrs. She died after being cruelly tortured with them.

At Antioch, St. Seraphion, bishop. He was noted for his learning.

At Capua, St. Germanus, bishop and confessor. He was a man of great sanctity and St. Benedict saw his soul, at the hour of death, being carried by angels into Heaven.

At Potenza in Lucania, St. Gerard, bishop.

The Thirty-first Day of October

The Vigil of All Saints.

The Commemoration of the holy martyrs, and of the other saints, whose bodies or relics are preserved in our churches. *A totum duplex feast.*

At Rome, St. Ampliatus, Urban, and Narcissus, whom St. Paul mentions in his Epistle to the Romans.[5] They were slain by Jews and Gentiles for the Gospel of Christ.

[5] Romans, 16, 8, 9, 11.

At Constantinople, St. Stachys, bishop. He was ordained the first bishop of that city by the Apostle St. Andrew.

Near the imperial city of Vermandois,[6] in Gaul, St. Quintinus, a Roman citizen of senatorial rank. He underwent martyrdom at the time of the Emperor Maximian, and, through the revelation of an angel, his body was found fifty-five years later, still incorrupt. *A memory.*

At Milan, St. Antoninus, bishop and confessor.

At Ratisbon in Bavaria, St. Wolfgang, bishop.

At Palma on the island of Majorca, St. Alphonsus Rodriguez, lay-coadjutor of the Society of Jesus, and confessor. He was noted for his humility and his continual zeal in mortification. He was canonized by the Sovereign Pontiff, Leo XIII.

At Rome, the transferal (of the relics) of St. Nemesius, deacon, and his daughter the virgin Lucilla, who were beheaded on August 25.

[6] The city, *Augusta Veromanduorum,* was later named after the saint, Saint-Quentin.

NOVEMBER

The First Day of November

The Festival of All Saints. Pope Boniface IV dedicated the Pantheon temple "in honor of the Blessed Virgin Mary, Mother of God, and in honor of the holy martyrs," and he decreed that every year this feast should be fittingly and generally observed throughout Rome. A somewhat similar feast was already observed in various ways in other dioceses; hence Gregory IV decreed that the feast, now extended to include all saints, should be forever solemnly celebrated in the Universal Church on the first day of November. *A totum duplex feast of the first class with a solemn octave.*

In Persia, the holy martyrs John, bishop, and James, priest, under King Sapor.

At Terracina in Campania, the birthday of St. Caesarius, deacon. He was harshly treated in prison for many days; afterward, with St. Julian, priest, he was placed in a sack and cast into the sea.

In the town of Dijon, the priest St. Benignus. He was sent into Gaul by St. Polycarp to preach the Gospel. Later, in the reign of the Emperor Marcus Aurelius, he was repeatedly subjected to the most inhuman tortures by the judge Terence. Finally, it was ordered that his neck be beaten with an iron bar and his body pierced with a spear.

At Damascus, the suffering of SS. Caesarius, Dacius, and five others.

On the same day, the servant-girl St. Mary. In the reign of the Emperor Hadrian, she was accused of professing the Christian religion. Accordingly, she was severely whipped, stretched on the rack, and mangled with iron hooks. In this manner, she completed her martyrdom.

At Tarsus in Cilicia, SS. Cyrenia and Juliana, martyrs, in the time of the Emperor Maximian.

In Auvergne in Gaul, St. Austremonius, who was the first bishop of that region.

At Paris, the death of St. Marcellus, bishop.

At Bayeaux in Gaul, St. Vigor, bishop, in the time of Childebert, King of the Franks.

At Angers in Gaul, the death of St. Licinius, bishop, a holy old man.

At Tivoli, St. Severinus, monk.

At Larchant in north central Gaul, St. Mathurin, confessor.

The Second Day of November

The Commemoration of All the Faithful Departed. *A feast of nine lessons.*

(*If November 2 falls on a Sunday, the announcement concerning the Faithful Departed is not read today. It is read in the first place on the following day.*)

At Pettau in Upper Pannonia, the birthday of St. Victorinus, bishop of that city. After publishing many of his writings, as St. Jerome informs us, he was crowned with martyrdom in the persecution of Diocletian.

At Trieste, the suffering of blessed Justus, who suffered martyrdom in the same persecution under the governor Manatius.

At Sebaste in Armenia, the martyrs, SS. Carterius, Styriacus, Tobias, Eudoxius, Agapius, and their companions, in the time of the Emperor Licinius.

In Persia, the holy martyrs Acindynus, Pegasus, Aphthonius, Elpidiphorus, and Anempodistus, with many companions.

In Africa, the birthday of the holy martyrs Publius, Victor, Hermes, and Papias.

At Tarsus in Cilicia, St. Eustochium, virgin and martyr. In the reign of Julian the Apostate, she underwent horrible tortures and died while engaged in prayer.

At Laodicea in Syria, St. Theodotus, bishop. He was adorned not only with eloquence, but also with deeds and virtues.

At Vienne in Gaul, St. George, bishop.

In the monastery at Saint-Maurice in Gaul, St. Ambrose, abbot.

At Cyrus in Syria, St. Marcian, confessor.

The Third Day of November

At Sant'Arcangelo near Rimini (Italy), Blessed Simon (Ballachi), confessor, of the Order of Preachers. Although he came of a distinguished family, he chose to become a lay-brother. By his humility and self-denial, he set a marvellous example even to his extreme old age. *A semi-duplex feast.*

At Milan, the birthday of St. Charles Borromeo, cardinal, Bishop of Milan, and confessor. Pope Paul V numbered him among the saints because of his outstanding holiness and miracles. His feast, however, is celebrated on November 4.

On the same day, the birthday of St. Quartus, a disciple of the Apostles.

At Viterbo, the holy martyrs Valentine, priest, and Hilary, deacon. In the persecution of Maximian, because they confessed Christ, they were weighted down with a rock and cast into the Tiber. However, they were miraculously rescued by an angel. Eventually, they received the crown of martyrdom by being beheaded.

At Caesarea in Cappadocia, the holy martyrs Germanus, Theophilus, Caesarius, and Vitalis. They courageously underwent martyrdom in the persecution of Decius.

At Saragossa in Spain, the countless holy martyrs who so admirably laid down their lives for Christ, in the time of Dacian, governor of Spain.

In England, St. Winifred, virgin and martyr.

In the monastery of Clairvaux in Gaul, the death of St. Malachy, Bishop of Connor in Ireland. He was enriched with many virtues and his life was written by Abbot St. Bernard.

On the same day, St. Hubert, Bishop of Tongres.

At Vienne in Gaul, St. Domnus, bishop and confessor.

Also, the death of St. Pirmin, Bishop of Meaux.

At Urgel in Spain, St. Hermengaud, bishop.

At Rome, St. Sylvia, mother of Pope St. Gregory.

The Fourth Day of November

St. Charles Borromeo, cardinal, Bishop of Milan, and confessor, who went to Heaven on November 3. *A duplex feast.*

At Bologna, SS. Vitalis and Agricola, martyrs. Vitalis had been the slave of Agricola but was afterward his companion and associate in martyrdom. The executioners used every kind of torture against Vitalis, so that there was no part of his body left unwounded. Notwithstanding, Vitalis endured them with firmness to the very end and, while in prayer, gave up his soul to God. They slew Agricola by nailing him to a cross with numerous spikes. St. Ambrose was present at the transferral of their bodies and he relates how he gathered up the nails of the martyr, his triumphal blood, and the wood of the cross, and buried them under the sacred altars. *A memory.*

In the monastery of Cerfroid near Meaux, the birthday of St. Felix of Valois, founder of the Order of the Most Holy Trinity for the redemption of captives. By a decree of Pope Innocent XI, his feast is observed on November 20.

On the same day, the birthday of SS. Philologus and Patrobas, disciples of the Apostle St. Paul.

At Autun, St. Proculus, bishop and martyr.

At Myra in Lycia, the holy martyrs Nicander, bishop, and Hermes, priest, under the governor Libanius.

In the district of Vexin in Gaul, St. Clarus, priest and martyr.

At Ephesus, St. Porphyrius, martyr, under the Emperor Aurelian.

At Rodez in Gaul, Blessed Amantius, bishop, whose life was outstanding for his splendid sanctity and miracles.

At Rome, the birthday of St. Pierius, a priest of Alexandria. Deeply versed in the Holy Scriptures, and most pure in his life, he stripped himself of all his goods that he might devote himself to Christian philosophy. In the time of the Emperors Carus and Diocletian, when Theonas governed the Church of Alexandria, he taught with great distinction and published various treatises. After the persecution, he spent the remainder of his life at Rome where he died a peaceful death.

In Bithynia, St. Joannicius, abbot.

At Stuhlweissenburg in Hungary, the death of Blessed Emeric, confessor, son of St. Stephen, King of Hungary.

At Treves, St. Modesta, virgin. ✠

The Fifth Day of November

At Lima in South America, Blessed Martin de Porres, a tertiary of the Order of Preachers. Having pronounced his solemn vows to God, he united integrity of life so perfectly with the most severe penances, that both before and after death he merited to become famous for his miracles. *A duplex feast.*

St. Zachary, priest and prophet. He was the father of St. John the Baptist, Precursor of the Lord.

Also, St. Elizabeth, the mother of the aforesaid holy Precursor.

At Terracina in Campania, the birthday of the holy martyrs Felix, priest, and Eusebius, monk. Eusebius buried the holy martyrs Julian and Caesarius, and he converted many persons to the faith of Christ, while St. Felix baptized them. As they could not be intimidated, they were imprisoned, and on their refusal to offer sacrifice were beheaded that very night.

At Emesa in Phoenicia, the holy martyrs Galatio and Epistemis, his wife. In the persecution of Diocletian, they were flogged; in addition, their hands, feet, and tongues were amputated. They finally completed their martyrdom by being beheaded.

Also, the holy martyrs Domninus, Theotimus, Philotheus, Silvanus, and their associates, in the reign of the Emperor Maximinus.

At Milan, St. Magnus, bishop and confessor.

At Brescia, St. Dominator, bishop.

At Treves, St. Fibitius, at first an abbot, and later Bishop of Treves.

At Orleans in Gaul, St. Laetus, priest and confessor.

The Sixth Day of November

In the kingdom of Tonkin (Indo-China), the Blessed martyrs Jerome Hermosilla and Valentine Berrio-Ochoa, both bishops; Peter Almato, Francis Gil de Federich, Matthew Alphonse Leziniana, Hyacinth Castañeda, Vincent Liem, priests and missionaries of the Order of Preachers; also Joseph Khang, a catechist of the Third Order of our Father St. Dominic. Although these martyrs died at different times, they were all united by the same strength of soul, and confirmed the faith they preached by the shedding of their blood. *A duplex feast.*

At Barcelona in Spain, St. Severus, bishop and martyr. For confessing the Catholic faith, a spike was driven into his skull and he thus won his crown of martyrdom.

At Tunis in Africa, the birthday of St. Felix, martyr. He confessed the faith of Christ and was removed for torture, but the next day he was found dead in his prison. So declared St. Augustine, when explaining a certain psalm to his flock on the feast day of St. Felix.

At Theopolis, now called Antioch,[1] ten holy martyrs, who are said to have suffered at the hands of the Saracens.

In Phrygia, St. Atticus, martyr.

At Berg in Flanders, the death of St. Winoc, abbot. He was famed for his virtues and miracles, and he ministered for a long time to the brethren subject to him.

At Fondi in Latium, St. Felix, monk.

At Limoges in Aquitaine, St. Leonard, confessor. He was a disciple of Bishop St. Remigius. Though of noble birth, he chose a solitary life, and was enriched with holiness and miracles. His goodness manifested itself especially in liberating captives.

The Seventh Day of November

At Turin (in Italy), Blessed Peter of Ruffia, (martyr) of our Order. Appointed Inquisitor in Turin, he did not cease to shine by his great vir-

---

[1] When Justinian rebuilt Antioch (middle of 6th cent.), he named it Theopolis. The name, however, did not last.

tues, and especially by his zeal in defense of Catholic truth. Finally, on the day consecrated to the Purification of the Blessed Virgin Mary, a day most auspicious for himself, he was slain by heretics, and so merited to enter the temple of Heaven. *A semi-duplex feast.*

At Padua, the death of St. Prosdocimus, who was the first bishop of that city. He was ordained bishop by St. Peter the Apostle, and sent to that city to preach the Word of God. He died a holy death at Padua, adorned with many virtues and miracles.

At Perugia, St. Herculanus, bishop and martyr.

At Schwelm in Germany, the suffering of St. Engelbert, Bishop of Cologne. He was on his way from Cologne to Essen to consecrate a church, when he was attacked on the road by assassins and slain by numerous wounds. Thus, he suffered martyrdom for defense of the liberty of the Church and the authority of the Church of Rome.

On the same day, St. Amaranthus, martyr. He underwent loyally the test of his faith. At Albi in Gaul, his body lies buried, but he lives in eternal glory.

At Melitina in Armenia, the suffering of SS. Hieron, Nicander, Hesychius, and thirty others, who were crowned in the persecution of Diocletian, under the governor Lysias.

At Amphipolis in Macedonia, the holy martyrs Auctus, Taurion, and Thessalonica.

At Ancyra in Galatia, the suffering of SS. Melasippus, Anthony, and Carina, under Julian the Apostate.

At Alexandria, Blessed Achilles, bishop, who was distinguished for his learning, faith, conduct, and purity of life.

In Friesland, the death of St. Willibrord, Bishop of Utrecht. He was ordained bishop by Blessed Pope Sergius, and preached the Gospel in Friesland and Denmark.

At Metz in Gaul, St. Rufus, bishop and confessor.

At Strasbourg, St. Florentius, bishop. ✠

The Eighth Day of November

The Octave of All Saints. *A solemn octave.*

At Rome, on the Via Lavicana, at the third milestone from the city, the suffering of the holy martyrs Claudius, Nicostratus, Symphorian, Castorius, and Simplicius. They were first cast into prison, and then severely flogged with scorpions. Since they could not be turned away from the faith of Christ, by the command of Diocletian, they were thrown headlong into the river.

234

At the same place, on the Via Lavicana, the birthday of the Four Holy Crowned Brothers, Severus, Severian, Carpophorus, and Victorinus. Under the same Emperor, they were flogged to death with blows from leaden-tipped scourges. Since their names could not then be learned (they were divinely revealed years later), it was decreed that their anniversary should be kept along with the five martyrs mentioned above, under the name of the Four Holy Crowned Ones. This has continued to be done in the Church even after their names were revealed. *A memory*.

Also at Rome, Pope St. Deusdedit, who had such great merit that he healed a leper of his disease by a kiss.

At Blexen on the river Weser, in Germany, St. Willehad, who was the first Bishop of Bremen. He, together with St. Boniface, whose disciple he was, spread the Gospel in Friesland and Saxony.

At Soissons in Gaul, St. Godefrid, Bishop of Amiens, a man of great sanctity.

At Verdun in Gaul, St. Maurus, bishop and confessor.

At Tours in Gaul, St. Clarus, priest, whose epitaph was written by St. Paulinus.

The Ninth Day of November

In Rome at the Lateran, the Dedication of the Basilica of the Most Holy Saviour, which is the mother and the head of all the churches of Rome and of the world. *A totum duplex feast of the second class*.

At Amasea in Pontus, the birthday of St. Theodore, soldier. In the reign of the Emperor Maximian, he was severely beaten and thrown into prison, for confessing the Christian faith. There the Lord appeared to him and encouraged him to be steadfast and brave, and his spirits were raised. Finally, he was stretched on the rack and torn with iron hooks until his insides were visible; he was then placed in a raging fire to be burned to death. St. Gregory of Nyssa celebrated his name in a famous panegyric. *A memory*.

At Tyana in Cappadocia, the suffering of St. Orestes, under the Emperor Diocletian.

At Thessalonica, St. Alexander, martyr, in the reign of the Emperor Maximian.

At Bourges in Aquitaine, St. Ursinus, confessor. He was ordained by the successors of the Apostles and was appointed the first Bishop of Bourges.

At Naples in Campania, St. Agrippinus, bishop, famed for his miracles.

At Constantinople, the holy virgins Eustolia, a Roman maiden, and Sopatra, the daughter of the Emperor Mauritius.

At Beirut in Syria, the commemoration of the image of the Saviour which, being nailed to a cross by some Jews, poured forth blood so abundantly that the Churches of the East and West both received an ample share of it.[2]

The Tenth Day of November

At Naples in Campania, the birthday of St. Andrew Avellino, Clerk Regular and confessor. He was renowned for holiness and zeal in promoting the salvation of his neighbors. Noted for his miracles, he was canonized by the Sovereign Pontiff, Clement XI.

On the same day, the birthday of the holy martyrs Tryphon and Respicius, and Nympha, virgin.

At Rome, the birthday of Pope St. Leo I, confessor and Doctor of the Church, who, by reason of his outstanding qualities, is surnamed the Great. During his pontificate, the Council of Chalcedon was held at which, through his legates, he condemned Eutyches; afterward, he confirmed the decrees of this Council by the weight of his authority. By the many laws he passed and by his numerous writings, he deserved well of the Holy Church of God and of the entire flock of the Lord as their good shepherd. His feast, however, is observed on April 11.

At Iconium in Lycaonia, the holy women Tryphenna and Tryphosa. By the preaching of St. Paul and the example of St. Thecla, these women made the greatest progress in Christian training.

At Antioch, SS. Demetrius, bishop, Anianus, deacon, Eustosius, and twenty other martyrs.

At Agde in Gaul, the holy martyrs Tiberius, Modestus, and Florence. In the reign of Diocletian, they were subjected to various tortures and so gained martyrdom.

At Ravenna, St. Probus, bishop, noted for miracles.

At Orleans in Gaul, St. Monitor, bishop and confessor.

In England, St. Justus, bishop. Pope St. Gregory sent him together with Augustine, Mellitus, and others, to England to preach the Gospel. There, renowned for his sanctity, he died in the Lord.

In the town of Melun in Gaul, St. Leo, confessor.

On the island of Patmos, St. Theoctiste, virgin. ✠ *An Anniversary.*

The Eleventh Day of November

At Tours in Gaul, the birthday of Blessed Martin, bishop and confessor.

[2] Needless to say, this story is regarded as a fable by many historians.

His life was so resplendent with miracles that he merited to raise three dead men to life. *A totum duplex feast.*

At Cotyaeus in Phrygia, the celebrated suffering of St. Menas. He was an Egyptian soldier who, in the persecution of Diocletian, cast away his military insignia and withdrew to the desert to wage an interior war for his heavenly King. Presenting himself before a public gathering, he loudly announced that he was a Christian. He was first subjected to severe tortures. Finally, as he was kneeling in prayer and giving thanks to the Lord Jesus Christ, he was put to the sword. After his death, he became famous for miracles. *A memory.*

At Ravenna, the holy martyrs Valentine, Felician, and Victorinus, who were crowned in the persecution of Diocletian.

In Mesopotamia, St. Athenodorus, martyr. He was tortured with fire and tried by other punishments. Finally, he was condemned to capital punishment. When the executioner fell to the ground and no one dared to strike him with the sword, the martyr, while engrossed in prayer, went to his rest in the Lord.

At Lyons in Gaul, St. Veranus, bishop, whose life was noteworthy for his faith and the merits of his virtue.

At Constantinople, St. Theodore, Abbot of Studium.[3] He fought zealously for the Catholic faith against the Iconoclasts and became famous throughout the Universal Church.

In the monastery of Grottaferrata on the site of Tusculanum, the Abbot St. Bartholomew, a companion of St. Nilus, whose life he wrote.

In the province of Samnium (Central Italy), Blessed Mennas, anchorite. Pope St. Gregory has commemorated his virtues and miracles.

The Twelfth Day of November

The Feast of All the Saints of our Order. *A totum duplex feast of the second class.*

St. Martin I, pope and martyr, whose birthday is commemorated on September 16.

At Vitebsk in Poland, the suffering of St. Josaphat, of the Order of St. Basil, a Polish archbishop and martyr. He was cruelly slain by the schismatics in their hatred of Catholic unity and truth. He was numbered among the martyrs by Pope Pius IX. His feast, however, is kept on November 14.

At Alcalá in Spain, the birthday of St. Didacus, confessor, of the Order

[3] Studium was the name of a famous monastery at Constantinople; it was built in the year 463 by the Roman consul Studius.

of Friars Minor, who was noted for his humility. He was canonized by the Sovereign Pontiff, Pope Sixtus V; his feast is celebrated on November 13.

In Asia, the suffering of the holy Bishops Aurelius and Publius.

At Eachen in Belgium, St. Livinus, bishop and martyr. He had converted many persons to the Christian faith when he was slain by the heathens. His body was later transferred to Ghent.

At Gnesen in Poland, the holy hermits and martyrs Benedict, John, Matthew, Isaac, and Christian. They were engaged in prayer when they were savagely attacked by robbers and put to the sword.

At Sergines near Sens, St. Paternus, monk and martyr. He met some robbers in the nearby forest and when he tried to persuade them to correct their lives, they put him to death.

At Avignon, St. Rufus, who was the first bishop of that city.

At Cologne, the death of St. Cunibert, bishop.

At Tarazona in Aragon, Blessed Emilian, priest. He was remarkable for his many miracles. St. Braulio, Bishop of Saragossa, wrote his admirable life.

At Constantinople, St. Nilus, abbot. In the reign of Theodosius the Younger, he had been prefect of that city and then became a monk. He was distinguished for his learning and holiness.

The Thirteenth Day of November

The Patronage of St. Thomas Aquinas over Catholic Schools. *A totum duplex feast of the first class.*

St. Didacus, confessor, of the Order of Friars Minor, whose birthday is observed on November 12.

At Ravenna, the birthday of the holy martyrs, Valentine, Solutor, and Victor, who suffered in the reign of the Emperor Diocletian.

At Aix in the province of Narbonne, Blessed Mitrius, a most famous martyr.

At Caesarea in Palestine, the suffering of St. Antoninus, Zebina, Germanus, and Ennatha, virgin. At the time of Galerius Maximus, Ennatha was scourged and then burned alive; the others were beheaded because they had fearlessly and loudly accused the governor Firmilian of idolatry in offering sacrifice to the gods.

In Africa, the holy Spanish martyrs Arcadius, Paschasius, Probus, and Eutychian. In the Vandal persecution, they refused positively to join the Arian heresy. They were first proscribed by the Arian king Genseric, and then exiled. They were treated with atrocious cruelty and finally put to death in various ways. At that time, too, was seen the constancy of

Paulillus, the little brother of SS. Paschasius and Eutychian. Since all efforts failed to turn him away from the Catholic faith, he was subjected to a long clubbing and then condemned to the vilest slavery.

At Rome, Pope St. Nicholas I, preeminent for his apostolic vigor.

At Tours in Gaul, St. Britius, bishop, who was a disciple of Blessed Bishop Martin. His memory is recalled on November 14.

At Toledo in Spain, St. Eugene, bishop.

In Auvergne in Gaul, St. Quinctian, bishop.

At Cremona in Insubria, St. Homobonus, confessor. He was renowned for miracles and was canonized by Pope Innocent III.

The Fourteenth Day of November

At Caccamo in Sicily, Blessed John Liccio, confessor, of the Order of Preachers. He was notable for his eloquence in speaking of divine things, for charity toward his neighbor, for the propagation of the Rosary, for striving after regular observance, and for other virtues. At the age of one hundred and eleven, he quietly rested in the Lord. *A semi-duplex feast.*

St. Josaphat, of the Order of St. Basil, a Polish archbishop and martyr, whose birthday is remembered on November 12.

At Gangra in Paphlagonia, St. Hypatius, bishop. While on the way home from the great Nicene Council, he was stoned by Novatian heretics and thus died a martyr.

At Heraclea in Thrace, the birthday of the holy martyrs Clementinus, Theodotus, and Philomenus.

At Alexandria, St. Serapion, martyr. In the reign of the Emperor Decius, the executioners inflicted on him the most cruel sufferings. After they had broken the joints of all his limbs, they flung him off the roof of his house, and so he became a glorious martyr of Christ.

At Troyes in Gaul, St. Venerandus, martyr, under the Emperor Aurelian.

In Gaul, St. Veneranda, virgin. She received the crown of martyrdom under the Emperor Antoninus and the governor Asclepiades.

At Emesa in Phoenicia, the suffering of many holy women. They were most brutally tortured and slain for the Christian faith under the cruel Arab chief Mady.

At Bologna, St. Jucundus, bishop and confessor.

At Eu in Gaul, St. Laurence, Bishop of Dublin.

At Tours in Gaul, St. Britius, bishop, who, on November 13, died in the Lord. *A memory.*

At Algiers in Africa, Blessed Serapion. He was the first one of the Order of our Lady of Ransom to merit obtaining the palm of martyrdom.

Because he redeemed the faithful from captivity and preached the Christian faith, he was crucified and then cut to pieces limb from limb.

The Fifteenth Day of November

At Cologne, St. Albert surnamed the Great, at one time Bishop of Ratisbon, and confessor, of the Order of Preachers. Radiant by the holiness of his life, by his zeal for the salvation of souls, and by his surpassing doctrine, he enlightened the Church. Pope Pius XI declared him to be a Doctor of the Universal Church (and Pius XII constituted him patron before God of students of the natural sciences).[4] *A totum duplex feast of the first class.*

St. Gertrude, virgin, of the Order of St. Benedict, who was called by her heavenly Spouse to eternal happiness on November 17.

On the same day, the birthday of St. Eugene, Bishop of Toledo and martyr. He was a disciple of Blessed Dionysius the Areopagite. Having finished the course of martyrdom near Paris, he received from the Lord the crown of his blessed suffering. His body was afterward transferred to Toledo in Spain.

At Nola in Campania, Blessed Felix, bishop and martyr. From the age of fifteen, he was remarkable for his miracles. Under the prefect Marcianus, he completed, together with thirty companions, the course of martyrdom.

At Edessa in Mesopotamia, the suffering of St. Abibus, deacon. He was mangled with hooks under the Emperor Licinius and the governor Lysanias, and was then burned alive.

In the same place, the holy martyrs Gurias and Samonas, under the Emperor Diocletian and the governor Antoninus.

In Africa, the holy martyrs Secundus, Fidentianus, and Varicus.

At Archingeay, in the territory of Saintes, the birthday of St. Malo, Bishop of Aleth in Gaul. Born in England, he was famous for his miracle from his earliest years.

At Verona, St. Luperius, bishop and confessor.

At Klosterneuburg near Vienna, in Austria, St. Leopold, margrave of the same province of Austria. He was canonized by Pope Innocent VIII.

The Sixteenth Day of November

At Ferrara (in Italy), Blessed Lucy of Narni, virgin, of the Order of

[4] The clause "and Pius XII, etc." is taken from the 1952 Supplement of the Roman Martyrology.

our Father St. Dominic. Her incorrupted body is held in the greatest reverence at Ferrara. *A semi-duplex feast.*

At Edinburgh in Scotland, the birthday of St. Margaret, widow, Queen of the Scots. She was conspicuous for her love of the poor and her voluntary poverty. Her feast is kept on June 10.

In Africa, the holy martyrs Rufinus, Mark, Valerius, and their companions.

On the same day, the holy martyrs Elpidius, Marcellus, Eustochius, and their associates. Elpidius, who was of senatorial rank, confessed the faith with great firmness before Julian the Apostate. He, with his companions, was first tied to wild horses and dragged by them; then he was cast into the fire and thus completed a glorious martyrdom.

At Lyons in Gaul, the birthday of St. Eucherius, bishop and confessor. He was a man of admirable faith and learning. Although he enjoyed the most noble senatorial rank, he exchanged it for the religious life and the religious habit. He had himself walled up in a cave where for a long period of time he served Christ by prayer and fasting. Then, because of a revelation made by an angel (to the faithful), he was solemnly made Bishop of Lyons.

At Padua, St. Fidentius, bishop.

At Canterbury in England, St. Edmund, archbishop and confessor. He was driven into exile for defending the rights of his church, and he died a most holy death at Provins, a town near Sens. He was inscribed in the canon of saints by Pope Innocent IV.

On the same day, the death of St. Othmar, abbot. ✠

The Seventeenth Day of November

At Neocaesarea in Pontus, the birthday of St. Gregory, bishop and confessor. He was celebrated for his learning and sanctity. Because of the signs and miracles he performed with great glory to the Church, he is called the Wonderworker. *A simplex feast.*

At Helfa in Saxony, the birthday of St. Gertrude, virgin, of the Order of St. Benedict, who was noted for the gift of revelations. Her feast is celebrated on November 15.

In Palestine, the holy martyrs Alpheus and Zachaeus. In the first year of Diocletian's persecution, they received capital punishment after having undergone many tortures.

At Cordoba in Spain, the holy martyrs Acislus and Victoria, brother and sister. In the same persecution, they were most savagely tortured by order of Dion the governor, and merited crowns from the Lord for their remarkable suffering.

At Alexandria, St. Dionysius, bishop. A man of the greatest learning, he was renowned for his many confessions of the faith. He was extraordinary in the diversity of the sufferings and tortures he endured. However, he lived to an advanced age and died a peaceful death.

At Orleans in Gaul, St. Aignan, bishop. His death was precious in the sight of the Lord, as many miracles showed.

In Britain, St. Hugh, bishop. He was called from the state of a Carthusian monk to govern the Church of Lincoln. He was renowned for numerous miracles and died a holy death.

At Tours in Gaul, St. Gregory, bishop.

At Florence, St. Eugene, confessor. He was the deacon of St. Zenobius, bishop of that city.

The Eighteenth Day of November

At Rome, the Dedication of the Basilicas of the Apostles St. Peter and St. Paul. The Basilica of St. Peter was solemnly consecrated on this day by the Sovereign Pontiff Urban VIII, after it had been rebuilt on a larger scale. The Basilica of St. Paul had been entirely destroyed by an unfortunate fire; it was rebuilt in a more imposing manner and was consecrated with solemn ritual by Pius IX on December 10; its annual commemoration was transferred to this day. *A totum duplex feast.*

At Antioch, the birthday of St. Romanus, martyr. During the reign of the Emperor Galerius, when the prefect Asclepiades attacked the Church and tried to destroy it completely, St. Romanus encouraged the other Christians to resist him. After he had endured terrible tortures, his tongue was cut out, but even without it, he spoke the praises of God. Then he was strangled with a noose in prison and so was crowned by a famous martyrdom. Ahead of him there suffered a young boy named Barula. He was asked by the governor whether it were better to worship one God or many gods; the boy replied that one must believe in the one God whom the Christians worship. For this answer, he was flogged and then ordered to be beheaded.

Also at Antioch, St. Hesychius, martyr. He was a soldier, and when he heard the order that anyone who would not offer sacrifice should lay aside his military insignia, he immediately did so. For this action, a huge rock was fastened to his right hand and he was flung into the river.

On the same day, SS. Oriculus and his companions, who suffered for the Catholic faith in the Vandal persecution.

At Mainz, St. Maximus, bishop. In the time of Constantine, he underwent many sufferings at the hands of the Arians. He died a confessor.

At Tours in Gaul, the passing of Blessed Odo, Abbot of Cluny.

At Antioch, St. Thomas, monk. In an annual solemnity, the people of Antioch were accustomed to reverence him for having ended a plague by his prayers.

At Lucca in Tuscany, the transferal of the relics of St. Frigidianus, bishop and confessor. ✠

The Nineteenth Day of November

In the town of Marburg in Germany, the death of St. Elizabeth, widow, daughter of King Andrew of Hungary, and (a member) of the Third Order of St. Francis. She was sedulously devoted to works of piety and went to the Lord, renowned for her miracles. *A duplex feast.*

St. Pontian, pope and martyr, whose birthday occurs on October 30.

At Samaria in Palestine, St. Abdias, Prophet.

At Rome on the Appian Way, the birthday of St. Maximus, priest and martyr. He suffered in the persecution of Valerian and was buried at St. Sixtus.

In the city of Ecija in Spain, Blessed Crispin, bishop, who obtained the glory of martyrdom by being beheaded.

On the same day, St. Faustus, a deacon of Alexandria. In the persecution of Valerian, he was first sent into exile with St. Dionysius. Later, in his old age, he suffered martyrdom, being slain by the sword.

At Caesarea in Cappadocia, St. Barlaam, martyr. Although he was an ignorant countryman, yet, strengthened by the wisdom of Christ, he conquered the tyrant, and by his unshaken faith he rose superior to the fire. St. Basil the Great delivered a famous panegyric to the people on his birthday.

At Vienne in Gaul, the holy martyrs Severinus, Exuperius, and Felicianus, whose bodies, after the course of many years, were found by their own revelation. Their bodies were reverently removed by the clergy and people of that city and given an honorable burial by the bishop.

In Isauria, the suffering of SS. Azas and his one hundred and fifty fellow soldiers, under the Emperor Diocletian and the tribune Aquilinus.

The Twentieth Day of November

St. Felix of Valois, priest and confessor. He founded the Order of the Most Holy Trinity for the Redemption of Captives. He died in the Lord on November 4. *A duplex feast.*

In Persia, the martyrdom of SS. Nersas, bishop, and his companions.

At Messina in Sicily, the holy martyrs Ampelus and Caius.

At Turin, SS. Octavius, Solutor, and Adventor, martyred soldiers of the Theban Legion. At the time of the Emperor Maximian, they fought wonderfully (for the faith) and were crowned with martyrdom.

At Caesaria in Palestine, St. Agapius, martyr. In the reign of the Emperor Galerius Maximian, he was condemned to the beasts. As he was not injured by them, he was flung into the sea with stones attached to his feet.

At Silistria in Rumania, St. Dasius, martyr. He was put to death by the governor Bassus, because he would not take part in the shameless rites of the Saturnalia.

At Nicaea in Bithynia, the holy martyrs Eustace, Thespesius, and Anatolius, in the persecution of Maximinus.

At Heraclea in Thrace, the holy martyrs Bassus, Dionysius, Agapitus, and forty others.

In England, St. Edmund, king and martyr.

At Constantinople, St. Gregory Decapolites, who suffered much because of his veneration of the holy images.

At Milan, St. Benignus, bishop. During a great incursion of barbarians, he governed the Church committed to his care with great firmness and piety.

At Chalons in Gaul, St. Silvester, bishop. In the forty-second year of his priesthood, rich in days and virtues, he died in the Lord.

At Verona, St. Simplicius, bishop and confessor.

At Hildesheim in Saxony, St. Bernard, bishop and confessor. He was canonized by Pope Celestine III.

The Twenty-first Day of November

At Jerusalem, the Presentation in the Temple of the Blessed Virgin Mary, Mother of God. *A totum duplex feast.*

On the same day, the birthday of Blessed Rufus, whom St. Paul the Apostle mentions in his Epistle to the Romans.[5]

At Rome, the suffering of SS. Celsus and Clement.

At Rheims in Gaul, St. Albert, Bishop of Liege and martyr, who was killed for defending the liberty of the Church.

Near Ostia, the holy martyrs Demetrius and Honorius.

In Spain, the holy martyrs Honorius, Eutychius, and Stephen.

In Pamphylia, St. Heliodorus, martyr, in the persecution of Aurelian, under the governor Aetius. After his execution, his executioners themselves were converted to the faith and were drowned in the sea.

At Rome, Pope St. Gelasius I, famed for his learning and holiness.

[5] Romans, 16:13.

At Verona, St. Maurus, bishop and confessor.

In the monastery of Bobbio, the death of St. Columban, abbot. He founded many monasteries and was the spiritual father of a very great number of monks. Eminent for his many virtues, he died peacefully at a good old age. ✠

The Twenty-second Day of November

St. Cecilia, virgin and martyr. Purpled with her own blood, she departed to her heavenly Spouse, on September 16. *A duplex feast.*

At Colossae in Phrygia, SS. Philemon and Apphias, disciples of St. Paul. In the reign of the Emperor Nero, on the feast of Diana, the heathens burst into the (Christian) church and seized Philemon and Apphias, while the rest of the congregation fled. By orders of the governor Artocles, they were flogged; after which, they were buried up to their waists in a pit and then stoned to death.

At Rome, St. Maurus, martyr. He came from Africa to visit the tombs of the Apostles, and suffered martyrdom under Celerinus, governor of Rome in the reign of the Emperor Numerian.

At Antioch in Pisidia, the suffering of SS. Mark and Stephen, in the days of the Emperor Diocletian.

At Autun, St. Pragmatius, bishop and confessor.

The Twenty-third Day of November

The birthday of St. Clement I, pope and martyr. He was the third pope after St. Peter the Apostle. In the persecution of Trajan, he was exiled to the Chersonese; there, an anchor was fastened to his neck and he was cast into the sea and so was crowned with martyrdom. During the time of the Sovereign Pontiff, Hadrian II, his body was taken to Rome by two brothers, SS. Cyril and Methodius, and buried with honor in the church which had been built and named after him. *A duplex feast.*

At Rome, St. Felicitas martyr, the mother of seven martyred sons. At the command of the Emperor Marcus Antoninus, she was beheaded for Christ after her sons had been martyred.

At Cyzicus in the Hellespont, St. Sisinius, martyr. In the persecution of the Emperor Diocletian, he was put to the sword after he had endured many tortures.

At Merida in Spain, St. Lucretia, virgin and martyr, who gained martyrdom in the same persecution under the governor Dacian.

At Iconium in Lycaonia, St. Amphilochius, bishop. He was the companion of SS. Basil and Gregory of Nyssa in the desert and their colleague in the episcopate. After suffering many trials for the Catholic faith, he died a peaceful death, famed for holiness and learning.

At Agrigento (in Sicily), the death of St. Gregory, bishop.

In the town of Hasbain in Belgium, St. Trond, priest and confessor. Both the monastery he erected there on his own land, and the town which shortly after arose, were later named after him.[6]

The Twenty-fourth Day of November

St. John of the Cross, priest, confessor, and Doctor of the Church. He was the associate of St. Teresa in the reform of Carmel. His birthday is mentioned on December 14. *A duplex feast.*

On the same day, the birthday of St. Chrysogonus, martyr. For his unwavering confession of Christ, he endured for a prolonged period chains and imprisonment. By orders of Diocletian, he was brought to Aquileia, there beheaded, and his body thrown into the sea, thus completing his martyrdom. *A memory.*

At Rome, St. Crescentian, martyr. He is mentioned in the martyrdom of Blessed Pope Marcellus.

At Corinth, St. Alexander, martyr. Under Julian the Apostate and the governor Sallust, he fought for the faith of Christ, even unto death.

At Perugia, St. Felicissimus, martyr.

At Ameria in Umbria, St. Firmina, virgin and martyr. In the persecution of Diocletian, she was tortured in various ways. At last, she was hung up and burned with flaming torches until she gave up her spotless soul to God.

At Cordoba in Spain, the holy virgins and martyrs Flora and Mary, who, in the Arab persecution, after long imprisonment were put to the sword.

At Milan, St. Protasius, bishop. At the Council of Sardica and in the presence of the Emperor Constans, he defended the cause of Athanasius. He died in the Lord, after he had performed many labors both for the Church committed to him and for religion.

In the province of Auvergne, St. Portianus, abbot. He was celebrated for his miracles in the reign of King Theodoric. He has given his name both to the monastery of which he had charge, and to the town which afterward was built in that place.[7]

In the district of Blaye in Gaul, St. Romanus, priest. The praise of his holiness is declared by the glory of his miracles.

[6] Saint-Trond or Sint-Truiden, near Hasselt.
[7] Saint-Pourçain-sur-Sioule, near Vichy.

The Twenty-fifth Day of November

At Alexandria, St. Catherine, virgin and martyr. In the reign of the Emperor Maximian, she was cast into prison for confessing the Christian faith. Then she was flogged for a long time with scorpions, and finally completed her martyrdom by being beheaded. Her body was miraculously carried by angels to Mount Sinai, and is there piously venerated by huge gatherings of Christians. *A totum duplex feast.*

At Rome, St. Moses, priest and martyr. While he was detained in prison together with other Christians, he was often encouraged by letters from St. Cyprian. With undiminished courage, he resisted not only the pagans but also the schismatics and Novatian heretics. Eventually, as Pope St. Cornelius testifies, he was crowned with a famous and admirable martyrdom in the persecution of Decius.

At Antioch, St. Erasmus, martyr.

At Caesarea in Cappadocia, the suffering of St. Mercurius, soldier. By the protection of his guardian angel, he conquered barbarians and overcame the cruelty of Decius. Enriched with the trophies of many tortures, he passed into heaven, crowned with martyrdom.

In Emilia, a province of Italy, St. Jucunda, virgin.

The Twenty-sixth Day of November

At Mantua, Blessed James Benefatti, bishop and confessor, of the Order of Preachers. On account of his having perfectly fulfilled the duties of a good shepherd, he earned for himself the name "Father of the Poor," as well as the love of his flock. *A semi-duplex feast.*

At Fabriano in Piceno, Blessed Silvester, abbot, founder of the Congregation of Silvestrine Monks.

At Alexandria, the birthday of St. Peter, bishop of that city and martyr. He was adorned with every kind of virtue. He was beheaded by command of Galerius Maximian.

Also at Alexandria, there suffered in the same persecution the holy martyrs Faustus, priest, Didius, and Ammonius; also Phileas, Hesychius, Pachomius and Theodore, Egyptian bishops, with six hundred and sixty-six others. All gained heaven by the sword of persecution.

At the village called Fratta [8] near Rovigo, St. Bellinus, Bishop of Padua and martyr. He was an excellent defender of the rights of the Church. He was cruelly attacked by assassins who, having inflicted many wounds on him, killed him.

[8] Fratta Polesine.

At Nicomedia, St. Marcellus, priest. In the reign of Constantius, he was flung headlong from a cliff by the Arians and thus died a martyr.

At Rome, St. Siricius, pope and confessor. Eminent for his learning, piety, and zeal for religion, he condemned various heretics, and restored ecclesiastical discipline by his most salutary decrees.

At Autun, St. Amator, bishop.

At Constance in Germany, St. Conrad, bishop.

At Rome, St. Leonard of Port Maurice, priest, of the Order of Friars Minor, and confessor. He was noteworthy for his zeal for souls and his missionary journeys throughout Italy. He was canonized by the Sovereign Pontiff, Pius IX.

In the district of Rheims, the birthday of St. Basolus, confessor.

At Adrianople in Paphlagonia, St. Stylian, hermit, noted for miracles.

In Armenia, St. Nicon, monk.

The Twenty-seventh Day of November

At Antioch, the holy martyrs Basileus, bishop, Auxilius, and Saturninus.

At Sebaste in Armenia, the holy martyrs Hirenarchus, Acacius, priest, and seven women. Hirenarchus was moved by the constancy of these women and was converted to Christ. Under the Emperor Diocletian and the governor Maximus, Hirenarchus together with Acacius was slain with an axe.

At the river Cea in Galicia, SS. Facundus and Primitivus, who suffered under the governor Atticus.

In Persia, St. James, a famous martyr surnamed "Dismembered." In the days of Theodosius the Younger, he denied Christ to secure the favor of King Isdegerd; whereupon, his mother and wife avoided his company. Repenting of his deed, James approached King Vararanes, the son and successor of Isdegerd, and confessed that he was a Christian. Hence, the angry monarch sentenced him to this death: his limbs were to be cut off one by one and finally he was to be beheaded. At that time and in the same place, innumerable other martyrs were slain.

At Aquileia, St. Valerian, bishop.

At Riez in Gaul, St. Maximus, bishop and confessor. He was endowed with every grace and virtue from his earliest years. He was at first the superior of the monastery at Lerins, and later Bishop of the Diocese of Riez. He was renowned for his signs and miracles.

At Salzburg in Germany, St. Virgil, Bishop and Apostle of Caranthia. He was canonized by the Sovereign Pontiff Gregory IX.

In India, near the Persian border, SS. Barlaam and Josaphat, whose wondrous deeds are narrated by St. John Damascene.

At Paris, the death of St. Severinus, monk and hermit.

The Twenty-eighth Day of November

At Corinth, the birthday of St. Sosthenes, a disciple of the Apostle St. Paul, whom the same Apostle mentions in his Epistle to the Corinthians.[9] He had been a ruler of the synagogue but was converted to Christ. Cruelly flogged before the governor Gallio, he thus hallowed the first-fruits of his faith by an admirable beginning.

At Rome, St. Rufus. Diocletian made him and his whole family martyrs of Christ.

In Africa, the holy martyrs Papinian and Mansuetus, bishops. At the time of the Vandal persecution by the Arian King Genseric, these bishops defended the Catholic faith. For so doing, their bodies were seared with red-hot iron plates until they had completed their glorious contest. At the same time, other holy Bishops Valerian, Urban, Crescens, Eustace, Cresconius, Crescentian, Felix, Hortulanus, and Florentian, all were condemned to exile where they finished their earthly days.

At Constantinople, the holy martyrs Stephen the Younger, Basil, Peter, Andrew, and three hundred and thirty-nine fellow-monks. Under Constantine Copronymus, they were tortured in various ways because of their veneration of the holy images. They confirmed Catholic truth by shedding their blood.

At Naples in Campania, the death of St. James of Piceno, priest, of the Order of Friars Minor, and confessor. He was famed for the austerity of his life, apostolic preaching, and the many diplomatic missions he performed for the Church. He was canonized by the Sovereign Pontiff, Pope Benedict XIII.

The Twenty-ninth Day of November

The Vigil of St. Andrew the Apostle.

At Rome on the Via Salaria, the birthday of the holy martyrs Saturninus, an old man, and Sisinius, deacon, under the Emperor Maximian. After they had been imprisoned for a long time, the prefect of the city ordered them to be raised upon the rack and stretched; then they were flogged with thongs, clubs, and scorpions. After fire had been applied to them, they were taken down from the rack and beheaded. *A memory.*

[9] I Cor., 1:1.

At Toulouse, St. Saturninus, bishop. In the reign of Decius, he was taken by the pagans to the capitol of that city and flung down the steps of the highest stairway. His skull was crushed, his brains dashed out, and his entire body mangled. Thus, he offered his worthy soul to Christ.

Also the suffering of SS. Paramon and three hundred and seventy-five companions under the Emperor Decius and the governor Aquilinus.

At Ancyra in Galatia, St. Philomenus, martyr. In the persecution of the Emperor Aurelian, under the governor Felix, he was tried by fire. Then his hands, feet, and lastly his head were pierced by spikes and he completed his martyrdom.

At Veroli in the Hernican mountains, the holy martyrs Blaise and Demetrius.

At Todi in Umbria, St. Illuminata, virgin.

The Thirtieth Day of November

At Patras in Achaia, the birthday of St. Andrew the Apostle. He preached the sacred Gospel of Christ in Thrace and Scythia, and was arrested by Aegeas the proconsul. After imprisonment, he was barbarously scourged and finally hung on a cross; he lived for two days, during which he did not cease to teach the people. He asked God not to permit him to be taken down from the cross, and he was then surrounded with a great light from heaven. When the light finally disappeared, he gave up his soul. *A totum duplex feast of the second class.*

At Rome, the suffering of SS. Castulus and Euprepes.

At Constantinople, St. Maura, virgin and martyr.

Also, St. Justina, virgin and martyr.

At Rome, St. Constantius, confessor. He fought bravely against the Pelagians and from that faction suffered many injuries, which made him a fellow of the holy confessors.

Near Saintes in Gaul, St. Trojan, bishop. He was a man of great holiness. He made it clear, by the many miracles he worked, that he lives in Heaven even though his body was buried on earth.

In Palestine, Blessed Zosimus, confessor. He was renowned for holiness and miracles, in the days of the Emperor Justin.

December

At Montpellier in Gaul, the birthday of Blessed John of Vercelli, the sixth master-general of the Order of Preachers. He was eminent both by his learning and his virtues. He restored religious discipline in his monasteries, and labored untiringly as an arbitror for peace, in the name of and by the authority of the Roman Pontiff, in reconciling kings and cities. *A duplex feast.*

St. Nahum, Prophet, who was buried at Beth-Gabre.

At Rome, the holy martyrs Diodorus, priest, and Marian, deacon, together with many others. In the days of the Emperor Numerian, while the Christians were celebrating in the catacombs the anniversaries of their martyrs, the persecutors walled up the entrance to the crypt and heaped a great mass of stones against it. In this manner, the Christians gained the glory of martyrdom.

Also at Rome, the suffering of SS. Lucius, Rogatus, Cassian, and Candida.

At Narni, St. Proculus, bishop and martyr. After he had accomplished numerous exceptional deeds, Totila king of the Goths ordered him to be beheaded.

In the city of Casale, St. Evasius, bishop and martyr.

On the same day, St. Ansanus, martyr. At the time of Diocletian, he confessed Christ at Rome. He was cast into prison and then taken to Siena in Tuscany, where he completed his course of martyrdom by being beheaded.

At Ameria in Umbria, St. Olympiades, a man of consular rank. He was converted to the faith by St. Firmina; under Diocletian, he was tortured on the rack and so achieved martyrdom.

At Arbela in Persia, St. Ananias, martyr.

At Milan, St. Castritian, bishop. At a time of great disturbance in the Church, he was eminent by reason of his virtues and his deeds piously and religiously performed.

At Brescia, St. Ursicinus, bishop.

At Noyon in Belgium, St. Eligius, bishop. A multitude of miracles gave approbation to his admirable life.

At Verdun in Gaul, St. Agericus, bishop.

On the same day, St. Natalia, the wife of the Blessed Martyr Adrian. For a long time she ministered to the holy martyrs imprisoned at Nicomedia in the reign of the Emperor Diocletian. When their contest was completed, she went to Constantinople where she died a peaceful death. ✠

The Second Day of December

At Rome, the suffering of St. Bibiana, virgin and martyr. Under the wicked Emperor Julian, she was flogged with whips tipped with lead until she expired. *A simplex feast.*

At Imola in the province of Aemilia, the birthday of St. Peter, surnamed Chrysologus, Bishop of Ravenna, confessor, and Doctor of the Church. He was distinguished for his learning and holiness. His feast is observed on December 4.

On Sancian, an island of China, the birthday of St. Francis Xavier, priest of the Society of Jesus, confessor, and Apostle of the Indies. He was famed for his conversion of the heathens, his supernatural gifts and miracles. Rich in merit and good works, he died in the Lord. The Sovereign Pontiff, Pius X, chose and appointed him the heavenly patron of the Society and the work for the Propagation of the Faith. By order of Pope Alexander VII, his feast is celebrated on December 3.

At Rome, the holy martyrs Eusebius, priest, Marcellus, deacon, Hippolytus, Maximus, Adria, Paulina, Neon, Mary, Martana, and Aurelia. They all completed their martyrdom in the persecution of Valerian, under the judge Secundian.

Also at Rome, St. Pontianus, martyr, and four others.

In Africa, the birthday of the holy martyrs Severus, Securus, Januarius, and Victorinus, who were there crowned with martyrdom.

At Aquileia, St. Chromatius, bishop and confessor.

At Verona, St. Lupus, bishop and confessor.

At Edessa in Syria, St. Nonus, bishop, by whose prayers Pelagia the penitent was converted to Christ.

At Troas in Phrygia, St. Silvanus, bishop, renowned for miracles.

At Brescia, St. Evasius, bishop.

The Third Day of December

St. Francis Xavier, priest of the Society of Jesus, confessor, Apostle of the Indies, and heavenly patron of the Society and work of the Propagation of the Faith. He died a peaceful death on December 2. *A totum duplex feast.*

In Judea, St. Sophonias, prophet.

At Rome, the holy martyrs Claudius the tribune and his wife Hilaria, their two sons Jason and Maurus, and seventy soldiers. The Emperor Numerian ordered Claudius to be fastened to a huge stone and cast into the river, while the soldiers and the sons of Claudius were to be punished by being beheaded. Blessed Hilaria buried the bodies of her sons; shortly after, she was seized by the pagans while she was praying at their sepulchre. She was cast into prison where she died.

At Tangier in Morocco, the suffering of St. Cassian, martyr. For a long time he held the position of public clerk, but eventually he was impressed by the fearless answers and unshaken firmness in the faith of Christ of the centurion St. Marcellus. Then inspired by grace, he felt it was a hateful thing to take part in the slaughter of Christians. He therefore resigned his office, confessed the Christian faith, and merited to obtain the palm of martyrdom.

Also in Africa, the holy martyrs Claudius, Crispin, Magina, John, and Stephen.

In Hungary, St. Agricola, martyr.

At Nicomedia, the suffering of SS. Ambicus, Victor, and Julius.

At Milan, St. Mirocles, bishop and confessor, whom St. Ambrose occasionally mentioned.

At Dorchester in England, St. Birinus, who was first bishop of that city.

At Chur in Germany, St. Lucius, an English king. In the time of St. Eleutherius, he was the first of the English kings to receive the faith of Christ.

At Siena in Tuscany, St. Galganus, hermit. ✠

The Fourth Day of December

St. Peter Chrysologus, Bishop of Ravenna, confessor, and Doctor of the Church, whose memory is recalled on December 2. *A duplex feast.*

At Nicomedia, the suffering of St. Barbara, virgin and martyr. In the persecution of Maximian, she was kept for a long time in prison, burned with torches, mutilated, and subjected to other tortures. She gained martyrdom by being put to the sword. *A memory.*

At Constantinople, SS. Theophanes and his associates.

In Pontus, St. Melitus, bishop and confessor. He was a man of remarkable learning but he was even more remarkable by reason of the virtue of his soul and the sincerity of his life.

At Bologna, St. Felix, bishop, who was once deacon of the Church of Milan under St. Ambrose.

In England, St. Osmund, bishop and confessor.

At Cologne, St. Anno, bishop.

In Mesopotamia, St. Maruthas, bishop. In Persia, he restored the churches of God that had fallen into ruin during the persecution of King Isdegerd. He was famous for his many miracles and was held in honor even by his enemies.

At Parma, St. Bernard, cardinal, and bishop of that city. He belonged to the Congregation of Vallombrosa of the Order of St. Benedict.

The Fifth Day of December

In Judea, St. Sabas, abbot. He was born in the town of Mutalaska in Cappadocia. He gave a splendid example of holiness and labored most zealously for the Catholic faith against those who attacked the holy Council of Chalcedon. He died peacefully in the laura of the Diocese of Jerusalem, which afterward was called after him the Laura of St. Sabas.

At Nice near the river Var, St. Bassus, bishop. In the persecution of Decius and Valerian, he was tortured for his faith by the governor Perennius. First he was stretched on the rack, then burned with red-hot bars, beaten with clubs and scorpions, and cast into the fire. When he came forth unhurt, he was pierced with two spikes and thus completed his illustrious martyrdom.

At Pavia, St. Dalmatius, bishop and martyr, who suffered in the persecution of Maximian.

At Corfinium among the Pelignians,[1] St. Pelinus, Bishop of Brindisi. In the time of Julian the Apostate, the temple of Mars crashed to the ground at his prayers. The priests of the temple most grievously flogged him and inflicted eighty-five wounds on his body; thus he gained the crown of martyrdom.

Also, St. Athanasius, martyr. Because of his ardent desire for martyrdom, he delivered himself of his own free will to the persecutors.

At Thagura in Africa, the holy martyrs Julius, Potamias, Crispin, Felix, Gratus, and seven others.

At Thebeste in Numidia, St. Crispina, a most noble woman. In the time of Diocletian and Maximian, she was beheaded by command of the proconsul Anolinus because she refused to offer sacrifice. St. Augustine often praised her.

At Treves, St. Nicetius, bishop, a man of marvellous holiness.

[1] See note under April 28.

At Polyboton in Asia (Minor), St. John, bishop, surnamed the Wonder-worker.

The Sixth Day of December

At Myra, the capital of Lycia (in Asia Minor), the birthday of St. Nicholas, bishop and confessor. Among his many remarkable miracles, this memorable one is told: although he was far away, he appeared to the Emperor Constantine, and by his warnings and threats induced him to have mercy on, instead of executing, some men who had invoked the assistance of the saint. *A duplex feast.*

On the same day, St. Polychronius, priest. In the time of the Emperor Constantine, while he was at the altar celebrating Mass, he was attacked by the Arians, who cut his throat.

In Africa, St. Majoricus, son of St. Dionysius. He was a youth who was afraid of torture, but his mother encouraged him by looks and words; whereupon he became more courageous than the rest and gave up his life during the tortures. His mother embraced his body, buried him at home, and made it a practise to pray unceasingly at his tomb.

In the same place, the holy women Dionysia, mother of St. Majoricus the martyr, Dativa, and Leontia; likewise, a religious man named Tertius, Emilian, a physician, Boniface, and three others. In the Vandal persecution under the Arian king Hunneric, they all suffered innumerable and horrible tortures in defense of the Catholic faith, so that they deserve to be associated with the band of holy confessors of Christ.

At Rome, St. Asella, virgin. St. Jerome wrote that she had been blessed from birth. She spent her whole life, even to old age, in fasting and prayer.

At Granada in Spain, the suffering of Blessed Peter Paschal, Bishop of Jaen and martyr. He belonged to the Order of Our Lady of Ransom for the Redemption of Captives.

The Seventh Day of December

The Vigil of the Immaculate Conception of the Blessed Virgin Mary. The octave of St. Andrew the Apostle. *A memory.*

St. Ambrose, bishop, confessor, and Doctor of the Church. He died in the Lord on April 4; but his feast is observed today—the day on which he took charge of the Church of Milan. *A duplex feast.*

At Rome, blessed Eutychian, pope. With his own hands, he buried three hundred and forty-two martyrs in various places. He himself was joined to them by being crowned with martyrdom in the reign of the Emperor Numerian, and was buried in the cemetery of Callistus.

At Alexandria, the birthday of Blessed Agatho, soldier. In the persecution of Decius, he prevented some men from making sport of the bodies of the martyrs. Quickly a cry against him arose from the rabble. He was brought before the judge, and since he remained firm in his confession of Christ, he was sentenced to death for his reverence.

At Antioch, the holy martyrs Polycarp and Theodore.

At Tuburbum in Africa, St. Servus, martyr. In the Vandal persecution under the Arian King Hunneric, he was beaten with clubs for a long time, repeatedly lifted on high by pulleys, then swiftly dropped, with all the weight of his body, on flints. Then he was scraped with very sharp stones until he had gained the palm of martyrdom.

At Teano in Campania, St. Urban, bishop and confessor.

Near Saintes in Gaul, St. Martin, abbot, at whose tomb numerous miracles take place.

At Farmoutiers in the territory of Meaux, the commemoration of St. Fara, also called Burgundofara, abbess and virgin. Her birthday is celebrated on April 3.

The Eighth Day of December

The Immaculate Conception of the glorious and ever Virgin Mary, Mother of God. On this day, the Sovereign Pontiff, Pius IX, solemnly defined that, by a singular privilege of God, she was preserved free from all stain of original sin. *A totum duplex feast of the first class.*

At Treves, St. Eucharius, who was a disciple of St. Peter the Apostle, and first Bishop of Treves.

At Alexandria, St. Macarius, martyr. In the time of Decius, the judge tried by many arguments to persuade him to deny Christ, but he confessed the faith with all the greater firmness. Finally, he was ordered to be burned alive.

In Cyprus, St. Sophronius, bishop. He was a wonderful protector of wards, orphans, and widows, and a helper of all the poor and oppressed.

In the monastery of Luxeuil in Gaul, St. Romaricus, abbot. He had very high rank at the court of King Theodebert, but, forsaking the world, he excelled others in his observance of the monastic life.

At Constantinople, St. Patapius, hermit, who was renowned for his virtues and miracles.

At Rome, the finding of the bodies of the holy martyrs Nemesius, deacon, his daughter the virgin Lucina, Symphronius, Olympius the tribune, Exuperia, his wife, and Theodulus, his son. Commemoration of them is made on August 25.

At Verona, the ordination of St. Zeno, bishop.

The Ninth Day of December

At Carthage, St. Restitutus, bishop and martyr. On his feastday, St. Augustine delivered to his congregation a panegyric on him.

Also in Africa, the holy martyrs Peter, Successus, Bassianus, Primitivus, and twenty others.

At Toledo in Spain, the birthday of St. Leocadia, virgin and martyr. During the Diocletian persecution, the prefect of Spain, Dacian, imprisoned Leocadia for a long time and treated her harshly. When she heard of the terrible sufferings of St. Eulalia and other martyrs, kneeling in prayer, she yielded her pure spirit to Christ.

At Limoges in Aquitaine, St. Valeria, virgin and martyr.

At Verona, St. Proculus, bishop. He was beaten with fists and clubs in the persecution of Diocletian, and was driven from the city. Eventually, he was restored to his church and died a peaceful death.

At Pavia, St. Syrus, who was the first bishop of that city. He was celebrated for his apostolic powers and virtues.

At Apamea in Syria, Blessed Julian, bishop, who in the time of Severus was eminent for his holiness.

At Gray in Burgundy, St. Peter Fourier, a Canon Regular of our Saviour, and founder of the Canonesses Regular of our Lady for the teaching of children. He was famed for his virtues and miracles, and was canonized by the Sovereign Pontiff Leo XIII.

At Perigueux in Gaul, St. Cyprian, abbot, a man of great holiness.

At Nazianus in Cappadocia, St. Gorgonia. She was the daughter of Blessed Nonna and the sister of SS. Gregory the Theologian and Caesarius. St. Gregory has described her virtues and miracles.

The Tenth Day of December

St. Melchiades, pope and martyr, whose birthday is recalled on January 11.

At Rome on the Via Ostiensis, the Dedication of the Basilica of St. Paul the Apostle. The annual commemoration of this dedication, with that of St. Peter the Prince of the Apostles, is observed on November 18.

On the same day, the holy martyrs Carpophorus, priest, and Abundius, deacon. In the persecution of Diocletian, they were first inhumanly beaten with clubs and then thrown into prison where they were denied food and drink. They were tortured for a second time on the rack and again cast into prison for a long period. Finally, they were slain by the sword.

At Alexandria, the holy martyrs Mennas, Hermogenes, and Eugraphus, who suffered under Galerius Maximian.

At Lentini in Sicily, the holy martyrs Mercurius and his fellow soldiers. In the time of the Emperor Licinius, under the governor Tertyllus, they were put to the sword.

At Ancyra in Galatia, St. Gemellus, martyr. After he had sustained savage torture under Julian the Apostate, he completed his martyrdom by being crucified.

At Merida in Spain, the suffering of St. Eulalia, virgin. In the reign of Maximian, when Eulalia was only twelve years old, by orders of the governor Dacian, she was subjected to many tortures for confessing Christ. Finally, she was placed on the rack, her body torn with iron claws, and flaming torches applied to her sides. As she inhaled the flames, she gave up her soul to God.

Also, at the same place, St. Julia, virgin and martyr. She was a companion of Blessed Eulalia and refused to leave her when she was hurrying to her martyrdom.

At Rome, Pope St. Gregory III, who died distinguished for his sanctity and miracles.

At Vienne in Gaul, St. Sindulph, bishop and confessor.

At Brescia, St. Deusdedit, bishop.

At Loretto in Piceno, the transferal of the Holy House of Mary the Mother of God. It was in this house that the Word was made flesh.

The Eleventh Day of December

At Rome, St. Damasus I, pope and confessor. He condemned the heresiarch Apollinaris and restored (to his see) Peter, Bishop of Alexandria, who had been forced to flee. He found many bodies of holy martyrs and wrote their epitaphs in verse. *A simplex feast.*

Also at Rome, the suffering of St. Thrason. At his own expense, he provided food for the exhausted Christians who were slaving in the public baths and other places, or who were detained in prison. By orders of Maximian, he was arrested and crowned with martyrdom, together with two others, Pontianus and Praetextatus.

At Amiens in Gaul, the holy martyrs Victoricus and Fuscian, under the same Emperor. The governor Rictiovarus ordered that iron rods should be driven into their nostrils and ears, and their temples pierced with red-hot spikes. Their eyes were then torn out and, later, their bodies were pierced with javelins. Together with their guest St. Gentian, they were beheaded and so went to their Lord.

In Persia, St. Barsabas, martyr.

In Spain, St. Eutychius, martyr.

At Piacenza, St. Sabinus, bishop, who was famed for miracles.

At Constantinople, St. Daniel Stylites. ✠

The Twelfth Day of December

At Alexandria, the holy martyrs Epimachus and Alexander. In the reign of the Emperor Decius, they were kept in chains for a long time and subjected to various punishments. As they remained unshaken in the faith, they were finally burned alive. The feast of St. Epimachus, together with that of St. Gordian the martyr, is celebrated on May 10.

At Rome, St. Synesius, martyr. He was ordained lector in the time of Pope St. Sixtus II. He had converted many persons to Christ when he was accused before the Emperor Aurelian. Being put to the sword, he gained the crown of martyrdom.

On the same day, the holy martyrs Hermogenes, Donatus, and twenty-two others.

At Treves, the holy martyrs Maxentius, Constantius, Crescentius, Justin, and their associates. All suffered in the persecution of Diocletian, under the governor Rictiovarus.

At Alexandria, SS. Ammonaria, virgin, Mercuria, Dionysia, and another Ammonaria. The first Ammonaria, in the persecution of Decius, obtained a happy ending to her life; after enduring unheard-of tortures, she was put to the sword. The judge felt humiliated to be overcome by women, and doubted that he would be able to conquer their firmness if he used the same torments on them. He therefore ordered them to be beheaded without delay.

The Thirteenth Day of December

At Syracuse in Sicily, the birthday of St. Lucy, virgin and martyr, in the persecution of Diocletian. At the command of the proconsul Paschasius, she was handed over to procurers that she might be degraded; but when they tried to lead her away, they were unable to budge her, even with ropes or many oxen. She was plunged into boiling pitch, resin and oil, without sustaining any hurt. At last, her throat was severed with a sword and she thus completed her martyrdom. *A duplex feast.*

At Moulins in France, St. Jane Frances Fremiot de Chantal, widow, foundress of the Nuns of the Visitation of St. Mary. She was eminent for her noble birth, the sanctity of the life she led in a fourfold state,[2] and for the gift of miracles. She was canonized by the Sovereign Pontiff, Clement XIII. Her holy body was taken to Annecy in Savoy and buried with solemn pomp in the first church of her Order. Pope Clement XIV directed that her feast should be observed by the Universal Church on August 21.

In Armenia, the suffering of the holy martyrs Eustratius, Auxentius, Eugenius, Mardarius, and Orestes, during the persecution of Diocletian. Eustratius and Orestes were subjected to cruel tortures, first under Lysias, then at Sebaste under the governor Agricolaus. Eustratius died on being thrown into a furnace, but Orestes died when he was placed on a red-hot iron bed. The rest suffered the most inhuman tortures from the governor Lysias at Arabrace, and completed their martyrdom in different ways. Their bodies were afterward taken to Rome and honorably buried in the church of St. Apollinaris.

On the island of Solci, near Sardinia, the suffering of St. Antiochus, under the Emperor Hadrian.

At Cambrai in Gaul, St. Aubert, bishop and confessor.

In the district of Ponthieu in Gaul, St. Judoc, priest and confessor.

In the territory of Strasburg, St. Odilia, virgin.

The Fourteenth Day of December

At Ubeda in Spain, the birthday of St. John of the Cross, priest and confessor, the associate of St. Teresa in the reformation of the Carmelites. He was canonized by the Sovereign Pontiff, Benedict XIII, and Pope Pius XI declared him to be a Doctor of the universal Church. His feast is celebrated on November 24.

At Rheims in Gaul, the suffering of St. Nicasius, bishop, his sister Eutropia, virgin, and their fellow-martyrs, who were killed by barbarous enemies of the Church.

At Alexandria, the holy martyrs Heron, Arsenius, Isidore, and Dioscurus, all boys. In the persecution of Decius, the judge ordered the first three children to be mangled by various tortures. When he saw them all equally unmoved, he ordered them to be burned alive. The fourth child, Dioscurus, was flogged again and again until God willed him to be released (from this life) to the consolation of the faithful.

At Antioch, the birthday of the holy martyrs Drusus, Zosimus, and Theodore.

On the same day, the suffering of SS. Justus and Abundius. Under the Emperor Numerian and the governor Olybrius, they were cast into the flames. When they emerged unhurt, they were killed by the sword.

[2] That is to say, she was successively a virgin, wife, widow, and religious.

On the island of Cyprus, the Blessed Spiridion, bishop. He was one of those confessors whom Galerius Maximian condemned to the mines, after his right eye had been dug out (with a dagger) and his left leg hamstrung. He was famed for his gift of prophecy and power of miracles. In the Council of Nicaea, he refuted and converted a Gentile philosopher who had scoffed at the Christian religion.

At Bergamo, St. Viator, bishop and confessor.

At Pavia, St. Pompey, bishop.

At Naples in Campania, St. Agnellus, abbot. He was renowned for his power to perform miracles. When Naples was besieged, he was often seen saving the city from the enemy by the banner of the cross.

At Milan, St. Matronian, hermit.

The Fifteenth Day of December

The Octave of the Immaculate Conception of the Blessed Virgin Mary. *A solemn octave.*

At Rome, the holy martyrs Irenaeus, Anthony, Theodore, Saturninus, Victor, and seventeen others, who died for Christ in the persecution of Valerian.

In Africa, the suffering of SS. Faustinus, Lucius, Candidus, Caelian, Mark, Januarius, and Fortunatus.

In the same place, St. Valerian, bishop. In the Vandal persecution, under the Arian King Generic, St. Valerian (then over eighty years of age) was ordered to surrender the sacred vessels of his church. When he steadfastly refused to do so, he was expelled from the city and everyone was forbidden to allow the Bishop to enter their house or to dwell in their field. As a result, he lay a long time on the public road without shelter, and thus finished the course of his life in the confession and defence of Catholic truth.

In the territory of Orleans, St. Maximin, confessor.

Among the Iberians beyond the Euxine sea, St. Christiana, a servant, who, in the time of Constantine, converted that people to the faith of Christ by her miracles.

At Vercelli, the ordination of St. Eusebius, bishop and martyr. ✠

The Sixteenth Day of December

At Genoa, Blessed Sebastian Maggi, confessor, of our Order. By the example of his virtues and by his preaching of the Word of God, he firmly established solid piety in several cities of Italy. *A semi-duplex feast.*

St. Eusebius, Bishop of Vercelli and martyr. His birthday is commemorated on August 1, and his ordination on December 15.

The Three Holy Youths, Ananias, Azarias, and Misael, whose bodies were buried in a cave near Babylon.

At Ravenna, the holy martyrs Valentine, a military officer, Concordius his son, Navalis, and Agricola. They suffered for Christ in the persecution of Maximian.

At Formia in Campania, St. Albina, virgin and martyr, (who died) during the reign of the Emperor Decius.

In Africa, the suffering of many holy virgins in the Vandal persecution at the time of the Arian King Hunneric. They were hung up with weights attached to their feet, and red-hot iron plates were placed against their bodies. They successfully completed the contest of martyrdom.

At Vienne in Gaul, Blessed Ado, bishop and confessor.

In Ireland, St. Bean, bishop.

At Gaza in Palestine, St. Irenion, bishop. ✠

The Seventeenth Day of December

At Rome, the birthday of St. John of Matha, priest, confessor, and founder of the Order of the Most Holy Trinity for the Redemption of Captives. By a decree of Pope Innocent XI, his feast is observed on February 8.

At Marseilles in Gaul, Blessed Lazarus, the brother of SS. Mary Magdalen and Martha. In the Gospel, our Lord called him His friend and even raised him from the dead.[3]

At Eleutheropolis in Palestine, the holy martyrs, Florian, Calanicus, and their fifty-eight companions. In the days of the Emperor Heraclius, they were killed by the Saracens because of their Christian faith.

In the monastery of Fulda, St. Sturmius, abbot and Apostle of Saxony. Pope Innocent II canonized him during the second Council of the Lateran.

At Grand-Bigard near Brussels in Brabant, St. Wivina, virgin, whose great sanctity is attested to by frequent miracles.

At Constantinople, St. Olympias, widow.

At Andenne (on the Meuse) near the seven chapels,[4] blessed Begga, widow, who was the sister of St. Gertrude.

On the same day, the transferal of the relics of St. Ignatius, bishop and

[3] John 11:1, 43.
[4] When St. Begga returned from a pilgrimage to Rome, she built seven chapels at Ardenne to represent the seven basilicas of Rome. Near the chapels, she erected her monastery.

martyr. He was the third (bishop) after the Apostle St. Peter to rule the Church of Antioch. His body was brought to Antioch from Rome, where he had suffered a glorious martyrdom under Trajan on December 20. It was buried in the cemetery of the church outside the Gate of Daphne. At this solemnity, St. John Chrysostom preached the sermon to the people. Later, however, his relics were again taken back to Rome and buried with great reverence in the church of St. Clement, together with the body of most Blessed Clement, pope and martyr. ✠

The Eighteenth Day of December

At Philippi in Macedonia, the birthday of the holy martyrs Rufus and Zosimus. They were of that number of disciples who founded the primitive Church among the Jews and Greeks. St. Polycarp, in his Epistle to the Philippians, describes their happy martyrdom.

At Laodicea in Syria, the suffering of SS. Theotimus and Basilian.

In Africa, St. Quinctus, Simplicius, and others, who suffered in the persecution of Decius and Valerian.

In the same place, St. Moses, martyr.

Also in Africa, the holy martyrs Victurus, Victor, Victorinus, Adjutor, Quartus, and thirty others.

At Mopsuestia in Cilicia, St. Auxentius, bishop. He had once been a soldier under Licinius, but rather than (perform a pagan rite, namely) offer grapes to Bacchus, he laid aside his military insignia. He became a bishop who was noted for his merits. He died a peaceful death.

At Tours in Gaul, St. Gratian, bishop. He was ordained the first bishop of that city by Pope St. Fabian I. Renowned for many miracles, he died in the Lord.

The Nineteenth Day of December

In Morocco, St. Timothy, deacon. After enduring a harsh imprisonment for the faith of Christ, he was thrown into the fire and so gained martyrdom.

At Alexandria, Blessed Nemesius, martyr. He was first falsely denounced to a judge as a thief. Being found innocent of that charge, he was soon afterward accused to the judge Emilian of being a Christian; this was during the persecution of Decius. The judge subjected him to redoubled tortures and ordered him to be burned alive with some thieves. Thus, he resembled the Saviour who also bore the cross with thieves.

At Nicaea, SS. Darius, Zosimus, Paul, and Secundus, martyrs.

At Nicomedia, the holy martyrs Cyriacus, Paulilus, Secundus, Anastasius, Sindimius, and their companions.

At Gaza in Palestine, the suffering of SS. Mauris and Thea.

At Rome, the death of Pope St. Anastasius I, a man rich in poverty and in apostolic solicitude. St. Jerome wrote that the world did not deserve to possess him long lest with such a bishop the world's head should be cut off; for not long after his death, Rome was captured and destroyed by the Goths.

At Auxerre, St. Gregory, bishop and confessor.

At Orleans in Gaul, St. Adjutus, abbot, illustrious for his spirit of prophecy.

At Rome, St. Fausta. She was the mother of St. Anastasia, and was eminent for her nobility and piety.

At Avignon, Blessed Pope Urban V. He merited well of the Church by restoring the Apostolic See to Rome; by bringing about a union of the Greeks and the Latins; and by converting unbelievers. The Sovereign Pontiff, Pius IX, ratified and confirmed his ancient cult.

The Twentieth Day of December

The Vigil of St. Thomas the Apostle.

In Spain, the death of St. Dominic of Silos of the Order of St. Benedict, greatly celebrated for his miracles in liberating captives. *A duplex feast.*

At Rome, the birthday of St. Zephyrinus, pope and martyr, whose feast is observed on August 26.

In the same city, the suffering of St. Ignatius, bishop and martyr. He was the third (bishop) after the Apostle St. Peter to govern the Church of Antioch, and in the persecution of Trajan, was condemned to the beasts. He was sent in chains to Rome. There, in the very presence of the Senate, he was first subjected to the most inhuman tortures and then thrown to the beasts. Being ground by their teeth, he became a host for Christ.[5] His feast is observed on February 1.

At Rome, the holy martyrs Liberatus and Bajulus.

In Arabia, the holy martyrs Eugene and Macarius, priests. For rebuking the impiety of Julian the Apostate, they were most savagely wounded, and, taken to an immense desert, were put to the sword.

At Alexandria, the holy martyrs Ammon, Zeno, Ptolemy, Ingenes, and Theophilus, soldiers. While on duty at a court of justice, they saw a certain Christian waver during his torture; when he was almost at the point

[5] The allusion is to the saint's famous epistle: "I am God's grain and I am to be ground by the teeth of wild beasts that I may be found the pure bread of Christ."

of forsaking his faith, they attempted by their expressions, gestures, and nods to strengthen him. Whereupon, an uproar from the crowd rose against them. The soldiers pushed forward and declared that they too were Christians. By their victory, Christ, Who had given them firmness of character, was gloriously triumphant.

At Gelduba in Germany, St. Julius, martyr.

At Antioch, the birthday of St. Philogonius, bishop. By the will of God, he was called from the legal profession to govern the Church of Antioch. Together with the Bishop Alexander and his associates, he first began the battle for the Catholic faith against Arius. Celebrated for his merits, he died a peaceful death. On his annual feast day, St. John Chrysostom extolled him in a famous panegyric.

At Brescia, St. Dominic, bishop and confessor. ✠

The Twenty-first Day of December

At Salamina,[6] the birthday of St. Thomas the Apostle. He preached the Gospel to the Parthians, Medes, Persians, and Hyrcanians, and at length went to India. He had already instructed the people of that country in the Christian religion when, by order of the king, he was killed by being pierced with spears. His relics were first taken to Edessa in Mesopotamia and later to Ortona of the Frentani.[7] *A totum duplex feast of the second class.*

At Antioch, St. Anastasius, bishop and martyr. At the time of the Emperor Phocas, in a riot instigated by the Jews he was most brutally slain by them.

At Nicomedia, St. Glycerius, priest. In the persecution of Diocletian, he was tested by many tortures and at last thrown into the fire, thus gaining his martyrdom.

In Tuscany, the holy martyrs John and Festus.

In Lycia, St. Themistocles, martyr. In the reign of the Emperor Decius, he offered himself in place of Dioscorus whom they were seeking to kill. He was tortured on the rack, dragged about and beaten with clubs, until he gained the crown of martyrdom.

At Treves, St. Severinus, bishop and confessor.

The Twenty-second Day of December

The Feast of the Patronage of the Most Blessed Mary ever Virgin. *A totum duplex feast.*

[6] Scholars have been unable to identify this place.
[7] See note for July 3.

At Rome, on the Via Lavicana, between the two laurels, the birthday of thirty holy martyrs. All were crowned with martyrdom on the same day during the persecution of Diocletian.

Also at Rome, St. Flavian, an ex-prefect. He was the husband of the martyred St. Dafrosa, and the father of the holy virgin martyrs, Bibiana and Demetria. Under Julian the Apostate, for Christ he was condemned, branded, and sent into exile at Acquapendente in Etruria, where he gave up his soul to God while engaged in prayer.

In Egypt, St. Chaeremon, Bishop of Nilopolis, and many other martyrs. While the persecution of Decius was raging, some (of these Christians) were dispersed in their flight and, wandering in uninhabited places, were killed by wild beasts; others perished of hunger, cold, and exhaustion. Others were killed by savages and thieves, and were crowned with the same glory of martyrdom.

Near Ostia, the holy martyrs Demetrius, Honoratus, and Florus.

At Alexandria, St. Ischyrion, martyr. Attempts were made by insults and injuries to force him to sacrifice; when he showed no fear (of their threats), the middle of his body was pierced with a sharpened stake and he was left to die.

At Nicomedia, St. Zeno, soldier. He mocked Diocletian when the latter was offering sacrifice to Ceres; whereupon, his jaw was broken, his teeth knocked out, and he was then beheaded.

The Twenty-third Day of December

At Alba in Northern Italy, Blessed Margaret of Savoy, widow. Though sprung of a royal house, she spurned the preeminence of the world. Firmly refusing a (second and) most advantageous marriage, she joined the (Third) Order of St. Dominic. She courageously endured calumnies, illnesses, and persecutions previously revealed by Heaven to her under the symbol of three lances. Her road to Paradise was the narrow road of patience. *A semi-duplex feast.*

At Rome, St. Victoria, virgin and martyr. She was espoused to a pagan named Eugene, and she refused either to marry him or to offer sacrifice. She performed many miracles by which numerous virgins were gathered to God. In the persecution of the Emperor Decius, at the demand of her fiancé, the executioner pierced her heart with a sword.

At Nicomedia, the suffering of SS. Migdonius and Mardonius, (martyrs). In the persecution of Diocletian, one was burned alive while the other met death by being thrown into a pit. At the same time, there also suffered the deacon of St. Anthimus, Bishop of Nicomedia. He was taking letters to the (imprisoned) martyrs when he was arrested by the pagans and stoned to death, thus going to his Lord.

At the same place, the birthday of twenty holy martyrs. The same persecution of Diocletian made them martyrs of Christ, after they had endured the most severe tortures.

At Crete, the holy martyrs Theodulus, Saturninus, Euporus, Gelasius, Eunician, Zeticus, Leomenes, Agathopus, Basilides, and Evaristus. In the persecution of Decius, they underwent cruel tortures and were beheaded.

At Rome, St. Servulus. St. Gregory declared that, from early years to the end of his life, Servulus was paralyzed and lay on a porch near the church of St. Clement. Finally, invited by the hymns of angels, he passed to the glory of Paradise. At his tomb, God frequently performed miracles. ✠

The Twenty-fourth Day of December

The Vigil of the Nativity of our Lord Jesus Christ.

At Cracow in Poland, the birthday of St. John Cantius, priest and confessor. He was noted for his learning, zeal in spreading the faith, virtues, and miracles. He was canonized by the Sovereign Pontiff, Clement XIII. His feast is observed on October 20.

At Spoleto, St. Gregory, priest and martyr. At the time of the Emperors Diocletian and Maximian, he was first beaten with knotty clubs; then, after he endured the gridiron and imprisonment, he was struck across the knees with iron bars and his sides burned with flaming torches. Finally, he was beheaded.

At Tripoli in Phoenicia, the holy martyrs Lucian, Metrobius, Paul, Zenobius, Theotimus, and Drusus.

At Nicomedia, St. Euthymius, martyr. In the persecution of Diocletian, after he had prepared many others to sustain martyrdom, he himself was run through with a sword, and followed them to a heavenly crown.

At Antioch, the birthday of the forty holy virgins, who, in the persecution of Decius, completed their martyrdom after suffering various tortures.

At Bordeaux, St. Delphinus, bishop, who was eminent for his holiness at the time of Theodosius.

At Rome, the birthday of St. Tharsilla, virgin, and aunt of Pope St. Gregory. He stated that when she was dying she saw Jesus coming to her.

At Treves, St. Irmina, virgin, daughter of King Dagobert.

The Twenty-fifth Day of December

(The community stands while the reader reads the following) [8]

In the year five thousand one hundred and ninety-nine from the creation of the world, when God in the beginning created heaven and earth;

In the year two thousand nine hundred and fifty-seven from the flood;

In the year two thousand and fifteen from the birthday of Abraham;

In the year one thousand five hundred and ten from Moses and the going forth of the people of Israel from Egypt;

In the year one thousand and thirty-two from the anointing of David as king;

In the sixty-fifth week according to the prophecy of Daniel;

In the one hundred and ninety-fourth Olympiad;

In the year seven hundred and fifty-two from the founding of the city of Rome;

In the forty-second year of the rule of Octavian Augustus;

In the sixth age of the world, when the whole world was at peace: [*here the voice is raised:*]

Jesus Christ, eternal God and Son of the eternal Father, being pleased to hallow the world by His most gracious coming, having been conceived of the Holy Ghost, and nine months having passed since His conception, having become Man, was born at Bethlehem in Juda of the Virgin Mary.

[*All prostrate themselves: at the signal of the superior, they arise.*]

The Nativity of Our Lord Jesus Christ according to the flesh. *A totum duplex feast of the first class.*

On the same day, the birthday of St. Anastasia. In the reign of Diocletian, she suffered harsh and cruel imprisonment at the hands of her husband Publius, during which she was greatly consoled and comforted by Chrysogonus, a confessor of Christ. Next, she was subjected to a long imprisonment by Florius, prefect of Illyria. At last, on the island of Palmaria, she was fastened to posts with her hands and feet stretched apart, and a fire was enkindled about her. Thus she completed her martyrdom. There had been deported to this island with her two hundred men and seventy women, who gained their martyrdom by being killed in various ways. *A memory.*

At Barcelona in Spain, the birthday of St. Peter Nolasco, confessor, and founder of the Order of our Lady of Ransom for the Redemption of Captives. He was noted for his virtues and miracles. His feast is celebrated on January 28.

[8] See the *Caeremoniale O.P.*, par. 1347.

At Rome, in the cemetery of Apronianus, St. Eugenia, virgin. She was the daughter of St. Philip the martyr. In the time of the Emperor Gallienus, she showed many signs and virtues and added holy choirs of virgins to Christ. She suffered for a long time under Nicetus, prefect of the city, and at last her throat was cut with a sword.

At Nicomedia, the sufferings of several thousand holy martyrs who on Christmas day were assembled at Mass. The Emperor Diocletian ordered the doors of the church to be shut and a fire to be prepared around the building. A tripod with incense was set before the door. Then a herald proclaimed that they who desired to escape the fire should come out and offer incense to Jupiter. When the Christians unanimously declared they would gladly die for the sake of Christ, the church was set on fire and they were burned alive. Thus, they were held worthy to be born in Heaven on the very day on which Christ was pleased to be born on earth for the salvation of the world.

The Twenty-sixth Day of December

At Jerusalem, the birthday of St. Stephen the Protomartyr, who was stoned to death by the Jews soon after the Lord's Ascension. *A totum duplex feast of the second class.*

At Rome, St. Marinus, a man of senatorial rank. In the reign of the Emperor Numerian and the prefect Marcian, he was arrested on the charge of being a Christian. Though a senator, he was racked and torn by iron claws as if he were a slave. He was then cast into a cauldron, but the fire turned to dew and he remained unharmed. Next, he was thrown to the wild beasts but they refused to injure him. Then he was brought back to the altar, but at his prayer the idols fell to the ground. He gained the triumph of martyrdom by being put to the sword.

In the same place, on the Appian Way, the death of Pope St. Dionysius. He undertook many labors for the Church and was famed for his writings concerning the faith.

Also at Rome, St. Zosimus, pope and confessor.

In Mesopotamia, St. Archelaus, bishop. He was celebrated for his learning and sanctity.

At Majuma in Palestine, St. Zeno, bishop.

At Rome, St. Theodore, sacristan of the church of St. Peter. Pope St. Gregory mentions him.

The Twenty-seventh Day of December

At Ephesus, the birthday of St. John the Apostle and Evangelist. After he had written his Gospel, he was sent into exile where he wrote the inspired Apocalypse. He lived even to the time of Trajan, and established and guided Churches over all Asia. Overcome by old age, he died in the sixty-eighth year after the Passion of our Lord and was buried near the aforesaid city. *A totum duplex feast of the second class.*

At Constantinople, the holy confessors Theodore and Theophanes, brothers. They were reared from childhood in the monastery of St. Sabas. Afterward, they contended zealously against Leo the Armenian in their defence of the veneration of holy images. By Leo's orders, they were flogged and driven into exile. After Leo's death, they also resisted the Emperor Theophilus who adhered to the same impiety; again they were beaten and driven into exile, where Theodore died in prison. When peace was at last restored to the Church, Theophanes became Bishop of Nicaea. Celebrated for the glory of his confession, he died peacefully in the Lord.

At Alexandria, St. Maximus, bishop, who was quite illustrious and outstanding by reason of his confession of the faith.

At Constantinople, St. Nicaretes, virgin, who, at the time of the Emperor Arcadius, was distinguished for her holiness.

The Twenty-eighth Day of December

In Bethlehem of Juda, the birthday of the martyred Holy Innocents, who were slain for Christ by king Herod. *A totum duplex feast of the second class.*

At Lyons in France, the birthday of St. Francis de Sales, bishop of Geneva, and confessor. Because of his learning and his ardent zeal for the conversion of heretics, Pope Alexander VII canonized him. His feast is celebrated on January 29, the day on which his holy body was removed from Lyons to Annecy in Savoy. The Sovereign Pontiff, Pius IX, declared him to be a Doctor of the Universal Church.

At Ancyra in Galatia, the holy martyrs Eutychius, priest, and Domitian, deacon.

In Africa, the birthday of the holy martyrs Castor, Victor, and Rogatian.

At Nicomedia, the holy martyrs, Indes, a eunuch, the virgins Domna, Agape, and Theophila, and their companions. In the persecution of

Diocletian, after they had sustained prolonged tortures and been put to death in various ways, they received the crown of martyrdom.

At Neocaesarea in Pontus, St. Troadius, martyr, in the persecution of Decius. St. Gregory the Wonderworker was with him in spirit during his trial and strengthened him to endure his martyrdom.

At Arabissus in Lower Armenia, St. Caesarius, martyr, who suffered under Galerius Maximian.

At Rome, St. Domnio, priest.

In the monastery of Lerins in Gaul, St. Anthony, monk, noted for his miracles.

The Twenty-ninth Day of December

At Canterbury in England, the birthday of St. Thomas, bishop and martyr. For his defence of justice and ecclesiastical immunity, he was put to the sword in his basilica by a band of evil men, and thus went to Christ as a martyr. *A duplex feast.*

At Jerusalem, St. David, king and prophet.

At Arles in Gaul, St. Trophimus, whom St. Paul mentions in his Epistle to Timothy.[9] He was ordained bishop by that Apostle and was first sent to Arles to preach the Gospel of Christ. As Pope St. Zosimus writes, it was from the preaching of Trophinus, as from a fountainhead, that all Gaul received the streams of the faith.

At Rome, the holy martyrs Callistus, Felix, and Boniface.

In Africa, the suffering of the holy martyrs Dominic, Victor, Primian, Lybosus, Saturninus, Crescentius, Secundus, and Honoratus.

At Constantinople, St. Marcellus, abbot.

In the district of Ouche in Gaul, St. Evroult, abbot and confessor, in the days of King Childebert I.

At Vienne in Gaul, the commemoration of St. Crescens, bishop and martyr. He was a disciple of St. Paul the Apostle and first Bishop of Vienne. His birthday is celebrated on June 27.

The Thirtieth Day of December

At Rome, the birthday of St. Felix I, pope and martyr. He governed the Church at the time of the Emperor Aurelius. His feast is celebrated on May 30.

At Spoleto, the birthday of the holy martyrs Sabinus, Bishop of Assisi, Exuperantius and Marcellus, deacons, and Venustian the governor, with

[9] 2 Timothy, 4:19.

his wife and children. They were martyred in the reign of the Emperor Maximian. Marcellus and Exuperantius were first stretched on the rack and grievously beaten with clubs. Next they were torn with iron claws and their sides roasted by fire until they gained their martyrdom. Shortly after, Venustian was killed by the sword, together with his wife and children. St. Sabinus had his hands cut off and was confined in prison for a long time; then he was flogged to death. Although the martyrdom of these saints took place at different times, they are all remembered on one day.

At Alexandria, SS. Mansuetus, Severus, Appian, Donatus, Honorius, and their fellow martyrs.

At Thessalonica, St. Anysia, martyr.

At the same place, St. Anysius, bishop of that city.

At Milan, St. Eugene, bishop and confessor.

At Ravenna, St. Liberius, bishop.

At Aquila, among the Vestinian people,[10] St. Rainer, bishop.

The Thirty-first Day of December

At Rome, the birthday of St. Silvester I, pope and confessor. He baptized the Emperor Constantine, and it was he who approved the Nicene Synod. After performing many other deeds in a most saintly way, he died in peace. *A duplex feast.*

Also at Rome on the Via Salaria, in the cemetery of Priscilla, the holy martyrs Donata, Paulina, Rustica, Nominanda, Serotina, Hilaria, and their companions.

At Sens, Blessed Sabinian, bishop, and Potentian. They had been sent there by the Roman Pontiff to preach the Gospel, and they rendered illustrious that city by the martyrdom following their confession of faith.

At Catania in Sicily, the suffering of St. Stephen, Pontian, Attalus, Fabian, Cornelius, Sextus, Flos, Quinctian, Minervinus, and Simplician.

At Sens, St. Columba, virgin and martyr. In the persecution of the Emperor Aurelius, she overcame the fire and was slain by the sword.

On the same day, St. Zoticus, a Roman priest, who went to Constantinople and dedicated himself to the work of taking care of orphans.

At Ravenna, St. Barbatian, priest and confessor.

At La Louvesc, in the diocese of Vienne in Dauphine, the death of St. John-Francis Regis, priest, of the Society of Jesus, and confessor. He was a man of extraordinary charity and patience in procuring the salvation of souls. He was canonized by Pope Clement XII.

[10] See note for July 24.

At Retiers, St. Hermes, exorcist.

On the same day, St. Melinia the Younger. She departed from Rome with her husband Pinian and went to Jerusalem; there she devoted herself to the religious life among women consecrated to God, while her husband joined the monks. Both died a holy death.

V. And elsewhere, many other holy martyrs, confessors, and holy virgins.

R. Thanks be to God.

index of
special feasts

Feasts of the Lord

Ascension	
Christ the King	Last Sunday of October
Circumcision	Jan. 1
Corpus Christi	Thursday after Trinity Sunday
Crown of Thorns	April 24
Easter	
Epiphany	Jan. 6
Exaltation of the Holy Cross	Sept. 14
Family, Holy	Sunday within octave of Epiphany
Finding of the Holy Cross	May 3
Heart, Most Sacred	Friday after octave of Corpus Christi
Nativity of our Lord	Dec. 25
Name of Jesus	Sunday after Circumcision
Pentecost	
Precious Blood	July 1
Transfiguration	Aug. 6
Trinity Sunday	Sunday after Pentecost

Feasts of Our Lady

Annunciation	April 25
Apparition of Blessed Virgin (Lourdes)	Feb. 11
Assumption	Aug. 15
Commemoration of Our Lady of Victory (see Rosary)	
Compassion	Friday after Passion Sunday
Conception, Immaculate	Dec. 8
Heart of Mary, Immaculate	Aug. 22
Mary, Mediatrix of all Graces	May 31
Mount Carmel, Our Lady of	July 16
Name of Mary, Most Holy	Sept. 12
Nativity of Blessed Virgin	Sept. 8

Patronage of Blessed Virgin	Dec. 22
Presentation of Blessed Virgin	Nov. 21
Purification	Feb. 2
Ransom, Our Lady of	Sept. 24
Rosary, Most Holy	First Sunday of October
Seven Dolors, Our Lady of	Sept. 15
Snows, Our Lady of	Aug. 5
Visitation	July 2

St. Joseph, Patron of Universal Church	Mar. 19
Solemnity of St. Joseph, Patron of Universal Church	Second Wed. after Low Sunday

index of
dominican feasts

A

Agnes of Monte Pulciano	April 20
Aimo Taparelli	Aug. 18
Albert of Bergamo	May 11
Albert the Great	Nov. 15
All Saints of our Order	Nov. 12
Alphonse Navarrete and his companions	Sept. 10
Alvarez of Corduba	Feb. 19
Ambrose Sansedonio	March 20
Andrew Abellon	May 17
Andrew Franchi	May 30
Andrew of Peschiera	Jan. 26
Anniversary of Dedication of our own Church	Oct. 22
Anniversary of those buried in our cemeteries	July 12
Anniversary of our deceased brothers and sisters	Nov. 10
Anniversary of our deceased friends and benefactors	Sept. 5
Anniversary of our deceased parents	Feb. 4
Anthony della Chiesa	July 28
Anthony Neyrot	April 10
Anthony Pavone	April 9
Antoninus	May 10
Augustine of Biella	July 24
Augustine of Lucera	Aug. 3

B

Bartholomew Breganza	Oct. 23
Bartholomew of Cerverio	April 22
Benedict XI	July 7
Benvenuta Bojani	Oct. 30
Bernard Scammacca	Feb. 16
Bertrand of Garrigua	Sept. 6

C

Catherine de'Ricci	Feb. 13
Catherine of Racconigi	Sept. 4
Catherine of Siena	April 30
Ceslaus	July 17
Christopher of Milan	March 1
Clara Gambacorti	April 17
Columba of Rieti	May 20
Commemoration of St. Dominic in Suriano	Sept. 25
Commemoration of the Saints whose relics are preserved in our churches	Oct. 31
Constantine of Fabriano	Feb. 25

D

Dalmatius Moner	Sept. 26
Damian Furcherio	Oct. 26
Diana, Cecilia, and Amata	June 9
Dominic	Aug. 4
Dominic and Gregory	April 26
Dominic Henares and companions	July 11
Dominic Spadafora	Oct. 12

E

Egidius. *See* Giles	
Emily Bicchieri	Aug. 19

F

Francis de Capillas	Jan. 15
Francis Gil and companions	Nov. 6
Francis of Possadas	Sept. 20

G

Giles of Portugal	May 14
Gonsalvo of Amarantha	Jan. 16
Gregory and Dominic	April 26
Guala	Sept. 3

H

Henry Suso	March 2
Hyacinth	August 17
Hyacinth Castañeda and companions	Nov. 6

I

Ignatius Delgrado	July 11
Imelda	May 13
Innocent V	June 22
Isnard of Chiampo	March 22

J

James Benefatti	Nov. 26
James of Mevania	Oct. 23
James Salomoni	June 5
James of Ulm	Oct. 11
James of Voragine	July 13
Jerome Hermosilla and companions	Nov. 6
Joan of Aza	Aug. 8
Joan of Orvieto	July 23
Joan of Portugal	May 12
John Dominic	June 10
John of Gorcum and companions	July 9
John Liccio	Nov. 14
John Massias	Sept. 18
John of Salerno	Aug. 9
John of Vercelli	Dec. 1
Jordan of Pisa	March 6
Jordan of Saxony	Feb. 15
Joseph Diaz Sanjurjo and companions	July 27
Joseph Khang and companions	Nov. 6

L

Lawrence of Ripafratta	Sept. 28
Louis Bertrand	Oct. 10
Louis-Marie Grignon de Montfort	April 28
Lucy of Narni	Nov. 16

M

Magdalen Pannatieri	Oct. 13
Mannes	July 30
Marcolino of Forli	Jan. 24
Margaret of Castello	April 13
Margaret of Hungary	Jan. 19
Margaret of Savoy	Dec. 23
Maria Mancini	Jan. 30
Mark of Modena	Sept. 23
Martin de Porres	Nov. 5
Mary Bartholomew	May 28
Matthew Alonzo and companions	Nov. 6
Matthew Carreri	Oct. 7
Melchior Garcia Sampedro and companions	July 27

N

Nicholas of Palea	Feb. 14

O

Osanna of Cattaro	April 27
Osanna of Mantua	June 20

P

Patronage of St. Thomas Aquinas	Nov. 13
Peter Almato and companions	Nov. 6
Peter Gonzales	April 14
Peter Geremia	March 10
Peter Martyr	April 29
Peter of Ruffia	Nov. 7
Peter Sanz and companions	June 3
Peter of Tiferno	October 21
Pius V	May 5

R

Raymond of Capua	Oct. 5
Raymond of Penafort	Jan. 23
Reginald of Orleans	Feb. 17
Rose of Lima	Aug. 30

S

Sadoc and companions	June 2
Sebastian Maggi	Dec. 16
Servatus	May 22
Sibyllina Bicossi	March 23
Simon Ballachi	Nov. 3
Stephana Quinzani	Jan. 2
Stephen Bandelli	June 12
Stigmata of St. Catherine of Siena	April 1

T

Thomas Aquinas	March 7
Translation of St. Catherine of Siena	Thurs. after Sexagesima
Translation of St. Dominic	May 24

V

Valentine Berrio-Ochoa and companions	Nov. 6
Villana de'Botti	Feb. 28
Vincent Ferrer	April 5
Vincent Liem a Pace and companions	Nov. 6

W

William and companions	May 29

Z

Zedislava de Berka	Jan. 3

A NOTE ON THE TYPE
IN WHICH THIS BOOK WAS SET

This book has been set in Granjon, a lovely Linotype face, designed by George W. Jones, one of England's great printers, to meet his own exacting requirements for fine book and publication work. Like most useful types, Granjon is neither wholly new nor wholly old. It is not a copy of a classic face nor an original creation, but rather something between the two—drawing its basic design from classic Garamond sources, but never hesitating to deviate from the model where four centuries of type-cutting experience indicate an improvement or where modern methods of punch-cutting make possible a refinement far beyond the skill of the originator. This book was composed and printed by The York Composition Company, Inc. of York, Pa., and bound by Moore and Company of Baltimore. The design and typography are by Howard N. King.